Church and Community in the Diocese of Lyon 1500–1789

Philip T. Hoffman

Yale University Press
New Haven and London

Designed by Nancy Ovedovitz and set in Garamond 2 type. Printed in the United States of America by Edwards Brothers, Inc., Ann Arbor, Michigan.

Library of Congress Cataloging in Publication Data

Hoffman, Philip T., 1947–
    Church and community in the Diocese of Lyon, 1500–1789.

    Bibliography: p.
    Includes index.
    1. Counter-Reformation. 2. Catholic Church—Europe—Clergy—History. 3. Catholic Church. Diocese of Lyon (France) I. Title.
BR430.H64 1984   282′.4458   83-23404
ISBN 0-300-03141-6 (alk. paper)

10   9   8   7   6   5   4   3   2   1

Contents

List of Illustrations and Tables vii

Acknowledgments ix

Introduction 1

1 Rapprochement with the Elite: The Parish Clergy in the City of Lyon from 1500 to 1595 7

2 The Rural Priests from 1500 to 1614 45

3 Christian Discipline: The Reforms of the Clergy 71

4 Agents of Counter Reformation 98

5 The Aftermath of the Reforms 139

6 Conclusion 167

Appendix 1. Tobit and Probit Analysis of the Wills 171

Appendix 2. The Evidence from Criminal Records 185

List of Abbreviations 189

Notes 191

Bibliography 227

Index 233

Illustrations and Tables

Illustrations

1 Lyon in the sixteenth century (courtesy of the University
Research Library, UCLA)   9
2 Major churches and male religious orders in Lyon   12
3 The diocese of Lyon   46

Tables

1 Percentage of urban testators making pious bequests by wealth
class, 1521–95   24
2 Percentage of testators requesting processions, psalms,
attendance of clergy, or bells at funerals   29
3 Complaints about the clergy in the 108 northeastern parishes
that received three successive visits   100
4 Death inventories of priests outside Lyon which mention libraries   102
5 Number of 108 northeastern parishes reporting devotional
confraternities during the pastoral visits of 1613–14,
1654–62, and 1700–19   110
6 Percentage of rural testators making pious bequests by
wealth class   120
7 Percentage of urban testators making pious bequests by
wealth class, 1596–1715   122
8 The relationship between population and the probability of having
a devotional confraternity among the 108 northeastern parishes   127
9 Criminal complaints before the *bailliage* of Beaujolais   147
10 Priest–parishioner cases concerned with the tithe   148
11 Criminal complaints to the *sénéchaussée* of Lyon:
rural and urban cases   150
12 Defendants in priest–parishioner criminal cases   153
13 Geographic recruitment of curés: sixteenth and
eighteenth centuries   157

14 Social origins of the secular clergy according to the *Titres Patrimoniaux,* 1691–1717 and 1759–62   158
15 Tobit estimates for pious bequests in rural wills, 1512–1737   175
16 Effect of unit change in selected explanatory variables on pious bequests in rural wills, 1512–1737   177
17 Tobit estimates for pious bequests: rural wills with additional explanatory variables, 1512–1737   178
18 Tobit analysis of urban wills, 1521–95   180
19 Effect of a unit change in selected explanatory variables: urban wills, 1521–95   181
20 Probit analysis of requests for selected funeral rituals in urban wills, 1521–95   182
21 Tobit analysis of seventeenth-century urban wills   183

Acknowledgments

Yale University, the French government, the National Endowment for the Humanities, and the Humanities and Social Sciences Division of the California Institute of Technology supported my forays into the archives; without their assistance, this study would not have been possible.

Several tables and a small portion of appendix 2 have already appeared in print. This material is reprinted from Philip T. Hoffman, "Wills and Statistics: Tobit Analysis and the Counter Reformation in Lyon," *Journal of Interdisciplinary History* 14 (1984): 818-20, 822-23, and tables 1, 2, 3, with permission of *The Journal of Interdisciplinary History* and The MIT Press, Cambridge, Massachusetts.

Like most other historians, I have benefited from the help of numerous scholars, archivists, and friends both in France and in the United States. On the other side of the Atlantic, my principal debt is to Professor Jean-Pierre Gutton of the Université de Lyon-II. In the course of his seminar and in a number of conversations with him, I profited greatly from his extensive knowledge of the Old Regime and of the Lyon region. His suggestions led me to a number of important but little-known documents, such as the *fonds des communes* at the Rhône archives, the manuscripts of the municipal library in Roanne, the collections of the Diana in Montbrison, and the records of the Seminary of Saint-Irénée in Francheville, and his comments had a great impact on my thoughts. The late Richard Gascon also provided me with much useful counsel, and I am indebted as well to Chanoine J. Jomand, who kindly allowed me access to the archdiocesan archives and discussed their contents with me. At the Seminary of Saint-Irénée, the librarian, M. Martins, facilitated the consultation of documents, and the members of the *Société de la Diana* (especially M. Garnier and M. Paret) gave me a warm welcome in Montbrison. Finally, I shall remain forever grateful to the staffs of the Ain, Loire, and Rhône archives, especially Madame Annie Charnay of Lyon, who first acquainted me with the importance of criminal court records.

Here in the United States I must thank the graduate students and the faculty of the Yale history department who commented on an earlier version of this study. Jane Abray, Jill Felzan, Corrina Herrera, Fabio Sampoli, and

Jeff Merrick lent support, and professors Harry Miskimin, Roberto Lopez, John Merriman, and John Brewer contributed sage advice. Robert Harding's guidance proved crucial throughout my work, and a number of my colleagues at the California Institute of Technology offered suggestions that I deeply appreciated: Robert Bates, John Benton, Lance Davis, Peter Fay, J. Morgan Kousser, George W. Pigman, and Eleanor Searle. Natalie Davis, Lynn Hunt, Keith Luria, and Geoffrey Parker generously went over the text at one stage or another, and an anonymous reader's perceptive comments influenced me greatly. If I have not followed every bit of the advice these readers have given me, it is not out of ingratitude; indeed, some of their ideas I shall reserve for future research.

The staff of Yale University Press, particularly Charles Grench and Lawrence Kenney, deserve thanks for making this a better book. I also wish to thank Edith Huang, who helped me with the technicalities of word processing, and the John Randolph Haynes and Dora Haynes Foundation, which graciously helped defray the costs of preparing my manuscript. My largest debt, though, is to Kathryn Norberg, who provided encouragement and counsel at every stage of this project.

Church and Community in the
Diocese of Lyon, 1500—1789

Introduction

Although the Protestant Reformation has long attracted historians interested in literacy, urbanization, or the origins of capitalism, its Catholic counterpart has sorely lacked any such social history—at least until recently. One occasionally heard accusations that the Counter Reformation brutally choked social and economic development, but for years most social historians simply ignored the Counter Reformation, as if it were some vast cloud of incense that briefly cast a shadow over Catholic Europe and then dissipated without lasting social or economic effects. This lack of interest in social history, of course, merely reflected the preoccupations of the scholars who wrote on the Counter Reformation during the first half of this century. Concerned with the origins of reforms in the Catholic Church or with actions taken by the Church hierarchy, they focused on the papacy, the Council of Trent, and illustrious spiritual leaders, from Loyola and Spanish mystics to French *dévots*. While these writers produced distinguished works of scholarship—such as Jedin's history of the Council of Trent or Brémond's celebrated literary study of spirituality in France—they generally paid no attention to society, the economy, or popular culture, and they gave the social historian little reason to suspect that resurgent Catholicism drastically affected the lives of everyday people.[1]

My desire to investigate the social consequences of the Counter Reformation inspired this book. It examines what was, for the vast majority of the people in Catholic Europe, the crucial event of the Counter Reformation: the reform of the parish clergy. The clerical reforms transformed parish priests into important cultural intermediaries, who helped transmit the Counter Reformation to the laity at the local level. The priests in fact became the agents who institutionalized the Counter Reformation in towns and villages, and they also bore the brunt of lay resistance when the populace defended traditional spirituality, institutions, and morality against the Counter Reformation's encroachments. I have therefore taken up not only the issue of how the parish clergymen were reformed and what these remade clerics did, but also the question of what effect their actions had upon the laity.

In choosing this topic, I owe a certain debt of gratitude to historians who, since the 1960s, have begun to explore the social history of resurgent

Catholicism. Jeanne Ferté and Louis Pérouas in particular and other scholars have attempted local histories of the Counter Reformation.[2] Jean Delumeau and John Bossy have mined these local histories in order to speculate about the relationship between the Counter Reformation and early modern society. Delumeau has advanced the provocative hypothesis that the Catholic Reformation (along with its Protestant counterpart) amounted to the first real christianization of the European common people. By rooting out "paganism" and educating the faithful, Delumeau argues, the Catholic reformers gave the populace their first taste of orthodox spirituality and theology. In the process, the Catholic reformers and the Church hierarchy gained control of religion at the parish level, and as John Bossy maintains, this brought the Church into conflict with local institutions such as kinship groups and the family.[3]

I must also acknowledge a debt to historians of popular culture such as Carlo Ginzburg, Yves-Marie Bercé, Robert Muchembled, and Peter Burke, for they have suggested that the Counter Reformation fits into a much broader campaign to transform popular beliefs and rituals and to discipline the populace.[4] The Church's efforts to eradicate unorthodox superstitions, to suppress customary festivities, and to reshape time-honored devotions thus appear to be part of a widespread drive under way in both Protestant and Catholic lands. This movement cut down maypoles in England and snuffed out summer solstice fires in France, and it seemed to enjoy the support of lay and religious reformers throughout early modern Europe.

Although the writers on popular culture and the local historians of the Counter Reformation have begun to shed light upon the social implications of resurgent Catholicism, it is certainly possible to improve upon their work and accomplish things that none of them has attempted. To begin with, we can avoid a number of flaws and omissions which, to a greater or lesser degree, afflict both the local histories and Delumeau's synthetic work. All of these writings suffer (as Natalie Davis has observed) from an overly hierarchical view of religion.[5] When Ferté, Pérouas, and Delumeau describe the Counter Reformation's extensive campaign to suppress popular rituals (ringing the bells for the dead on Halloween, for example, or going on a pilgrimage to the shrine of some local healing saint), they often treat the popular customs simply as "disorders" or as pagan "superstitions," without asking what these customs meant to the populace. They fail to recognize that such customs themselves constituted a religion, a religion rich in meaning for ordinary people. One wonders, therefore, whether Ferté, Pérouas, Delumeau, and the others are correct in depicting the Counter Reformation as an effort to christianize a superstitious, irreligious population. Was it not instead a drive to replace an old, indigenous Christianity with a new orthodoxy?

Similarly, Ferté, Pérouas, and Delumeau imply that the Counter Reformation was the work of the Church hierarchy alone, even at the local level. In their view, reforming bishops and leaders of regular houses imposed the

Counter Reformation upon the lower clergy, and the priests then mechanically thrust it upon the faithful. Although such a perspective corresponds to the structure of the Catholic Church, it completely ignores the important yet little-known role that the laity played in the Counter Reformation. Worse, it implies that religious innovation and reform are one-way processes, moving from the clerical elite down to the populace.

The local studies by Ferté, Pérouas, and others suffer from other problems as well. Almost without exception, they ignore the sixteenth century in order to focus on the reforms undertaken after 1600.[6] Emphasis on the seventeenth century is certainly understandable, since many of the reforms that institutionalized the Counter Reformation on a local level (the establishment of seminaries, for example, or the creation of confraternities and catechism classes) were scarcely under way by 1600. But even in France, where the Wars of Religion delayed the work of the Church, it is nonetheless true that the resurgence of Catholic preaching and piety began well before the end of the 1500s.

In addition to neglecting the sixteenth-century background, the authors of these local studies also fail to make the most of their material. They seem to recoil from drawing possible conclusions about society and popular culture or from making connections with trends in politics, the economy, or society as a whole. Restricting themselves almost exclusively to ecclesiastical sources, they describe the Church's accomplishments on the local level from a narrow, ecclesiastical perspective. We can, of course, always turn to Bossy or Delumeau or to the historians of popular culture for fascinating speculation about the social impact of the Counter Reformation. But even their generalizations, which are often only provisional, leave many questions unanswered.

It is not at all clear, for example, how the campaign against popular culture fitted into the Tridentine reforms. Despite helpful suggestions by Burke and Muchembled, we still do not know which elements of Counter-Reformation spirituality helped justify this drive for order. Who supported this campaign remains equally murky, despite some evidence in the literature on popular culture. Was it solely a clerical initiative, or did laymen join the clergy in the movement to reshape popular culture? If so, what sort of laymen and clergymen were involved and what motives or beliefs mobilized them to participate?

We can, in fact, raise similar questions about the Counter Reformation as a whole, not just the campaign against popular culture. None of the existing works—not the local histories nor Bossy nor Delumeau—reveals who rallied to resurgent Catholicism, and the works on popular culture also slight this subject. And finally there is the matter of resistance. Bossy mentions the difficulties which the Counter Reformation faced at the hands of families and kinship groups. Similar allusions crop up in the book by Bercé. But neither of these authors sheds much light on what sort of individuals resisted the

Church. Nor is it clear what issues were involved or what the consequences were. We do not know, for example, whether the Tridentine reforms poisoned the relationship between priests and their parishioners or whether the reforms drove some individuals away from the Church.

In what follows, I have tried to avoid the omissions and pitfalls in the recent literature on the Counter Reformation. While my book is not a study of the entire Counter Reformation (such a history would be an impossibly ambitious task), it does weave together the major strands of the Counter Reformation's social history: the reform of the clergy, the spread of a new spirituality which the priests extolled, the campaign against popular culture in which they participated, and the questions of lay resistance and support. Previous historians have failed to unite these disparate elements in the story of resurgent Catholicism, and my account will therefore interest not just historians of the clergy or students of the Counter Reformation, but anyone intrigued by early modern social history.

Such a study of the parish priests' social and cultural role and the effects it had upon their relationship with the laity requires detailed research in local archives, for only local archives contain the documents that can bring back to life, say, an obscure village pastor or his long-forgotten flock. I therefore chose to make my history a study of the clerical reforms in one region. After spending several months considering nearly every bishopric in France and a number of episcopal sees in Germany, I finally selected the diocese of Lyon as the site for my research. My reasons were simple. In the first place, Lyon had witnessed all the changes that Delumeau and other historians consider representative of the Counter Reformation, from Jesuit missions and new seminaries to regular parish visits and more frequent diocesan synods. Second, while early modern Lyon has attracted a number of gifted historians—the names of Natalie Davis, Maurice Garden, Richard Gascon, and Jean-Pierre Gutton immediately come to mind—the story of the local Counter Reformation remains largely unknown. Finally, and most important, Lyon and its environs boast archives that are second to none. Before I chose Lyon, I went through the relevant archival inventories for nearly every diocese in France, and I did the same for a number of German regions as well. I also consulted archivists and secondary authorities. This exercise made it very clear that the source material for the diocese of Lyon was among the best available. Subsequent work in other archives has only reaffirmed this judgment.

Although I chose to do a local history, I have sought to avoid the parochialism that afflicts so many local studies by making comparisons with other regions in Europe whenever the scanty literature makes this possible. Such comparisons must be made with care, of course, for in the diocese of Lyon the Counter Reformation took a path a bit different than it did in, say, central Europe, where papal legates wielded an influence on the local level that was unheard of in Gallican France.[7] My goal has always been to balance a sensitivity to these local variations with an awareness that the events in the diocese of Lyon were part of a larger process unfolding throughout the whole of Catholic Europe.

While the geographical scope is narrow, the chronological scope is quite broad. The transformation that forms my subject was accomplished with excruciating slowness, and a long time scale (the *longue durée* as the French would say) is the only feasible way to study it. Unlike the other local studies, mine begins early in the sixteenth century. This is so for two reasons. First of all, it is impossible to understand the social impact of the seventeenth-century reforms of the clergy without first looking at the parish priests' role in sixteenth-century communities. Second, parish priests in the city of Lyon felt the effects of the Counter Reformation well before 1600.

I was convinced also that I had to pursue my topic deep into the eighteenth century. Extending a work on the Counter Reformation past 1700 will no doubt shock many historians, who do not customarily associate the Counter Reformation with so late a period. Modern scholarship demonstrates, however, that the Counter Reformation was "certainly not over in 1700," and this generalization holds in particular for the reforms of the clergy.[8] In Lyon and in many other dioceses, for example, the diocesan seminaries, which were the main instrument for reforming the priesthood, were scarcely established (and in some dioceses still nonexistent) in the first decades of the eighteenth century. The Counter Reformation itself thus demands that research be pushed up to at least 1700 or 1725. My own research goes still further, for even after the Counter Reformation itself had faded, its legacy continued to affect society. Parish priests, for instance, continued until the end of the Old Regime to carry out the role that the Counter-Reformation Church had assigned them, despite the problems that this role caused them during the last half of the eighteenth century. Since these problems on the eve of the French Revolution were an outgrowth of the reforms of the clergy, I continued my research up to 1789.

I should perhaps caution the reader about several peculiarities of vocabulary in the chapters that follow. In the first place, unless otherwise stated, the adjective *urban* will apply only to the metropolis of Lyon, and not to the small cities and market towns of the diocese. While in other contexts one might well consider even the market towns as urban, for our purposes they seem far closer to villages. Lyon, after all, was the only community in the diocese with over ten thousand inhabitants, and it alone had an intendant, a cathedral, a seminary, and a large Protestant population.

I shall also speak of *the* Counter Reformation in the singular, even though reform in the Catholic Church consisted of so many different and at times conflicting movements that it might be better to speak of "Counter Reformations," as Ranke did.[9] The plural might better describe a campaign that embraced men as different as Loyola and Borromeo and that produced theologies as diverse as Molinism and Jansenism. But the singular is now customary usage, and we already have the sample of *the* Reformation, a term that is stretched to cover both Luther and Thomas Müntzer. Similarly, the reader should know that the terms *Catholic Reformation, resurgent Catholicism,* and *Tridentine Catholicism* will be used as synonyms for the Counter Reformation. I realize that this may discomfit a few sensitive persons. After all, the term *Counter Reformation* is sometimes reserved for the Church's defensive reaction against Protestantism, while *Catholic Reformation* is employed to stress Catholicism's own internal reform. More important, *Tridentine Catholicism* bears connotations different from the other terms because it often refers specifically to the hierarchical, episcopal model of reform approved at the Council of Trent and later enacted throughout Europe. This vision of episcopal reform (which would preserve the Church's structure) conflicted with the less conservative model of missionary work supported by the Jesuits, missionary work that was very important in the early stages of the Counter Reformation.[10] I use all of these expressions synonymously merely for the sake of variety.

While I shall focus upon the parish priests in what follows (and in particular upon their role as agents of the Counter Reformation), I shall not hesitate to discuss either the regular orders or the local ecclesiastical hierarchy when necessary. Similarly, I shall devote considerable attention to lay piety and lay reactions to resurgent Catholicism, since this is necessary to any understanding of the priests' social role. Knowing which elements of Tridentine Catholicism attracted the laity and which laymen resisted the Counter Reformation affords us a much firmer grasp on the relationship between priests and parishioners. Without this knowledge, one would repeat the errors of earlier historians, who gazed down upon the Counter Reformation from a perch high in the ecclesiastical hierarchy and never saw the faithful or those closest to them, the parish clergy.

1
Rapprochement with the Elite: The Parish Clergy in the City of Lyon from 1500 to 1595

When Henry II and Catherine de Médicis entered Lyon on a Sunday late in September 1548, the city greeted them with what was, in the words of a knowledgeable eyewitness, "by unanimous judgment one of the most lovely entry ceremonies ever staged for the king of this realm, and perhaps for any prince in any other place."[1] One of the financial capitals of Europe, Lyon was at the peak of its commercial power, and it had drawn upon the fantastic wealth of its foreign banking community to welcome the king. The city's artists and poets, who supervised the affair, made the ceremony a lavish spectacle of Renaissance magnificence, adorning the king's path along the western bank of the languid river Saône with a host of ornate constructions. Arches, gates, and wine-spouting statues graced the monarch's way, and as his cortege moved south along the narrow street that hugged the river's edge, he viewed an Italian comedy, a mock naval battle, and a combat of gladiators.[2]

The procession escorting the king into Lyon that day numbered some seven thousand persons, including representatives of nearly every privileged group in the city. First to march by was the urban militia: the musketeers and the guards who represented the force of order in the neighborhoods. At their rear strutted twenty ranks of richly costumed craftsmen, ranging from lowly butchers and teamsters to the printers and textile tradesmen who made the city famous throughout Europe. A short distance behind them came the foreign "nations," the commercial magnates and bankers from Germany, Lucca, Florence, and Milan, whose Italian velours and satin robes distinguished them as the wealthiest group in Lyon. Next to file past were the judges and lawyers of the archbishop's seignorial court and then the royal officers: the king's tax officials and the magistrates from the city's royal court (the *sénéchaussée*). Parading behind them were the city "notables," a small group of prosperous merchants who advised the city council; then the city youth (*enfants de la ville*), Lyon's organization of well-to-do young men; and the city council itself, a body dominated by an urban patriciate of rich, native-born merchants. Near the end came the royal governor, who, along with his lieutenant, was the monarch's chief representative in Lyon, the archbishop, Hippolyte d'Este, followed by the court, and last of all the king.

Almost half a century after that Sunday in 1548, at a time when France was only beginning to recover from three decades of devastating civil war and religious strife, Lyon witnessed another, nearly identical entry parade. This time, in September 1595, it was King Henry IV who entered Lyon, and, like Henry II, he was escorted into the city by a resplendent cavalcade of the city's notables and privileged classes. Although the order of this second procession was almost precisely the same as in 1548, the two ceremonies differed in an important way. One prestigious group, conspicuously absent in 1548, was obtrusively present in 1595: the city clergy. Actually, the city's ecclesiastics had greeted the king before the parade started in 1548, but save for the archbishop, the clergy did not march in the procession with Henry II. In 1595, however, the clergy strode at the front of the procession. Having raised statues and a huge triumphal arch in honor of "Henry the Great, the divinely crowned and most Christian king of France and Navarre," the priests presented him with a spotless white damask canopy at the conclusion of the parade and in general outdid every other social group in the city in lavishing praise upon their monarch.[3]

More than a mere detail, this contrast between the two processions was a telling sign of the clergy's changing role in the city during the last half of the sixteenth century. Marching in a royal entry parade (as opposed to simply greeting the king before or after his entry) meant a great deal to contemporaries, and as we shall see, the clergy cared deeply about such rituals. Their absence in 1548 was in fact symptomatic of their lack of influence in city government and their exclusion from much of the city's life at that time. Although they were far from politically impotent, they were at odds with the city council and had no influence over it at midcentury. Worse, they were unable to meet the spiritual needs of a number of social groups, and they found themselves alienated from many laymen. Their conspicuous presence in 1595, on the other hand, bore striking witness to a momentous rapprochement between the urban clergy and the lay community, a rapprochement effected after the 1560s. Under the twin pressures of the need for solidarity against the Protestants and the incipient movement to reform the Catholic Church, the divisions between the clergy and the urban laity (or at least the lay elite) were overcome, and the ecclesiastics gained a political importance they had not enjoyed since the Middle Ages. This reconciliation would shape the role of the parish priests during the two centuries to come, but before we examine it, we should first look at sixteenth-century Lyon, the city's inhabitants and its numerous clergymen.

The City of Lyon and Its Inhabitants

Lyon stood at the confluence of the Saône and the larger, swifter river Rhône, which ran into the city from the plains to the northeast (figure 1). The Saône and the Rhône divided the city into two distinct parts. One, the tongue of land between the two rivers, which was called the peninsula, was made up of bustling neighborhoods of traders and artisans. The other, the right bank, lay across the Saône from this newer section of the city. Wedged between the river and the steep hills to the west, this district was the medieval city, the cramped quarters of the cathedral and law courts. It was also the residence of many of the city's wealthiest merchants.

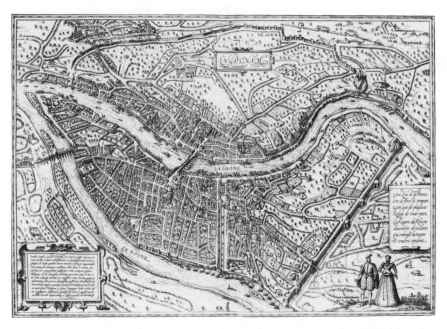

Figure 1. Lyon in the sixteenth century. This reduction of the twenty-five-plate *plan scénographique* is from Georg Braun and Franz Hogenberg, *Civitates orbis terrarum* (Cologne, 1572).

Sixty to seventy thousand persons dwelled in these two districts at mid-century, making Lyon the third largest city in France and, by sixteenth-century standards, a great city. As the artistry displayed in the entry ceremony of 1548 suggests, Lyon was a center of the Renaissance, the place where Rabelais had printed *Gargantua* and *Pantagruel,* the home of poets like

Louise Labé and Maurice Scève. Lyon was also a notable commercial center, where four annual fairs attracted businessmen from throughout Europe to exchange spices from the Orient, silks from Italy, woolens from Holland, England, and France, leather, hardware, arms, linen, and thread from Lyon's hinterland, and books, velvet, and taffetas from the city itself. The buyers and sellers were drawn to the fairs by the freedom from taxes and the favorable legal climate of a city long hospitable to trade. They were drawn too by the credit instruments the city put at their disposal, for after the sale and purchase of goods at the fairs, merchants and bankers met to settle and renegotiate loans and bills of exchange, making Lyon a money market that even kings sought to tap. The foreign merchants residing in the city, especially the Italians, controlled the international side of this trade as well as the sophisticated banking operations. Native merchants concentrated on domestic trade, selling French goods to foreigners for export and purchasing foreign goods for resale within the kingdom. Lyon's economic vitality also attracted a host of artisans and journeymen, who immigrated to Lyon from towns and villages throughout France and the rest of Europe.[4]

Since the city was so devoted to business, it is not at all surprising that merchants dominated the social and political hierarchy. Lyon's wealthiest merchants were the foreign bankers and traders. Though barred from holding municipal offices (unless they were naturalized), their loans to the city and to the king gave them considerable influence in municipal affairs. Just below them in the hierarchy of wealth and power stood the city's native merchants, from the rich members of the urban patriciate, who controlled the city government, to modest shopkeepers. Occupying roughly the same social strata were the lawyers and the officials of the city's seignorial and royal courts and the tax administration, a group that embraced lowly sergeants at law, modest petitioners, clerks and attorneys, and the prosperous tax collectors, barristers, and magistrates of the sénéchaussée. The artisans, some of whom had a slight voice in city affairs, clung to the social ladder on rungs below the merchants, lawyers, and officers. At the bottom of the social hierarchy were the "common people," to use the contemporary expression: the less prosperous artisans, the journeymen, and day laborers, distinguished by their lack of property and their financial insecurity. Constituting a majority of the urban population, this body of men and women had no voice in city affairs, save when they threatened to riot.[5]

The Clergy and Churches of the City

Like the lay estates, ecclesiastical society in sixteenth-century Lyon was large, complex, and hierarchical. To count precisely all the Catholic clergymen serving these churches in the city at midcentury would be impossible, for their numbers varied, and the same person often occupied several posts. But we can offer some rough estimates. Several hundred ecclesiastics (not all of them priests) were attached to the cathedral, four collegiate churches, and twelve parishes of the city. These included over one hundred canons, thirteen priests who worked as pastors (curés or their equivalent), and a larger number of vicars, curates, and stipendiary priests. Perhaps two hundred more clergymen were associated with the city's nine monasteries and religious houses and its numerous chapels. These ecclesiastics were not a homogenous collection of individuals. Contemporaries did at times regard the city clergy as one powerful body, but they also recognized it as a disparate group, composed of a variety of individuals who had diverse backgrounds and varying powers and who were associated with a number of different churches.[6]

At the pinnacle of ecclesiastical society in Lyon stood the clergy of the cathedral of Saint-Jean. Nestled between the foot of the hillside and the Saône River, Saint-Jean lay in the heart of the city's medieval quarter (see figure 2 for the location of this and other churches), and its thirty-odd canons were, along with the archbishop, the richest and most powerful ecclesiastics in Lyon. Since the fifteenth century, the canons of Saint-Jean had styled themselves counts because of the jurisdiction they held over the county of Lyon. While not all the canon-counts were priests, each one was obliged to prove his descent from four generations of nobility, and thus it is not surprising that the canon-counts were drawn from the most illustrious families of the local nobility. In fact, cathedral chairs often passed down from uncle to nephew in the "best" families, such as the d'Albons.

The cathedral and its adjacent "daughter" churches, Saint-Etienne and the parish of Sainte-Croix, housed still more clerics with a welter of titles and duties.[7] Among them were four *custodes,* who served as pastors, seven *chevaliers,* who looked after the cathedral's legal affairs, a *théologal,* who gave sermons and instructed young clerics of the cathedral in doctrine, and twenty curates, who said masses and helped assure the divine service. These clergymen, nearly all priests, were almost invariably well educated, and before assuming their posts they were required to contribute between 100 and 200 *livres* to the chapter's endowment—a sum large enough to restrict the social recruitment of the cathedral clergy. The expected contribution was sufficient to buy an office of sergeant at law at the sénéchaussée, and it certainly exceeded the means of journeymen in the building trades, some of the best paid among the common people. It was thus to be expected that the custodes, chevaliers, théologaux, and curates were the sons of well-off merchants or officers from Lyon and the surrounding region. For example, Jean and Etienne du Choul, custodes in the first half of the century, were the offspring of a seignorial judge, and Antoine de Bresse, a curate in 1527, was the nephew of the cathedral treasurer. The custodes and even the curates often held additional posts with the archbishop or as canons in the other collegiate churches of the city. Thus Jean Cyberand, custode of Sainte-Croix until his

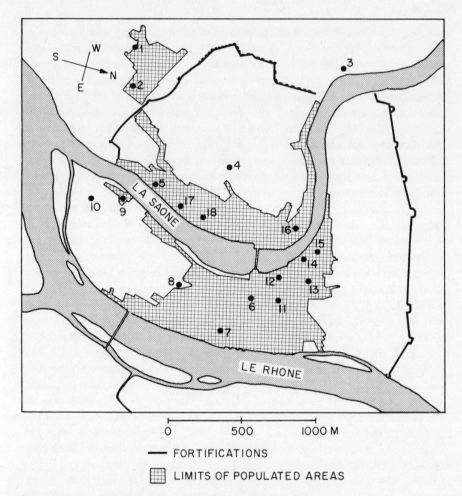

Figure 2. Major churches and male religious orders in Lyon

1. Church of Saint-Irénée
2. Church of Saint-Just
3. Observant Franciscans' Convent
4. Church of Saint-Thomas-de-Fourvière
5. Church of Saint-Georges
6. Church of Saint-Nizier
7. Franciscans of Saint-Bonaventure Convent
8. Dominicans' Convent
9. Church of Saint-Michel
10. Abbey of Saint-Martin-d'Ainay
11. Church of Saint-Pierre-et-Saint-Saturnin
12. Church of Notre-Dame-de-Platière
13. Carmelites' Convent
14. Augustinians' Convent
15. Church of Saint-Vincent
16. Church of Saint-Paul
17. Church of Saint-Pierre-le-Vieux
18. Cathedral of Saint-Jean and Associated Churches of Saint-Etienne and Sainte-Croix

death in 1572, was a canon in two other collegiate churches and served as a judge in the archdiocesan officiality. Most of the custodes and the curates had risen from the ranks of the cathedral's thirty or more stipendiary priests, who labored saying masses in the church's numerous chapels. Of course, many of the stipendiary priests, who usually began their careers by singing in the church choir, never managed to become custodes or curates. It was among them that one could find the only priests in the cathedral who came from more modest social strata, from families of artisans.

To support this multitude of clergymen, the cathedral drew upon an enormous portfolio of land holdings, tithe rights, annuities, and seignorial jurisdictions. It owned buildings in Lyon, and its property spilled over into the hinterland, reaching north into Beaujolais, west into Forez, and east into Bresse and Dauphiné. With land, pensions, and tithe rights in over sixty-seven villages and seignorial justices in nearly all of these, Saint-Jean could fund scores of chapels, prebends, and benefices. In particular, the cathedral canons held direct patronage rights to some eighty-four parishes. Such wealth and associated patronage rights contributed greatly to the cathedral's power. So did the canon-counts' seigniories. Along with the archbishop, who exercised seignorial jurisdiction over the city of Lyon and ten nearby communities, the canon-counts of Saint-Jean were, in fact, the preeminent lords of the region.[8]

The four other collegiate churches in Lyon all served as parishes, with a canon or officer in each one holding the post of pastor. The canons in these four churches were in turn assisted by an army of curates and stipendiary priests, who performed many of the pastoral duties, as early baptismal registers testify.[9] One of these four churches—Saint-Thomas-de-Fourvière—played little active role in the religious life of the city, but the other three—Saint-Just, Saint-Paul, and Saint-Nizier—deserve more attention. Like the cathedral, these three collegiate churches obliged their canons and priests to contribute to the collegiate endowment when they assumed their offices. This requirement helped restrict recruitment of their canons to the local elite, although none of the clerics at the collegiate churches could boast such illustrious pedigrees as the august canon-counts of Saint-Jean. At Saint-Just, the canons were often children of recently ennobled judges or officeholders from Lyon. For example, Antoine Bellièvre, canon at Saint-Just in 1556, and Andrieu du Lange, canon in 1560, both came from prominent local magistrates' families. At Saint-Paul, the canons were drawn from the Lyon patriciate and from wealthy lawyers' families, and at Saint-Nizier, which was a bit less prestigious, they tended to be the sons of affluent merchants. In any case, at all of these collegiate churches one could find men with relatives on the city council or in the royal courts.[10]

The curates and stipendiary priests associated with the collegiate churches had less exalted origins. At Saint-Just, the curates were the offspring of local lawyers, while at Saint-Paul and Saint-Nizier they were drawn from families of lesser merchants. The stipendiary priests, who usually rose from the ranks of the church choir, came from even more modest social strata. Of nineteen choirboys who entered Saint-Nizier in the years 1548–56, for example, eight were fathered by artisans, while only three were the children of merchants, lawyers, or officeholders.[11] These choirboys did not come from afar, either. Of the nineteen, nine had grown up in Lyon itself, four in the surrounding diocese, and all but one of the others in the nearby provinces of Dauphiné or Burgundy. The stipendiary priests who began their careers in the choir no doubt had similar origins.

Like those at the cathedral, the canons and priests at the collegiate churches were generally well educated. At Saint-Paul and Saint-Nizier, for instance, most of the curates and stipendiary priests had graduated from a university, and canons were even more likely to possess a diploma.[12] Large personal libraries were common. Phillippe Docheis, a priest at Saint-Just, left only 4 books when he died in 1496, but his colleague Claude Monthelein, a canon, owned 27 volumes in 1498. At least 10 of these were printed (rather than manuscript), and apart from a hymnal and several other liturgical works, most of Monthelein's books dealt with canon law. François Pupier, a canon who died in 1578, seemed positively learned. Besides some canon law and civil law, his library of over 213 volumes included works in Greek, Hebrew, and Italian, and it ranged from Aristophanes, Xenophon, and Virgil to Boccaccio, Erasmus, Budé, and the Catechism and Breviary of Trent.[13]

To support their ecclesiastics, the collegiate churches relied upon income from real estate. None of the churches was as rich as the cathedral, but Saint-Just and Saint-Paul together possessed land, tithe rights, and seignorial justices in over fifty parishes. Saint-Nizier lacked such extensive rural holdings, but along with the other collegiate churches, it owned both buildings and numerous annuities owed by property owners in Lyon. The three collegiate churches also exercised patronage rights over seventy-four rural parishes.[14]

In addition to the cathedral and the four collegiate churches, the city had seven other parishes: Saint-Irénée (actually a priory), Notre-Dame-de-Platière (also a priory), Saint-Georges, Saint-Pierre-le-Vieux, Saint-Vincent, Saint-Michel, and Saint-Pierre-et-Saint-Saturnin, the annex of a luxurious Benedictine convent. Often the priests at these parishes held prebends at the cathedral or at the collegiate churches. Thus Guillaume de la Barge, one of the canon-counts, served as curé of Notre-Dame-de-Platière in 1559, and Clement Maistret, a canon of Saint-Nizier, ministered to the faithful as vicar of Saint-Georges. In general, the parish clergymen came from backgrounds similar to those of the clergy at the collegiate churches. Born into local families of merchants or artisans, they were usually well educated as well.[15]

The parish clergymen were of course not the only ecclesiastics who filed about the streets of the city. Priests were also attached to the hospital and to the numerous chapels of the city, and a large squadron of monks and friars—regular clergymen—helped meet the spiritual needs of the faithful. Oldest among these regular communities was the abbey of Saint-Martin-d'Ainay, to which the parish of Saint-Michel was attached. Ainay sheltered sixteen monks, who were usually nobly born or recruited from the mercantile elite of Lyon. The monks occasionally served as aides to the archbishop, but otherwise they did not play an active part in the life of the city. The same cannot be said of the members of the five mendicant houses in Lyon: the Augustinians, located near the parish of Saint-Vincent; the Carmelites, in the parish of Notre-Dame-de-la-Platière; the Dominicans (known locally as the Jacobins) and the Franciscans of Saint-Bonaventure (known as the Cordeliers), both in the parish of Saint-Nizier; and the Observant Franciscans, on the banks of the Saône beyond Saint-Paul.

In several important respects, these mendicants differed from their colleagues among the secular clergy. First of all, whereas natives to Lyon or the nearby countryside predominated among the seculars, the mendicants came from distant provinces. At Saint-Nizier, we recall, nearly one-half the clerics entering the choir were natives of Lyon, and only a quarter arrived from outside the diocese. At the Cordeliers, by contrast, only one-fifth of the brothers were born in Lyon, and nearly three-quarters hailed from beyond the diocesan borders. Many of these had migrated from provinces as far away as Savoy, Paris, or Champagne, whereas the choirboys at Saint-Nizier usually came from no further than Dauphiné or Burgundy. Newcomers to Lyon also abounded at the Dominicans.[16]

While the meager records do not allow us to say much more about the friars save that they were generally well educated, it is clear that the mendicant houses lacked the enormous wealth and power of the cathedral and the collegiate churches. Together, the five friaries possessed only a few scattered parcels of land outside Lyon, and they held no significant patronage rights. The friaries owned some annuities and property within the city, but their holdings were dwarfed by those of the cathedral and the collegiate churches. A 1555 list shows, for instance, that the various mendicant houses earned between 13 and 162 livres a year from annuities payed by urban property owners. Saint-Paul and Saint-Nizier, by contrast, received 686 and 949 livres a year, respectively, and the cathedral got over 1,000.[17]

Despite the differences in wealth and power within the First Estate and the disputes which occasionally erupted between various ecclesiastical corps, a certain unity prevailed among the clergy. Priests shuttled from benefice to benefice at Lyon's ecclesiastical institutions, and as we have seen, it was not unusual for a cleric to serve the archbishop, a collegiate church, and even another parish at the same time. Among the secular clergymen, the sense of unity was reinforced by bonds to lay society in Lyon. After all, many of these secular clergymen had grown up in Lyon, and they retained ties to their families and local friends. Antoine Bellièvre, a canon at Saint-Just, presided at his nephew's nuptials in 1556, and other clerics, from canons to stipendiary priests, attended relatives' marriages or served as godfathers for kith and kin.[18]

The links between the various churches and the clerics' ties to the local community united Lyon's ecclesiastics—or at least its seculars—and hardened the clergy to outsiders. In this chapter, we shall therefore broaden our definition of the city's parish clergy to cover all of the ecclesiastics attached to the cathedral and to the collegiate churches, from the lofty canon-counts to the lowly stipendiary priests. Our justification for doing so is the overriding unity that joined the clergymen and the fact that even the canons had religious duties to perform. We shall discuss the mendicants as well, since they played a major role in the spiritual life of the city. With a clear sense then of who the clergymen were in Lyon, let us now consider the various problems their Church faced at midcentury. One of these problems was strife between the clergy and the laity.

Troubles Between Laymen and the Parish Clergy

Probably the most striking feature of the clergy's relationship with the urban laity was the deep-rooted enmity between the cathedral and city hall, an abiding political tradition that, by association, created ill will between the laity and much of the parish clergy. The origins of this hostility, which bonds of blood and acquaintance between individual clergymen and laymen did not dispel, go back as far as the thirteenth century, when the city's merchants battled the archbishop and canons—the seigniors of the city—in order to win a municipal charter.[19] Although Lyon finally gained its charter, strife between cathedral and city hall persisted into the sixteenth century. The archbishop and the canon-counts argued continually with the municipal government over precedence, fiscal privileges, property rights, and their seignorial prerogative of policing the city. Worse, they resented their exclusion from Lyon's political life. Although they were rich and powerful seigniors, the archbishop and canon-counts had little influence over the merchants who controlled the city government in the sixteenth century, and from time to time they found themselves barred from general assemblies of the city's privileged inhabitants. Even when they were not excluded from these assemblies, they often feared to attend, lest they and the rest of the clergy be forced to contribute to the city's coffers.

The archbishop and the canon-counts did not simply acquiesce in this loss of power and influence. In the 1540s and 1550s they intervened in a number of political squabbles in an effort to influence the city council's policies and put an end to their exile from urban political life. They sought, first of all, to push the council toward repression of the growing Protestant community.

Second, there were fiscal disputes. When, for example, the council considered raising money by means of an indirect tax on necessities, the archbishop and the canon-counts joined the resulting fray on the side of the common people, whose real wages were being reduced by inflation and who protested that other merchandise ought to be taxed. These battles culminated in 1558, when the archbishop and the canon-counts allied with the city's lawyers (who had their own grievances against the municipal government) in a lawsuit denouncing the policies of the city government and claiming that the city council was monopolized by a clique of rich merchants.

The archbishop and canon-counts undoubtedly had justice on their side. Their accusation that thirty rich merchants controlled city government and manipulated municipal expenditures and taxes in their own self-interest rang largely true. Seventeen affluent families, nearly all of them involved in trade, did dominate the city council and through it the other institutions of municipal government. These merchants indulged themselves when spending the city's money, profited from lower property tax rates, and benefited from the city's decision to levy duties not on the cloth or spices they sold, but on necessities such as food and wine. The clergy could thus claim that this urban patriciate was enriching itself and impoverishing the common people, against all principles of "Christian charity . . . and the duty . . . of magistrates."[20]

The clergy's action, though, was itself hardly devoid of self-interest. The archbishop and the canon-counts themselves produced substantial amounts of grain and wine on their own rural lands. They therefore stood to lose heavily if Lyon taxed food and drink which they or their tenants sold in the city. It was apparently this levy rather than the hardship of the common people that most worried the archbishop and the canon-counts, for in settling their lawsuit in 1559 they abandoned the commoners and in effect agreed to let the city tax food and wine so long as all produce from their own and other clerical lands was declared tax-exempt. They even went so far as to exploit this exemption by importing duty-free wine into Lyon and selling it at the tax-inflated price. Nor was the rest of the settlement the archbishop and canon-counts reached with the city council in 1559 any more mindful of the common people; indeed, in the settlement the commoners were largely forgotten.[21]

In the end, the archbishop and the canon-counts gained little besides the tax exemption from their repeated campaigns. The city council continued its policy of religious neutrality, for even the Catholic majority among the councilmen agreed that this policy was best for trade. Neutrality, moreover, was in keeping with the city's "laic tradition": a tradition that had as its focus the conflict between the cathedral and city hall and that was reinforced early in the sixteenth century when the city council took over secondary education and public welfare in Lyon. The settlement of the 1558 lawsuit did give the archbishop, the canon-counts, and the rest of the city's clergy the right to attend the general assemblies and witness the rendering of the city's accounts.[22] However, the outbreak of the Wars of Religion soon nullified this arrangement, and the Church was again impotent before the hostile urban patriciate.

The magistrates' antiecclesiastical tendencies were typical of Lyon's elite. The attitude of Jean Guéraud, a merchant draper and city notable, was probably representative. Though a devout Catholic, he found the canon-counts' suit against the city infuriating, and in his diary he railed against the clergy on a number of occasions. The extent to which this ill will extended beyond the cathedral varied, of course, from church to church. Saint-Paul, for example, was not usually at odds with the city, but Saint-Just traditionally was. In any case, disputes between city hall and various churches over property rights and the use of Church land for urban renewal were common, and these disputes could involve even the mendicants. And when the city councilors settled the lawsuit of 1558 they had to sign the unpleasant agreement along with representatives not just of the canon-counts but of nearly all the city's chapters and parishes.[23]

If political strife divided the canon-counts and perhaps some of Lyon's other clergy from the wealthy merchants on the city council, then social and economic barriers isolated the upper clergy from the artisans and the common people. The canons, after all, were recruited from prosperous local families. As canons, they were property owners and landlords in the city. They therefore had little in common with the poor artisans, journeymen, or day laborers (the same statement in fact applies to most of the parish clergy, save for some of the stipendiary priests). It is clear too that the canons scarcely led lives of poverty. We have only to consider the estate left by Claude Damour, a priest and canon at Saint-Nizier in the late sixteenth and early seventeenth centuries. Damour did not eat his meals on wood, iron, or pottery, like the humble; nor was his dinner served on bourgeois tin. He dined on silver, like aristocrats and the richest of merchants. The rest of Damour's belongings—a clock, money from France and Italy, chests full of clothing—are by no means extraordinary, and his estate was valued at only 1,157 livres, a substantial but not enormous sum. Yet if Damour was not rich, his silver plates suggest a manner of living that even most of Lyon's merchants would have found a bit ostentatious. Nor was Damour exceptional, for even greater opulence prevailed at the other collegiate churches and at the cathedral. At Saint-Just, canon François Pupier owned silver, tapestries, and rich robes of silk and velvet. Canon Pierre de Masso's moveable property alone was worth nearly 2,300 livres in 1593, almost twelve years' salary for a journeyman in the construction trades. Such affluence was enjoyed by other clerics at Saint-Just as well.[24]

While wealth isolated the upper clergy from the common people, another social barrier separated the parish clergy as a whole from the city's large immigrant population. As we have seen, only the mendicants recruited priests from afar. Most of the parish clerics, from canons to stipendiary priests, were natives to Lyon or to nearby provinces. By contrast, many of the immigrants in the city, who ranged from maidservants and journeymen to wealthy merchants, came from more distant provinces or from foreign countries. As Natalie Davis has argued, the native Catholic clergy and the Church as a whole failed to welcome these numerous immigrants and to integrate them into urban society. In fact, some native clergymen felt a certain ambivalence toward the immigrants, and in times of danger their ambivalence could turn into actual distrust.[25]

A final problem that beset the relationship between the parish clergy and the laity was the behavior of the lower clergy. The curates, stipendiary priests, and less prestigious curés were often arrogant and shockingly immoral, and their conduct repelled many laymen and women. At Saint-Nizier, a merchant from the parish complained to the canons in 1593 that he had seen one of the church's curates in the company of a band of drunks; he found this conduct "scandalous" because of the priest's "clerical estate." In 1573, parishioners of Saint-Nizier denounced priests who left services early. Other breaches of decorum on the part of the chapter's lower clergymen abound in the capitulary registers. During a procession in 1584, curate Jacques Bellache got into an argument with Claude Mellier, the priest who was directing the procession. Bellache shouted at Mellier that he was an "ass" and a "fool" and that he could "go to the moon," words so unbecoming of a priest that they reportedly shocked the "numerous people" present. At Saint-Georges in 1572, over twenty parishioners went before the officiality (the ecclesiastical court) to file a complaint against the pastor and the other priests of their church. According to the complaint, the pastor and his vicars did not reside in the parish; high mass was never said; and, worst of all, when in need of their curé, the parishioners had to fetch the wanton fellow from "a house of prostitution and scandal."[26]

Additional examples of dubious behavior can be cited at other parishes: at Saint-Just in particular. Consider the case of Pierre Jarrolier, one of the chapter's curés in the sixteenth century. Hauled before Saint-Just's seignorial justice in 1543, this fellow was denounced by one of his parishioners, whom he had beaten up to collect a debt. Ten years later, he was disciplined for his unseemly habit of consorting with prostitutes. Laymen were disgusted by such failures to live up to the ideals of priestly conduct, and hypocrisy and arrogance only compounded the lower clergy's shortcomings. Claude Le Grand, another curé of Saint-Just, filed a complaint with the chapter's seignorial justice that led to the prosecution of tavernkeeper Benoist Chalon and his wife for serving meat on the eve of the feast of Saint Bartholomew, in violation of the rules of the jurisdiction. Three years later, Le Grand himself was stripped of his post as curé for being a notorious "fornicator, scandalous and incorrigible." Such appalling conduct was not confined simply to the curés of Saint-Just; other members of the church's lower clergy were just as guilty. In 1579, the curate Jean Thomas, in the company of two canons and several other clerics, encountered the parishioner Claude Robert in a neighborhood butcher shop. The clergymen began to ridicule Robert, and Thomas seized his hat. A fight broke out, and Thomas smote the layman with a sword, despite Robert's protestations that this was hardly proper conduct for a man of the cloth.[27]

Whether it was immorality or violence, contemporaries considered such ecclesiastical behavior reprehensible. In the fifteenth century, François Garin, a prosperous Lyon merchant, had devoted two hundred lines of verse to denouncing the sexual sins of clergymen, and Jean Guéraud grumbled when a misbehaving cleric at Saint-Paul seemed to evade punishment for his role in a robbery.[28] Garin and Guéraud belonged to the city's elite, but the concerns they shared were not peculiar to the well-to-do. The twenty laymen from the impoverished parish of Saint-Georges who excoriated their pastor's misdeeds were by no stretch of the imagination patricians, and the same applies to Claude Robert and the other laymen who complained of violence at Saint-Just.

Given the grievous shortcomings of many parish priests and the long tradition of ill will between the cathedral and city hall, it is not surprising that layfolk might occasionally strike out in anger against the clergy. At the entry parade of Archbishop d'Este in 1540, a fight broke out between the city youth and the priests representing the churches of Lyon. The youths disrupted the clergy's parade order and roughed up some of the priests so severely that they had to be taken to the hospital. A few of the injured clergymen were hurt so badly that the cathedral and collegiate churches took up a collection on their behalf. In addition, the churches decided to sue the city government, since the city youth apparently acted under the council's auspices.

Even the devout Catholic notable Jean Guéraud could take pleasure in the fact that the clergy had been beaten up during the 1540 parade. The members of the city council no doubt shared Guéraud's opinion, for they did nothing to discipline the city youth and made every effort to keep the clergy from marching in subsequent parades during the 1540s and 1550s. The clergy desperately wanted to join these entries (instead of simply greeting visiting dignitaries outside the city), but the city councilors adamantly refused, arguing that since they paid for the entries the clergy had no right to participate in them.[29]

The incident in 1540 and the disputes over subsequent entry parades go to the heart of the hostility that divided Lyon's clergy from its lay elite. To the clergy, the city seemed to be interfering with the Church's rightful and immemorial place of honor in municipal affairs. To the city councilors, the clerics appeared guilty of unjust and even outrageous pretensions. Despite all the family ties linking the clergy and the lay elite, despite several attempted reconciliations, enmity toward ecclesiastics was thus widespread among the urban patricians, among Catholics as well as Protestants. To what extent lesser merchants, artisans, and the common people shared these feelings of ill will is hard to say. All we know is that a social gulf separated many of the people from the clergy and that commoners actually complained of ecclesiastical misconduct. In any event, hostility toward the clergy was spread wide enough in Lyon (as in many other cities) to have deeply troubled the Church.

Urban Piety

In addition to a strained relationship with the laity, the Catholic clergy faced another serious and not unrelated problem: the whole set of spiritual difficulties that afflicted Catholicism in the sixteenth century. To understand these difficulties and to grasp fully the role played by the clergy in religious life, we must first step back and examine Catholic piety in its prime, before it faltered and began to wane at midcentury. In particular, we must examine a complex of rituals that flourished at the end of the Middle Ages and in the decades before the Council of Trent. These rituals gave expression to pre-Tridentine spirituality, at least as it was experienced by most lay persons, and for a believer, the rituals had considerable value. They could help him cope with the responsibilities of life or the tragedy of death or remind him of the role that the sacred had in the world. And of course they could further his salvation.

Among these ceremonies, perhaps the most important for salvation were votive masses and other rites of burial. Confession could of course absolve one's sins, but a man still had to do penance for his misdeeds. If he failed to make amends on earth, he would expiate his sins in the fires of Purgatory. Fortunately, masses, prayers, and good works would purge a Christian's guilt and thereby spare him the torments of Purgatory. Belief in the efficacy of these acts had gained widespread currency in the late Middle Ages, and throughout Christendom men and women therefore sought to earn God's mercy by prayer, alms, and, most important of all, masses. Often they commissioned these good works and religious services in their wills, so that they would benefit after death, when their souls hung in the balance. The whole movement reached its peak at the end of the fifteenth century and in the early decades of the 1500s, and it was apparently most pronounced in cities.[30]

Lyon was no exception to this trend. Many of the city's residents apparently took to heart the lurid revelations made during a much-publicized exorcism in 1527, when a spirit was cast out of Antoinette de Grolée, a Benedictine nun in Lyon. This spirit, who communicated through Antoinette, was reportedly the soul of another nun returned from Purgatory. Before crowds, the spirit maintained that masses and prayers for the dead could win relief for the souls in Purgatory, and she denounced Lutherans who cast doubt on these rituals. The Lyonnais by and large agreed with her claims, for most of them wagered on the effectiveness of prayers, alms, and masses when they drew up their wills.[31]

When, for example, Genefe Henry made out her will in Lyon in 1544, she incorporated a host of prayers and masses designed to further her salvation. This widow of a Lyon merchant began her testament by recommending her soul to "God our savior and redemptor . . . and to the Blessed Virgin Mary, to my Lord Saint Michael the angel and archangel, and to all the saints . . . of Paradise." Asking to be buried beside her late husband in the chapel of Saint-Laurent at the parish of Notre-Dame-de-Platière, she requested that the parish priests hold a vigil after her death and that eight of them read the Psalms over her body. In elaborate detail, she then commissioned four solemn high masses, during which *salve reginas* would be sung and alms and candles passed out to the faithful in attendance; three requiems with distributions of candles, wine, and bread; and a total of forty-two low masses. These masses she wanted said at Notre-Dame-de-Platière at the time of her death or shortly thereafter. She also asked for a mass one month later and a yearly solemn high mass in her burial chapel on the anniversary of her death. And so that fellow Christians might pray for her during the services at Notre-Dame-de-Platière, she requested that the bells of the church be rung three times, once at her death, once at her burial, and once a year later.

Nor was this all Genefe Henry had done to further her salvation. According to her will, the Carmelite friars were to hold a vigil for her, and they and the four other mendicant convents were to say a total of forty-five low masses. In addition, all the mendicants were to join the funeral procession from her house to Notre-Dame-de-Platière. Six poor girls, dressed in white and bearing candles, were to help conduct her body to Platière as well; in return, Genefe Henry paid for their shoes and robes and arranged to give each girl a sou. To the charitable institutions which would supply the six paupers, Madame Henry gave 20 livres, and she left several other charitable bequests to local hospitals. Finally, she required her four sons to have a total of one hundred twenty masses offered for the repose of her soul.[32]

Only after she had orchestrated this elaborate ritual of religious services and good works did Genefe Henry turn to the business we would associate with her will, the division of her estate among her heirs. Her primary concern was evidently to assure her own salvation, and every step she took seemed directed toward this goal. Her invocation of Michael the archangel suggests that she expected to face divine judgment, for according to legend, Michael led the souls of the dead before God. Common wisdom had it that God judged souls soon after death, and Genefe Henry apparently agreed, for she concentrated most of her masses at the time of her demise or during her burial for greatest effectiveness. The prayers and other rituals in her testament were also marshaled for greatest effect. The Psalms she requested had in fact been the first prayers said to release the spirit of the dead nun from Purgatory in the 1527 exorcism. Her gifts to poor girls not only qualified as alms but would lead the paupers to intercede with God on her behalf. And her stipulation of church bells would move other Christians to pray.[33]

Genefe Henry's will thus tells us a great deal about her spirituality and her deep attachment to pre-Tridentine Catholicism. It does so because, as Michel Vovelle and Pierre Chaunu have amply demonstrated, the religious clauses in her will and in most other early modern wills were not dictates of rigid custom but rather matters of choice and deliberation that illuminate the religious beliefs of the testators.[34] When Genefe Henry elected to have priests say masses for her soul or when she left money for other pious bequests, she demonstrated her faith in pre-Tridentine Catholic piety.

A sample of wills registered with notaries in Lyon indicates that many of Genefe Henry's contemporaries shared her faith. Among wills from the years 1521–55, fully 84 percent included some pious bequest, be it a request for masses or prayers or charitable donations to hospitals and the poor. To be sure, not everyone devoted as much money to piety as Genefe Henry, who lavished a total of over 70 livres on her charitable and religious legacies. Poorer folk or testators with larger numbers of needy heirs simply could not afford to match her ornate funeral, with its costly procession, and they certainly did not commission as many masses. Nonetheless, we can find occasional artisans who designed funerals nearly as elaborate as Genefe Henry's, and even among artisans, 80 percent of wills contained some pious bequest in the years before 1555 (table 1).[35]

Like pious bequests, the sacraments of penance and the Eucharist could also affect a believer's salvation. Despite their importance in official Church piety, though, few ordinary men and women had made these two sacraments regular spiritual exercises before the end of the sixteenth century. How often men or women actually confessed to a priest we cannot say, but absolution at Easter and upon the deathbed was no doubt ordinary. Many layfolk probably dreaded anything more than this minimal revelation of their sins. As for communion, most men and women received it no more than four to six times a year, if the purchases of hosts at the parish of Saint-Paul are indicative. It was therefore probably reserved for major feast days.[36] This is not to say that penance, the Eucharist, or the other sacraments lacked any significance whatsoever. Baptism, for example, was extremely important, for it not only removed original sin but also blessed familial alliances through the choice of godparents. The marriage ceremony had analogous social functions.

Votive masses, burial rites, and the sacraments were not the only focus of pre-Tridentine piety. Catholicism was also rooted in shrines and holy places, and in observances that demarcated the ecclesiastical calendar and the passage of the seasons. Some of the holy places were ancient. The churches of

Saint-Just and Saint-Irénée, which loomed over the city from the hills west of the Saône, occupied sites that had attracted processions since the Middle Ages, if not before. Other shrines were of more recent origin, like the chapel of Saint-Roch, erected outside the western gates of the city after the plague swept through in 1577. Churches and chapels, however, were not the only loci of holiness, for simple objects such as relics or statues also embodied the sacred. On each Saint Stephen's Day Eve, for instance, a stone figure in one of the cathedral's chapels drew worshipers wearing their shirts reversed—until a priest ordered the figure destroyed in the early sixteenth century because he considered it a source of popular idolatry.[37]

Table 1 Percentage of urban testators making pious bequests by wealth class, 1521–95

Period	Officers, large- and medium- scale merchants	Small-scale merchants and officers; richer artisans	Other artisans	Common people	All classes
1521–55	87%	78%	80%	100%	84%
	(55)	(18)	(51)	(8)	(132)
1556–75	68%	76%	61%	57%	67%
	(25)	(29)	(31)	(7)	(92)
1576–95	87%	60%	48%	17%	65%
	(38)	(15)	(27)	(6)	(86)

Source: Sample of urban wills described in appendix 1.

Note: For this table, information from tax records in Gascon, 1: 351–406, was used to arrange occupations in a hierarchy of wealth, and testators were then classified by occupation. The class of large- and medium-scale merchants includes bourgeois and nobles. Richer artisans include such prosperous tradesmen as goldsmiths and jewelers. The figures in parentheses are the absolute number of testators in each category.

Of the periodic religious rituals in the city, processions probably drew the greatest attention from contemporaries. Some of the processions were organized by the clergy in response to natural calamities or political crisis: plague, famine, flood, drought, and even a frightening peasant rebellion in nearby Dauphiné. During the Wars of Religion (and even before) long lines of chanting priests and marching layfolk beseeched God to crush the "heretics."[38] Even more common, though, were the processions in honor of holy days. In the parish of Sainte-Croix, for example, processions for feast days coiled about the church at least fourteen times in 1571. Sometimes these processions brought together all the churches of the city. Before Ascension Sunday, for example, the clergy made the procession of Rogations to solicit agricultural prosperity during the coming year. This meant trekking back and forth for three days, visiting every church in the city, filing out into the countryside and returning each evening for a mass and vespers at the cathedral—all a prelude to the grand festival of Ascension Sunday, when boats took the clergy and crowds of lay people up the Saône to the old abbey of the Ile-Barbe.[39]

Still other holy days were honored with special ceremony. The canon-counts, for example, feted the feast of Saint John the Baptist, the patron saint of the cathedral, with a lavish ritual known as the Pardon of Saint John. The observances began with a procession on the Sunday prior to the feast: as bells tolled, clergy from all the city parishes marched through the streets bedecked with banners and colored cloth. On the eve of the feast day itself, the clergy of all the collegiate churches gathered with throngs of people in the cathedral, which was decorated for the occasion with wild thyme and other herbs, to hear a High Mass. Layfolk flocked to this ceremony from near and far, not only for the pomp, but also for the indulgences they would gain if they made a donation in honor of John the Baptist, whose very jawbone rested in the cathedral.[40]

At Saint-Nizier, the priests celebrated their own luxurious "pardon," with their relics on display and the church swathed in silk. At Sainte-Croix, the parish of the cathedral, the vicar presided at a festival known as the *royaume* of Saint Christophe. After a High Mass in honor of the saint, the chance to be king or queen of the festival of Saint Christophe was auctioned off to parish children. Merchants, royal officers, and even Lyon's governor purchased these festival offices for their children. In the less prosperous neighborhood of Saint-Georges, the priests also helped celebrate royaumes, and mock dignities of the parish feast day went to more modest folk. At Saint-Pierre-et-Saint-Saturnin, the curé took part in the quarter's celebration of Pentecost, the occasion for a banquet, a dance, and two processions, all organized by a group of lesser merchants and young men from the neighborhood. The curé led the processions, and then he and the abbess of the convent adjoining the parish church opened the customary dance.[41]

This band of youths and modest merchants in the parish of Saint-Pierre-et-Saint-Saturnin was actually a confraternity, which we can define as a laymen's association organized for reasons that were at least in part religious. In Lyon, confraternities must have seemed nearly ubiquitous. The city council summoned thirty local confraternities to a meeting in 1496, and we can enumerate over five dozen of them in the sixteenth century. They included neighborhood associations, devotional or charitable groups, and mutual aid societies of artisans or tradesmen that served as professional associations in a city practically free of official guilds. Besides the one at Saint-Pierre-et-Saint-Saturnin, there were, among several brotherhoods at the Augustinians, a dockers' confraternity, a fishermen's confraternity, and one dedicated to the

Passion. Saint-Nizier housed confraternities of gardeners, weavers, and stone-cutters, that of the Pilgrims of Saint-Jacques, and a confraternity of the Trinity, whose members were largely urban notables. And this list is hardly complete.[42]

As in much of Catholic Europe, these confraternities played a highly significant role in the religious and social life of Lyon—a fact that contemporaries were quick to recognize.[43] Typically, each confraternity had the use of an altar or chapel in a church or a friary, where it had masses said in memory of its dead or in honor of its patron saint. Members of a confraternity could elect burial in the group's chapel, as Pierre Placard did in the chapel of his fellow rope makers in 1552, and the confreres would conduct a dead brother's body to his tomb. For artisans, the professional confraternities thus offered members the masses, candles, tolling bells, and processions that they might not otherwise be able to afford. And in effect, these and other confraternities even supplanted the parish. The silk weavers and embroiderers, for instance, apparently heard Sunday mass not in their parishes but in their confraternity chapel at the Cordeliers, and members of other professional brotherhoods did the same.[44]

It was among the confraternities that the limits of the clergy's role in Catholic spirituality come most clearly into focus. In general, these groups were highly independent of the clergy. From silk weavers and embroiderers at the Cordeliers to the notables in the Confraternity of the Trinity at Saint-Nizier, the confreres almost invariably managed their own affairs without clerical supervision. More important, ecclesiastics figured only peripherally in the activities of the confraternities. To be sure, the priests performed religious ceremonies for the confraternities and even proclaimed royaumes on confraternity feast days. But with a few exceptions they apparently did not enter into the rest of the confraternity celebrations on feast days or other occasions. For example, the important festivities sponsored by the vocational confraternities escaped almost completely the influence of the clergy. On the feast day of a trade's patron saint, the confreres filed out of the house of their lay director to the sounds of fifes and tambourines. Masked and in costume, bearing muskets and carrying huge loaves of bread adorned with the insignia of their craft, they marched to the confraternity chapel. There they heard mass, and then they returned to a tavern or to a brother's house for a raucous banquet. Save for the mass, the clergy usually took little part in these ceremonies.[45]

The same statement in fact applies to virtually all the city's popular recreations. The mummeries, charivaris, and satiric parades, which played as large a cultural role in Lyon as in other early modern cities, were staged by "abbeys of misrule," neighborhood associations or professional groups of artisans and small merchants. The clergy had practically no part in them (apart from the Augustinians' involvement in a few mystery plays), and the clerics therefore found themselves by and large excluded from this significant realm of urban popular culture.[46]

The priests' isolation from the realm of festive life reinforces what we know about the economic and social gap between the clergy (or at least the secular clergymen) and the bulk of Lyon's population. Many canons and priests, we recall, enjoyed opulence inconceivable among artisans and the common people. But more important than these differences in wealth were the social barriers entailed by the very organization of traditional Catholic piety. Catholic spirituality in the pre-Tridentine era was deeply rooted in tightly knit social groups and local institutions. Burial rituals, we know, engaged a number of local institutions and associations, from the parish whose bells tolled for the dead man to the confraternity whose members accompanied the corpse to its grave. Baptism and marriage, of course, linked families and friends, and the very ritual of the mass served to unite parishioners in prayer. Processions, for their part, reaffirmed a sense of community among Catholics, and confraternities both presupposed and encouraged the existence of vocational or devotional groupings.[47]

The problem, though, was that a number of the associations and institutions which supported traditional piety could not cope with the massive influx of people into sixteenth-century Lyon. Immigrants after all constituted perhaps one-half of the city's population at midcentury, and although they may have married, made friends, and developed family ties, they probably found the confraternities less than receptive. Worse yet, the parishes made little effort to integrate the newcomers. Parish clergymen were native born, and the important parishes, such as Saint-Nizier, were simply too large to make a migrant feel at home. The parish rituals—processions, for example—were too closely tied to local geography to permit easy assimilation of outsiders, and the parish clergy did not preach to or confess foreigners in their native tongue.[48]

What could a newcomer do? Some, like the rich Florentine merchants and bankers, formed their own pious associations, but this solution obviously exceeded the means of many immigrants, who were poor artisans. Often, the newcomers turned away from overwhelmed parishes and toward the mendicants. The wealthy Florentines formed their confraternity at the Dominicans, and the Genoese assembled at the Carmelite friary. Not surprisingly, testators born outside Lyon were more likely than natives to favor the mendicant houses in their wills and less likely to remember their parishes. In our sample of wills, newcomers to Lyon were 8 percent more prone than natives to elect burial at a mendicant community and 17 percent less likely to choose a grave in a parish. Among the testators who dictated their wills before 1555, the immigrants bequeathed 60 percent more money than the Lyonnais to the Dominicans, Carmelites, Augustinians, and Franciscans, and they left 86 percent less to the parishes.[49]

One might explain the immigrants' beneficence toward the mendicants by saying that they disposed of greater wealth or had to care for fewer heirs. While such differences may account for a large portion of the newcomers' favoritism toward the mendicants, it does not elucidate their niggardliness toward the parishes. Indeed, a statistical analysis shows that an immigrant testator of average wealth was 28 percent less likely to make a pious bequest to his parish than an equally wealthy and otherwise identical native. The sum he did bestow upon his parish was 24 livres smaller as well.[50]

Perhaps the mendicants drew more newcomers than the parishes because the friars themselves had often come from outside the city walls.[51] Perhaps the attraction of the mendicants was the welcome they offered associations of immigrants or the fact that their style of piety was more cosmopolitan and less specifically local than the parish rituals and devotions. Or perhaps their hold over newcomers derived from their spiritual zeal—a subject we will consider later. In any case, Lyon's parishes did not assimilate the city's new migrants, and the failure to absorb this large population clearly betokened something of a spiritual dilemma for traditional Catholicism.

But even worse signs of spiritual crisis clouded the horizons in the middle of the sixteenth century, posing serious problems for Lyon's clergy. The funeral rituals and votive masses, which flourished so in the later Middle Ages and in the early decades of the sixteenth century, began to wane in the late 1530s. By the 1550s the decline became precipitous. The issue here was not simply a mindless shift in fashion, for as we have seen, these rituals formed an integral part of traditional piety. Their decline in fact marked a significant turning point for pre-Tridentine Catholicism in Lyon, which had once appeared so strong but which now found itself threatened by doubt and, eventually, by heresy.

The collapse in the demand for religious services left its mark in the churches and friaries, where wealthy donors ceased to commission masses and endow chapels. At Saint-Nizier, the chapel of Notre-Dame-de-Grace recorded five foundations of annual or weekly masses between 1481 and 1530, but after 1530, no further requests were received until the seventeenth century. The story was little different at the Dominican friary. There, Florentines and other benefactors established prebends and altars with gusto in the late fifteenth and early sixteenth centuries, yet their activity came to a halt in the 1530s. Even burial rituals apparently lost their luster. When the affluent merchant Jean Paffy died in 1558, Jean Guéraud noted that his elaborate funeral was "as honorable as was seen fifty years ago." Paffy's great wealth no doubt permitted an extraordinarily lavish ceremony, but Guéraud's remark suggests that rites of mourning had faded over the preceding fifty years.[52]

These examples concern only the well-to-do, but in fact the decline of traditional piety was widespread and cut across class lines. In our sample of wills, for instance, 60 percent of the testators before 1536 asked for funeral processions, but only 35 percent did so in the years 1536–55. The proportion continued to drop, falling still lower after 1555 (table 2). Requests for psalms, tolling bells, and the attendance of the clergy also collapsed. Too dramatic to be a mere chance result, this drop in the elaborate and sometimes costly funeral rites did not result from the immiserization of the testators, either, or from greater demands placed on their estates by heirs, or from any other shift in the composition of the sample.[53]

Table 2 Percentage of testators requesting processions, psalms, attendance of clergy, or bells at funerals

Year	Total wills	Processions	Psalms	Mendicant clergy	Secular clergy	Bells
1520–35	20	60%	40%	50%	60%	10%
1536–55	112	35%	15%	29%	27%	17%
1556–75	92	22%	5%	20%	9%	3%
1576–95	86	16%	3%	17%	9%	1%

Source: Sample of urban wills described in appendix 1.

Along with lavish funerals, pious bequests also diminished at midcentury. While 84 percent of the testators in the years 1521–55 left money for masses or charity, only 67 percent did so during the subsequent two decades, when both the rich and the poor hesitated to make pious bequests (table 1). In fact, a smaller fraction of estates was going to the church or to charity. Merely 16 percent of the cash mentioned in the wills ended up reserved for pious bequests in the years 1556–75, versus 24 percent before 1555. The average testator in 1561 actually left 72 livres less for masses and charity than an otherwise identical predecessor of equivalent wealth twenty years before. Once again, these differences were far too large to be mere statistical flukes.[54]

The waning of traditional piety may have left its mark even at the communion rail. At Saint-Paul, purchases of hosts rose precipitously in the period from 1515 to the late 1520s, only to drop to a level consonant with population growth thereafter. Confraternities were probably affected as well, for they too seemed in decline at midcentury.[55]

Why then did these traditional rituals begin to fade away, and what did their disappearance signify? Did a worsening economy prompt testators both rich and poor to eschew expensive funerals and trim costly pious bequests? The fact is, though, that just as fluctuations of wealth do not account for the plainer funerals and reduced religious bequests, neither do indices of Lyon's economic fortunes. Quite simply, the religious stipulations in the wills declined long before Lyon began to slip into economic torpor, late in the 1560s. And no other economic or legal reasons exist for the testators' changing behavior.[56]

The evidence thus points to a stunning shift in religious attitudes, beginning in the late 1530s and reaching crisis proportions by 1555. The conclusion seems inescapable that a number of men and women from all social
classes had come to question the efficacy of Catholic ritual. Perhaps the
processions, alms, and masses which had been offered in ever increasing numbers through the 1530s were merely symptoms of a gnawing spiritual
anxiety—anxiety that eventually gave way to doubt. Perhaps Protestantism
(which we shall see was growing at this time in Lyon) released these individuals from the treadmill of good works for the sake of salvation, but our
testators were all at least nominal Catholics. Many in fact protested their
attachment to the Roman Church at the same time they spurned funeral rituals and votive masses.[57] It is more likely, therefore, that Protestantism profited from this anxiety, as well as from other religious problems, in making
converts, but that many of those who had doubts about the rituals remained
within the Church.

The spiritual crisis clearly posed a severe problem for the Catholic clergy. If
the rituals they conducted lost their effectiveness, what good were they? Many
laymen, of course, were still attached to the Church, as the testators' protestations suggest. Sacred objects and rituals, from the Host to local processions,
had by no means ceased to attract devotion, and masses and prayers for the
dead always had ardent defenders.[58] Nevertheless, the growing doubt did
amount to a crisis, striking as it did both at the heart of traditional Catholic
spirituality and at the role of the clergy. The problem seemed to afflict the
parish clergy more than the regulars, for bequests to the parishes fell more
rapidly than those to the friaries and monasteries. And the difficulties
assumed their gravest proportion among Lyon's newcomers, who showed
more disaffection than natives for the rituals of Catholicism.[59]

Surely, the spiritual dilemma facing the pre-Tridentine Church was only
aggravated by the recurrent enmity that divided the clergy and the lay elite
and by the social gulf that separated secular clergymen from the common
people and immigrants. These social barriers in turn served to hamper the
Catholic clergy in the fight against Protestantism, which was thriving upon
the doubt and anxiety prevalent among the laity at the middle of the
sixteenth century.

The Changing Role of the Parish Clergy

The Parish Clergy and the Struggle against the Protestants

The rise of Protestantism constituted probably the most serious of all the
problems the clergy faced in Lyon in the sixteenth century. Calvinism
spread swiftly in Lyon during the 1540s and 1550s, swelling the Protestant

community to perhaps one-third of the city's population and reaching almost every class of the social hierarchy, from the common people to the urban patriciate.[60] Although they were always a minority in the city, the Calvinists profited during the years 1560–62 from the municipal government's avowed policy of religious neutrality and toleration. By this time they were also spared serious persecution by the sénéchaussée (the court with jurisdiction over cases of heresy) because the sénéchaussée's magistrates were too divided between proponents of toleration and advocates of repression to pursue Protestants with any zeal. In addition, the Calvinists benefited from the politics of the royal government, once the queen mother Catherine de Médicis adopted a policy favorable toward the Huguenots early in 1561. In September of that year she even removed the lieutenant of the governor in Lyon, the abbé Antoine d'Albon, because he was hostile to the Protestants.[61] With their sense of security heightened by d'Albon's removal, the Huguenots began, for the first time, to worship in public within the walls of the city.

Yet all was not peaceful, for as in other French cities confessional violence was multiplying ominously. Butchers and boatmen in the parish of Saint-Vincent attacked Huguenots returning from services, or so Protestants claimed.[62] The Corpus Christi procession at Saint-Nizier in 1561 witnessed a particularly gruesome incident, touched off when a young Protestant painter, Denis de Valois, tried to throw the Sacred Host to the ground. Although he was immediately arrested, the common people, "shocked and angered," forced the procession to continue and then "rose up . . . striking, killing and mutilating all those they suspected of being Huguenots." The riot spread and cost the city council the lives of three musketeers it had sent in to restore order. This only further embittered the relationship between the municipal government and the clergy, for the city councilors suspected the clergy of fomenting the disorders, which they feared would spark a revolt.[63]

While Lyon crackled with religious violence, the canon-counts labored in vain for the repression of Protestantism, lest Lyon become, to use their words, a "second Geneva." They tried to have Protestant services banned within the city. Along with ardent Catholic laymen, they asked that city councilors sign a profession of Catholic orthodoxy, but the council, dismissing this request, refused to budge from its policy of toleration of the Huguenots and hostility toward the clergy.[64] In addition, the canon-counts labored to arouse popular feeling against the Protestants. While no evidence exists to support the city council's suspicion that the canons or other ecclesiastics fomented the Corpus Christi day riots (indeed, the riots no doubt expressed the Catholic population's sense of outrage at the magistrates' unwillingness to restrain Protestants), the city's clergy did intervene on behalf of Catholic rioters who had been arrested. Furthermore, the canon-counts held several processions to drum up feeling against the Huguenots and beseech God for their destruction. Protestants also charged that the canon-counts were circulating inflammatory letters against them, and there is some independent evidence to substantiate their accusation.[65]

Unable to persuade the authorities to adopt a policy of repression, the canon-counts and the other members of the parish clergy assembled nervously for a number of meetings. In March of 1561, representatives of the archbishop and the regular clergy, five canon-counts, and clergymen from several other collegiate churches and parishes met to discuss the Protestant menace. They dispatched one of the canons of Saint-Paul to the king in the hopes of urging him to prohibit the bearing of arms in the city, a practice that was becoming distressingly common among members of both confessions. In September the canon-counts met with the governor's lieutenant, d'Albon, to discuss the danger, and in November canons from the cathedral, Saint-Paul, Saint-Just, and Saint-Nizier assembled to see if there was anything they could do about the Protestants, who (so they complained) were openly carrying arms in the city and disrupting Catholic processions. By December the canon-counts were discussing the same problem with de Saulx, d'Albon's replacement. Receiving no help from him, they hired their own soldiers to protect the cathedral.[66]

But their efforts came to naught. Unable to influence the city council, the canon-counts had even less luck with the lieutenant de Saulx. He remained unbendingly faithful to the policy of toleration, even when royal support for that policy began to waver. Personally convinced that the Protestants were the ones in danger, he decided to dismiss the canon-counts' troops, and he also disarmed most other Catholics. Profiting from the weakness of the Catholics and citing an ineffective Catholic attempt at rearmament as their justification, the Protestants finally staged a coup in April 1562: on the night of the twenty-ninth they seized control of Lyon.[67]

With the help of the baron des Adrets, the infamous mercenary for the Protestant cause, and later the Huguenot soldier Soubise, the Protestants controlled Lyon until the spring of 1563, when the end of the first War of Religion deprived them of their military support. Catholic members of the city council (and many other Catholics as well) fled during this Protestant takeover of Lyon, and Church buildings suffered considerable damage. Des Adret's soldiers seem to have been responsible for chiseling the images from the front of the cathedral, but the native Protestants also undertook certain projects of fortification and urban renewal at the expense of Catholic churches, most notably that of Saint-Just, which was razed in order to strengthen the city's defenses.[68]

On their return in June of 1563, clergymen and Catholic authorities were outraged to find their churches damaged and "polluted."[69] Catholics feared the threat of another Protestant takeover, and many were eager for revenge against the Huguenots. Marshal Vieilleville, whom the crown sent to Lyon to maintain peace between the two religions, intervened in city council elections and managed for a short time to preserve a fragile truce. But it was not long before Lyon's older irenic tradition foundered beneath a wave of religious extremism. Two new, pro-Catholic lieutenant generals (Jean de Losses, appointed in 1564, and his successor, Réné de Birague, appointed in 1565) organized Catholic forces in the city with the aid of the magistrates of the sénéchaussée, who were already won over to the Catholic camp. Although the crown intervened in the municipal elections until 1566, it eventually allowed the Catholics to predominate in the city council. In fact, the whole composition of the council began to change at the expense of moderation. Catholic extremists won seats in the council, while moderate Protestant and Catholic families who had once controlled it retreated from city government. By 1567 the Catholic extremists had gained complete control of the municipal government.[70]

The triumph of the extremists meant revenge upon the Protestants, whom Catholics still considered a threat to the city, and the outbreak of the second War of Religion in 1567 only bolstered Catholic fears. Three Calvinist ministers were expelled from Lyon in 1565, and in 1567 rioters sacked the Protestant church. Excluded from the city council, wealthy Protestants were subject to forced loans, and the lieutenant general Birague ordered the confiscation of Protestant property. Members of the reformed community were spied upon, and their houses were searched. The number of Protestants in the city declined drastically, as they fled or converted. In a number of cases, it must be noted, the conversions were actually sincere and done for reasons unrelated to the persecution. Calvinist printers' journeymen, for example, having grown disillusioned with the hierarchical administration of the Protestant consistory and its harsh moral surveillance of the Protestant congregation, freely chose to return to the Catholic Church. Disenchantment may have produced additional conversions among other groups of Protestant artisans and journeymen. Those Huguenots who only masqueraded as Catholics had to contend with watchful vicars and curés, whom the lieutenant of the governor had ordered to be on guard against feigned conversions. Converts had to be wary of vigilant laymen as well, like the rich bookseller Guillaume Rouille, chief of his quarter's unit in the city guard, who kept watch at the communion rail for slackers among the new converts. Worst of all for the Protestants was the appalling massacre of 1572, which repeated, after a delay of several days, the tragic events of Saint-Bartholomew's Day in Paris. Although it was apparently Catholic artisans who wielded the knives, the murders were committed with the complicity of the city council and perhaps even Governor Mandelot. After this tragedy, the Protestant community was reduced to a tiny minority of the city's population. As for the clergy's role in the persecution of the Huguenots, while they did not direct the massacre or any of the other acts of repression, they at least gave their support to what was going on by granting absolution to the murderers and celebrating the killings with a procession.[71]

The triumph of the extremists had momentous consequences for the relationship between the city council and Lyon's clergy. By 1565, the time was ripe for a patching up of differences and the forging of a new alliance between these two groups. Most of the traditional issues that divided the Cathedral and city hall had now been decided. The agreement ending the 1558 lawsuit had settled the matter of the clergy's fiscal privileges, while the Protestants had already executed the urban renewal projects that required Church land during their occupation of the city. The king had suppressed the archbishop's seignorial jurisdiction over Lyon in 1563, and the policing of the city was therefore no longer the Church's concern.[72]

With these traditional conflicts finally resolved, the family ties that linked the merchants and officers on the city council and members of the upper clergy could finally help effect a rapprochement between city hall and the Church. Shared hostility toward the Protestants and Catholic zeal quickly dissolved any lingering animosity and brought the city council and Lyon's clergymen even closer together. Between 1565 and 1567, the council and the cathedral clergy agreed to place the Jesuits in control of Lyon's College of the Trinity so that students could be "instructed in the Catholic Religion"—a break with the old tradition of secular control of secondary education. Later, the clergy's lawyers began to gain election to the council, and bit by bit the unenforced provisions of the 1558 suit were put into effect: as early as 1565 the canon-counts were attending and participating in the general assemblies, where the city councilors met with urban notables and representatives from the trades, and by the end of the century they were reviewing municipal accounts.[73]

Eventually, representatives of the upper clergy were also included in the Lyon *conseil d'état,* a new and important council of local notables presided over by the governor or the lieutenant general. Created by lieutenant general de Losses in 1565 as part of the effort to organize Catholic forces in the city, the conseil d'état supervised almost all aspects of the city's administration until nearly the end of the sixteenth century. Its first members were Catholic magistrates and city councilors, but representatives of the upper clergy soon joined them. Besides the archbishop, canons from the cathedral and Saint-Nizier were playing an active role in the conseil d'état deliberations in the 1580s and early 1590s.[74]

Obviously, the new alliance between the clergy and the city elite was still not perfect, for political differences and bickering over issues such as the use of Church property never disappeared. But the old antagonism between cathedral and city hall had nonetheless come to an end. Shared fears of the Protestant threat were partially responsible for this astounding rapprochement between the urban elite and the clergy—this "miracle," as Richard Gascon calls it—but a budding movement of reform also contributed greatly. By harnessing the Catholic laity's desires for religious reform, the movement to renew the Catholic Church would, as we shall see, complete the reconciliation between the city's upper classes and the parish clergy.[75]

The Beginnings of the Counter Reformation

According to conventional wisdom, the Counter Reformation (that is, the Church's efforts to proselytize and reform itself) did not cross the Alps into France until the seventeenth century, when saintly bishops founded seminaries and imposed reform from above. Although this bit of received wisdom contains some truth, especially insofar as the countryside is concerned, the fact is that the Counter Reformation was under way in France well before 1600. It began in the cities and was not simply thrust upon the laity by the ecclesiastical authorities on high, as events in Lyon will show.[76] Indeed, while the Counter Reformation may well have been imposed upon the peasantry or even the common people in the cities, it enjoyed strong and early support among urban lay elites.

The first efforts of Catholic reform in Lyon actually date back to the early decades of the century. In the 1520s and early 1530s the Dominican Santo Pagnini, a humanist and student of Savonarola, preached against the Protestants in the city and advocated a reform of relief for the poor. At roughly the same time, a provincial Church council discussed reforms of the clergy and the vexing first signs of the Reformation in the region, and the suffragan bishop publicized the exorcism of Antoinette de Grolée, since the spirit possessing her had "come back" from hell to denounce "heresy." And even before the 1520s the collegiate churches had made sporadic attempts to discipline their unruly clergy.[77] None of these isolated gestures had much effect, though. It was not until the 1550s that the Counter Reformation gathered momentum and not until after the return of the Catholic authorities in 1563 that a vigorous campaign was unleashed by the city's canons, its preachers, and its lay elite.

The canons redoubled their efforts to reform the behavior of the lower clergy associated with the collegiate churches. At Saint-Nizier, the canons strove from at least the 1550s onward to ensure that all the parish's clergymen attended services, dressed modestly, and comported themselves in a manner becoming ordained men of God. Similar reforms were pressed with renewed vigor at the other chapters. At the cathedral, canon Gabriel de Saconay argued that an end to scandal and spiritual "nonchalance" among the clergy was the first step toward renewal of the Catholic Church.[78]

The disciplinary measures never managed to correct completely behavior that, we well know, continued to outrage laymen and laywomen to the end of the sixteenth century, but these efforts did reveal a concern for the priests' image in the eyes of the laity. Good behavior, the chapters emphasized, was necessary in order to spare the lay people any scandal. Proceedings against errant priests who quarreled or sneaked away from services to guzzle wine in a tavern reflected the concern that those of the "ecclesiastical estate" not appear "scandalous to the people." The diocesan statutes of 1566 and 1577 reiterated these prescriptions, also ordering an end to ostentation and luxurious dress lest the laity be shocked.[79]

More important than these defensive measures was the revival of Catholic preaching. Beginning in the 1550s and then with even greater force after the Catholics' return in 1563, Catholic preachers battled the Calvinists from the pulpits of the parish churches. In contrast to those in Paris, the most noted pulpit orators in Lyon were almost never parish priests. They were Dominicans, Franciscans, or Carmelites, or else they wore the habits of the new orders established in Lyon after the 1550s: the Minimes, the Jesuits, and the Capuchins.[80] It was these friars or Jesuits who were invited to the parishes to preach on the numerous holy days or during the long liturgical cycles of Advent–Christmas and Lent–Easter. To be sure, an occasional parish priest did make a mark for himself in the pulpit. André Amyot, the custode of Sainte-Croix, assisted the famed Jesuit preacher Edmond Auger when Auger preached at his parish during a horrible plague in 1564. But the surviving records of Sainte-Croix demonstrate that in the sixteenth century the custodes and the vicars of the parish normally spoke only on ordinary Sundays, which suggests that their sermons (the sermons themselves do not exist in print) were less elaborate than those delivered by regulars. Similarly, although the théologaux at Saint-Jean occasionally gave sermons, none were preachers of renown. On important feast days, Sainte-Croix and Saint-Jean depended on Jesuits or mendicants. The same was true at Saint-Nizier, where a friar or a member of one of the new orders always gave the Advent and Lenten sermons, from the Catholic restoration of 1563 to the end of the sixteenth century.[81]

Why did these members of the regular orders dominate the pulpits? In the first place, there was throughout Europe a long tradition of preaching among older mendicant orders. The Minimes and Capuchins actively expanded upon this tradition, and the Jesuits of course gained renown as the shock troops of the Counter Reformation for their sermons and evangelizing. In Lyon, these new orders filled pulpits with orators as skilled as the Jesuit Auger or the Minime Jean Ropitel, who engaged in a heated polemic with the Protestant minister Pierre Viret. The preachers from the regular orders also seemed able to draw upon the renewal of Catholic theology. Auger wrote a celebrated catechism, and one of his Jesuit colleagues in Lyon, the Italian Antonio Possevino, won a reputation throughout Catholic Europe both for his sermons and for his knowledge of biblical and patristic exegesis. In addition, the preachers encouraged devotions that eventually won favor among the

Lyonnais—a fact that must have further augmented their appeal. The Dominican Pierre de Bollo, for example, promoted the cult of the Virgin and the Rosary. The Jesuits did the same.[82]

One final virtue the preachers had was flexibility. The regular orders did not have to await the commands of the diocesan hierarchy to move into action, and their missionary activity was supple enough to respond to lay initiatives. Admittedly, the archbishop still played a role in the revival of preaching. For example, archbishops d'Este and de Tournon (along with canon-count de Vichy) were instrumental in bringing the Minime preachers to Lyon. But by the same token, it was lay Italian merchants who attracted the Jesuit Possevino to Lyon—no doubt so that they could hear his sermons in Italian. Italians also enabled the Capuchins to locate in the city.[83]

More evidence of the laity's part in the revival of Catholic preaching comes from the largest parish in the city, Saint-Nizier, where laymen were deeply involved with the parish priests in the process of selecting preachers for Advent and Lent. At Saint-Nizier, parish laymen had been meeting with canons to discuss repairs to the church as early as the 1530s. By 1542, but apparently not earlier, these vestry assemblies had begun to choose Advent and Lenten preachers, and the practice of having parishioners meet with canons to discuss preachers became even more important in the 1550s and 1560s. Whether it was the clergy or the laity who initiated these assemblies is not clear. In any case, the laymen present did not simply defer to the canons' opinions. On one occasion, for example, when the canons mysteriously resisted a popular preacher the laymen had proposed (the Carmelite and suffragan bishop Jacques Maistret, whom some of the lower clergy at Saint-Nizier also favored), the laymen responded with the thinly veiled threat that they and other zealous parishioners would withhold contributions which had been promised for repairs to the church if the canons prevented Maistret from preaching. In general, however, the canons and the laymen agreed on most matters, and the canons sought the laymen's advice on a wide variety of subjects besides the selection of preachers.[84]

These regular consultations between the canons of Saint-Nizier and parish laymen provide additional evidence of the rapprochement between the parish clergy and the Catholic elite, for most of the laymen who met with the canons came from the city's upper classes. The majority were prosperous merchants, often members of the urban patriciate, and zealous Catholics as well. Of the eight who assembled with the canons in April of 1564, for instance, five were merchants of considerable importance, and two of these (Claude Valleton and Claude Platet) ran mercantile operations large enough to be involved in the international fairs of Lyon. Four of the eight (Platet, Valleton, and the merchants Humbert Faure and Jacques de Grimond) were, or would be, members of the city council. The first two were elected in 1566 and proved themselves to be extremely zealous defenders of Catholicism while in

city government. Laymen who met on other occasions with the canons came
from similar social strata. They included notables like Guillaume Rouille, the
rich bookseller and city councilor whom we met scouting for Protestants from
his post as neighborhood chief of the city guard.[85]

The meetings at Saint-Nizier also bore witness to the Catholic lay elite's
extraordinary enthusiasm for resurgent Catholicism. This enthusiasm not only
bound the clergy and the lay elite more closely together, it also vaulted the
laymen to the forefront of the local Counter Reformation. Further evidence of
the Catholic elite's religious zeal abounds. Besides the decision to turn the
city's college over to the Jesuits, the city council voted subsidies for the
Catholic preaching orders in order to "further the Catholic religion." In its
cahiers for the Estates-General of 1576, the council was ready to demand
that parish priests watch for noncommunicants and Protestants, that the
clergy be reformed, and that the decrees of the Council of Trent be published
in France.[86]

More important, the elite supplied the fervent membership of several new
devotional confraternities in Lyon. The first of these was the Confraternity of
the Penitents of Confalon, known as the White Penitents because of the
hooded white robes that the members donned during devotional exercises.
Hallmarks of the Counter Reformation, such Penitents' confraternities had
proliferated in the later sixteenth century all over the Catholic Mediterranean
and beyond. In Lyon, where Italianate facades and Florentine courtyards
testified to a traditional readiness to embrace Mediterranean culture, the local
chapter of the White Penitents of Confalon was founded in 1577. According
to Claude de Rubys, a Catholic zealot, city government official, and one of
the early members of the confraternity, the Penitents were established by two
city notables: Justinian Panse, scion of a family in the urban patriciate, and
Maurice du Peyrat, a member of a wealthy old family that had abandoned
trade for offices and seigniories. Other early leaders included the city councilor
Jacques de Grimond, who was among the devout laymen active at Saint-
Nizier. A number of prosperous officers and merchants, often members of the
city government, were also active in the group. With all these ties to the
city's governing classes, the White Penitents of Confalon were also linked to
the pious Catholic clergy. The Jesuit preacher Edmond Auger and the
preacher and suffragan bishop Jacques Maistret seem to have lent a hand at
the foundation of the organization, Maistret having consecrated the group's
chapel. And although ecclesiastics were not present at the Penitents' business
meetings (this was, after all, an autonomous lay organization), Archbishop
Epinac and several members of the mendicant orders attended their numerous
processions.[87]

Besides processions the Penitents performed several other notable duties
which were typical of Counter-Reformation confraternities and which would
have important implications for the parish clergy. First, the Penitents were to

confess monthly. This requirement was a characteristic novelty of the Counter Reformation, which sought to promote more frequent reception of the sacraments than the yearly confession customary in the past. The Penitents were also to comport themselves decently, eschew "public houses . . . and taverns," and monitor one another's behavior, lest any member provoke some "scandal in public." Such moral austerity well suited this association, which replaced the drinking and tumultuous banquets customary in medieval confraternities with somber prayers and fasting. Finally, on holy days the Penitents were to gather for prayers to the Virgin and then go to mass at their home parishes. Seemingly innocuous, this latter obligation was in fact another novelty of the Counter Reformation that attempted to focus religious life on the parish. It is true that the White Penitents had a chapel that was served by the Cordeliers and not attached to any parish church; services at this chapel did tend to draw the confraternity's members away from their parishes and the parish clergy. In the seventeenth century, such separate chapels and religious services, which were always common in Penitents' confraternities, would earn them the enmity of bishops and parish priests throughout France. But this was not the case in sixteenth-century Lyon. The White Penitents took pains to ensure that their members frequented the parishes and that their rituals did not conflict with parish services. Not only were the Penitents to attend parish mass on all holy days, but also each Penitent was obliged, whenever he heard mass in the confraternity's chapel, to go to a second mass at his home parish. If we consider the practices of most contemporaneous vocational confraternities, which usually avoided any connection with the parishes, the conclusion is inescapable that the Penitents marked a first step toward bringing religious life closer to the parishes and to the parish clergy.[88]

A second, similar confraternity, the black-robed Penitents of the Crucifix, was founded somewhat later, in 1589, at about the same time that Lyon gave its formal adherence to the Holy League, the Catholic alliance for the extirpation of Protestantism in France, which had grown into a revolution against the monarchy. The Black Penitents of the Crucifix had the approval of the papal legate in France, of Jacques Maistret, and of another zealous local clergyman, the canon-count Etienne de la Barge, who, like Maistret, gained infamy as a champion of the League. The Penitents of the Crucifix counted among their members a similar group of prosperous and fervid Catholic laymen, like Pierre Austrein, an officer of the sénéchaussée and a member of the city council.[89] Only two years later, in 1591, an older confraternity, that of Saint-Bonaventure, sprang back to life in Lyon, thanks to the efforts of the Franciscan friar Martin Valletier, the city councilor Jacques d'Aveyne, and a number of other ardent laymen. This confraternity had once been a somewhat festive association for the patrician city youth, but d'Aveyne wanted it transformed into an austere and purely devotional organization much like the White Penitents. The other laymen who helped him breathe new life into the Confraternity of Saint-Bonaventure included a prestigious retinue of officers, city councilors, and devout notables who took part in the assemblies at Saint-Nizier. Many were furiously active in the League, and they enjoyed such a close relationship with the city council that the municipality delegated official representatives to the meeting at which the confraternity was revived.[90]

The testaments provide one final confirmation of the lay elite's growing attachment to resurgent Catholicism. Whereas pious bequests made by members of the city's upper classes had been dropping precipitously at mid-century, thereafter they leveled off and showed signs of rising. Among officers and prosperous merchants, the fraction of wills containing pious bequests rose from the low of 68 percent in the years 1556–75 to 87 percent in 1576–95 (table 1). A more precise statistical analysis (one which takes into account the actual amounts the elite testators left to churches or charity, as well as other factors influencing their legacies, such as their wealth and the number of their heirs) suggests that the turning point came even earlier than 1575, that it happened in the 1560s. In such a tiny sample these slight changes might conceivably be the result of chance or of greater economic prosperity among the upper classes. But the statistical analysis demonstrates that this is not the case. After the late 1550s, the decline in pious bequests did begin to slow among the wealthy, and in the top layers of the lay elite, the religious and charitable legacies actually began to rise again. The depression Lyon suffered after the 1560s did not reverse this trend.[91]

While pious bequests increased among the upper classes, the old funeral ceremonies, from psalms and processions to tolling bells, continued to fade away. In the emphasis the elite placed on votive masses and individual charity, which rose at the expense of traditional group rituals, we can perhaps see the first glimmerings of a new piety, a piety that was more Christocentric and individualistic than pre-Tridentine spirituality. In any event, the pious bequests did leave an ineffaceable mark at some of the city's churches. The Minimes, for example, experienced a flood of foundations by wealthy donors in the 1580s and 1590s.[92]

If enthusiasm for Tridentine Catholicism tightened the alliance forming between the city elite and the urban clergy, what about the rest of the populace? Did the Catholic resurgence leave a mark upon the less prosperous classes of the city's population and thereby shape their relationship with the parish priests and the urban elite? Certainly the sermons were aimed at the common people, and some of the numerous pro-Catholic pamphlets churned out by the city's presses had a wide audience among the city's literate artisans. Efforts were also made to exploit miracles and "successful" exorcisms that reflected well upon the Catholic cause. In 1582 the well-known Franciscan preacher Jean Benedicti cast out devils who "blasphemed" in the style of Huguenots; the exorcism was performed before a crowd of people and was publicized at the time. Similarly, the Saint-Nizier canon Emmanuel Chalon, the Dominican preacher de Bollo, and the zealous Catholic printer Jean Pillehotte spread news about the miraculous "punishment" that the Virgin Mary had meted out to a blasphemous soldier. No wave of new confraternities spread among the mass of people, as the Penitents did among the elite, but one devotional confraternity did form among artisans living near the Cordeliers' friary.[93]

Furthermore, Catholic leaders made a concerted effort to exploit popular pageants and festivities. The canon-counts engaged the Jesuits Auger and Antonio Possevino to address the throngs that had gathered for the festival of the Pardon of Saint John the Baptist, and the canon-counts themselves multiplied their gaudy processions against the Huguenots. At Saint-Nizier, the canons restored the Corpus Christi procession with all the pomp of the years before the Protestant seizure of power.[94] The ardent Catholic Claude de Rubys praised a number of other popular festivities, and some Catholics lent support to the satiric parade (the *chevauchée de l'âne*) organized by the abbeys of misrule in 1566, at a time when Protestant artisans were becoming disenchanted with the Reformed Church and voluntarily returning to Catholicism. Catholics supported or at least tolerated these celebrations because they struck at the Protestants' Achilles heel. Calvinists did indeed despise such frivolities, and this contempt cost them support and even bred hostility among the artisans and common people.[95]

One must not, however, overestimate the populace's attachment to resurgent Catholicism. Despite all the efforts to woo the artisans and common people, their testaments showed no sign of growing attachment to Tridentine Catholicism. While pious bequests among the elite began to rise, they continued to fall among the rest of the populace (table 1), and once again the differences in behavior did not result from changing or contrasting economic circumstances. One reason, perhaps, for this difference between the populace and the elite was that the craftsmen who returned to the bosom of the Church usually professed a Catholicism more tolerant and more moderate than that of the city fathers and the clergy. They thus diluted somewhat the strength of Catholic enthusiasm among the people.[96] Whatever the explanation, the artisans and common people clearly did not follow the elite and rush to embrace Tridentine Catholicism.

If the Catholic Reformation failed to attract the lower classes, neither did it bring them any closer to the urban elite or to the parish clergy. Between the populace and these two groups there still yawned an awesome social chasm. The city council admittedly did take steps to consult the people by meeting more frequently with city notables, neighborhood chiefs of the city guard, and representatives from the crafts. Through these intermediaries, the municipal government's policies were assured of some support from the artisans and from the common people.[97] But the intermediaries between the council and the people were themselves members of the elite, and throughout all the council's dealings with the artisans and the common people fear and hostility lingered in the background, and the social gulf, though bridged, was never closed.

And what could one expect, given the obvious social and cultural differences and Lyon's long history of conflict between the city council and the people over the issue of taxation, a tension that religious solidarity had not dispelled? Moreover, the tradition of popular rebellion remained a nightmare to the city fathers.[98] Any truce the clergy and the elite made with the common people was bound to be always a bit uneasy.

What was true of the urban elite in general holds, in particular, for the parish clergy. Resurgent Catholicism did little to bring them closer to the common people. Although parish clergymen revived processions and subsidized preachers, they left most of the actual work of stimulating the zeal of the masses to the mendicants and to the Jesuits. After all, these priests of the religious orders delivered the sermons and (along with certain laymen) wrote most of the religious pamphlets. By contrast, the parish clergy in the city remained a bit aloof from the common people. They were more concerned with consolidating their rapprochement with the elite than with satisfying the spiritual needs of the common people.

The Aftermath of the Wars of Religion

The collapse of the Catholic League and the end of the Wars of Religion conceivably could have destroyed the alliance between Lyon's elite and the city's clergy. After all, the Catholic Church was deeply involved in the League, and in the aftermath of the Wars of Religion there was a widespread reaction against churchmen who had been compromised in League activities. In Paris, League preachers were driven into exile, the Jesuits were expelled, Penitents' confraternities were suppressed, and in a gesture of hostility to the papacy, the Parlement of Paris blocked the publication in France of the decrees of the Council of Trent.[99] The end of the civil wars in Lyon witnessed a similar reaction against the Catholic League and some of its ecclesiastical allies. Mobs burned in effigy figures of "sorcerers" that represented the League. Royalists harassed and threatened Jesuits and Capuchins because of their reluctance to recognize Henry IV. They forced Claude de Rubys and a number of magistrates and city councilors compromised by League activities to leave town, and several clergymen active in the League suffered the same fate. The suffragan bishop Jacques Maistret and the canon-count Etienne de la Barge, both of whom championed the League, were exiled from Lyon, and Archbishop Epinac also left the city for a brief period.[100]

Yet this reaction after the Wars of Religion did not break or even weaken the alliance between Lyon's elite and the clergy. After Lyon surrendered to royalist troops in February of 1594, the conseil d'état continued to meet for over a year under the supervision of Henry IV's emissaries, and its assemblies continued to bring together representatives of the city elite and of the local churches. The royalist city councilmen and urban notables who sat on the conseil d'état and controlled municipal institutions after the League's demise rejected neither rapprochement with the clergy nor the nascent Counter Reformation. They even asked the clergy's opinion when it came time for punishing the most rabid partisans of the League in city government. When this problem was discussed by the conseil d'état, canon-count Claude de Talaru de Chalmazel and Saint-Nizier canon Emmanuel Chalon, the clergy's representatives, agreed wholeheartedly with the body's decision to banish a number of League sympathizers from the city.

Admittedly, the king's emissaries and the royalists on the conseil d'état did criticize several Catholic preachers who continued to rail against Henry IV for his failure to recognize the pope. But when the problem of these troublesome preachers was raised at a meeting of the conseil d'état, Chalmazel and Chalon responded apologetically (and the royalists present did not really disagree) that the recalcitrant preachers were only a small minority, mostly from the Dominicans or the new religious orders. The two canons agreed to watch over the city's preachers and expel those guilty of delivering rash sermons. Delivering a statement that must have seemed especially reassuring, canon Chalon declared that he had told the clergy "to preach the Gospel and not at all touch upon what concerned the State, to preach obedience to superiors, and fidelity and goodwill to our region and our fellow citizens."[101]

To preach obedience to superiors: this was wholly consonant with the desires of the royalists present at the meeting, as their own statements show. These royalists did not want to silence the pulpit—in fact, they themselves engaged priests to give sermons. Rather, they sought a religion stripped of all revolutionary potential, a religion that would only support, and never threaten, the monarchy and the local ruling elite. And on these terms alliance with the clerics, themselves eager to prove their loyalty, was still possible. Thus when Henry IV entered Lyon in September 1595, the city's clergy joined the royal parade as they so conspicuously had not in 1548. And the clergy outdid the other urban groups in lavishing praise upon the king; Henry IV himself remarked that although they had spurned him in the past, the priests of Lyon would no doubt be "among the most faithful and devoted in his obedience" in the future.[102]

The alliance with the urban elite was preserved, then, because the clergy professed their loyalty to the king. No other sacrifices were required of them, for the royalists who held power in Lyon were enthusiastic Catholics. One sign of this enthusiasm was the fact that when the city council acted after the League's collapse to forbid slander of Henry IV, it forbade calumny of the Catholic Church as well, a measure that met with the approval of lay notables and the king's representatives in Lyon. The royalist councilmen, city notables, and representatives of the clergy swore at the same time to live and die in the Roman religion and wrote a protestation of orthodoxy to Pope Clement VIII. Moreover, these royalists took no steps to disturb the institutions of the Counter Reformation. The Penitents' confraternities, for example, were not abolished in Lyon; they still attracted members among the city elite and would continue to do so into the seventeenth century. And the city's cahiers for the meeting of the Estates-General in 1614 show that enthusiasm for the Catholic Reformation thrived among the urban elite in the early seventeenth century. According to the cahiers, the elite wanted to found seminaries, improve the quality of parish clergymen and increase their numbers, and punish those who dared to blaspheme God or the saints.[103]

Resurgent Catholicism had thus forged a durable alliance between Lyon's clergy and its lay elite. This rapprochement between the two groups spelled the end of the city's laic tradition, which had for decades limited the clergy's role in urban government and religion's impact upon municipal affairs. In the seventeenth century, the bonds between clergy and urban laity were to be drawn even tighter, and the ethic of resurgent Catholicism came to exert a great influence over decisions made by the urban elite. The seventeenth-century monarchy supported this sort of alliance between clergy and urban elites, which became common throughout France. As a result, the clergy, the urban elite, and royal officials all worked in concert for the great social measures of the Counter Reformation. This cooperative effort entailed significant changes in the role of the diocese's parish priests. But before examining these changes, we must turn to the countryside, where, in contrast to the city, the Counter Reformation was not under way by the end of the sixteenth century and where the parish clergy's relationship with the common people was far closer than it was in the city.

2
The Rural Priests from 1500 to 1614

The Landscape of the Sixteenth-Century Countryside

Large by French standards, the diocese of Lyon contained some 783 parishes in the sixteenth century, all but a dozen of them outside the walls of Lyon.[1] It encompassed nearly all the land that makes up the present-day departments of the Rhône and the Loire and included, in addition, the eastern half of the Ain, enclaves in the Isère and the Jura, and tiny parcels in the Haute-Loire and the Saône-et-Loire (see figure 3). Divided into western and eastern wings by the Saône and the Rhône rivers, the diocese was shaped roughly like a butterfly. In the southeast, it extended beyond Morestel in Dauphiné. In the northeast, the tip of its wing stretched past Saint-Claude to Bois-d'Amont on the border of the Swiss cantons and to Les-Rousses, where the parish church sat on the boundary between the watersheds of the Rhône and the Rhine. Near Lyon this eastern wing of the diocese was gentle countryside: the swamps of the Dombes, the moraines of Bas-Dauphiné, the plains and boxwood-covered hillocks of Bresse. But a woodcutter returning from Lyon to Saint-Claude, cr Protestants fleeing Lyon to seek refuge in Geneva, would soon pass over this flat country and arrive in the more rugged and sparsely settled Bugey and Franche-Comté, where highland pastures and mountain forests formed the eastern boundary of the diocese. Here parishes were often inaccessible to wagons or even to men on horseback; they could be reached solely by slogging upward on foot, and then only in good weather.

Part of this eastern wing of the diocese—Bresse and Bugey—belonged to the House of Savoy and did not become irrevocably French until 1601. The corner of the diocese in the Franche-Comté was not attached to France until even later in the seventeenth century. But these political frontiers were hardly a barrier to trade with Lyon.[2] Peasants in the Savoyard Bresse, like those in French Dauphiné, not only supplied Lyon with food but also harvested flax, spun thread, and wove linen, all for the Lyon market. As for urban manufactures, there were no large cities in the eastern wing of the diocese—Bourg-en-Bresse, no doubt the largest, could hardly count four thousand habitants in the period 1560–1613—but the region did boast many small cities and market towns with populations usually on the order of one thousand persons.[3] In some of these small urban centers, such as Saint-Rambert-en-Bugey or Bourg-en-Bresse, artisans and small-scale merchants wove cheap linens which Lyon merchants bought for resale abroad.

On the other side of the Saône, the western wing of the diocese reached north into the hills of Beaujolais almost as far as Beaujeu. On the left bank of the Loire, the diocese stretched past Roanne to the village of Melay. From there, the western boundary followed the wooded crest of the Monts du Forez south to their end, near the small, fortified city of Saint-Bonnet-le-Château. Here the marauding troops of the Protestant general des Adrets had passed in 1562, leaving thirty corpses to mummify in the church crypt.

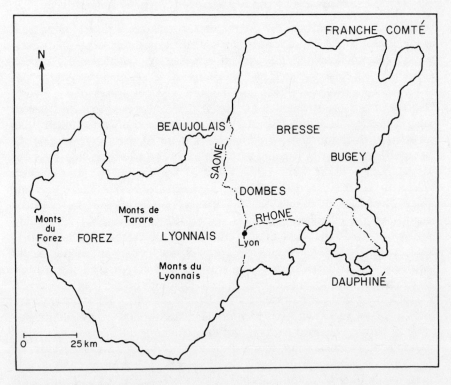

Figure 3. The diocese of Lyon

As in the east, the largest settlements in the western wing of the diocese were simple market towns and small cities, whose populations usually did not surpass several thousand souls. Saint-Etienne, which grew significantly in the sixteenth century, was probably the largest of these small western municipalities by a considerable margin. But even its population (eight thousand at most) remained well under the figure of ten thousand inhabitants that distinguished small cities and market towns from urban centers of medium or large size. In the sixteenth century, some of these western cities and towns were the sites of thriving industries. In Saint-Etienne and neighboring towns in the southwest of the diocese, metalworkers forged arms and hardware, while other artisans stretched and fulled cloth. And in small cities and villages throughout Forez, Lyonnais, and Beaujolais, weavers made linens and woolens. But it was Lyon that stimulated and directed this flourishing trade in hardware and textiles. Only by virtue of Lyon's existence did the small cities and market towns have access to larger markets.[4]

The peasants in the west of the diocese also produced for the market in Lyon, just like the artisans of the more prosperous market towns. Along the west bank of the Saône and the Rhône, they grew wheat and flax, and, especially near Lyon, harvested grapes for wine. In the hilly regions further west—Monts du Lyonnais, Monts du Tarare, western Beaujolais, and Monts du Forez—they practiced a more varied agriculture. Here stock raisers sent hides to Lyon and to local market towns. Other peasants spun flax into thread or wove linen cloth for sale in Lyon.[5]

Despite the presence of large numbers of Protestants in neighboring Geneva, in Dauphiné, and to the southwest of the diocese of Lyon, these rural portions of the diocese were largely Catholic. A few Protestants did live in the north of the diocese, toward Mâcon. In Belleville, for example, the Protestants purchased their own burial ground in 1566, after they had been barred from using the Catholic cemetery. A small number of Protestant settlements survived also in the eastern wing of the diocese, in towns like Pont-de-Veyle or Saint-Amour.[6] The west of the diocese sheltered even fewer Protestants. Meetinghouses did exist in Feurs, Saint-Bonnet-le-Château, Saint-Etienne, and Saint-Galmier, but many of the Protestant merchants and artisans in these towns left to seek refuge in Geneva. In short, despite these enclaves scattered throughout the countryside, the Protestants were a pitifully small minority outside the city of Lyon, and a dwindling one at that because of conversion and exodus.[7]

With only a small number of Protestants, the countryside around Lyon witnessed little religious violence, save for the depredations of Protestant and Catholic troops, who from time to time wreaked havoc in the area. Admittedly, there were a few outbursts of anti-Protestant feeling, and several isolated reprisals were taken against Calvinists by local Catholics. In 1569, for instance, Catholics in Belleville held a procession to ask divine aid for Spanish troops who were off to fight the "heretics." In the late 1570s, the duke of Savoy ordered pro-Catholic "white processions" in Bresse, in which participants wore white robes and walked barefoot. Some Calvinists who mocked these processions were hanged. And in 1596 Pierre Harenc de la Condamine, the curé of Saint-Etienne, persuaded landlords in his parish not to rent to

Protestants. He also apparently convinced the shoemakers of Saint-Etienne to harass Protestant cobblers, and he himself, so the Protestants complained, was in the habit of running after and beating suspected heretics who sneaked away from religious processions. But such lamentable violence was extremely rare outside Lyon. No Saint Bartholomew's Day massacre bloodied the countryside, as was the case in some rural districts in France.[8] Nor did fervor for the Catholic League ever seize hold of rural portions of the diocese. This lack of fervor for the ultra-Catholic cause did not mean that the peasants and townsmen harbored any affection for Protestantism. They no doubt hated the Huguenots. But they left the League to nobles and officeholders, who battled as much among themselves as against the threat of a non-Catholic king.[9]

The Rural Clergy

The faithful outside Lyon were far more dependent on the parish clergy than were their Catholic brethren in the city, who, we know, often frequented the churches of the mendicants. Some monasteries and friaries did exist outside Lyon, especially in the small cities, and clergymen from religious orders occasionally preached in rural churches. But there were simply not enough of these monks and friars to minister to the vast number of parishes in the diocesan hinterland.[10] As in the rest of Catholic Europe, the friaries in France were predominantly urban institutions, and this meant that the country dwellers had to turn to the parish clergy.

The parish priests included not only curés and vicars but also clerics from several collegiate churches and from *sociétés de prêtres*—groups of priests established in the later Middle Ages to recite the daily office and perform the liturgical duties entailed by pious foundations. Sociétés existed in nearly all the small cities of the diocese and in a few villages as well. Sharing the revenues of the pious endowments, the priests in these sociétés (and in rural collegiate churches as well) spent much of their time offering masses and prayers for the souls of the parish dead and for the welfare of the community.[11] Priests in the sociétés were almost always required to be natives of the parish they served, and sometimes the requirements for admission were even more restrictive. In Saint-Bonnet-le-Château, an ecclesiastic seeking admission to the société was not only supposed to be native born and baptized, but also had to win the approval of the town government. When, for instance, the young priest Jehan Goulte was received into the société in 1571, he had to obtain the assent of the town lieutenant (the seignior's agent) and the town consuls (the heads of the municipality).[12]

If the sixteenth-century sociétés were firmly bound to their communities, the same was true of the curés and vicars. These curés and vicars were themselves often natives of the parishes they served. For example, in Saint-Just-en-Chevalet, a small city of roughly two thousand inhabitants in the west of

the diocese, all six of the priests known to have presided over the parish during the years 1541 to 1607 were natives, and so were the five vicars who assisted them during the years 1557 to 1606. Because young men from small cities took holy orders in large numbers, Saint-Just-en-Chevalet and most other parishes of the same size had little difficulty filling local ecclesiastical posts with native sons.[13] But even smaller communities managed to find local men who were priests. In Saint-Romain-d'Urfé, a western village with less than half the population of nearby Saint-Just-en-Chevalet, one of the three known curés for the years 1564–1612 and both known vicars for the years 1546–1617 were natives. If a parish could not furnish enough locals to fill priestly offices, it often drew priests from those nearby market towns and small cities which were centers of ecclesiastical recruitment. Thus all six curés of the village of Saint-Priest-la-Prugne during the years 1563–1622 came from nearby Saint-Just-en-Chevalet.[14]

More general evidence confirms that most parish priests were local men, and this fact helps explain how the priests managed to win acceptance in their villages, which were usually suspicious of, and hostile to, outsiders. Documents known as *prises de possession,* which certified that a priest had taken over a parish, were often accompanied by letters of ordination that allow a sedulous reader to track down the new priest's birthplace or at least his parish of origin. Although only a fraction of the prises de possession were recorded in this way by ecclesiastical notaries, they do provide information on the geographical origins of some twenty-four typical curés who assumed posts in the countryside during the years 1579–1596.[15] Seven of the priests were either native sons or came to their parishes from adjacent towns. Such were Anthoine Symon, curé in 1585 of his hometown, Roche, in the mountains of Forez, and Jehan Precieu, a native of the western village of Saint-Laurent-sous-Rochefort, who became curé of neighboring Rochefort.[16] Eight others arrived in their parishes from towns merely five to fifteen kilometers away—easily within a day's walk, whatever the terrain. And only nine of the twenty-four curés hailed from communities over fifteen kilometers away. If these twenty-four curés were representative of their fellow clergymen (an assumption that is plausible despite the small sample size), then it appears that a sixteenth-century parish priest was indeed likely to be a native of the region around his parish.

Since many of the priests were local men, they naturally became godfathers of children in their parishes. In particular, if they had family in their parishes, they could be godfathers for their relatives. Thus in Montarcher, a tiny parish of one village and seven hamlets in the mountains of Forez, the vicar Claude Fermier belonged to a family group that linked eight of the twelve households in the village. He was godfather to eighteen relatives in the late fifteenth century. The fertile relatives of Mathieu Meigret seem to have followed him to the small parish of Chevrières when he became curé there early in the seventeenth century. Thereafter other Meigrets were often curés and vicars, and nearly all signed the baptismal records as godfathers of infants named Meigret. And Vicar Fresne, who died in the western parish of Feurs in 1627, was godfather to sixty-seven children during his fifty-four years in the parish.[17] If not all the families were related to the vicar, they at least wished to make him an ally and a friend—a sure sign that the curés were caught in the web of family alliances in their parishes.

Local men, often with ties to local families, the rural priests were as yet hardly affected by the Counter Reformation. As late as the 1613–14 episcopal visitation of the parishes, the curés, vicars, and priests in rural sociétés had scarcely been touched by the Tridentine reforms. To be sure, clerical concubinage, which episcopal visitors noted in some 17 percent of the diocese's parishes in the late fourteenth century, had nearly disappeared by 1613–14: in none of the parishes inspected did the visitor catch the pastor or his assistant living in sin.[18] Priestly concubinage seemed to survive in the diocese of Lyon only as a sporadic exception, no longer as the widespread custom it had been in the Middle Ages. But the keeping of concubines was only one of the problems that Trent sought to solve, and the others seemed largely untreated, even in 1614. For example, despite the Tridentine fathers' advocacy of the catechism, few priests in the hinterlands of the diocese were teaching it at the time of the 1613–14 visit. Indeed, Archbishop de Marquemont and the other visitors had to admonish nearly every curé they met to catechize.

The visitors were also infuriated that the curés failed to dress and behave in ways becoming a priest. Pierre Morard, pastor of Passin, drew the archbishop's ire not only for the greasy linen on his altar, but also for his distinctly nonclerical demeanor: he was "clothed in an extremely indecent costume, with a huge mustache like a soldier—which we made him shave off on the spot."[19] In other parishes, the pastors frequented taverns and gambled in the presence of laymen: curé Estienne Roux of the village of Balan, for example, was notorious for haunting taverns and whiling away his hours playing games of chance. Absenteeism was also a problem. In 6 percent of the parishes visited in 1613–14, both the pastor and his assistant were absent; in others the curé scarcely set foot in his parish, leaving his parishioners at the mercy of an often incompetent vicar in order to pursue a more glamorous and lucrative second office. One such negligent pastor was Antoine Lacourt, curé of Saint-Genest-de-Malifaux from 1550 to 1572. He entrusted his flock of parishioners to a vicar and spent most of his time in the city of Le Puy, where he was a cathedral canon and head of the ecclesiastical court of the diocese. Other curés occupied benefices in Lyon and leased out their rural parishes to local priests for a fixed fee.[20]

Perhaps the most grievous shortcoming of the rural clergymen was their lack of education. During the 1613–14 visitation, the archbishop and his aides decried the ignorance of the priests in 55 of the 368 parishes they visited, and they found few others whose learning they could praise. Priests such as Jacques Mesard, the "extremely ignorant" curé of Niost-de-Gourdon, knew "neither Latin nor how to administer the sacraments." Similarly, the curé of Couzance, Nicolas Crippon, knew neither "the form of absolution nor how to administer the other sacraments, and even had difficulty reading [the Latin]." Crippon was told to carry a little card bearing "the form of the aforementioned absolution so that he can read it when he wishes to absolve someone in confession."[21] These priests were not illiterate, for Crippon and others like him were able to keep baptismal registers (in French) and to read their "cue cards" bearing the formula of absolution. But they were uneducated: although they could read French, they knew no Latin and hence only dimly understood the ritual they conducted. This is what angered the archbishop and the other visitors, for to the ecclesiastical hierarchy it meant that the ignorant curés and vicars only went through the motions. It also evidenced their lack of exposure to Catholic theology, for in the sixteenth century most serious Catholic religious writing was in Latin.

Finally, the parish priests were in no way members of the intellectual elite. Even though they read French, their ignorance of Latin placed them on the populace's side of the great rift that divided the learned from the people. But what could be expected in an age when seminaries did not exist and when most candidates for the priesthood honed their minds by apprenticing themselves to benighted neighbors or untutored relatives who were already in the ranks of the clergy?

Of course, a few priests in the countryside did have a smattering of learning, and some even owned a small number of books. These better-educated clergymen could be found not only in the market towns and small cities (two of the canons in Bourg-en-Bresse held doctorates, for example), but also in some villages. Curé Jehan Valliezy of Beligny, for instance, who died in 1605, possessed a library of nine volumes. Except for a Latin–French dictionary, each of his books was concerned with pastoral duties: a missal, a catechism, a book of sermons, etc. All but two of the volumes (the exceptions were a catechism and a book of excerpts from the Gospels) were in Latin. The 1613–14 visits and the complaints of the diocesan hierarchy suggest, however, that priests of Valliezy's high caliber were a distinct minority.[22] Valliezy's many colleagues who were not so learned could no doubt work their way through a passage in French, but no enormous cultural gulf separated them from their parishioners. Their dress differed little from that of their flock, and they commonly passed their time in taverns alongside the layfolk. Some curés even lived with their relatives, evidence that joining the priesthood entailed no break with the secular world: for example, Pierre Pallon, curé of Ranchal, who in 1587 shared a house and a herd of livestock with his brother and sister-in-law.[23]

Rural clerics thus seem to have lived on closer terms with their parishioners than did the priests in Lyon. Admittedly, many clergymen in the city had relatives among the urban laity, and like priests in the countryside, they retained their ties to kith and kin by presiding at marriages or serving as godfathers. But these clerics in Lyon were cut off from the city's large immigrant population, while their rural counterparts faced no such troubling newcomers in their parishes. Furthermore, whereas wealth isolated the upper clergy in Lyon from the city's common people, the priests in the villages lived in relative modesty, to judge from the few death inventories we have.[24] The rural curés were certainly not poor, but their benefices would not support the sort of ostentatious wealth enjoyed by canons in Lyon. Finally, the clergymen in the countryside often dressed and behaved like their parishioners; no cultural barrier separated them from the laity. As yet, seminaries and education had not driven a wedge between the priests and the people.

The Priest and the Rituals of Community Life

Like the village clergy, rural laymen were largely untouched by the Counter Reformation before 1615. In this respect, the religious situation in the countryside differed sharply from that in Lyon. There, we recall, the Catholic Reformation was under way among the city's upper classes as early as the 1560s. Members of the urban elite were forming new devotional confraternities, and they reversed a decline in pious bequests, which had fallen from a late medieval peak. Nothing of the kind, though, took place in the countryside. The parish visits of 1613–14 reveal few of the new devotional confraternities in the villages, and parish records provide little or no evidence of a change in rural piety either.

Pious bequests in wills tend to confirm this picture of rural spirituality. Rural testaments, though, are rare items in notarial registers before 1550; too few of them exist to draw absolutely certain conclusions about trends in village piety at midcentury. A number of rural wills from the early sixteenth century and before do survive amidst the records of ecclesiastical or civil courts, but because these testaments were in many cases preserved by the courts precisely because they contained pious bequests, no ready comparison with the later wills in the notarial registers is possible. The paucity of rural testaments before 1550 makes it particularly difficult to determine whether the countryside experienced the same decline in traditional spirituality which beset Lyon in the middle of the sixteenth century. Whether religious legacies in the countryside subsided from some late medieval peak (as they did in Lyon) is therefore unclear, although the surge of votive masses we associate with late medieval piety apparently made only small ripples outside Lyon and other cities. If rural testaments before 1550 thus remain shrouded in mystery, the end of the sixteenth century definitely witnessed no dramatic rise in pious bequests in the countryside. Overall, only 13 percent of a sample of rural wills drawn up before 1600 (nearly all of these date from 1550–1600) included pious legacies, versus fully 72 percent of urban testaments.[25] Although greater wealth among urban testators explains part of this difference, it does nevertheless suggest that Catholic spirituality in the villages was not entirely the same as in Lyon.

Fortunately, other documents can depict sixteenth-century rural piety in greater detail. While Catholic spirituality in the countryside resembled that of the city in some ways, it bears describing, and certain features of rural piety deserve particular attention, for they would later draw the ire of priests who were eager to remake village religion.

In the countryside, the rites of Catholic spirituality bound a curé to the lay persons of his parish. Even the sacraments brought him closer to his parishioners. Since he alone had the power to administer the sacraments, they ought to have isolated him from the laity. But they did not do so, for a web of paraliturgical ritual accompanied each sacrament and drew the curé into the life of his village. Baptism, for example, was the occasion for a number of ceremonies accompanying childbirth. After the birth and the christening, the curé administered a blessing to the infant's mother. The family and the godparents of the child then gave a banquet to celebrate the birth, and the local priests all attended the feast. And the baptism itself served not only to mark the removal of original sin but also as a sign of membership in the community. Hence the church bells were rung afterward in order to signal the admission of a new Christian into the village.[26]

Other sacraments administered by the curé also united priest and faithful. Paraliturgical ritual made the sacraments acts which partook more of group sanctification than of individual salvation. Confession, for instance, was not yet a secret dialogue between the curé and the penitent. Churches lacked confessionals, and the priest gave absolution in the open. In the east of the diocese, whole groups of people (such as the adolescent males of the parish) even confessed in unison.[27] Holy Communion also entailed a group ritual that bound together the priest and the faithful. In rural areas (as in cities) Catholics took Communion only several times a year, most notably at Easter, when nearly everyone received the Eucharist. At the Easter Communion it was customary for many towns and villages to furnish wine to help the lay people wash down the host. Although this wine, purchased by the laity, was apparently not consecrated, it was distributed by the priest and it was an integral part of the most important Communion ceremony of the year.[28] As for the sacrament of marriage, it was accompanied by pealing carillons, banquets, and dancing in front of the church. The parish priests blessed these festivities and even frolicked with the newlyweds.[29]

We know very little about extreme unction, the last of the Catholic sacraments, but rituals of mourning gave the priests an additional opportunity to mix in the affairs of parish groups. Testators asked the curés or the sociétés de prêtres for burial rites and memorial masses; families did the same. Vocational groups called upon priests to lament their dead as well. When a bonnet-maker died in sixteenth-century Saint-Just-en-Chevalet, each of his fellow tradesmen attended his funeral and payed the curé for a requiem. Parish vestries had their part to play in the mourning too. They often determined the manner in which the bells rung when the priest led a funeral procession to the graveyard, and they even stipulated the number of candles to be burnt at the funeral. Village confraternities also joined in the memorial services for the dead. At the request of donors, they had the curés offer mass *in perpetuum* "for the salvation of the souls of the current confrères, of their predecessors and successors," to quote from a typical foundation.[30] As we shall see, the membership of such a confraternity could encompass nearly the entire parish; such bequests in effect provided masses for all the residents of the village and their ancestors. The masses the curé said thus preserved a link between his parishioners and their departed ancestors—this in a Catholic society, in which purgatory was a deeply entrenched article of faith and the dead were in many ways yet another "age group" in society.

All the various ceremonies the priest conducted were of great significance in the sixteenth-century countryside, where, among illiterate peasants, ritual and gesture took the place of the written word. If such ceremonies left little trace on parchment and paper, it was because they were commonplace, a part of every man's life, and therefore not normally worthy of mention. As we shall see, however, they were hardly meaningless actions, and they may have assumed even greater importance in the villages than similar ceremonies did in the city of Lyon. In fact, by mixing the sacred and the secular, the rituals held together the local units of rural society. They bound man to man, placated God, gave expression to joy, sorrow, and anger, and helped each participant overcome crises in his life. In the absence of schools, they instilled and perpetuated local values and traditions.

The curés and vicars were deeply involved in all of the village rituals, not simply the ceremonies accompanying the sacraments or rites of mourning. Consider, for example, the numerous processions, which wound through the countryside as often as they did in Lyon itself and which always included the curés. The great holy days, such as Easter and Pentecost, all witnessed processions directed by curés; so did lesser feasts. Some of these processions honored patron saints of parishes. In Chevrières, for instance, the parishioners customarily made a procession on their knees on the parish feast day.[31] Others honored the saints of confraternities. On the feast day of Saint Eloy, the patron of the local blacksmiths' confraternity, the chanting priests of Saint-Bonnet-le-Château led a procession from the choir to the saint's chapel in the nave of the church. Such celebrations of parish and confraternity feast days could be nearly weekly events. In Feurs, for example, the calendar was graced with at least nineteen such feast days, in honor of the patron saints of the parish, of two hamlets, and of sixteen professional and devotional confraternities.[32]

Often these various processions left the church and went far outside the city walls to a revered local cross or hallowed shrine. Throughout the sixteenth century, for example, the curé and the faithful of Feurs walked twenty kilometers each Monday after Pentecost to the famed statue of the Black Virgin in Saint-Germain-Laval, and during the week of Rogations, this parish, like others, went in procession to neighboring towns. This was a common means of uniting a community with its neighbors, and symbolic exchanges of wine or bread with the residents of the surrounding towns were often involved.[33]

Just as in the city of Lyon, the long lines of chanting priests and marching layfolk were also remedies against danger and disaster. In 1609, a plague struck Saint-Bonnet-le-Château, prompting the worried curé and the priests of the local société to lead a procession to another hallowed statue of a Black Virgin, this one in the chapel of Our Lady in Valfleury, near Saint-Chamond. If the skies threatened hail—as they frequently did in the Rhône valley—the priest and the lay people filed out of the church with the Eucharist in order to exorcise the clouds and save the crops. A drought in 1556 led to numerous white processions from the countryside into the city of Lyon, and on other occasions there were processions to reconsecrate defiled cemeteries and to protect communal lands against encroachment.[34] A procession of priests was even part of the ritual in which a leper was symbolically driven from the community. In 1558, an anonymous priest in Belleville scribbled in his parish register that a poor young woman afflicted with leprosy

> was removed from the company of human beings . . . and these funeral ceremonies were done by the canons . . . and other secular priests, with the great bells ringing in the manner that is customary in such a case. . . . We led her and turned her over to the Hospital and Leprosarium of Belleville, there to use up the rest of her days, which God by his goodness allow her to spend and finish with patience.[35]

Processions led by priests thus signaled expulsion, staved off calamities, brought a community together with its neighbors, and united the members of a parish or a confraternity to celebrate a holy day or a patron saint's feast day. The processions illustrate very well how the parish church and the parish clergy were drawn into the life of the rural communities. The church bells, which tolled so sadly when the priests escorted the young woman to the leprosarium, provided yet another link between the parish church and the community. Indeed, the bells seemed the very voice of the village. They called the laity not only to baptisms, marriages, funerals, and masses, but to confraternity ceremonies, village fairs, and community assemblies. And the rapid ringing of the bell, the feared tocsin, warned him of danger. In Feurs, not far from the Loire River, the bells rang out whenever a flood threatened nearby hamlets. In Belleville the tocsin sounded when, in 1621, it was rumored that Protestant troops were approaching the town gates; the result was a riot. The bells were so important to the community that a new one always received a ritual baptism. Given both a name and god-parents—usually the local seignior or other village notable—the bell was cus-tomarily blessed with holy water by the curé.[36]

A multitude of other customs blended the sacred with the secular and thus involved the pastors in the life of their communities. Laymen built crosses to adorn holy places and mark village boundaries, and they bought religious banners that served as parish insignia when the community went on proces-sion. In 1614, for example, the municipal officers and principal inhabitants of the market town of Saint-Rambert-en-Forez rebuilt one such stone cross on a little hill outside their town. During the parish visit of the same year this cross was blessed and then kissed by the visitor, by the town's inhabitants, and by the canons and curé. In 1598 in the village of Longes, the curé blessed a cross that a pious father and son had erected on a hill in the parish. And in Chambost-Longessaigne the married men of the parish helped pur-chase a banner for processions. Another community practice that called for the curé's participation was *pain bénit,* bread that the parishioners shared at mass. Every Sunday they took turns bringing bread to church, and even the curé would have his turn once a year. Before mass the priest blessed this bread and then distributed it to the parishioners at the offertory. In a sense, the pain bénit was a symbolic meal that united the whole parish. Perhaps this is why it attracted more frequent participation than the other ritual breaking of bread—for Communion.[37]

Parish priests in the countryside also took part when the villages presented mystery plays. In 1599, for instance, the youths of Feurs played *l'Enfant pro-digue* before the portals of the church. The curé led a procession to celebrate the occasion. In Montbrison, one of the local priests played the role of Christ in the three-day Passion play in 1533, and in 1539 one of the parish clergy-men and six laymen from the town staged a farce and morality play after a confraternity banquet.[38]

In the seventeenth century the Catholic Church and the curés would con-demn such popular religious theater, and in general they would strive to separate the sacred and the secular in rural life. In the sixteenth century, however, no such winnowing had taken place. The sacred embraced work and play; work and play in turn mingled with what was holy. Crosses stood in the fields to protect agricultural labors. Processions initiated raucous parish dances. Churches, with their porches and the open spaces before them, were the scenes of markets, assemblies, and fairs. The mass itself was commonly an occasion to gossip or talk of business, and even before the end of the service the congregation would at times slip back to the doorway or walk outside in order to socialize, dance, or play. In La Bruyère, a village northeast of Lyon, a chapel used for Sunday services was also a storehouse: in 1614 it housed twelve wooden chests belonging to local peasants. Elsewhere, livestock grazed in cemeteries and creaking wagons passed over hallowed ground. In Saint-Jean-des-Aventures, dancing at the parish festival spilled out over the burial ground, and in Saint-Amour the cemetery was a place of work: the peasants used it to dress the flax they had harvested and to dry their laundry and the cloth they had woven.[39]

One could argue that similar rites in Lyon drew urban priests equally close to their own parishioners, and this undoubtedly happened in smaller parishes in the city and in ones that had links to neighborhood organizations, such as Saint-Pierre-et-Saint-Saturnin. Urban clergymen participated in celebrations accompanying marriages and baptisms, and they too led processions. But the rural curés played a far greater role in popular culture than did their urban counterparts. While urban clergymen were by and large excluded from this realm of profane affairs, the rural curés openly drank, gambled, and socialized with members of the community. They had a hand in popular theater as well, and they danced at parish festivals and joined in parish games. The diocesan statutes of 1577 railed against priests in the countryside who took part in such festivities: priests like Jean Reydellet, vicar of the village of Tossiac, who was "always at the dances."[40]

Evidence from other areas of France provides more vivid confirmation that rural curés were only too ready to gambol at parish festivities and participate in all sorts of other local games. In *Propos rustiques,* Noël Du Fail's sixteenth-century fiction, village curé Jacquinot was an insatiable dancer at parish celebrations: "Brisk and filled, perhaps, with a bit of lust, he [the curé] spun his partners so vigorously that the ladies felt the lamb [they had eaten] rise in their throats; and all the while the curé shouted, 'On! On! Never shall we frolic together any younger, and so let us take time as it comes and may the devil take anyone who collapses.'" The other characters in *Propos rustiques* saw nothing shocking in this conduct, and Jacquinot, modeled after the beloved pastor in Du Fail's own home parish in Brittany, was depicted in the *Propos rustiques* as a good man and an exemplary priest. While this Breton curé was only a character in a work of fiction, albeit realistic fiction, we also have the example of a real curé in the matter-of-fact diary kept at midcentury by the Norman squire Gilles de Gouberville. According to Gouberville's diary, this Norman curé spent the hours between Sunday mass and vespers playing ninepins with the young men of the parish or trying his hand at *boules* with them at the rectory. He and the vicars even took part in violent games of football with neighboring villages, and they entered wrestling contests, which pitted the married men of the parish against the unmarried.[41]

The Priest and the Community in the Sixteenth Century

In the seventeenth and eighteenth centuries, the Church and the parish priests would battle with, and even fight to suppress, the communal institutions of the towns and villages, but in the sixteenth century, the rural curés participated enthusiastically in nearly all of their multitudinous activities. To understand these subsequent battles and to grasp fully the priests' place in village life before the onslaught of the Tridentine reforms, we must examine the various communal organizations and institutions of government in the sixteenth-century towns and villages.

By comparison to the highly organized local government of Provençal communities, village government in the diocese of Lyon was vague and undeveloped. Often the only institutions of community government were informal village assemblies. These meetings took place periodically (only several times a year in small villages) in the cemetery or the public square, in the church or on a porch attached to it, or perhaps in a town hall. The right to attend was customarily limited to the family heads, and in some communities only to those possessing property; however, the latter requirement was not very restrictive in the sixteenth century, when ownership of at least a parcel of land was more widespread than in centuries to follow. Those present at the assemblies chose consuls who collected and apportioned the *taille,* or direct tax. They also selected syndics and *procureurs* to represent the community in dealings concerning communal property, and they coped with the troops who often imposed upon the village's hospitality. If the town's population exceeded a thousand residents, the assembly might also collect indirect taxes and run a community hospital or even a tiny school. Such a larger market town or small city held more frequent assemblies, and it was usually endowed with a town council and sometimes a civic charter, which gave it a recognized municipal government.[42]

In some communities, the seignior or his agent authorized and presided over the village assemblies. Seigniors commonly policed rural communities as well. However, many of the communities in the diocese of Lyon were relatively independent of the seignior, a situation common further south in France, and local seigniors therefore played a smaller role in the village affairs.

In addition to town or village assemblies, there were meetings of the property owners of the parish, at which the business concerned ecclesiastical matters such as the upkeep of the church or the management of glebe land. These meetings constituted the parish vestry. The parishioners who attended them also chose churchwardens who looked after the vestry's interests.

Of course, this is an overly simplistic picture of village institutions, for when the villagers assembled to treat fiscal matters (the most common order of business), their meeting was properly called the assembly of the *communauté d'habitants,* and it drew the family heads who resided in the *parcelle fiscale,* the village considered as a taxpaying district. When the villagers discussed more general matters, their meeting was termed the assembly of the parish, and the family heads in attendance came from the parish. What complicated matters was that, as a geographical entity, the parcelle fiscale did not always coincide with the parish or even with the seigniory. A further complication was that the vestry and the assembly of the communauté d'habitants were often hopelessly intertwined, especially in the sixteenth century. In the diocese of Lyon this confusion of vestry and communauté d'habitants did not reach the extremes that it did in the north of France, where one often cannot tell whether a given assembly was that of the communauté d'habitants or of the parish, or whether a plot of communal land belonged to the vestry or to the communauté. But even around Lyon the two institutions overlapped, so that the consuls chosen by the communauté d'habitants often served as churchwardens, and the word *parish* in legal practice was synonymous with communauté d'habitants.[43]

To make matters more confusing, the parish vestry and the communauté d'habitants were themselves often merely reflections of another organization that lay at the heart of commmunal life: the village confraternity. In part mutual aid societies and in part surrogate families, these confraternities were the oldest communal organizations in the towns and villages. Their members included the village's male property owners, whose names are the only ones on the surviving documents, occasionally the property owners' wives and children, and perhaps even the poor, although the confraternities sometimes levied an entrance fee. They usually bore the name of confraternities of the Holy Spirit, although they could have other patrons and were sometimes referred to simply as "the confraternity of such and such place," as if everyone knew what was meant.[44] In the later Middle Ages and the first half of the sixteenth century, these associations of the Holy Spirit were the most common confraternities in the diocese of Lyon and in much of southern and eastern France. They could be found in small cities, towns, villages, and even hamlets. Nonetheless, they have left few traces in the archives, partly because they fell on hard times and were usually suppressed before the end of the Old Regime and partly because their activities, governed by the dictates of an immemorial spoken tradition, demanded few written records. In fact, in the eighteenth century, when the Catholic Church and the royal intendants required that the remaining village confraternities produce titles and charters to justify their existence, the best the members of such *confréries* could do was to wave a single dusty medieval will beneath the nose of the intendant's or bishop's agent and lament that their organization was "so ancient . . . that they could not furnish its original title."[45]

The village confraternities stood close to the center of communal life and government, and they had many ties to the other village institutions. In market towns and small cities with actual town councils, the council assemblies often took place in the confraternity's house, beneath its primitive frescoes of the Holy Spirit and the parish patron saints. In the eastern market town of Ceyzeriat, for example, the municipal government used the confraternity's building for meetings and for storing its worm-eaten records.

In Rive-de-Gier, a tiny walled city in the southwest of the diocese, the "building of the inhabitants' confraternity" stood at the center of town, across from the church and near the dwelling of the seignior's agents. It housed not only the confraternity but the parish priest as well and also served as the seat of communal administration.[46]

Sharing a building was not the only overlap of other village institutions. In Pérouges, a town northeast of Lyon, the Confraternity of the Holy Spirit was the vestry, and in l'Hôpital-le-Grand the vestry itself managed the property of the Holy Spirit confraternity. Elsewhere it was the confraternity and the government of the communauté d'habitants that were bound together. In the small city of Saint-Symphorien-le-Château in the fifteenth century, the two lay rectors of the Confraternity of the Holy Spirit sat on the six-man city council and administered the city with the four other councilors. In Condrieu, the communal government of the consuls was at one time identified with the Confraternity of the Holy Spirit, and in many places the syndics or consuls of the community oversaw the confraternity's property and income. In 1534 in Saint-Cyr-au-Mont-d'Or, a village northwest of Lyon, the village syndics pursued certain debtors of the local Holy Spirit confraternity. Although in 1597 rectors directed the affairs of the confraternity of Saint-Cyr, they did nothing without the approval of an assembly of the inhabitants and consuls of the village. And in 1610 the village consuls of Saint-Cyr included the lands of the still active confraternity in a declaration of the village's communal property.[47] Often the entire communauté d'habitants took up the business of managing the village confraternity's lands and rentes. Thus in 1581 the heads of families in Saint-Genis-Laval signed a contract with their seignior to assure he would pay an annuity that he owed the confraternity, and in Verrières a community assembly in 1588 approved a property transaction involving a piece of the Holy Spirit confraternity's land.[48]

Such a bewildering variety of local custom makes impossible any rigid definition of the village confraternity's role and powers which would hold true for every community in the diocese. Yet clearly in the small communities the confraternity and the communauté d'habitants were nearly identical. In market towns and smaller cities, on the other hand, the situation was more complicated. Here, syndics and elected town councils constituted a formal municipal government that handled most of the tasks of local politics. With their political role thus somewhat reduced, the confraternities still had significant ceremonial duties, and they also served as the embodiment of the municipal citizenry. The market town of Ceyzeriat, for example, enjoyed an enfranchised municipal government, which the citizens were perfectly ready to use for judicial battles with their seignior or with their sovereign, the duke of Savoy. But what conferred citizenship and membership in the community was not any act of the municipal government but rather admission to the confraternity. Only after the property owners admitted a newcomer to the confraternity did he become a bourgeois of Ceyzeriat and gain the right to use communal property. Thus in 1601, Bastian Vignon and a *sieur* Naiz, two "non-natives and outsiders" who lived in Ceyzeriat, sought entry into the confraternity because they wanted to "join in with the others of the aforesaid Ceyzeriat so that they might enjoy the confraternity and communal lands, like those who are already bourgeois, confrères, and members in common of the town." After the two paid a fee, the assembled town syndics and property-owning heads of families admitted them and their heirs into the confraternity and granted them "each and every liberty, immunity and right of the communality and confraternity." These rights included citizenship and access to communal land and grazing, a sign that the confraternity controlled access to the communal property. The very language of the document—the linking of "bourgeois" and "confrères"—suggests that the confraternity was identified with the citizenry.[49]

Like other pious confraternities, the village associations marched in processions with the clergy, erected crosses, and brought pain bénit to church for blessing.[50] Like professional confraternities, they also held annual banquets. The curés naturally attended these banquets and offered a blessing before the meal began, just as they did at the feasts of the rural professional confraternities. But the banquets of the village confraternities differed from those of the professional guilds. First, the feasts of the village confraternities attracted a far larger number of guests: not just the members of a single trade but nearly the whole community supped together. In the small city of Saint-Symphorien-le-Château, the guests at the banquet included the "confrères-citizens of the town and other guests." The "confrères-citizens" were the property-owning family heads, the men who formed the communauté d'habitants; their families probably attended too. The other guests included, at the very least, the noblemen in the vicinity, according to the terms of a 1403 will that subsidized the meal. The banquets of these village associations were also likely to be far more elaborate than those of professional confraternities. At Saint-Symphorien-le-Château, the guests feasted like gluttons on bread, wine, six "fat cattle," and a "sufficient number" of lambs, in addition to other, unnamed servings. Their Rabelaisian meals went on for three full days.[51]

The other characteristic activity of the village confraternities was the almsgiving, the charitable donation of food to the poor which the confraternities usually performed at Pentecost. In Renaison, the curé distributed the Holy Spirit confraternity's alms. In Neuville it was the confraternity's lay rectors who handed out bread and wine after the Pentecost High Mass. In Sainte-Foy-les-Lyon the alms were more elaborate: bread, vegetable soup, and cooked lard. Those who received this food were poor in the medieval sense of the word: poor meant anyone who stretched forth his hand to accept the gift, whether he was wealthy or indigent. At the distribution in Saint-Genis-Laval, for instance, every family in the community was given salt, and anyone who happened to be present at the Pentecost procession received wine and bread.[52]

In addition, the confraternities helped stage the village festivals, again with the participation of the curé. These explosions of dance and revelry normally took place on the feast day of the parish's patron saint and sometimes at Pentecost as well. In Montarcher, a tiny mountain community just over the western boundary of the diocese, the village confraternity organized festivals on the feast of Saint Pantaleon, the community's patron saint, and perhaps at Pentecost too. The festivals at Montarcher followed the confraternity's banquets, and on Saint Pantaleon's day the parish's well-fed inhabitants danced to the music of "three trumpet or reed players and two horns." Near Montbrison, in the small parish of l'Hôpital-le-Grand, the village confraternity held its banquet on the parish feast and helped the "fiddlers" and "tambourine players"—there were five of them in 1538—who goaded on the dancers. Villages even built sheds to shelter the musicians and wine sellers, and the rural festivals (though less elaborate than traditional festivities in Lyon) sometimes became scenes of riotous masquerade, where armed horsemen and mock dignitaries presided over masked revelers.[53]

These celebrations were expressions of the parish's solidarity and of the people's willingness to defend their community. In mock combats during the festivals or in real skirmishes afterward, the villagers battled for their parish's honor against interlopers from neighboring towns. Military activities flourished as rowdy young men fired their muskets in feigned battles.[54] Village celebrations were also an occasion for the acculturation of the rural youth; in fact, these festivities fulfilled an important educational function, given the lack of even rudimentary schools or catechism classes. At the parish festival in Du Fail's *Propos rustiques,* the older men demonstrated the dance steps to the young people of the village. After the dancing had stopped, everyone retired to a nearby field, where the elders, their tongues loosened by a bit of hard cider, gave the young men moral lessons, spoke to them of the "happy vocation of agriculture," and counseled them to avoid excessive riches. The festivals were also crucial to the sexual lives of the village young people, for it was during the dancing at these celebrations that courtship began. Although the Church and the curés would later wage war against the sexual mingling and violence of the rural festivals, the sixteenth-century churchmen were rather indulgent. They usually began the festivals by celebrating a mass or leading a procession, before joining in the merrymaking alongside their parishioners.[55]

During the rural festivals, the curé usually presided over the boisterous ceremonies known throughout central France as *royaumes* or *reinages.* In these half-religious, half-secular rituals, which we have already encountered in parishes in Lyon, the curé auctioned off the right to be king or queen or *dauphin* or *connétable* of the parish feast day—the list of offices for sale was endless. The origin of this widespread custom is far from clear. In the village of Montarcher, where a royaume first appeared in the records in 1494, the king of the royaume and the other dignitaries took over the task of organizing the parish feast day from the chief of the village confraternity. On the basis of this example, Jean Pierre Gutton, one of the few French historians who has written on royaumes, suggests that the village confraternities gave birth to these celebrations in the late fifteenth century. Some royaumes, however, date back as far as the early fourteenth century and others seem to have had little to do with the village confraternities.[56]

The king and the other dignitaries of the royaume financed and helped stage the parish festivals, often with the assistance of the village confraternity. This was part of the fee they paid for their festival office. Thus in l'Hôpital-le-Grand the parishioners met the expenses of their parish feast day by means of a customary "royaume, for the sake of which each year there is selected a queen, a number of confrères [from the village confraternity and also a king of the feast day], all for the support of the festival, which is burdened with fiddlers and tambourine players." The king of the festival in l'Hôpital-le-Grand paid for the parish's celebrations and hired the musicians; the queen and the members of the village confraternity were obliged to reimburse him with payments of money and wine. The priest of l'Hôpital-le-Grand, and other rural priests like him, blessed the king and queen of the royaume and sanctified their financial obligations in a ceremony conducted in the parish church. In l'Hôpital-le-Grand, this ceremony saw the king, queen, and other festival dignitaries assemble before the altar so that the parish priest, who was only a vicar, could inscribe their names in a register. Then, taking turns, they all placed their hands between the vicar's cupped palms and swore a solemn oath to fulfill their obligations toward the festival.[57]

But the royaumes were not simply a means of making money. The king and queen wore crowns and actually presided over the festival, and in some instances they had the right to judge misdemeanors for a brief period. Their election, accompanied by fifes, drums, and musket fire, exemplified the ritual inversion of social and political hierarchies that was so common in early modern celebrations, inversion that gave the participants an opportunity to enjoy a fleeting sense of equality and a chance to laugh at existing social and political structures.[58] The royaumes also had religious significance. Not only were the king and queen escorted into the church to hear mass or to receive a blessing, but their coronation and the auction itself often took place there. Adding to the religious importance was the fact that the king and queen usually gave candle wax to the curé or to the parish church as part of the fee they paid for their offices. In return for furnishing this wax, they gained the cherished right to decorate the chapel of the saint whose feast day was being celebrated or to carry the saint's statue or banner in a procession. Those who bought the offices of king and queen even spoke of the purchase as a religious act: they usually said they had been moved to do so out of devotion to the honored saint.[59] And the parish clergy was, of course, deeply involved in the entire ceremony of the royaume.

The young unmarried men of the community also aided the confraternities and the royaume dignitaries in organizing the parish festivals. Associations of youths were common in communities throughout Europe, and the diocese of Lyon was no exception. In Saint-Claude, Bourg-en-Bresse, Saint-Bonnet-le-Château, and some of the other small cities of the diocese, the bachelors formed clearly defined groups known as the city youth (enfants de la ville, as in Lyon) or the youth abbeys. But in most rural communities, the youth organizations were less formal and less likely to have left any records. They were called simply the young men of the parish. In general, recruitment in these groups cut across class lines. In contrast to the enfants de la ville in Lyon, whose members came from prominent families, the youth groups in the villages and even those in some of the small cities of the diocese drew young men from all social classes.

The youth's vigorous role included battling outsiders during parish festivals, not only to maintain their community's honor but also to keep the interlopers from courting the parish's small pool of girls eligible for marriage. They also upheld the community's marriage standards. They exacted small fines from people who took spouses outside the parish, and they conducted charivaris, rituals that symbolically punished those whose marriages violated community norms. After an unseemly marriage—a widow or widower who took a second spouse or a bride who suffered from a bad reputation—the masked youths and older married accomplices beat pots and pans outside the newlywed's door and harassed the couple until the young men and their accomplices were propitiated with a gift of drink or money. The youth also held their own celebrations. On the first Sunday of Lent, for example, they might expose the recently married village males to a ritualistic ordeal. The bridegrooms might have to hitch themselves to a cart laden with firewood and then drag the heavy vehicle about town. The youths would use the wood to build a bonfire, and they customarily frolicked before the flames to the amusement of a laughing crowd that included even the curé.[60]

These unmarried males helped organize the parish festivals, for after all it was there that they courted their future wives and learned of village traditions from their elders. They also had ties to other organizations responsible for the festivals. The village confraternities may have been linked to the young men. In Boen, for instance, frescoes in the confraternity's house depicted not only the Holy Spirit and the parish's patron saint, but also Saint Nicholas, the patron of youth. The ties between the youths and the various royaumes were stronger still. Some of the royaumes seemed expressly reserved for the village youths. In the town of Oullins the parish festivals witnessed the choice of a "king of the children of Oullins," and in Montarcher the king and queen who organized the parish festival were usually local young people. Elsewhere, it was the young men who ritualistically delivered to the curé or the vestry the candle wax from the sale of the office of king. And at the feast day in Charlieu, just north of the diocese, the young men, armed with muskets, customarily escorted the "king and queen of the parish's confraternity" into church for a mass celebrated by the curé.[61] The youth sometimes even held royaumes of their own, apart from those of village or professional confraternities. In Condrieu, the proceeds of such a youths' royaume went to the curé; in return, their king received as an emblem of his powers a bouquet that either his peers or the curé had to deliver to the king's beloved. The village youths were in fact so deeply involved in the royaumes of the village confraternities that some historians believe the royaumes were, at least on occasion, merely the local form of youth organization, the local variant of the youth abbeys.[62]

The demand for the parish priest's liturgical services and for his participation in festivals and royaumes naturally raises the question of his power in the villages of the diocese. One might assume that the call for his services gave him great power in the parish, all the more so since rural curés faced little competition from regular clergymen. Could not his near monopoly of sacerdotal functions or an implicit threat to withhold his participation in paraliturgical rituals have enabled him to issue orders to his parishioners? Could he not derive tremendous informal authority from his post as the community's confessor?

If one defines power as making one's will prevail against resistance, then the sixteenth-century curé clearly had no power over the laity. Perhaps medieval priests had been able to compel parishioners to follow their orders. One thinks, for example, of curé Clergue in Emmanuel Le Roy Ladurie's *Montaillou,* who was a near despot in his early-fourteenth-century village.[63] Rural priests in the sixteenth century, however, wielded no such coercive authority.

A definition of power more relevant to the parish clergy would be the potential for exerting influence. A curé would have power over lay people if, within limits, social relationships made the laity's behavior dependent on the curé's own actions. In this sense of the word, it is clear that a priest did have some power over the laity, for his monopoly of sacerdotal functions undoubtedly gave him the ability to influence his parishioners. However, this power was in fact limited. A curé could not excommunicate parishioners or place them under interdict, for usage of these ecclesiastical penalties was severely restricted in the sixteenth century.[64] He could not, in other words, simply deprive the laity of the sacraments. Moreover, some of the curé's informal means of affecting the laity's behavior were equally ineffective. What authority did a confessor have when parishioners received absolution only once a year and when, in some parishes, absolution was granted to groups of people?

Curés also lacked power inside parish organizations. Only rarely, for example, did they take part in the community assemblies. They may have pulled strings behind the scenes, but the visible mechanisms of power—the assemblies themselves—were largely off limits to the clergymen. The evidence from dozens of village assemblies is practically unanimous on this point. Despite their presence at all the village cultural events, the sixteenth-century priests almost never appeared at the meetings where the family heads made decisions about the collection of the taille and the management of communal debts and property. The curés often did not participate even when the assemblies touched upon matters seemingly within their competence. In the eastern parish of Pont-de-Veyle, the curé did approve a new schoolmaster in 1581, but this was not the practice everywhere. In the market town of Belleville, for instance, the family heads met in 1599 and chose Bartholomé de Vaulx to be the new town schoolmaster. Although they questioned de Vaulx about religion to see if he was a good Catholic, the parish priest did not attend the meeting. And in Belleville and other towns and small cities, the assemblies often selected Christmas and Lenten preachers without their parish priest's assistance. At times the priests were even formally excluded from decisions concerning the communal institutions in the larger towns. In Bourg-en-Bresse, for example, an agreement made in 1442 between the municipal syndics and the curé forbad the curé a voice in the nomination of the rector of the town hospital or school; this right of nomination was reserved exclusively for the syndics.[65]

The curés were equally powerless in the village confraternities, despite their role in all the associations' ceremonies. In lists of annuities and rentes owed these confraternities, the curés hardly ever appeared, except occasionally as witnesses. Power of the purse in these confraternities lay securely in the hands of the laymen. In Saint-Cyr-au-Mont-d'Or, the villagers themselves or lay rectors under their control managed the financial affairs of the confraternity from the 1540s through the early seventeenth century. In Neuville, a town just north of Lyon, it was the lay rectors of the Confraternity of the Holy Spirit who customarily distributed the alms of bread and wine. They also assembled the curé and neighboring priests for an annual mass in honor of the "departed of the confraternity," and they ensured that the annuities and rentes due to the confraternity were payed. When the Neuville confraternity lay in shambles in 1585, the laymen—not the curé—stepped in and restored it. In that year many of the Neuville confraternity's rentes were unpaid. Negligent administration, the death of a notary, and the Wars of Religion had cost the confraternity many of the documents confirming these obligations, and unscrupulous individuals and new landowners (many from Lyon) had taken advantage of the situation by refusing to pay the rentes that burdened their lands. A village assembly gave Claude Morel, the seignior's agent, the task of bringing the confraternity back to life. He burrowed in ancient documents, made a list of the confraternity's property and annuities, tracked down absentee landlords, collected debts, pursued the recalcitrant in court, revived the almsgiving, rebuilt the confraternity's cross, and in general ensured the respect for the "intentions and desires of the former members" of the confraternity, former members whose foundations and rentes funded its activities. One hundred years later in Neuville and in other towns, the curé, and only the curé, would be entrusted with such tasks, but at the end of the sixteenth century it was layman Morel who directed the confraternity.[66]

Rural professional confraternities were just as independent of the parish clergy. The bonnet-makers of sixteenth-century Saint-Just-en-Chevalet reviewed their accounts and named their own officers without any interference from the curé; so did professional confraternities in Bourg-en-Bresse. The parish priests did not even have much to say in the financial affairs of the vestries and in the nomination of churchwardens. They did not usually receive the accounts of the vestry wardens, as they would in the eighteenth century. And although curés occasionally witnessed the act drawn up to acknowledge that annuities were due the vestry, this was not always so. In fact, wherever vestries and parish assemblies can be distinguished from assemblies of the village, they were dominated by laymen, even though the curés might attend their meetings. In the parish of Quincié in Beaujolais, the inhabitants stipulated in 1548 that the curé maintain a lamp always illuminated before the altar; when he failed to do so in 1552, the parishioners banded together, gave the operation of the lamp to the vestry, and assessed the curé for the cost of the lamp oil. In Isernore, lack of power drove the curé, Jean Chardon, to make an exceptionally bitter complaint. In 1613 he remarked that a local notary had taken over the office of churchwarden and usurped church revenues—a common occurrence during and after the Wars of Religion. The notary threatened to swallow the parish's revenues and make the wardenship a family office, acts "which gravely harmed the dignity of the curé." As disgruntled curé Chardon lamented during the parish visit in 1613, "this is how—because we lack support, are distant from our superiors and also have no means of defending ourselves—the strong, the wily, and the powerful of this world encroach upon the property of the Church, cause numerous abuses and harm the divine service, all the while laughing at priests." When Chardon said "we," he felt he was speaking for all the parish clergymen, whom he believed to be powerless before lay notables who were perfectly willing to defy their curé.[67]

The clergy's influence and power were thus limited. But power was not the only dimension of a curé's role, for much of parish life was based not on relationships of power but on a shared community of feeling. Men and women marched in processions, mourned the community's dead, and rejoiced at banquets and festivals not because they had been commanded to do so but because they shared notions of what was important in their lives. These parish rituals, in which the laity participated with enthusiasm, were evidence of communal solidarity in the towns and villages and a sign that people in fact believed themselves to be members of a community. May one deduce the existence of a sense of community from such ceremonies? The rituals were not meaningless actions, and the significance of communal banquets or parish festivals (where one of the chief activities was fighting with interlopers from other communities) is unmistakable. One might protest that the parishes in the diocese of Lyon lacked the extensive communal property or the strong institutions of village government that held together communities in other regions of France. Even the Holy Spirit confraternities, which had long served to reinforce communal solidarity in the towns and villages, were weakened by the nonpayment of annuities and a decline in charitable donations. Nonetheless, the parishes still formed communities, and parish institutions, though weakened, were still capable of sustaining communal solidarity. The village assemblies, the Holy Spirit confraternities, and the youth groups were able to maintain a sense of common identity and purpose. Festivals, banquets, royaumes, and other rituals reinforced this sense of community.[68]

But communal solidarity did not mean that the denizens of the countryside were cheerful altruists or that their lives were serene and egalitarian. Peasants were often extremely selfish, and inequality and internal strife were prominent features of village life, particularly as the sixteenth century drew to a close. Village property owners, we know, argued with one another and with the poor and less powerful over the apportionment of the community's tax burden and the management of communal lands. Village notables, along with urban elites, began to encroach upon communal property and to destroy whatever economic equality had existed. We have seen how Claude Morel worked to resuscitate the confraternity of Neuville after predatory landowners had sought "to suppress [the confraternity's] almsgiving, take advantage of its rights and grow rich from its rentes, all to the detriment of God's poor."[69] Grievous problems of the same sort afflicted many other towns and villages in France, especially in the last decades of the century.

The fact is that peasants and other village dwellers were crafty, self-interested individuals, as one recent theoretical work argues persuasively.[70] The village institutions—from assemblies and youth groups to confraternities—were therefore more than mere marks of solidarity; they were in fact the very ties that bound these disparate, selfish individuals. They accomplished this miracle by offering villagers not just access to communal lands, but also festivals, charity, blessings for their families and processions for their crops, and prayers for their souls after death. Outsiders and villagers who stood aloof would lose these precious benefits. Such recalcitrant individuals might also face ritualized shame or ostracism, such as the charivaris the youth groups meted out to those who transgressed communal wedding standards. The same institutions linked the residents not just of small villages, but of market towns as well, even though the market towns were endowed with more formal municipal governments. Indeed, in the market towns the confraternities, youth groups, and local cultural celebrations were most deeply entrenched. Only in large, cosmopolitan cities such as Lyon did they lose their power to unite an entire community, their strength sapped by population growth, mobility, and immigration.

Clearly, the clergymen in parishes outside Lyon reinforced all the bonds of community. The blessings they offered at village banquets and the processions they led on feast days helped cement the ties between individuals on the one hand and the parish, its youth groups, and confraternities on the other. Masses for confraternity members and requiems for the dead further strengthened solidarity and tightened the hold of local institutions. The curé was thus one of the chief links in the community. He provided many of the spiritual and psychological benefits that bound parishioners to the town or village.

Although the curé thus played a key role in the community, he did not always live on good terms with his parishioners. Indeed, he could easily be embroiled in conflict with his fellow villagers, just like any other member of the community. As in the rest of France, the tithe and the *casuel* (the offerings given a priest for his services) provoked arguments, particularly during the Wars of Religion. In the diocese of Lyon, though, disputes about the tithe usually pitted parishioners not against their curé but against the monasteries and urban collegiate churches that held the vast majority of the tithing rights.[71] Strife could also erupt over the costs of building or refurbishing a parish church. If a curé was guilty of immorality or serious misconduct, rural parishioners (like laymen in the city) would lodge a complaint with the diocese's ecclesiastical court. Thus the parishioners of Taluyers denounced their curé to the archbishop because of his "evil behavior, immorality," and failure to perform sacerdotal duties. Occasionally the parish priest might even be swept up in a village feud. In the village of La-Chapelle-en-Vaudragon, for example, curé Bartholemy Blanc was accused in 1580 of having a concubine and of fathering an illegitimate child. But his accuser, Etienne Commermond, was a convicted perjurer who was hated by a large number of people in the community. The episcopal court hearing the complaint against Blanc found the charges groundless, and from the testimony it seems clear that the accusation was an act of vengeance stemming from a village feud.[72]

In none of these instances of conflict, though, did the rural curés antagonize their parishioners by authoritarian attempts to reform popular religion or popular culture. The priests did not argue with their parishioners over remaking processions or other paraliturgical rites, nor did they earn their enmity by suppressing the festivals of confraternities or youth groups. Clashes of this sort, which were incompatible with the clergy's role as a mainstay of the village community, did not trouble the curés' relationship with the laity until the seventeenth century.[73] Only then did the priests break with the community and seek to dominate and interfere with village institutions.

The sixteenth-century curés thus argued with their parishioners, but they never elevated themselves above the community or withdrew their support for the institutions of popular culture. The diocese of Lyon was not the only place where this was so: parish clergymen in the sixteenth century shared in the life of rural communities in other regions of France, and in Italy, Austria, and Catholic Germany as well. Their clothing and comportment hardly differentiated them from laymen; they often had kin among their parishioners; and they were ready to join in the festivals of the parishes they served: confraternity banquets, feast day dances, royaumes, and the festivities of youth—none of these celebrations was peculiar to the diocese of Lyon or even to France.[74] As in the diocese of Lyon, so in the rest of Catholic Europe, priests maintained the local institutions that united each village internally but isolated it from the rest of society. The priest and, paradoxically, the "universal" Church were therefore among the forces that atomized the social and political organization of rural Europe. They helped perpetuate a fragmented society of parishes, each one turned in upon itself and suspicious of outsiders.

The tardy arrival in the countryside of the reforms of Trent would change all this. With the cooperation of urban elites and the absolutist monarchy, the Counter-Reformation Church made an about-face and sought to dash the rural confraternities, youth groups, and other communal entities it had tolerated and supported for so long. Spreading out from large, cosmopolitan cities, the Counter Reformation attempted to root out illiteracy, suppress local cultural traditions, and pry the villages open to the outside world. Already under way in the city of Lyon, it would make the curés the agents of a massive social, political, and religious campaign, and the result would be a clash between them and their parishioners.

3
Christian Discipline: The Reforms of the Clergy

In 1617 Châtillon-sur-Chalaronne received a new pastor, one Vincent de Paul. Already well known in devout Parisian circles, the future saint had taken the obscure post in Châtillon, a small walled city in the midst of the swampy Dombes northeast of Lyon, at the urging of the noted spiritual leader Bérulle. His reasons for doing so were complicated. The parish of Châtillon was in such a deplorable state that the church's patrons, the canon-counts of Lyon, had asked Bérulle to send them a dynamic young priest capable of ridding the parish of abuses and renewing its spiritual life. Bérulle had then recommended the promising young Vincent de Paul. The parish he was entering was indeed in desperate need of reform. The church building was in disrepair, and the conduct of the priests in the local *société de prêtres* left much to be desired. As one of Vincent de Paul's biographers later remarked, the church grounds "served both ecclesiastics and the laity as a site for promenades and banter, as if the place had been intended for ordinary and vulgar uses. . . . [The priests of the société] went to taverns and frequented bad company."[1] Worse yet, many of the little city's notables were Protestant, and local Catholics indulged in a number of cultural and religious practices that absolutely shocked Vincent de Paul when he arrived in Châtillon.

Undaunted by all of these problems, Vincent de Paul swiftly undertook a vigorous program of reform, beginning with the local clergy. Endeavoring with his somber dress and sober comportment to set an example for the priests in Châtillon's société, he persuaded them to give up their gallivanting in the taverns and adopt a regimen of work and prayer. He also had a deep effect upon the religion and the cultural practices of the parish laity. While he probably did not convert large numbers of Protestants (despite the exaggerated claims of hagiographers), his sermons, catechism lessons, and frequent visits to parishioners reshaped Catholic piety and popular culture as well. He convinced Catholics in Châtillon to behave in a more dignified manner during church services and halted public group confessions and other rituals frowned upon by the Counter-Reformation Church. He suppressed the customary *royaume* ceremonies, which he considered spectacles of "debauchery," diverted people from dances and parish festivals by putting the Eucharist on display, and converted the "abbot of misrule," the chief of a communal festive group, from "libertinage" to a life of celibacy and good works. At the same time, he convinced parishioners to help rebuild the church, and he attracted the wives of parish notables to charity work by founding a new confraternity for them, the Ladies of Charity, which would later spread throughout France.[2]

Vincent de Paul's labors in Châtillon lasted only a few months, for in 1618 he left the parish to minister to the prisoners in the galleys. He would go on to greater fame, but even at this early stage in his career he managed to embody the new ideal of the Counter-Reformation priesthood, an ideal which was slowly imposed upon all the clergy in the seventeenth century. As his accomplishments in Châtillon suggest, the new ideal was not simply a matter of higher standards of personal conduct for clerics. It also involved the institutionalization of the Counter Reformation on a local level, the reshaping of popular culture, and the dissemination of a new ethic in the parishes.

The new ideal enjoyed the support of urban lay groups who deeply influenced the reforms of the clergy, and it was embodied in seminaries and other institutions created to train parish priests. These institutions not only reshaped clerical behavior but also inculcated new spiritual and cultural values that reformed priests were to represent in their parishes. These values were of great importance, especially in the countryside, for the Counter-Reformation morality which the priests were to promote was an ethic largely foreign to the vast mass of the peasantry. It was the ethic of the devout urban elite, and it made the priests agents of a discipline that seemed terribly harsh to many residents of the diocese's towns and villages.

Lay *Dévots*

The Counter Reformation, which as we have seen was already under way in Lyon in the 1560s, gathered momentum in the seventeenth century. Signs of its progress marked every quarter of the city. A dozen new chapels and churches were built between 1627 and 1643, when a Protestant traveler in Lyon commented upon the natives' appetite for church services and their penchant for the new confraternities that were cropping up throughout the city. Religious communities also multiplied in Lyon: a score of male orders, societies of secular priests, and women's convents gained a foothold in the city in the first half of the seventeenth century. Devout laymen poured money into these institutions and into the new *hôpital-général,* where from the 1620s on the poor were locked up to work and pray.[3] In Lyon, as in other French cities, the advance of resurgent Catholicism was not seriously hindered by the fact that France never officially received the decrees of the Council of Trent, for the French clergy as a whole pledged itself to enforce the Tridentine decrees, and both diocesan statutes and royal legislation often echoed what the council had enacted.[4]

We have seen that the city's lay elite played a large role in the early stages of the Counter Reformation in Lyon. Their efforts on behalf of the Catholic Reformation grew even more important in the seventeenth century. One mark of their enthusiastic support for resurgent Catholicism was the increasing number of lay religious groups forming among the city's upper classes. A phenomenon with parallels in cities throughout France, the spread of these associations among the urban elite deserves particular attention. As we shall see, the lay associations reinforced the bonds between the urban clergy and the more prosperous urban classes; they contributed greatly to the enactment of the Counter Reformation on a local level; and they deeply influenced the seventeenth-century reforms of the parish clergy. Indeed, one cannot fully understand the clerical reforms or their impact upon life in both rural and urban parishes without first coming to grips with these associations for Lyon's pious elite.

Among the city's new religious groups for the upper classes were several newly formed devotional confraternities: the Penitents of Mercy, for example, and the Penitents of Our Lady of Loretto, whose members included the same sort of officers, wealthy merchants, and consular families who had been join- ing the White Penitents of Confalon and the Black Penitents of the Crucifix since the 1580s. In addition, the Jesuits had organized several lay groups, and one, the Congregation of the Messieurs, was specifically designed to recruit members among the city's upper classes. Lyon was also the home of a number of secret religious associations called, somewhat cryptically, the AAs. Although most of the AAs were composed of students and young clerics, one, formed by associates of the Jesuit Congregation of the Messieurs, attracted pious laymen from Lyon's prosperous classes.[5]

But the most influential and, for our purposes, the most important reli- gious association in the city was Lyon's chapter of the infamous Company of the Holy Sacrament, another secret society which brought together ecclesiastics and members of the urban lay elite and which exercised a decisive influence over the local course of the Counter Reformation. The Lyon company, like branches in other cities, was the offspring of the original Parisian Company of the Holy Sacrament, which was founded in 1627 by a pious nobleman, the Duc de Ventadour, and soon attracted the capital's most zealous ecclesiastics and most devout nobles and gentlemen. While in some ways it resembled a devotional confraternity, what distinguished the Company of the Holy Sacra- ment was its intense commitment to "good works" that would contribute to the extirpation of Protestantism and the revival of Catholicism in France. To accomplish this objective, chapters of the company were established in fifty-six cities throughout France. The daughter companies had the same objectives as their Parisian mother, and they attracted nobles, officers, and wealthy merchants, who stood ready to battle for resurgent Catholicism.[6]

Lyon's chapter was created in 1630 through the efforts of a priest who had been dispatched by the Parisian company. The first officers of the Lyon company included one of the canon-counts and a magistrate from the *sénéchaussée,* and although the city of Lyon lacked the large body of resident nobility and the august sovereign courts that supplied the aristocratic membership of the companies in Paris and Grenoble, Lyon's branch of the company did attract the officers, magistrates, bourgeois *rentiers,* wealthy merchants, and members of the city government who formed the municipal elite. Clergymen from urban churches and chapels also rallied to the company: canons, curates, stipendiary priests, and other ecclesiastics from the cathedral, Saint-Just, Saint-Paul, Saint-Nizier, and Saint-Thomas-de-Fourvière; curés, vicars, and other priests from Saint-Pierre-le-Vieux, Saint-Pierre-et-Saint-Saturnin, Saint-Vincent, Sainte-Croix, and Saint-Georges.[7]

Forming Lyon's circle of dévots, these laymen and ecclesiastics were determined to further the "glory of God," and their accomplishments in the city of Lyon were considerable. The company contributed substantially to reforms of the clergy, and it is hard to find any social reform or religious foundation after the 1630s in which the company was not involved. The dévots created schools and charities, helped establish confraternities like the Penitents of Mercy, and undertook a strenuous campaign to improve public morals. Unlike the Parisian company, suppressed by 1666 because first Mazarin and then Louis XIV viewed it with suspicion, Lyon's chapter remained active until 1731. It enjoyed the support of the diocesan hierarchy, apart from some obscure troubles with the archbishop during the years 1634–45, and influential members of the company won support for the group's projects from intendants, governors, the municipal government, and the local courts. The company bore witness to the urban elite's commitment to the Counter Reformation, and it confirmed the alliance between the elite and the urban clergy.[8]

The Reforms of the Clergy

The Council of Trent had voted to focus the Church's educational efforts not on the laity but on the clergy, and this program for clerical education entailed substantial reforms. The problem was not simply one of ridding the clergy of abuses but of transforming parish priests into a body capable of responding to the religious aspirations of a devout and zealous age. Here the Church had to start from scratch, for the Middle Ages had known no seminaries and had imposed practically no educational requirements on young men seeking ordination.[9]

The first major step in the reform of the parish clergy was the Tridentine decree enjoining bishops to establish diocesan seminaries. The seminaries were to receive youths aged twelve and older, shelter them from the baneful influence of the outside world, and teach them both theology and practical pastoral care in order to train them for the ministry. Although the Tridentine decrees were never officially received in France, the Ordinance of Blois (1579) contained a similar order, and royal legislation and provincial Church councils repeated this injunction during the following fifty years. At the Estates-General in 1614, all three orders called for the creation of seminaries.[10] It was a long way, however, from the promulgation of decrees or petitions of the Estates-General to the actual foundation of seminaries in each Catholic diocese, for throughout Europe serious obstacles blocked their establishment.

One major difficulty lay in deciding precisely what age group the seminaries were to serve. Although the Council of Trent had envisaged an institution that would lump together both young and old students, the Italian Carlo Borromeo and a number of leaders of the Counter Reformation in France thought it more effective to separate the younger clerics from the older candidates for the priesthood. The result of this indecision was a proliferation of different approaches to the training of priests in the seventeenth century.[11]

A lack of clear goals was not the only obstacle to the creation of effective diocesan seminaries. Teachers were in short supply, and it was sometimes difficult to convince young clerics to submit to the harsh discipline of the seminary. Many preferred the more relaxed atmosphere of colleges and universities, which still provided a pathway to holy orders. Universities themselves sometimes opposed the creation of seminaries which infringed on their monopoly of higher education. Worst of all, a shortage of money frustrated and delayed attempts to create seminaries and hire professors.[12]

In Lyon the process of establishing a seminary and of imposing increasingly stringent requirements on candidates for the priesthood was as slow and halting as in the rest of France. The diocesan hierarchy imposed standards for ordination only gradually, and it tried various approaches to the education of the clergy before finally deciding upon a solution. The first attempt to reform the education of the Lyonnais clergy occurred in 1565, at the height of the struggle against the Protestants in the city. Shortly before the Catholics in the city council turned the College of the Trinity over to the Jesuits, the canon-counts decided that the college would function as the sort of diocesan seminary which the Council of Trent had recently required. It never fulfilled this function, though, and in 1618 the canon-counts, worried about the education of the choirboys in the cathedral, entrusted the Oratorians (whom Archbishop de Marquemont had recently invited to Lyon) with the task of instructing these young clerics. The Oratorians' school was something of a seminary, since it did train clerics from the cathedral choir, but it collapsed during the plague of 1628.[13]

Meanwhile, most candidates for the priesthood continued to receive their training at the hands of the local curés or relatives in the clergy.[14] In 1577 the diocese took the first steps to regulate this informal instruction. The statutes adopted at a diocesan synod in that year required that candidates for holy orders undergo an examination and produce letters of recommendation from the curé of their home parish. By 1611, if not earlier, the diocesan hierarchy was actually imposing the examinations, and diocesan statutes enacted in 1614 make it clear what these exercises entailed. For the tonsure, candidates had to know how to read and write, and they had to be able to recite the Ten Commandments and a number of prayers. For minor orders, they had to demonstrate a rudimentary knowledge of Latin and the catechism. For major orders, they had to be "truly well versed in letters, Latin and catechism. . . ." Finally, priests named to pastorates would have to pass an examination in moral theology and the administration of the sacraments. Since numerous rural priests would obviously have been hard pressed to meet this last requirement, the 1614 statutes waived the examination for priests who were already curés, "provided that they are not completely ignorant and that their experience and good behavior make up for what they lack in [schooling]."[15]

The diocese actually did without seminaries until the middle of the seventeenth century. Then, in less than two decades, four seminaries were founded in Lyon. The first, the Oratorian Seminary, was established at Archbishop Camille de Neuville's invitation in 1654. About the same time, several pious diocesan clergymen were struggling to organize a company of priests in Saint-Julien-en-Jarez, near Saint-Chamond, in order to train ecclesiastics for missions. After a short time, the band of priests moved to the parish of Saint-Michel in Lyon, where Archbishop de Neuville had entrusted one of the group, a cleric named François Thomazet, with the post of curé. A member of the Company of the Holy Sacrament, Thomazet and the others worked with the archbishop's brother, Antoine de Neuville, a vicar general and a dominant figure in the company, to turn the group of clerics in the parish of Saint-Michel into a full-fledged seminary. Using his great influence over his brother, Antoine de Neuville got the archbishop to recognize the group at Saint-Michel in 1659. The archbishop also invited three priests from the famous Seminary of Saint-Sulpice in Paris to assist the Saint-Michel community, and in 1663 he officially recognized the community as a seminary—that of Saint-Irénée—under the directorship of the Sulpicians from Paris. With the aid of the archbishop and the financial support of the Company of the Holy Sacrament, the Seminary of Saint-Irénée slowly gained a secure footing in the city, and by the 1670s it was firmly installed in a neighborhood in the northeast of the peninsula.[16]

Lyon's third seminary, Saint-Joseph, grew out of another community of missionary priests, this one founded in the 1640s by Jacques Cretenet, a pious lay surgeon with connections in devout circles in Paris and Lyon.

Cretenet's community trained priests for missions in the countryside, and Camille de Neuville recognized it as a seminary in 1667.[17]

The fourth and final seminary in the city, Saint-Charles, was established in 1672. As in the case of Saint-Irénée, the Company of the Holy Sacrament was deeply involved in the establishment of Saint-Charles. The Seminary of Saint-Charles was in fact the offspring of the dévots' drive to found "little schools," free primary schools for the urban poor and the peasantry. Throughout France the Company of the Holy Sacrament promoted such schools as one of its good works, and the company's branch in Lyon was no exception. When a devout local priest named Charles Demia proposed creating little schools in the city in 1666, the company readily helped him start the first school in the parish of Saint-Georges, even providing him with subsidies. Demia, known in pious circles in Lyon and already enjoying the patronage of Antoine de Neuville, actually joined the Lyon Company of the Holy Sacrament in 1669, not long after the first little school was founded. With the support of the diocesan hierarchy, the Company of the Holy Sacrament, and members of the lay elite, he succeeded in establishing additional little schools throughout the diocese, and he managed to reform existing primary schools as well. In 1671, with the company's support, he created the Seminary of Saint-Charles to train teachers for the little schools. Although the graduates of Saint-Charles were to teach in the schools, Demia believed that teaching would be only a temporary career before they entered the priesthood. He therefore placed great emphasis on training students to be vicars and curés in the countryside, and the majority of the students at Saint-Charles ended up as priests in rural parishes. By the eighteenth century the training of future priests (who might teach a bit on the side) had in fact become the seminary's primary mission.[18]

The diocesan hierarchy first required its ordinands to attend seminary in 1657, when Archbishop Camille de Neuville imposed a ten- to fifteen-day retreat in a seminary before receipt of major orders. As the century wore on, these requirements were tightened. In 1670 Archbishop de Neuville obliged candidates for higher orders to pass examinations, given in the seminaries, on matters such as moral theology, and he later demanded that they take at least one course of philosophy. His successor, Claude de Saint Georges, went even further, imposing a number of new requirements on candidates for minor and major orders. The tonsure now involved six months of informal study with groups of ecclesiastics and an eight-day retreat at the Seminary of Saint-Irénée. Candidates for minor orders had to demonstrate a knowledge of Latin and spend ten days at Saint-Irénée. The three major orders required a total of one year at a seminary, and according to diocesan statutes of 1704 and 1715, that seminary was supposed to be either Saint-Irénée or Saint-Charles.[19]

In addition to taking in clerics for retreats or brief terms of study before ordination, the seminaries also accepted students for longer periods of time. At Saint-Charles, during the years 1679–93, 427 persons attended the seminary, or roughly 30 persons per year. Of these, 24 percent (7 per year on the average) stayed for one month or less, from which we can infer that they were in most cases taking the one- to two-week retreats required for ordination. The rest of the seminarians at Saint-Charles (a number that averaged 23 per year) were engaged in a longer course of study and residence that could last up to several years before they went on to become teachers and curés.[20]

At Saint-Irénée, the number on retreat before ordination is difficult to count accurately because those who took retreats were listed together with pious laymen and previously ordained clergymen who also availed themselves of retreats at the seminary. Between 1670 and 1682, some 1,200 persons, or about 100 per year, took such retreats at Saint-Irénée. Evidence suggests that roughly a quarter of these were either laymen not preparing for orders or vicars, curés, and other parish priests. Thus perhaps 75 persons a year came to Saint-Irénée during this period in order to take the required retreat before ordination. The number of long-term students at Saint-Irénée was smaller, ranging from 55 in 1675–76 to fewer than a dozen in 1684–85.[21]

Saint-Charles and Saint-Irénée were the two most important seminaries in the diocese, at least insofar as parish priests were concerned. The other two, the Oratorian Seminary and Saint-Joseph, suffered from accusations of Jansenism. The Jansenist sympathies of the Oratorians led Camille de Neuville to transfer diocesan students from their seminary to Saint-Irénée in 1674, and similar suspicions led the diocesan hierarchy to limit Saint-Joseph's role as a training ground for parish priests until the last half of the eighteenth century. The result was that Saint-Irénée and Saint-Charles trained most of the parish clergy. Sulpician Saint-Irénée, the larger of the two, drew more seminarians who were likely to be from urban backgrounds and august families than did Saint-Charles, which attracted students from outside Lyon and from less exalted origins. Together, the two institutions not only took in the ordinands of the diocese for the required retreats before holy orders but also subjected more than forty students a year to longer and more extensive training. This number amounted to roughly half of the priests ordained each year.[22]

The curriculum was roughly the same at Saint-Irénée and at Saint-Charles: classes were given in theology, philosophy, catechism, casuistry, and the Bible. Learning at the seminaries, however, was not restricted to academic matters, for both institutions showed great concern with "exercises of piety and mental preparations that the dignity and sanctity of holy orders require." Prayers and meditation occupied much of the seminarians' time, especially at Saint-Irénée, which assigned each student a spiritual director and enforced a strict disciplinary regime. Bound to observe silence even during meals, the seminarians at Saint-Irénée were forbidden to demonstrate even the slightest sign of friendship toward one another, and they could not leave the premises or receive visitors without permission. The harsh rules aimed to instill in the seminarians the conviction, dear to Bérulle and other leaders of the French

Counter Reformation, that the priesthood was a sacred calling different from any other vocation. The regime at Saint-Irénée was in fact so strict that it could not be enforced in all its rigor. As the seminary's director himself admitted, to have done so would have driven students away to other, less rigorous institutions.[23]

Besides preparing candidates for orders, Saint-Irénée was the site of various retreats for clerics who had already been ordained, retreats which were yet another means of upgrading the clergy. One sort of retreat, popular in the 1670s and early 1680s, brought pious individuals to Saint-Irénée for spiritual exercises lasting several days or weeks. The participants included not only clergymen (usually from the city's churches) but also devout laymen. Like the laymen, many of the clergymen were, or would be, active in the Company of the Holy Sacrament: clerics such as canon Manis of Saint-Paul in Lyon; Noël Chomel, a priest at the Lyon hospital and later curé of Saint-Vincent in Lyon; Guy Colombet, a pious curé from the city of Saint-Etienne; and even Charles Demia himself. The company in fact urged its members to take retreats, and on a number of occasions it even organized the spiritual sojourns at Saint-Irénée.[24]

In addition to these retreats for devout individuals, Saint-Irénée also hosted a second group of retreats organized for the curés of the diocese. Urged upon the curés in strong terms in the diocesan regulations of 1670, the biannual sojourns at Saint-Irénée brought together an average of more than one hundred curés and vicars per year from all parts of the diocese. Little is known about what transpired during these retreats for curés, but evidence shows that during the 1737 retreat, the clergymen heard a sermon, took communion, and read pastoral and inspirational literature, including François de Sales's regulations for his diocese of Geneva. In 1739 the readings touched upon ecclesiastical discipline, and in 1744 one of the subjects was moral "scandal." The activities thus consisted of spiritual exercises, sermons, and readings on pastoral care, discipline, and inspirational topics. As in the case of retreats by pious individuals, the Company of the Holy Sacrament was deeply involved in the retreats for curés. The company supervised the organization of the curés' gatherings and urged its members to discuss company projects with the curés when they assembled at Saint-Irénée.[25]

Another means of improving the parish clergy was the ecclesiastical conference, a regional meeting where curés prayed and discussed religious topics. In the seventeenth century, reforming bishops organized such conferences in dioceses throughout France. In Lyon Archbishop de Marquemont created the first conferences in the early seventeenth century by dividing the diocese up into thirty geographical districts and ordering the curés in each district to meet for discussions of moral theology. Camille de Neuville subsequently reorganized the conferences in 1663. Despite the attention given the conferences by the two archbishops, it took years before the practice of holding these meetings was firmly established, and on occasion the early sessions were devoted to ensuring that priests knew the liturgy. In Tarare, where ecclesiastical conferences apparently did not begin until 1676, the first meeting included a week of meditation and study of the diocesan ritual, followed by an examination on its contents. Elsewhere, priests at the conferences heard talks by their colleagues on subjects such as "moral cases involving restitution" or "the excessive affection that priests have for their relatives."[26] As in the case of the retreats, the documents rarely reveal the internal workings of the conferences, but on the basis of these few examples it does seem that the conferences continued the priests' training by giving them an opportunity to discuss topics of moral theology and ecclesiastical discipline.

The establishment of seminaries and the calling of retreats and conferences were but two manifestations of the massive institutional reform launched by the Council of Trent. Reforming bishops held more frequent synods, which issued diocesan regulations, and in order to measure the progress of the Catholic Reformation, bishops undertook visits of their dioceses as Trent had directed. In Lyon, after sporadic visits by Archbishop Epinac and his suffragan Maistret in the late sixteenth century, Archbishop de Marquemont made a lengthy visit in 1613–14, the first such general visit since the fifteenth century. Camille de Neuville did the same in 1654–62. Even more important than these visits by the archbishops were the more frequent and more regular visits by the vicars general and rural deans. By the early eighteenth century, these visits by the archbishop's delegates had become common occurrences in rural parishes, taking place as often as once every several years.[27] Such regular supervision ensured that the priests adhered to the ideals that the seminaries were trying to instill.

What role did the archbishops of Lyon play in the reforms of the clergy? Historians have usually given credit to dynamic bishops for many of the local initiatives in the French Counter Reformation, and it is clear that bishops such as Henri de Laval of La Rochelle or Etienne Le Camus of Grenoble had a great impact upon the reforms of the clergy and the Catholic Reformation in their dioceses. One might compare their accomplishments to those of archbishops de Marquemont or Camille de Neuville in Lyon. Known for his friendship with François de Sales, de Marquemont not only visited the diocese, but also attracted numerous religious communities to Lyon. Archbishop Camille de Neuville, who undertook his own pastoral visit, issued numerous diocesan regulations and, as we saw, presided over the establishment of the diocesan seminaries. Since he held the lieutenant generalship of Lyon in addition to the bishopric, de Neuville wielded a great deal of power in the diocese, and the creation of new religious institutions (the seminaries, for example) required his approval.[28]

Yet judging by the reforms of the clergy, we see that neither de Marquemont nor de Neuville exerted as great an influence on the local

Catholic Reformation as did bishops elsewhere. Although the devout de Marquemont and the more worldly de Neuville certainly contributed to religious reforms, they rarely initiated these reforms and only occasionally implemented them. De Neuville, for instance, approved and even encouraged the seminaries of Saint-Irénée and Saint-Charles, but the impetus for establishing the two seminaries came from local priests and from the Company of the Holy Sacrament. Nor did de Neuville design the curricula at the two seminaries. This was the work of Charles Demia at Saint-Charles and of the Sulpicians at Saint-Irénée. Even some of the diocesan regulations which de Neuville issued may have been suggested to him by his brother Antoine or by other members of the Company of the Holy Sacrament.[29] De Neuville, de Marquemont, and the other archbishops of Lyon were powerful, and their support was necessary for the success of any religious undertaking. But they were not the sort of charismatic religious leaders who completely dominated the reforms of the clergy and the Counter Reformation in other dioceses.

Ideals of Reformed Behavior

What then did the seminaries, retreats, and more stringent regulations aim to accomplish besides simply turning out greater numbers of well-educated parish priests? What were the new ideals for the parish clergy's behavior and for their relationship with the laity?

At the very least, the clerical reformers sought to wipe out abuses prevalent among the Catholic clergy: abuses that ranged from occasional concubinage and unseemly behavior to rampant ignorance. Such abuses provoked the collegiate churches of Lyon to mend the behavior of their curates and stipendiary priests in the sixteenth century. Diocesan statutes from 1560 through the seventeenth century attempted much the same thing. Priests were ordered to reside in their benefices and eschew young maidservants, who might raise the suspicion of concubinage. They were exhorted to make their conduct exemplary, and, as we know, they were required to pass examinations to test their knowledge of religious matters.[30]

The clerical reforms, though, went far beyond rooting out scandal in the ranks of the parish clergy. They were meant to sanctify the priesthood, to fashion priests who would behave like Vincent de Paul. Priests were therefore required to isolate themselves from the evil influences of secular society. Such attempts to cut the clergy's ties to the secular world certainly antedate the Catholic Reformation of the sixteenth and seventeenth centuries: they go back at least as far as the spread of Ockhamism and mysticism in the later Middle Ages, when bishops voiced similar complaints about clerical involvement in secular affairs, and their origins can in fact be traced to the Gregorian reforms of the eleventh century, if not before. The difference during the Counter Reformation was that, under the influence of the Council of Trent and the new conception of the priest's vocation, the Church hierarchy pressed these demands with much greater intensity and success.[31] Repeatedly, diocesan authorities in Lyon and in the rest of France called upon parish priests to don somber cassocks and cut their hair short—novelties even in the seventeenth century—so that they would be clearly marked off from laymen. As the diocesan statutes of 1657 explained, a tonsure, cassock, and decent clothing allow priests "to be recognized for what they are and distinguish them from laymen. . . . Those who appear in long curly hair or gaudy clothing . . . are not part of the ecclesiastical estate." The archbishops of Lyon also told priests to shun involvement in commerce and almost all secular festivities. They were to avoid taverns, card and dice playing, public games, festivals, and banquets. They were to eschew "all dances, mummeries, shows, displays of juggling, and comedies staged by actors and mountebanks, where there is licentiousness, lewdness and jesting." Singing popular songs was forbidden, and priests were not even to converse "with lay people," unless the conversation was "modest and conducted in such a manner that it does not bring scorn and ill will upon the clerical estate."[32]

The seminaries instilled the same standards. Saint-Irénée, with its emphasis on the priestly vocation and its regimen of silence and limited visits by outsiders, obviously encouraged clerics to consider themselves apart from the secular world. And at Saint-Charles, Demia himself counseled students to avoid women, gambling, hunting, theater, dances, festivals, taverns, public spectacles, and "excessive familiarity with the common people."[33]

The shock of these reforms was greatest in the countryside. In contrast to the jovial country curés who drank and played with laymen, the reformed priests were to "behave with all due gravity, humility and ecclesiastical modesty, wearing long cassocks and square bonnets and other black clothing, and avoiding all other colors." Priests were even supposed to cut their ties to their relatives. At the Saint-Charles Seminary and in ecclesiastical conferences they were counseled against being excessively attached to their families, and in 1705 curés were forbidden to serve as godfathers.[34]

Because the Tridentine Church viewed the curés as links between the Church hierarchy and the faithful, the clerical reforms also enlarged the curés' pastoral role, albeit gradually. Curés were expected to teach catechism (initially, the catechism of Trent), and they were ordered to preach to their flocks, just as Vincent de Paul had done. Preaching and catechism were necessary, so the hierarchy believed, in order to correct the woeful ignorance of the laity.[35]

In the sixteenth century, of course, the rural clergy's own ignorance had precluded their giving elaborate, sophisticated sermons. Leaders of the local Counter Reformation were fully aware of this problem. Indeed, they lamented how benighted the parish clergy was, most notably in 1577, when, for the first time, the diocesan statutes had to be printed in French because so many curés could not understand Latin. The Church hierarchy consequently advised parish priests to make only elementary sermons, which were probably nothing more than recitations of prayers and the Ten Commandments together with brief lectures on the catechism of the Council of Trent.[36]

In the seventeenth century, the curés' pastoral role expanded significantly. Parish priests were urged to act as directors of conscience and to guide each parishioner along the path toward salvation.[37] A few exemplary curés even began to make important contributions to the good works undertaken by Lyon's dévots, helping establish the little schools and other institutions favored by the Company of the Holy Sacrament. Noël Chomel, the curé of Saint-Vincent in Lyon who was a veteran of the Saint-Irénée retreats and an active member of the company, founded a little school for his parish with the aid of lay notables. Earlier, with the support of the company and several pious ladies, he had created a shelter for the rehabilitation of prostitutes and a home that protected unemployed maidservants and female silk workers from the risks of prostitution and "debauchery." Guy Colombet, curé of Saint-Etienne and also a veteran of the retreats and a member of the company, managed similar accomplishments in his parish. Encouraged by his friend Charles Demia, he even managed to endow Saint-Etienne with a hôpital-général like Lyon's, where the poor were locked up, given religious instruction, and forced to work. The Company of the Holy Sacrament favored such houses of confinement for the poor, and with the help of local dévots Colombet succeeded in confining the first "idlers" in 1682.[38]

Although most rural pastors were incapable of the sort of grand accomplishments realized by Noël Chomel and Guy Colombet, all parish priests were urged to support the good works of resurgent Catholicism. Such charitable activities had always been important in post-Tridentine Catholicism, but this was especially true in the last decades of the seventeenth century, when, as Louis Pérouas has noted, the French Catholic Church moved toward an even greater emphasis on good works.[39] The more humanistic focus of late-seventeenth-century Catholicism placed a special premium on the sort of worldly activism favored by the Company of the Holy Sacrament, and it encouraged priests to undertake similar actions in their parishes. But the tasks the curés were to assume extended far beyond simple acts of charity.

The Piety and Ethic of the Counter Reformation

The most dramatic addition to the curé's role was the task of imposing a new Catholic piety and a harsh new ethic upon the faithful. The parish priests were to become the agents who institutionalized the Counter Reformation on the local level and enforced a new Tridentine morality in the parishes. Again, the change would be most noticeable in the countryside, where parish priests had long been identified with the local community and local values. They were now to represent the external culture of the Counter Reformation, a culture of the Church hierarchy and the urban elites. To understand what the reformed clergymen were expected to accomplish, we must examine the new spirituality and morality of the Counter Reformation, weigh their effects on popular culture, and consider why the Tridentine sensibility received fervent support from the Church hierarchy and the urban lay elite.

One of the Church's chief spiritual goals was to assert the importance of the sacraments (and indeed all religious ritual) as acts of worship crucial to individual salvation. In part a reaction to Protestant criticism and in part the expression of a radically different view of human nature and divine grace, this emphasis on the sacraments entailed vast changes in religious practice, especially insofar as confession and Holy Communion were concerned. As noted above, before the Counter Reformation, the laity received these two sacraments only rarely: an annual confession and communion several times a year were the rule, except perhaps among the well-to-do in the cities. The Counter Reformation sought to make receipt of these sacraments more frequent— monthly, if possible. But greater reliance on the sacraments meant more than confessing and communing more often. It also involved linking the sacraments to the practices of meditation and the examination of one's conscience, for the sacraments, it was stressed, were more than mere rituals. They were individual acts of worship, and the faithful were urged to contemplate the meaning of the sacraments for their personal salvation.[40]

Though seemingly innocuous, this emphasis on contemplation and devotion marked a radical break with established custom, especially for the peasantry, who regarded the sacraments (and the mass as well) less as acts of personal salvation than as expressions of group solidarity. The divergence between popular traditions and the new Counter-Reformation ideal explains the vehemence with which the Church hierarchy condemned many popular practices surrounding the sacraments. Rural customs concerning penance, for example, were subjected to severe attack. A papal brief of 1575 ordered Archbishop Epinac to halt public group confessions, which were common in the eastern part of the diocese, and Vincent de Paul attacked the same practice when he was curé of Châtillon-sur-Chalaronne in 1617. Rather than a group exercise, penance was to be a dialogue conducted in private, as Jean Benedicti, a local Franciscan theologian and noted preacher, explained. This doctrine no doubt prompted Lyon's archbishops to have each parish procure one of the newly invented confessionals; the confessionals would isolate the conversation between the penitent and his confessor and thus facilitate the priest's role as director of the penitent's conscience.[41]

Practices surrounding the other sacraments provoked similar admonitions. Marriage, for instance, was to be celebrated "without tumult, mockery, taunts, scuffles, jokes, and foul and immoderate speech which is customary at betrothals and weddings." It was not to be entered into for the sake of passion, familial interest, or communal rejoicing, but for the glory of God.

Consequently, parish clergymen were to question the bride and groom concerning the tenets of the Catholic faith. The same standards were extended to nonsacramental rituals in order to make them individualized acts of worship. For example, in religious processions, which traditionally resembled joyous parades, marchers were to file off reverently, concerning themselves with their own internal mental state. They were to concentrate on developing an internal sense of devotion and humility during the procession.[42]

Incompatible with the celebrations of family and community that traditionally accompanied the sacraments and other religious rituals, the new Counter-Reformation spirituality called for a reorientation in the way ordinary people approached religion. After all, the church, especially in rural areas, had been a place for socializing, and religious rituals had traditionally reinforced bonds of community and family. The leaders of the Counter Reformation would tolerate little of this. According to them, the church was a place for holiness and prayer, where mingling and gossiping were decidedly inappropriate. Parish priests were therefore warned against allowing "lewd speech, vain and idle chatter, jesting, profane pacts and contracts, tumult and the crying of infants, insolence and ostentation" in their churches. Instead of using the house of the Lord for "assignations, flirting and intrigue," lay people were to remain silent in church, follow the services with "attention, contemplation and respect," and reflect upon the meaning of the priest's actions.[43]

Tridentine spirituality also elevated certain devotions, most notably the veneration of the Eucharist, a focal point of the new piety. While Counter-Reformation theologians defended the real presence in print, Catholic painters did so in art. Those who portrayed the Last Supper turned from the theme of betrayal to that of the consecration, which had been almost unknown in medieval art. To glorify the Eucharist in the parishes, Pius V ordered that the simple cabinets or ciboria, which had traditionally housed the consecrated hosts, be replaced with tabernacles, recent inventions that had gained great popularity in sixteenth-century Italy. Archbishop de Marquemont did the same in his parish visits of 1613–14. And confraternities and processions that honored the Holy Sacrament were encouraged by the Church hierarchy, by regular orders, and by the dévots.[44]

At the same time, the Tridentine Church restricted devotions to a number of traditional saints. Although the Church defended the cult of the saints as a whole, Pius V condemned the apocryphal stories of *The Golden Legend,* a popular medieval collection of saints' lives. The old legends, without disappearing completely, began to inspire fewer paintings. In their place, the Counter-Reformation Church promoted the cult of Saint Joseph and later those of resurgent Catholicism's own heroes, such as Ignatius Loyola, Teresa of Avila, and François de Sales.[45]

Devotion to the Virgin Mary received particular encouragement, especially in France, where it was favored by Bérulle and other spiritual leaders. In Lyon, as elsewhere, Rosary confraternities won support from the Church hierarchy, from the regulars, and from the dévots. The Virgin's chapel at Saint-Thomas-de-Fourvière on the bluffs overlooking the city grew immensely popular in the late sixteenth and seventeenth centuries, eclipsing the older devotion to Thomas à Becket. In 1643, the city government placed Lyon under her protection and vowed to make a yearly procession to Fourvière in her honor.[46]

In the towns and villages, the duty of promoting the devotions to the Eucharist and to the Virgin fell chiefly upon the shoulders of the parish clergy. While encouraging these devotions, the priests had to respect one other cardinal principle of Tridentine spirituality: worship was to be centered on the parish and controlled by the clergy. Although much of medieval religious life had of course focused on the parish, certain medieval religious organizations—confraternities, for example—were largely independent of the parish clergy, and some medieval devotions (distant processions, chapels at a convent or at a monastery) escaped the parish altogether. The Counter Reformation aimed to thwart such independence. The problem attracted the attention even of local dévots such as Noël Chomel. To keep religious life focused on the parish, Chomel recommended that curés distribute Saint François de Sales's *Les devoirs des paroissiens envers leurs églises* in parish schools and that priests celebrate the feast days of saints whose names were common among men and women in their parishes. By the same token, religious practices that drew the faithful away from the parish or from the control of their curé (distant processions, for example) invoked the ire of the diocesan hierarchy.[47]

The Penitents' confraternities ran into particularly serious problems because of their independence of the parishes and the clergy. Although the Penitents had once been at the forefront of the Catholic Reformation, and although many dévots continued to join their ranks during the seventeenth century, the Penitents proved too independent for the Counter Reformation's hierarchical, parish-centered spirituality. The Penitents built their chapels away from the parishes, and while their rules required attendance at parish services, the Church hierarchy came to believe that they actually detracted from parish religious life. As a result, bishops throughout France began to harass the Penitents in the 1640s in order to reduce their independence. In the city of Lyon, a concerted effort by the Penitents to avoid offending the diocesan hierarchy (and the fact that many influential notables belonged to the groups) spared the Penitents any trouble with the archbishop. Penitents outside the city, however, did suffer from the hostility of the archbishop and his underlings. Their processions were placed under restrictions, and their chapels were subject to interdict unless they could provide letters patent justifying their existence.[48]

Reining in the Penitents was part of a broader campaign which the Church hierarchy and the dévots launched against popular culture. An outgrowth of the Tridentine sensibility, this campaign was an earmark of the Counter Reformation. Its chief targets were the sort of popular customs that Vincent de Paul attacked: popular traditions and organizations that threatened either the desired hierarchical control of religious life or the vision of the sacraments (and religious rituals in general) as pious, individualized acts of worship. The campaign had a devastating effect on society and on the social role of the parish clergy, who were expected to implement it on the local level.

In Lyon the diocesan hierarchy took the first steps in the Church's campaign against popular culture. The diocesan statutes in 1566 placed confraternities under closer control and (in theory) outlawed the charivaris mounted against second marriages. Existing confraternities apparently exercised far too much independence, while the charivaris infringed upon the Church's control over marriage by subjecting this sacrament to the authority of a community group—namely, the parish youth who staged these affairs. Repeating the prohibition of the charivaris, the diocesan statutes of 1577 tightened the restrictions upon confraternities and excoriated their stubborn independence, as well as the excesses of their banquets, festivals, and dances. Noting that the church was to be a place for reverence, the statutes also denounced using it for dances, fairs, or comedies. Celebrations on the Feast of the Innocents (when junior clergy in churches throughout Europe elected mock bishops and conducted mock rituals) and profane festivities that disturbed church services were specifically condemned. Furthermore, curés were to exhort their parishioners to avoid the banquets and festivals that were commonly held on feast days. In 1614 the diocesan statutes decried dancing on feast days in even stronger terms.[49]

The attacks on popular culture grew fiercer in the second half of the seventeenth century. Diocesan statutes issued by Archbishop Camille de Neuville in 1670 banned royaumes until after the parish high mass, and in 1682 de Neuville ordered that churches be closed to fiddlers who accompanied the royaumes or who played at parish festivals. In 1687 he outlawed all parish festivals in the extensive lands where he was seignior. In 1705 his successor, Claude de Saint Georges, issued even more stringent regulations prohibiting confraternity banquets and festivals.[50]

The archbishops did not wage this campaign alone. Regular clergymen on missions warned against the dangers of dancing and parish festivals, and a number of Lyon's dévots railed against popular pastimes. Noël Chomel, for example, was obsessed with the abuses riddling popular customs. Although he tolerated the royaumes that supported parish vestries (at least until the faithful could be persuaded to make their contributions for "more pure motives"), he would not permit these "farces" to spill over into the church; nor would he allow the kings and queens to be blessed with holy water before the altar. Invoking an argument that was popular at the time, Chomel also denounced parish festivals and the celebrations of the village youths as remnants of paganism that defiled holy days:

> During these holy days, the air is filled with the worst sort of filth; impudence knows no bounds; and because of negligence great enough to make one cry, even the most moderate persons approve what on other occasions they would judge to be a scandal and an atrocious crime. . . . To see the lewd and violent gyrations of the girls mixed in dance with the young men, does it not seem that one is watching bacchantes and savages rather than Christians?[51]

Chomel's fellow dévot Charles Demia railed against yet another set of customs: popular rituals of death and mourning. In his guidebook used for training priests at the Saint-Charles Seminary, he urged curés and vicars to abolish twenty-four common death rituals. These rites of mourning ranged from having the eldest member of the family blow out a candle at the head of the deceased to the habit of avoiding the door through which the body passed to that of running, screaming, and groaning around the funeral bier.[52] While these practices were merely a way of coping with the horror of death and the passing of a loved one, Demia denounced them as superstitious abuses.

As could be expected, the Company of the Holy Sacrament was deeply involved in the campaign against popular culture. It denounced "indecent" conduct in churches, the celebrations of the carnival season, children's rejoicing in May, the charivaris of unmarried youths, popular theater and music, excesses during processions, and "disorders" during baptisms and funerals. The company was particularly troubled by the festivities of traditional communal bodies It condemned royaume ceremonies, celebrations at Pentecost (no doubt meaning those staged by Holy Spirit confraternities), dancing, and parish festivals. True to its goal of pursuing good works, the company did not restrict its actions to mere verbal tirades. The lay and clerical members of the company repeatedly voted to battle the popular customs they abhorred and to work for the suppression of the practices they considered abusive.[53]

As early as 1630, for example, the first year of the company's existence in Lyon, the members resolved to "work to prevent public dances on the patron saints' feast days in the villages." The members passed similar resolutions later in the century, and the company decided to pursue two general solutions to these and other problems: the appointment of inspectors in each *généralité* to enforce existing royal legislation against the festivals and other disorders and the foundation of additional little schools in market towns and large rural parishes. The network of inspectors was never established, but with the company's help the little schools were set up in market towns throughout the diocese, where they proved a useful weapon in the battle against popular culture. Supervised by a committee headed by Charles Demia and adhering to model regulations drawn up by Demia himself, the schools helped combat the festivals and many other popular customs. The regulations for Lyon's schools, for example, specifically advised that children be kept inside school during Mardi Gras "so as to remove by this means . . . every occasion of dissipation and debauchery."[54]

The company also undertook more specific measures against the festivals. In May of 1683 one of the company's lay members convinced judges at the sénéchaussée of Lyon to ban parish festivals in the Lyonnais. The company paid part of the court costs for the necessary court injunction against the festivals and had the injunction printed up as part of its campaign against festivals. Its members then tried to insure that the injunction would be enforced. The curé of Saint-Nizier of Lyon, for instance, talked to the father of a seignorial judge to make sure that the judge executed the sénéchaussée's ruling, and the company watched over the injunction's success in rural parishes. The company convinced seigniors such as the collegiate church of Saint-Just to forbid the festivals and dancing in rural parishes under their jurisdiction, and they appear to have been responsible for Archbishop Camille de Neuville's declaration against the festivals in areas where he was seignior. They persuaded the magistrates of the *bailliage* of Beaujolais to enact a similar ban against parish festivals in the Beaujolais, and they convinced the *procureur du roi* at the Lyon sénéchaussée to contact the Parlement of Paris about the possibility of a broader injunction. They even approached the intendant of Lyon to see if the king would enact legislation requiring seigniors to suppress the dancing and festivals.[55]

The company brought to the campaign against popular culture a wealth of contacts in the civil as well as the ecclesiastical hierarchy: members were either themselves seigniors, magistrates, municipal officers, or royal officials, or they could influence such personages. The company thus had at its disposal a vast network of fellow dévots and sympathizers whom it could draw upon to further the "glory of God," and it readily employed this same network when it undertook other "good works." The company also made good use of the parish clergy: not just those canons and urban curés who were active members of the company (the curé of Saint-Nizier, for example, or Noël Chomel of Saint-Vincent), but parish priests who held posts throughout the diocese. It had members in the diocesan hierarchy speak to the parish clergy about matters of interest—such as the problem of profane tapestries in churches—and the members of the company were invited to propose various good works to the curés when they came to take retreats at Saint-Irénée.[56]

The suppression of popular customs such as the festivals was only one aspect of the Counter Reformation's overall struggle against popular culture. This campaign also tried to replace traditional practices with sober ritual subject to the firm control of the Tridentine Church. Sunday vespers, for instance, were extolled as a means of drawing people away from traditional Sunday gatherings in taverns. In similar fashion, devotions to the Holy

Sacrament were praised, at least by the Company of the Holy Sacrament, as a means of competing with the "debauchery" of the carnival season. In the schools, Demia and other seventeenth-century educational reformers took care to replace the raucous contests and parades traditional among students with catechism disputations and solemn processions.[57]

Often traditional community bodies that sponsored offensive customs were replaced by reformed organizations whose rituals imitated, in an unobjectionable manner, the practices that the Church aimed to suppress—a subtle form of cultural "counterfeiting."[58] Some of the new devotional confraternities the dévots encouraged carried this process of counterfeiting to extreme lengths. For example, confraternities of the Blessed Sacrament, which promoted the devotion to the Eucharist, mimicked the royaumes of the traditional village confraternities, but in a way that the Church found completely acceptable. Their royaumes still had kings and processions, but the ceremonies were now somber and devout affairs, stripped of the customary revelry. Instead of the music and gunfire that had traditionally accompanied the king's procession, instead of the rowdiness that had formerly characterized the coronation, there was now a silent procession, the young men and everyone else in fixed order, carrying not muskets but candles and marching not for the sake of communal solidarity but in honor of the Eucharist.[59]

We should not oversimplify this Tridentine campaign against popular culture. Catholic attacks on popular customs did not make their first appearance during the Counter Reformation, although they certainly grew more intense at that time. Hostility to popular culture had an illustrious pedigree, antedating both the Reformation and the Counter Reformation. Medieval opponents of popular traditions included clerics such as Gerson in the late Middle Ages, eleventh-century writers such as Burchard of Worms, and even the Church fathers. But as Peter Burke has argued, medieval attempts to reform popular culture were merely sporadic efforts made by isolated individuals. It took the Reformation and the Counter Reformation to mount a sustained campaign against the cultural traditions of the populace.[60]

At least initially, the leaders of the Counter Reformation were far from unanimous in their opposition to popular culture and far slower to attack it than were the Protestants. Not until the 1560s did provincial Church councils and charismatic bishops such as Carlo Borromeo make the campaign against popular culture an organized movement within the Catholic Church, long after Calvinist consistories had begun an energetic battle against popular pastimes. Even after 1600, some champions of resurgent Catholicism, such as François de Sales, remained surprisingly lenient toward certain popular customs.[61]

Among Catholic authorities in Lyon also this ambivalence toward popular culture persisted until the early seventeenth century. In the heat of the Wars of Religion, no less staunch a Catholic than the city attorney Claude de

Rubys supported the urban festivities of the abbeys of misrule and other popular "topsy-turvy" celebrations, both because they were a safety valve that vented popular discontent and because they helped lure the populace away from Protestantism.[62] Not until the first decades of the seventeenth century, when many of these popular festivities in the city of Lyon had already disappeared, did such indulgent attitudes toward popular culture show clear signs of losing all support among Catholic authorities. In a municipal history published in 1604, de Rubys defended the city's traditional topsy-turvy festivals, lamenting the fact that they were succumbing to a certain "passion for order or to measures of economy." Claude Garon, a convert to Catholicism who was later part of the clientele of the governor of Lyon, undertook a similar defense of the moribund topsy-turvy festivals in 1609. The plaintive tone of these two works suggests that support for the traditional festivities of inversion was a minority opinion, at least among the Catholic elite.[63] Forty years later, of course, with the Company of the Holy Sacrament flexing its muscles, opposition to popular culture was entrenched among the city's upper classes.

The campaign against popular culture raises several obvious questions—questions that bear upon the Tridentine ethic priests were to impose. Why did these seemingly innocuous customs and festivities spark so much hostility? Why did the Counter-Reformation Church mount such a ferocious attack on popular culture, and why did this attack gain such fervent support among the urban lay elite?

Clearly, the campaign had roots in Counter-Reformation spirituality, to which the Church hierarchy and pious laymen were so zealously devoted. One objection to popular culture derived from the fact that the Counter-Reformation Church, far more so than the medieval Church, was determined to make a clear separation between the sacred and the profane. While Protestants had renounced the belief that certain days or certain places were holy, the Catholic Church insisted on preserving the sanctity of feast days and churches. Therefore any mingling of sacred and profane affairs or any profanation of holy days and holy places was strictly forbidden.

This conviction motivated the new standards of dress for the clergy, and it explained the archbishops' orders that the priests wall up their cemeteries, so that profane activities would not spill over onto hallowed ground. It also inspired attacks on popular culture. As Noël Chomel explained, popular celebrations "profane the holy days that we ought to sanctify."[64] Festivities intruded into the churches, hence the orders to expel musicians, royaume coronations, and other celebrations from church grounds. Even worse than intrusions onto church property was the fact that popular customs such as the royaumes or the parish festivals mixed devotion to the sacred with profane levity and enjoyment. Although the Church in the Middle Ages had shown a marked tolerance for mixing laughter and prayer, the dévots considered such mingling highly irreverent. The conflict with the Counter-Reformation view of religious ritual thus gave the dévots even greater reason to be infuriated by the festivals.

The campaign against popular culture drew additional inspiration from the Tridentine Church's desire to monopolize human access to the spiritual or the supernatural. A corollary to the Counter Reformation's hierarchical scheme of religious organization, the quest for monopoly stood out clearly in a sixteenth-century confessor's manual written by a local Franciscan, Jean Benedicti. His shrill warnings against village magicians, good luck charms, and a host of popular practices of white magic amounted to an assertion of a Church monopoly in the realm of the supernatural. Although Benedicti agreed (like most learned men in the sixteenth century, Catholic or Protestant) that sorcerers could derive real powers from pacts with the devil, he denied that the popular superstitions he condemned had any power whatsoever.[65] In his view, the evils of everyday life which these superstitions seemed to remedy were to be faced not by means of worthless popular customs or the intercession of powerless village magicians, but solely through the agency of the Church and its clergy. The same desire to monopolize the realm of the supernatural and the spiritual explains Charles Demia's concern with popular customs of mourning. For Demia, coping with death was not a matter for the family and the community and their "superstitious" burial practices, but for priests and priests alone.

An austere new sexual morality was a third ingredient in the Church's campaign against popular culture. Evidence of the new sexual morality appears throughout the Counter Reformation: bans upon nudity in religious art, harsher rules against illegitimacy, prostitution, and concubinage, and more "puritanical" standards of dress and behavior. To be sure, the medieval Church had never shown any indulgence toward sexual sins, but the harsh sexual morality of the Counter-Reformation Church had the support of the royal government and of the urban elites, who had in the past tolerated a great deal more sexual license.[66]

In Lyon concern over the new sexual morality was most evident in the workings of the Company of the Holy Sacrament, marking every page of the company's journals. From their very first meeting, the members of the company railed against prostitution, concubinage, male and female nudity, the mingling of the sexes at public baths, the use of churches for assignations and flirting, and even the common practice of allowing children of opposite sexes to share the same bed. A resolution to suppress what the company considered "scandalous nudity" is indicative of the dévots' prudishness: "Using confessors and preachers, we shall work to destroy lavish dress among women, their immodest manner of clothing themselves, [and] nudity of shoulders, throat and arms." It was not just women who were singled out for attack: "Public baths give rise to scandal because of the mingling of the sexes. One sees, in summer, boys of fifteen and twenty, and even full grown men completely nude, in full view along the river quais, on boats and ships, where everyone can see them, all of which constitutes a sordid spectacle for Christians and a great danger for the purity of young persons."[67] Concern for youthful purity caused Charles Demia and the dévots to imbue the little schools with the same "puritanical" morality. They rigorously separated the boys and girls and made certain that the children were taught to shun the ubiquitous evils of "debauchery."[68]

This austere sexual morality prompted much of the hostility toward popular culture, for as far as the dévots were concerned, popular customs were brimming over with lewdness. The Company of the Holy Sacrament complained of the lewd songs common at popular gatherings, and its prudish members believed that the dancing and courting at parish festivals constituted a veritable scandal. Noël Chomel, for example, denounced the "lewd gyrations" of dancers at festivals, and he warned parents to keep their daughters away from dances and other youthful gatherings in order to instill in them a love for sexual purity. Popular games and assemblies, he argued, were dangerous "occasions" of sin that each penitent had to renounce to gain absolution, and he made it clear that the risk the penitent ran was one of sexual sin. Catechisms reiterated this connection between popular celebrations and the dangers of sexual immorality. Of course, such fears were not unreasonable. Village festivals, after all, were occasions for courtship, and carnival was a time of "carnal" desire and intense sexual activity, if we may judge from demographers' curves of conceptions. Furthermore, sexual imagery undeniably pervaded both popular festivities and popular songs.[69]

Beyond the religious and moral objections to popular culture lay a host of cultural and political reasons that prompted lay dévots and other members of the urban lay elite to join the Church's campaign. In the first place, the sixteenth century saw elites in large cities throughout Europe withdraw from popular culture, in which they had once participated enthusiastically. This retreat from popular culture was fueled by both the Reformation and the Counter Reformation, and it owed something as well to the spread of Renaissance values. Lyon was no exception to this general trend. The city's elites early forsook the traditional festivals of the abbeys of misrule and other topsy-turvy celebrations for elaborate Renaissance entry parades and later, in the seventeenth century, decorous allegories celebrating the monarchy. Another sign of the cultural division between the urban elites and the populace was the growing scorn which the elites heaped upon popular beliefs in magic and witchcraft after the beginning of the seventeenth century. The prosperous city dwellers thus developed their own distinctive culture, which stressed rationality, decorum, and hierarchical order. Because of all the apparent crudeness and superstition of popular traditions, this cultural divorce made the reform of popular culture seem all the more reasonable and urgent to the urban elite.[70]

More important, the campaign against popular culture assuaged the urban elite's political fears and furthered some of its political ambitions. Here lies one of the ultimate causes of the lay elite's support for the Church's measures. Obsessed with the threat of popular violence in the aftermath of the Wars of Religion, the magistrates, royal officials, and other prosperous urbanites sought to establish political order in the fragmented body politic and to end chronic rebellion among the peasants and the common people in the cities. Popular culture, in their view, posed a particularly dangerous obstacle to their ambitions, for they believed that popular rituals mocked the political hierarchy and held the social order up to derision, that confraternities were dangerous cells of independence and revolt, and that festivals provoked disorder and rebellion. The law enshrined their fears. Legislative texts and legal usage lumped together charivaris and revolts, and royal ordinances and declarations of sovereign courts condemned popular theater, confraternities, and festivals not simply as moral dangers but as sources of contumacy, disorder, and sedition.[71]

As Yves-Marie Bercé has argued, these fears were often more perceived than real, more ideological projections of self-interest than actual physical threats. Except in the large cities, popular festivals lacked overt political content, and traditional confraternities and youth groups almost never incited revolt, certainly not in the diocese of Lyon, which was relatively unscathed by peasant uprisings. But even unfounded beliefs can exert a strong influence, and, in any case, the fears expressed by the urban elite were not completely preposterous. While the traditional confraternities and youth groups rarely incited rebellions, they were bastions of independence and village solidarity, independence and solidarity that lay at the heart of popular revolts and popular resistance to the monarchy and its urban-based officials. In nearby Dauphiné, the leaders and organizers of the uprisings in 1579–80 were members of confraternities and youth groups. By the same token, while the parish festivals never provoked an actual rebellion in the diocese of Lyon, the celebrations were often followed by brawls, fights between youths of different villages, or attacks on the forces of order.[72] Even the innocuous royaume ceremonies could seem to threaten the established order with their ritualized mockery of the political hierarchy.

Finally, a new sense of discipline won the urban elite over to the campaign and to the Counter Reformation in general. Akin to the "this-worldly asceticism" of Weber's Calvinists, this sense of discipline involved prizing industry and economical use of time. In Catholic lands it drew inspiration from the emphasis that the spiritual leaders of the Counter Reformation placed upon self-mastery and self-control. The need for discipline, of course, provided the urban elite with one more motive to enlist in the campaign against popular culture, for popular festivities were commonly believed to spawn all sorts of vanity and idleness. It also justified support for the little schools and the houses of confinement for the poor. Indeed, these institutions were expressly designed to extirpate idleness.[73]

In a larger sense, this concern for discipline formed part of a new ethic, a new moral code that lay at the heart of the campaign against popular culture and permeated the Counter Reformation's program of social reform. The goals that Charles Demia set for the little schools captured this ethic almost perfectly:

> [The schools will instill in students] a horror of idleness, falsehood, debauchery, theft and impurity, and will take particular care to exhort the students to love God and their neighbor, to be obedient and faithful, and to be diligent in their work, the goal we had in establishing these schools having always been that by teaching these poor children the principles of religion we could make them good subjects suited for work in the manufactures [or] as servants.[74]

It was an ethic that condemned idleness, sexual license, insubordination, and disorder, a morality that extolled diligence, abstemiousness, obedience to authority, and social and political order.

The definition of this moral code may appear to focus on what the Catholic reformers opposed. Such goals as diligence, abstemiousness, and order, however, were all positive values (and extremely important ones at that) in the reformers' eyes. In fact, these virtues derived from the very ideals of Counter-Reformation spirituality and the central tenets of Tridentine theology. To begin with, Catholic spirituality acknowledged that the world was the domain of Satan. This condemnation of the world of the flesh explained not only the reformers' desire to separate the sacred from the profane but also their austere sexual morality. Medieval ascetics had, of course, shared the same concerns, but what distinguished the leaders of resurgent Catholicism from most of their medieval predecessors was their belief in self-control and their extraordinary commitment to activism. Rather than fleeing into monasteries or retreating into contemplation, they subjected themselves to rigorous self-discipline and at the same time worked in the world to salvage other men's souls. Such an active pursuit of other men's salvation in turn easily justified the imposition of an austere morality that would make saving souls all the easier.[75]

Here of course the Catholic reformers drew upon Tridentine doctrines of grace, justification, and good works. God's grace, according to the theology of Trent, enabled man to perform good works, which in turn advanced man's salvation. These good works included not simply receipt of the sacraments or the practice of traditional charity, but efforts to discipline others as well. For the Catholic reformers, enforcing a discipline akin to their own self-control was, quite simply, a praiseworthy way to save men's souls. The diligence, abstemiousness, obedience, and order they advocated would further salvation and ward off the corruption of the flesh, while their upholding of these virtues would itself be an act of love of God. The imposition of an austere morality was thus an integral part of Counter-Reformation charity and spirituality. With no sense of contradiction, Vincent de Paul could therefore perform saintly labors among the poor, on the one hand, and stamp out popular culture in his parish in the Dombes on the other. Both deeds qualified as good works, and both were God's will.

That the suppression of festivals, the banning of nudity, and other efforts to enforce what we might call social control all counted as good works helps explain why resurgent Catholicism was such a potent force for mobilizing devout elites in early modern Europe. Normally, we might not expect elites to unify behind such a campaign against popular culture, no matter how much they favored disciplining the populace and no matter how much they stood to benefit from obedience and political order. Although it may at first glance seem paradoxical, individual members of the elite might well have declined to join the Counter-Reformation campaign for social control, for a lone individual's efforts would be too insignificant to make social control more likely, and, in any case, a person would enjoy the eventual fruits of social control whether he participated in the campaign or not. Difficulties of this sort—known to social scientists as "free rider" problems—are in fact likely to plague group action in pursuit of any collective good such as social control or political order. Quite simply, mutual interests do not guarantee that men and women will unite to pursue a common goal, if, as individuals, they can enjoy the benefits of achieving this goal without working for it.[76]

Tridentine theology, though, solved this problem of mobilizing individual members of the elite for collective action because the devout urban laymen, political authorities, and Catholic clergymen all had a powerful religious incentive for supporting the campaign for social control. Each individual who joined the campaign furthered his own salvation because the undertakings that made up the campaign qualified as good works. Indeed, these undertakings were morally essential, and they earned each participant all the spiritual benefits that Tridentine theology attached to charitable deeds. Conversely, individuals who declined to participate deprived themselves of these spiritual benefits and risked the pains of hell—an intolerable price to pay in such a devout age and among such a devout social class.

Thus Tridentine theology brought together the urban elite, political authorities, and the Church. Their alliance not only sustained the campaign against popular culture, but also produced an awesome fusion of civil law and moral obligation in seventeenth-century France. For the elite of the large cities, allying with the Church and supporting the campaign against popular culture were ways of protecting the social system and of imposing refined cultural standards, urban control, and an urban sense of order on the populace. For the political authorities, the alliance was a means of social control, a way of socializing the public so that they would obey and meekly pay taxes to the royal government. For each of the three allies, and for the Church in particular, it was a way to moralize the populace and instill the faith of the Counter Reformation.

Although the common people in the cities were to be subjected to this morality, the peasantry seemed even more important as a target, especially in the seventeenth century, for the Counter Reformation, long under way in the cities (at least among urban elites), had yet to affect the countryside. Vincent de Paul alluded to the need for religious reform in rural districts in an address delivered in 1641 to the Sisters of Charity, the women's religious order he had founded to carry on educational and charitable work. He told the sisters that they had to "apply themselves seriously [to the tasks of charity and education] . . . and do so chiefly in the countryside. The city is almost perfectly equipped with sisters. It is therefore fitting that you go and work in the fields." What was true of the Sisters of Charity applied very well to the Counter Reformation as a whole. Cities had the regular clergy, and it was in the large cities that formal associations of dévots such as the Company of the Holy Sacrament were headquartered. It is no wonder then that missions fanned out into the countryside, nor that the Parisian Company of the Holy Sacrament proposed in 1648 to encourage smaller branches of the company in small cities and market towns in order to "reestablish the cult of the Holy Sacrament and Christian discipline" in the countryside, which the company acknowledged to be "more deprived [than cities] of Christian wisdom."[77]

The rural communities would thus bear the brunt of the drive to impose the Tridentine spirituality and the austere Counter-Reformation morality, although the common people in the cities would be subject to proselytizing too. It was one more campaign of aggression from the cities, parallel to and supportive of the monarchy's efforts to levy taxes and establish political control in the countryside. The triumph of this austere fusion of moral obligation and civil law would assure the victory of Lent over Carnival.[78]

The burden of imposing the Tridentine ethic and making the Counter Reformation a permanent fixture among the faithful fell largely upon the curés, especially in rural areas. Noël Chomel acknowledged the difficulties inherent in this task and promised the curés the aid of the archbishop and of the Company of the Holy Sacrament if they experienced any difficulty or resistance in the struggle against popular culture.[79] The question was whether the graduates of the seminaries and retreats could manage to meet the goals that had been set for them.

4
Agents of Counter Reformation

Parish Priests: Behavior and Intellectual Level

On trial before the diocesan tribunal in 1684, Blaise Dusacq hardly conformed to the saintly ideal of the post-Tridentine clergyman. In fact, the only devotion that this curé from Saint-Bonnet-le-Coureau had ever displayed was an unrelenting passion for debauchery and dissipation. He swore, fought with his parishioners, attempted to seduce their wives, and frequently ended the day so befuddled by drink that he fell from his horse and had to be carried home. At times he seemed to revel in scandal. Arguing over a game of cards with a parishioner in a tavern, he blurted out to a crowd of onlookers what the man had revealed in confession. When the wife of a country innkeeper spurned his advances, he left the establishment without paying, shouting from horseback to the proprietor that he had "ravished" his wife in lieu of payment.[1]

Curé Dusacq was the last of a dying breed. Although few priests had engaged in such truly egregious behavior, certain lesser misdeeds Dusacq was charged with had once been common among the parish clergy, especially in the countryside: visiting taverns, gambling, dancing at parish festivals. But by the end of the seventeenth century this state of affairs had changed. The diocesan hierarchy had labored to suppress such behavior, and most curés and even rural laymen (as testimony in Dusacq's case shows) came to disapprove of priests who drank, gambled, or danced. Subsequently, the number of priests who indulged in these amusements dwindled, and clergymen guilty of other lapses in behavior—most notably absenteeism—grew increasingly rare. More and more frequently, the parish clergymen were noted for their piety and austerity, and their intellectual level improved as well.

These changes were most conspicuous among the curés and vicars outside the city of Lyon. In Lyon, despite an occasional peccadillo by a chapter curate or stipendiary priest, most parish clergymen had long since rallied to the Counter Reformation and to Tridentine standards of ecclesiastical behavior. In the urban parish of Saint-Just, for example, incidents of clerical misbehavior recorded in court documents were far less serious in the seventeenth and early eighteenth centuries than in the years before 1600. Among other things, brawls no longer erupted between clerics and laymen. Court records leave a similar impression for other city parishes as well. And as for the intellectual level of urban priests, it had never posed a problem.[2]

Outside the city, however, the improvement in the priests' conduct had been more recent and more dramatic. The diocese's rich collection of parish visits makes this abundantly clear, especially if we compare the visits made in the years 1613–14 by Archbishop de Marquemont with those undertaken in 1654–62 by Archbishop Camille de Neuville, or those ordered by archbishops Claude de Saint Georges and François Paul de Neuville in 1700 and 1719, respectively. Admittedly, these records of pastoral visits must be used with caution. The visits were conducted in haste, and the records were drawn up in a shorthand whose meaning is often obscure. Given this superficiality and the reticence that parishioners might have shown when asked to divulge the misconduct of their own curé, parish visits at times failed to uncover the shortcomings of a priest or the troubles that agonized a parish. This problem is compounded by the fact that records of visits always reflect the concerns of the clergyman making the inspection, and these concerns varied depending on the visitor, who could be the archbishop or one of the members of his entourage or one of the vicars-general and rural deans who in 1719 inspected parishes with the aid of printed questionnaires prepared by the diocesan hierarchy.[3]

Yet despite all the difficulties surrounding their use, the parish visits provide undeniable evidence of the Counter Reformation's progress among the parish clergy in the countryside. Consider, for example, the problem of nonresident curés. In 1613–14, the curé was reported absent in 6 percent of the 368 parishes visited; in some areas, such as the northeast of the diocese, the number of nonresident curés was even higher (table 3). By the middle of the seventeenth century, though, such reports of nonresidence were rare, and they had vanished completely by the beginning of the eighteenth century.

The evidence from the visits is reinforced by what we know about the decline of pluralism, the practice of holding more than one benefice, which was a major cause of absenteeism among sixteenth-century curés. Canons and members of the Church hierarchy commonly occupied pastorates in the sixteenth century, and since they did not reside, the best they could do was to hire vicars to perform their sacerdotal functions. The Council of Trent and French law forbad this sort of pluralism, and it disappeared during the seventeenth century. For example, among the ninety-two canon-counts who received their canonships at the cathedral during the years 1530–79, fifteen were simultaneously curés. Of the seventy canons who received their cathedral stalls during the years 1680–1720, however, none held pastorships. They might have been nonresident abbots, but they were not curés.[4]

The visits reveal other changes in the priests' behavior as well. Unlike the rural curés of the sixteenth century, who dressed like peasants and drank with their parishioners in village taverns, those of the early-eighteenth-century visits sought to keep the taverns shut and clothed themselves in long, black cassocks even in muddy, swampy Dombes. Socializing on familiar terms with lay people had thus come to an end, just as the Church hierarchy had hoped. More important, the charge that curés failed to teach catechism, common during the 1613–14 visits, was almost unheard of by the time of the visits of 1654–62, and in 1719 the visitors would note with monotonous regularity that every curé gave catechism lessons.[5]

Table 3   Complaints about the clergy in the 108 northeastern
parishes that received three successive parish visits

Date of visit	Curés reported absent		Curés or vicars reported ignorant of liturgy or basic theology	
	Number	Percent	Number	Percent
1613–14	11	10%	18	17%
1654–62	1	1%	0	0%
1700–19	0	0%	0	0%

Sources: Visites; AD Rhône, 1 G 49–53; AD Jura, G 10.

Note: The 108 parishes are those in the diocese that received one visit in each of three successive time periods: 1613–14, 1654–62, and again in either 1700 or 1719. These parishes are all located in the northeast of the diocese, in the Dombes, Bress, Bugey, and Franch-Comté. For a list of the 108 parishes, see Hoffman, "Church and Community," pp. 385–87.

Of course, there were always a few exceptions, curés who still acted like their predecessors in the sixteenth century. Jean Grand, the curé of Saint-Cyr-au-Mont-d'Or, continued to join his parishioners in games of *boules* and ninepins in the 1720s, a habit that caused one of his successors to look somewhat askance. But Grand was eighty years old and had been curé since 1683. His fondness for the games played "on Sundays and feast days, after the church services" was a relic of the past, highly unusual among the austere priests of the eighteenth century. Although one could always find an occasional Blaise Dusacq in a country rectory or a few misbehaving curates and stipendiary priests in the city of Lyon, the visits make it clear that the bulk of the parish clergymen had definitely reformed their ways.[6]

The general impression the visits give of the priests' behavior is confirmed by a study of the reasons why priests left their benefices. When an ecclesiastic assumed a benefice in the diocese, he was supposed to dispatch to the diocesan hierarchy a document known as a *provision de bénéfice*. Filed with some regularity beginning in the late sixteenth century, these provisions form by 1645 a nearly continuous set of registers recording most of the changes of benefices in the diocese, and each provision gave the reason why the benefice had been vacant. Usually the previous holder had died or resigned, but he might have lost his post for "extraordinary" reasons, which usually implied some misconduct or failing on his part: nonresidence, failure to perform divine services, conviction for a serious crime, ineligibility under canon law. Extraordinary reasons declined noticeably as a cause of vacancy, and this was especially true of benefices having charge of souls (*bénéfices à âmes*), the vast majority of which were pastorships, vicarates, or other posts for parish priests. The percentage of these benefices which changed hands for extraordinary reasons fell from 5.5 percent in the years 1595–1674 to 1.8 percent in 1675–1704, and it dropped to less than 0.4 percent after 1705.[7] In particular, failure to perform religious services, once a frequent cause of the loss of bénéfices à âmes, had disappeared entirely by the end of the seventeenth century. All of this constitutes further proof that the Tridentine reforms had improved the behavior of the vicars and curés.

The reforms (especially the retreats and sojourns in the seminaries) seem to have had an equally dramatic effect upon the curés' educational level. During the pastoral visits of 1613–14, the archbishop and his emissaries commonly encountered rural priests who were unable to say mass or give absolution. Such complaints concerning clerical ignorance were recorded in 15 percent of the 368 parishes visited in 1613–14, but they disappeared by the time of the visits of 1654–62. Among the 108 northeastern parishes that received three successive pastoral visits between 1613–14 and 1700–19, no complaints of clerical ignorance were registered in the later visits (table 3).

Parish priests were also likely to own larger, more erudite libraries in the eighteenth century—or at least this is what their death inventories would suggest. Unfortunately, death inventories are extremely rare for rural curés in the diocese of Lyon, and a search produced only fifteen of them. Eight of these mentioned books, but it is likely that the other seven estates included books as well, for notaries in the countryside often overlooked books when they drew up inventories, and in some cases books were removed before a death inventory was made.[8] Along with a published description of another priest's library, these inventories give us information on the book holdings of nine rural pastors. Among these nine priests, libraries were larger after the final decades of the seventeenth century (table 4). Admittedly, death inventories are hardly an ideal source, and one hesitates to generalize from a scant nine cases to the behavior of thousands of parish priests spread out over more than a century of time. Yet the inventories do testify to the rural priests' improved education, especially if we consider what volumes the priests owned. Most of the books were works of religion, although in 1679 curé Chassilon of Treffort possessed a travelogue, an Italian grammar, a book of philosophy, and at

Table 4 Death inventories of priests
outside Lyon which mention libraries

Date of inventory	Number of volumes	Name of curé	Parish	Source
May 28, 1605	9	Jehan Valliezy	Beligny	ADR, Bailliage de Beaujolais, Scellés . . . inventaires
April 28, 1629	9	Laurent Girait	Saint-Denis-lès-Bourg	AD Ain, 2 B
Oct. 30, 1661	16	Pierre Fontaine	S.-Rambert-l'Ile-Barbe	ADR, 10 G 3151
July 7, 1679	74	Chassilon	Treffort	AD Ain, B 245
1701	261	Jean Mouginot	Boen	BM Roanne, 3 G 6
Jan. 7, 1712	11	Benoit Gabriel Chussur	Cras	AD Ain, B 252
Dec. 27, 1712	4	Pierre Delisser	S.-André-le-Bouchoux	AD Ain, B 252
1755	66	Joseph Albaret	S.-Genest-Malifaux	•
Jan. 22, 1778	123	Jean Souchon	Jarnioux	ADR, Bailliage de Beaujolais, petite justice de Jarnioux

Note: ADR is an abbreviation for AD Rhône.
•Not an inventory, but a library description in Vanel, "Saint-Genest-Malifaux," pp. 99–111.

least one of Cicero's works. And in 1778 the erudite Jean Souchon, curé of
Jarnioux, owned several works on agronomy, geography, and medicine, as
well as Voltaire's *Le siècle de Louis XIV*. More important, the religious works
that predominated in these collections after the last decades of the seventeenth
century were precisely the books that the Church hierarchy and the *dévots*

urged upon the priests: not just the books of sermons, ritual, and paraphrases from Scripture that had formed Jehan Valliezy's library long ago in 1605, but the Bible itself, along with works of scriptural exegesis; confessor's handbooks, manuals for directors of conscience, and volumes of piety and spiritual meditation; letters of Saint François de Sales and weighty tomes of theology, such as the writings of Saint Augustine and the *Summa Theologica* of Thomas Aquinas; and, finally, the indispensable histories and catechisms of the Council of Trent.[9]

Clearly, an increasing number of rural curés had come to know the theology and spirituality of the Tridentine Church. In the sixteenth century, such "official" knowledge had been rare in the countryside, although it was common among regular clergymen and canons in the city. At the same time, priests who could scarcely read the liturgy (a significant minority in the countryside as late as 1613–14) had disappeared from rural parishes. This overall improvement in the clergy's educational level was certainly one of the Counter Reformation's great achievements, but it probably had one undesirable side effect insofar as the rural curés were concerned.[10] It no doubt put strains upon their traditional relationship with the rural laity, for the rural priests were now in contact with the literate, urban culture of the Tridentine Catholicism. The fact that these country priests behaved more soberly than their sixteenth-century predecessors must have further strained, if not severed, the bonds of familiarity between priests and parishioners in the countryside. The relationship was further weakened as the priests began to wield greater influence in their communities.

The Priests and Communal Institutions

Resembling many other sixteenth-century communities, the tiny city of Saint-Germain-Laval was endowed with periodic municipal assemblies, a vestry, and a Confraternity of the Holy Spirit. As usual in the sixteenth century, none of these institutions gave the parish clergy an important role to play. In the seventeenth century, however, the framework of communal life slowly changed in Saint-Germain-Laval, just as it did in many other communities. Reformed curés brought about some of these alterations in communal institutions, and other changes they exploited to promote resurgent Catholicism. In the process, the priests greatly expanded their role and influence in the parish.

In Saint-Germain-Laval, we can see the beginning of these changes as early as the 1620s. By that time, the parish boasted two new devotional confraternities: White Penitents and a Confraternity of the Rosary. The new confraternities testified to a Catholic resurgence in Saint-Germain, and perhaps this development explains why the young curé Jean Rajat took the unprecedented step of appearing before the municipal assembly in 1620 in order to request money to help establish the Oratorians in nearby Roanne. Curé Rajat, who participated in the earliest pious retreats at the Seminary of Saint-Irénée in Lyon, was perhaps the first example of a reformed curé in Saint-Germain-Laval. Like all good post-Tridentine curés, he wanted to draw religious life in Saint-Germain closer to the parish, the focus of Counter-Reformation spirituality. He worried, for instance, about the town's Confraternity of Penitents, which he considered to be too independent of the parish. These vexatious Penitents had a separate chapel, and instead of calling upon parish priests to say their services and act as chaplains at their meetings, they relied upon various clergymen, especially Saint-Germain's own *récollets*. In order to bring the Penitents closer to the parish, Rajat refused to let them display the Holy Sacrament in their chapel during Holy Week, and he tried to stop their independent services on feast days. Moreover, he sought to insinuate himself into the confraternity and take control of it. By the 1660s he had succeeded: he and the other parish clergy now served as the Penitents' chaplains, and in 1663 Rajat was even elected the confraternity's chief officer.

Yet curé Rajat, now an old man, did not stop here. Feeling that the Penitents' religious zeal had flagged somewhat, he invited the Capuchins to dispatch a mission to his parish in 1666. After a month of sermons and frenzied processions, the mission culminated in the foundation of a new devotional confraternity, that of the Blessed Sacrament, of which the curé was the "permanent director."

The process of change in Saint-Germain-Laval continued after Jean Rajat's death, for his successors further augmented the curé's influence in the community, using their increased powers for the benefit of resurgent Catholicism. As elsewhere in France, the deterioration of the community's traditional institutions allowed the priests to become dominant. In Saint-Germain, the old communal organizations were ailing by the end of the seventeenth century. The Confraternity of the Holy Spirit was moribund, the intendant was encroaching on the formerly autonomous municipal government, and rising royal taxes were provoking conflict in town assemblies. And a vestry warden, Claude Meysson, had appropriated the lands and rentes of the dying Holy Spirit confraternity. Although the municipality recovered the confraternity's lands by 1708, Meysson steadfastly refused to turn over the organization's papers, which were needed to regain payment of the rentes.

In this impasse in communal affairs, the man who cleared the way was curé Charles Valentin. That he did so clearly signals the parish priest's great influence in the community. At his suggestion, the inhabitants of Saint-Germain-Laval authorized him in 1726 to get the papers back from Meysson and begin collecting the money due from the rentes. Valentin promptly took Meysson to court, seized the papers, and resumed collection of the money due from the rentes, employing the funds to support Saint-Germain's paupers' hospital, of which the curé was a director. Later, in 1738, he proposed to the inhabitants of Saint-Germain that they spend the Holy Spirit confraternity's income to bring the nuns of Saint-Joseph-du-Puy to the parish "in order to provide [our] youths with an education, visit the sick and poor, and perform other acts of piety and charity."[11] The inhabitants agreed, and thus, thanks to the influence of the curé, the revenues of the dying old confraternity were diverted to pay for the sort of charitable and educational works so dear to resurgent Catholicism.

These events over the course of a century in Saint-Germain-Laval mirrored a more general transformation that affected the religious and communal life of many other communities. As in Saint-Germain, the reformed curés took on a host of new duties and responsibilities in their parishes, duties and responsibilities that reshaped the priests' social function and served the interests of the Tridentine Church. The priests' obligation to catechize, perhaps the most striking of these new duties, was only the beginning. As the Catholic revival swept over the diocese, it left in its wake a number of reformed institutions, which the parish clergymen were to supervise. In addition to these new bodies, there were myriad old institutions—vestries and ancient village confraternities, for example—that the priests were now to watch over and reform.

The assumption of these responsibilities within institutions both new and old gave the priests a platform from which they could militate in favor of the Catholic Reformation, just as the curés in Saint-Germain-Laval had done. It also expanded their power in local communities, and the clergymen used their newly acquired positions of influence to impose Tridentine discipline and order upon the populace. Again, the term *power* is used in a somewhat restricted sense. The curé's power consisted of a new set of social relationships that, within limits, made the behavior of the laity increasingly dependent on the priests' own actions: it was the ability to persuade the laity, to encourage certain actions, or to hold other forms of behavior in check. Having power did not mean, however, that the curés could make their will prevail when laymen firmly resisted. This distinction is important, for we shall see that the curés' new responsibilities often sparked hostility between the priests and their parishioners, who were sometimes less than eager to accept the priestly tutelage over religious affairs and local institutions. Indeed, resistance born of this hostility could at times grow strong enough to block the curés' desires.

Confraternities, Old and New

Of all the institutions that came under the curés' control, parish confraternities were perhaps the most noteworthy, for they underwent tremendous change over the course of the seventeenth century. Old Holy Spirit confraternities, once at the core of communal life, declined, and those that did survive came under the tutelage of the parish clergy. Simultaneously, there sprang up in the parishes new devotional confraternities promoted by the Counter-Reformation Church; they too were subject to the priests' control.

The old Holy Spirit confraternities succumbed to a variety of ills, including attacks led by the Counter-Reformation Church and the reformed parish clergy. The causes of their demise go back to the sixteenth century. The Wars of Religion destroyed deeds and papers belonging to Holy Spirit confraternities, and epidemics devastated the landowners and peasants whose property supported their annuities and rentes. Land changed hands, confraternity rectors grew negligent, heirs chafed under the burden of rentes their ancestors had founded, and privileged outsiders who used tax exemptions to purchase property in the villages saw no reason to pay the rentes at all. None of these ailments ceased to afflict the Holy Spirit confraternities in the seventeenth century, and as these beleaguered institutions sank into decadence, the Counter Reformation administered the coup de grace. The Church hierarchy frowned on the old confraternities' banquets and indiscriminate Pentecostal almsgivings; it considered them profligate, indecent, and debauched. When bishops discovered active Holy Spirit confraternities during parish visits, they accordingly suppressed them and ordered that their income be used to support the vestry, the parish school or charity, or some other pious work.[12] The curés of course were charged with the execution of the bishop's orders.

Curés themselves took up the struggle against those Holy Spirit confraternities that were not yet attached to vestries or charities. In Aillieux in 1671, the curé participated in a parish assembly that voted to join the local Holy Spirit confraternity to the vestry, to bring an end to its banquets, and to use its revenues for repairs on the church and the "relief of the poor." When in 1705 it appeared that the vestry wardens had revived the traditional Pentecost banquet, the curé battled to replace the old wardens and to have the banquet permanently suppressed.[13]

In Pérouges, the surviving Holy Spirit confraternity provoked a bitter clash between the parishioners and their curé. The inhabitants of this market town had preserved a Pentecost almsgiving and banquet (they called it the *frairie*) until well into the eighteenth century. Each Pentecost Sunday, the vestry wardens and town syndics distributed two pounds of bread and two jugs of wine to "each inhabitant with a house in the community." The annual feast continued unchallenged until the middle of the eighteenth century, when a new curé, Jean François Mollat, arrived in Pérouges. A frequent participant in the devout retreats at the Seminary of Saint-Irénée, he looked upon this custom as an impious squandering of community resources. He sued in 1751 to suppress the tradition and attach to the vestry the revenues which supported it, but the inhabitants (or at least some of them) refused to accept the demise of the banquets and almsgiving. The syndics and twenty-five men of the town assembled in 1751 and voiced unanimous opposition to suppression of the frairie. Demanding their "share and portion of the banquet" as an immemorial right, they empowered the town syndics to fight the curé in court, and they managed to preserve the almsgiving for at least five more years.[14]

Direct confrontation was not the only way parish priests dealt with the remaining confraternities of the Holy Spirit. A curé could also persuade the inhabitants to turn the old confraternity's income over to some pious project, as in Saint-Germain-Laval. Or the inhabitants might decide (perhaps of their own accord) that money once used for confraternity banquets or traditional almsgiving could be better spent on the parish's deserving poor, and the parish charity would then absorb the old Holy Spirit confraternity. In effect this often meant that the curé took control of the old confraternity's revenue, for as we shall see, the parish clergy now dominated many of the local charities. In this manner, the priests came to manage confraternity rentes and plots of land that had once been administered without the slightest ecclesiastical interference.[15]

If a curé did not suppress a Holy Spirit confraternity or merge it with a local charity, he could seek to purify the old association and strip it of its "indecent" practices, as curé Pierre Gaiffon sought to do in Sainte-Foy-les-Lyon. With a number of inhabitants of Sainte-Foy, he drafted new written rules for the parish's Holy Spirit confraternity in 1726. The mere existence of written regulations was a novelty for the confraternity, which, like other Holy Spirit brotherhoods, had governed its actions according to immemorial custom. But the rules drawn up in 1726 changed the whole character of the confraternity. Formerly open to anyone present on Pentecost Sunday, the reception of alms would henceforth be restricted to the deserving poor. The regulations went to even greater lengths to purge the confraternity's banquet of its objectionable aspects. Limited to one and a half hours, the frugal meal was no longer an occasion for fraternal conviviality, but a time for somber meditation under the supervision of the curé.

Unfortunately, the reforms undertaken by the curé and the confreres of Sainte-Foy-les-Lyon did not suffice for long. After a complaint concerning the "abuses that have slipped into the administration of . . . the Holy Spirit confraternities, also known as frairies, which are established in a number of parishes . . . in the diocese," Archbishop Tencin in 1749 imposed stringent new rules on all the remaining associations. Tencin's regulations, which completed the process of subjecting the Holy Spirit confraternities to strict clerical control, stipulated that the curé in each parish with a Holy Spirit confraternity was to convoke an assembly of the confreres. The assembly would name new rectors to manage the confraternity's financial affairs "under the supervision of the curé." The curé would preside over the confraternity's meetings, and to ensure that only the deserving poor benefited from the group's largess, he would supervise the confraternity's charitable activities.[16]

More important, Tencin's rules abolished altogether the "general and public almsgiving" on Pentecost, along with any "banquets or feasts that the confraternity sponsored on these occasions." Anyone who attempted to revive these characteristic activities was to be expelled from the confraternity. Finally, "to give a new motive" for the confraternity's existence, the group was to take on spiritual duties that would transform it into a purely devotional organization.

If the members refused to accept these new rules, the curé and vestry wardens were to take over the confraternity's property and distribute its income to the poor.[17]

The new regulations thus stripped the Holy Spirit confraternities of most of the features that had made them cells of communal solidarity. The confraternities lost their role as an organ of communal government, and they could no longer bind together villagers by offering them banquets, festivals, or a distribution of confraternity money. Similar regulations had been imposed upon Holy Spirit confraternities in the diocese of Besançon, and in a sense, these rules came close to capturing a major part of the Tridentine Church's approach to popular culture.[18] By suppressing the banquets and communal almsgiving, the new regulations tried to direct the confreres' energies away from the community and toward divine worship. Henceforth the members would have much less opportunity to enjoy a little conviviality or to cultivate fraternal solidarity. Such a sense of joy or earthly brotherhood, after all, detracted from the devotion owed God and spawned profligacy, rebellion, and sin. And to ensure that the confraternities of the Holy Spirit adhered to these rules, they were subjected to the direction of the parish curé.

When these regulations were imposed in Sainte-Foy-les-Lyon, the Confraternity of the Holy Spirit simply disbanded.[19] The members saw no point in continuing the association under the new rules, and the communal revenues that fed the old confraternity fell into the hands of the village officers, the vestry wardens, and the curé. Whether these statutes were enforced in other Holy Spirit confraternities in the diocese is not known. Few of the old brotherhoods remained now, and they disappeared entirely from the records after 1750. Financial ailments, the hostility of the Counter-Reformation Church, and campaigns by watchful curés had finally destroyed them.

While the old Holy Spirit confraternities were dying out, new devotional confraternities were proliferating in the diocese with the encouragement of the Counter-Reformation Church. These new devotional confraternities helped spread Counter-Reformation piety, and their broad and growing membership in parishes throughout the diocese furnishes some of the best evidence we have concerning the arrival of the Counter Reformation among the rural laity—a subject to which we shall return below. Naturally, the new devotional associations drew upon the energy of the reformed parish clergy. Reformed curés like Rajat of Saint-Germain-Laval promoted them, and if the actual establishment of the confraternities was frequently the work of a Jesuit or a friar, it was the parish priests who kept them under control.

The devotional confraternities in question here were the groups that the dévots and the Church hierarchy had extolled in the late sixteenth and seventeenth centuries: confraternities of the Rosary and of the Blessed Sacrament, most commonly, but also confraternities of the Scapulary and of Christian Doctrine, and the Penitents' confraternities, even though, as we noted above, the Penitents' independence incurred the disfavor of the ecclesiastical hierarchy after the 1630s.

In the city of Lyon, these confraternities included the devotional groups founded by the city's lay and clerical elite in the late sixteenth and seventeenth centuries. In addition to these associations of dévots, nearly all the city parishes could boast a Confraternity of the Blessed Sacrament in the seventeenth century.[20]

Outside the city of Lyon, the new devotional confraternities were a bit more novel and not so widespread. Usually they were established in parishes by members of religious orders from Lyon or other cities who were conducting missions in the countryside: Jesuits frequently set up the confraternities of the Blessed Sacrament, while the Rosary confraternities were commonly the work of Capuchins or Dominicans.[21] Before 1650, the parish clergy played little part in the creation of the new confraternities, but as the seventeenth century wore on, the curés, along with enthusiastic parishioners, became increasingly involved in such foundations. In doing so, the curés were acting just like parish priests elsewhere in France. At times, the curé's role in the establishment of a new confraternity amounted to little more than relaying the laity's wish for one of the new associations to the appropriate religious order. Thus, in the western parish of Sauvain in 1623, curé Jehan Goron and layman Pierre Crozet asked the Dominicans in Lyon for permission to set up a Confraternity of the Rosary in the parish. Elsewhere, the curés called in missions to start the confraternities, as in Saint-Germain-Laval and also in the parish of Tassin, where curé Picard summoned the Jesuits in 1721 in order to create a Confraternity of the Blessed Sacrament. In the western parish of Saint-Barthelemy-Letra, the curé himself harangued a crowd of parishioners and established a Confraternity of the Blessed Sacrament without any help from regular clergymen; and in Saint-Genis-les-Ollières, curé Dupellier led his parishioners on a procession to Lyon in order to found a branch of the same confraternity in his parish.[22]

Some time passed before the new confraternities spread throughout the countryside, but eventually the curés, regular clergymen, and pious laymen managed to establish them even in the most remote corners of the diocese. Of the 108 parishes in the northeastern part of the diocese that received three successive pastoral visits in 1613–14, 1654–62, and 1700–19 (the same parishes used in the study of the priests), only 1 had a Confraternity of the Blessed Sacrament in 1613–14, but 9 did by 1654–62. By the early eighteenth century, there were Blessed Sacrament confraternities in 42 of the 108 parishes (table 5). Confraternities of the Rosary proliferated at nearly the same rate. Of the same 108 parishes, only 2 boasted Rosary confraternities in 1614, but the number had climbed to 12 by the mid–seventeenth century, and it reached 28 by the early eighteenth century. The experience of other parts of the diocese was similar.[23]

As they spread throughout the diocese, the devotional confraternities enhanced the role of the parish clergy considerably. In the city of Lyon, the confraternities of the Blessed Sacrament carried on the practice, born in the early days of the Counter Reformation, of bringing together parish priests and lay notables to select preachers and adorn the parish church. In the countryside, the brotherhoods of Christian Doctrine encouraged the curés to teach, and the faithful to attend, catechism classes.[24] These new confraternities were also a means of focusing religious life on the parish. Except for the Penitents, whose independence had incurred the suspicion of the Church hierarchy, the devotional confraternities did not have chapels outside the parish church. Their services were subordinate to those of the parish, and their spiritual director was usually the vicar or the curé.

Table 5 Number of 108 northeastern parishes reporting devotional confraternities during the pastoral visits of 1613–14, 1654–62, and 1700–19

		Date of visit	
Confraternity	1613–14	1654–62	1700–19
Blessed Sacrament	1	9	42
Rosary	2	12	28
Penitents	0	3	7
Scapulary	0	3	8
Christian Doctrine	0	0	1
Other devotional confraternities	0	1	4

Sources: Visites; AD Rhône, 1 G 49–53; AD Jura, G 10.

As spiritual director, the parish priest had a moral responsibility for the devotional confraternity and its members. In the Blessed Sacrament confraternity of Les-Ardillats, the curé, along with the lay rector, issued warnings to any member who had "lapsed into crime and scandal." If the warnings failed, he and the group's lay officers expelled the misbehaving confrere. The curé also delivered a short sermon each year, urging the confreres to respect the rules of their confraternity. And since part of the Blessed Sacrament confraternity's mission was to encourage devout conduct in the parishes, the priest had the additional task of reciting a prayer, each octave of Corpus

Christi, "in order to atone for . . . the misdeeds, irreverences and acts of sacrilege, the profanations and impieties committed by the parishioners during the preceding year."[25]

The priest's responsibilities also included supervising the activities of the devotional confraternities. As we have noted, the new devotional brotherhoods were considered a potent weapon in the Tridentine Church's struggle against the village festivals, banquets, and excessive boisterous *royaumes,* for in the countryside the somber processions these confraternities held and their sober exercises of piety were designed to supplant the old communal celebrations, which the Church viewed as sources of scandal and debauchery. But the Catholic hierarchy lived in fear that the new confraternities might be diverted from their pious mission, that they might begin to sponsor banquets and raucous festivals like those of the Holy Spirit confraternities of the sixteenth century. The Church therefore entrusted the parish clergy with the task of watching over the new devotional confraternities, so that they would not revert to the behavior of the village confraternities of old. Thus the recommendations that the priests establish confraternities of the Rosary or Blessed Sacrament were always tempered with exhortations to vigilance, lest the new confraternity's feast days become occasions for games, dances, banquets, and fairs. The diocesan statutes of 1705, for instance, while encouraging the new devotional associations, told the curés to prevent "public dances, festivals and other amusements" on confraternity feast days; similarly, the confraternities were not to hold festive banquets. Instead of these "indecencies," so typical of sixteenth-century confraternities, the new devotional brotherhoods celebrated their holy days with masses and sermons. The hierarchy's fear of misbehavior was so great that by the beginning of the eighteenth century all confraternities, whether new or old, were subjected to increasingly stringent control. During parish visits of 1700 and 1719, the ecclesiastical inspectors repeatedly demanded that confraternities produce papers showing that their rules had been approved by the diocesan authorities; those confraternities unable to do so could not meet until they had secured the necessary episcopal approval.[26]

The Church's fears were not entirely unfounded. Penitents' confraternities, the oldest of the devotional associations, actually did seem predisposed to backsliding. At times, Penitents' confraternities in the diocese seem to have lost their devotional trappings altogether and to have become associations for drinking and socializing. The archpriest of the Dombes observed, after a visit to the parish of Trévoux in the early eighteenth century, that the Penitents there resembled Penitents' confraternities "everywhere else, . . . made up of men who frequent taverns." Similar complaints were made about the society of Penitents in Saint-Claude. The Penitents in Bourg-en-Bresse were even worse. They sponsored banquets on Holy Thursday and again on the feast of the Assumption—precisely the sort of practice that drove the Catholic hierarchy into a frenzy. Here, however, the group's chaplain, a canon and parish priest named Buisson, convinced the confraternity to suppress the banquet and use the money to support a series of public sermons.[27]

The most effective way to regulate the new devotional confraternities and assure that such scandalous relapses did not occur was to monitor their use of funds. This duty fell to the curé, and it was among his chief duties and a major source of his power in the confraternities. The priests had to inspect confraternity accounts to make sure that the confreres spent their money for masses and the upkeep of their chapel, not for banquets and festivities. A confraternity's rules might also stipulate that the curé had to preside over the group's meetings, since it was here that the officers reviewed the confraternity's finances. Even if he did not preside at the meetings, the parish priest was normally in attendance, and he signed the accounts of revenues and expenses presented by the confraternity's rectors. In Neuville, for example, the curés affixed their signatures to the accounts of the town's Rosary confraternity throughout the eighteenth century. When the group's officers gathered to approve financial records, they assembled at the curé's residence, and by 1788 curé Gacon had even assumed the task of drawing up the records of income and expenditure. In Neuville's Confraternity of the Blessed Sacrament, the curé exercised similar influence. He attended the group's assemblies, usually served as one of the confraternity's officers, and by the middle of the eighteenth century he acted as the association's treasurer.[28]

Yet despite these measures, the priests' grip over the confraternities was sometimes tenuous. The Penitents caused the most difficulties, (at least in rural parishes), no doubt because of their long tradition of recalcitrance. Although the curés in some communities did preside over the Penitents' assemblies (we saw this was the case in Saint-Germain-Laval), other Penitents' confraternities remained free from clerical control. In the parish of Bois-d'Oingt, for instance, the Penitents conceded that the curé, as "first rector" of the confraternity, could witness withdrawals from the trunk holding the group's papers, and they also granted his wish that none of the confraternity's lay offices be "posts held for life." But in return for these concessions, the Penitents obliged the curé to recognize that the confraternity could name any chaplain it wished, and they forced him to renounce any claims to power over their affairs.[29]

A strange sequence of events in Saint-Just-en-Chevalet reveals how a curé's efforts to subordinate a Penitents' confraternity could lead even to public protest—a sign that pursuing the Counter Reformation was not without its problems. The difficulties began in 1678, when a new curé, Jean Genebrier, arrived in this small western city. Benoite Poncet, the wife of a teamster in the parish, later described Genebrier as an "extremely worthy man," a mark perhaps of his devotion to Tridentine ideals of priestly behavior. To others in the parish he seemed haughty, authoritarian, and intransigent, and, significantly, he was also the first pastor in living memory who was not a native of Saint-Just. As might be expected of such a newcomer, Genebrier began to reform the parish institutions, which were not at all to his liking. Like curé Valentin of Saint-Germain-Laval, he pursued the parish's debtors, only in contrast to Valentin he did so ruthlessly, alienating a number of his parishioners in the process. He took a particularly keen interest in reforming the Penitents. In 1681 the Penitents complained that Genebrier and his vicar, Claude Perret, had twice disrupted their meetings, no doubt in order to assert authority over the confraternity. Then, like so many curés, he attempted to draw the Penitents closer to the parish: he refused to allow them to exhibit the Holy Sacrament in their chapel, which was separate from the parish church.

But the Penitents in Saint-Just-en-Chevalet did not acquiesce in Genebrier's demands. Fighting to maintain their independence, they complained to the archbishop that they had long enjoyed the right to display the Holy Sacrament in their chapel, and on January 23, 1682, Genebrier yielded, allowing the Penitents to put the Eucharist on display. But on February 15, the curé reneged and put their chapel under interdict. Retaliation by the Penitents was swift and took a symbolic form typical of early modern societies. The Saturday evening after Genebrier banned the chapel, a group of men gathered at a house in Saint-Just-en-Chevalet. A witness later said that they were "indulging in debauchery" (probably meaning that they were drinking) and that they were "singing shocking and indecent songs against the curé." Under the cover of darkness, the singers filed into the streets, carrying "large staves shaped like halberds," beating a drum, and chanting lines like "how the curé grumbles when he sees the world laugh." The music, the noise, and the halberds were reminiscent of a charivari, but this band of men aimed to embarrass not newlyweds but rather curé Genebrier and his vicar. Passersby swelled the revelers' ranks until it became a large crowd. Reviling the curé all the way, they marched down the street to the house of Perret, the vicar and Genebrier's accomplice in the harassment of the Penitents. There they fired pistol shots at his front door, shouted threats, and then disappeared into the night.[30]

Vicar Perret was so frightened by the incident that for a while it looked as if he would flee the parish. Perhaps this was what the perpetrators of the incident wanted, for driving the vicar away would place a great burden upon the curé's shoulders. Genebrier himself, the object of the crowd's derisive songs, was outraged by the incident. He denounced it in a sermon the next day, and he filed a complaint with the lieutenant of the *maréchaussée* in Roanne against six parishioners whom he felt were responsible for the ritualistic insult. Among the six men was Etienne Joseph Dubessey, a minor nobleman, *greffier* of the local seignorial court, and a man who had several times served as rector of Saint-Just's Confraternity of Penitents, most recently in

1679–81. We do not know if the other five men were Penitents too, but likely they were; at least they were allied with members of the confraternity.[31] Furthermore, the Penitents, not stopping at ritualistic violence directed against their parish priest, also threatened to take Genebrier to court. By June of 1683, the exhausted curé finally relented, allowed the Penitents the use of their chapel, and left them in relative peace for the rest of his tenure.[32]

It was not just the Penitents' confraternities that frustrated the curés' efforts to gain or wield power. Even confraternities of the Rosary and of the Blessed Sacrament proved troublesome on occasion. In the village of l'Arbrêle, for instance, curé Dumolin lamented the serious problems he had with the women of the parish's Rosary confraternity. Dumolin claimed that certain "scandalous troubles" besetting the confraternity were the work of a "cabal of several individuals . . . especially a number of women." In Dumolin's opinion, these women had "upset" the confraternity's "great work" by contesting the curé's control over the group's finances. They "revolted against their pastor, . . . and using as an excuse their desire to spend the confraternity's money according to their whims . . . they submitted proposals that tended to destroy the curé's authority and that of his successors." Dumolin had to put the confraternity under interdict "in order to eliminate any pretext for revolt and trouble in the future." Only a special devotion to the Virgin brought him through this terrible "crisis," Dumolin recorded, but in the end he seemed to have reestablished his authority over the Rosary confraternity. He permitted the women to resume their meetings, but only in order to say the Rosary, and only "when they meet with the consent of the curé and have obtained his permission for each individual meeting."[33]

A comic incident, no doubt, but it demonstrates how fraught with difficulty the reformed curé's role always was. Even minuscule matters could lead to real crises of authority. In Belleville, for example, conflict broke out over candles and a small amount of money! The confreres of the Blessed Sacrament there were supposed to pay curé Guy Estienne for the unused candles he let them collect at funerals. Unfortunately, the confraternity collected the candles but did not pay Estienne. When he protested, he was insulted by three members of the confraternity. Laughing in his face, the three told him that they "scoffed at" his order to pay for the candles and said that they "did not recognize in any way" his authority.[34]

Schools

Like devotional confraternities, primary schools also expanded the curé's role in communal affairs. Primary schools in the diocese tended to be of three types: communal schools that had been founded by a donor (often the curé), schools run by religious orders, and the little schools that Charles Demia and other dévots had promoted in the seventeenth century to teach reading and to imbue children with the Tridentine ethic. In 1672–73 Archbishop Camille de Neuville entrusted control over all these diocesan schools to the *bureaux des écoles,* a board of ecclesiastics and lay dévots headed by Demia, and this board exerted a great influence over primary education in the diocese, especially during the 1670s and 1680s. Thanks to the dévots and pious donors, primary schools of all three types (and especially the little schools) proliferated throughout the diocese by the eighteenth century. The city of Lyon had nine little schools for boys and ten for girls, and each suburb had at least one little school for children of each sex. Outside the city primary schools never spread to every parish, and financial difficulties often cut short the schools' existence. Nonetheless, little schools and communal schools were relatively common in the eighteenth-century countryside. They existed in roughly one-third of the parishes in Lyonnais and were only slightly less widespread in Beaujolais and Forez. In Bresse and Bugey, at least thirty-five parishes boasted schools, including all of the market towns and small cities.[35]

The parish clergy enjoyed a significant voice in the operation of these schools. In Lyon, urban curés sat alongside lay notables on the bureaux des écoles. In communities outside Lyon, the parish vicar, we know, often doubled as schoolmaster. As for the curé, he had the right to approve new schoolteachers—such power was rare in the sixteenth century—and he usually attended communal assemblies when school affairs were under consideration.[36]

Evidently the parish clergy both in Lyon and in the countryside supported the schools enthusiastically. To begin with, priests bequeathed money to the little schools. In those towns and large villages that still lacked schools, priests continued to work for their establishment well into the eighteenth century. In the 1780s, for example, curé Ranchon of Saint-Cyr-au-Mont-d'Or labored with the vestry wardens to found a school in his parish: Ranchon even supervised the construction work that transformed the town hospital into a school building.[37] Similarly, in Lyon in the late 1730s, curé Lyote of Saint-Vincent (one of the priests who sat on the bureaux des écoles) seconded efforts of pious laywomen to open a school for destitute girls in his parish, one of the few in the city that still lacked a girls' school. Later, Lyote and the other clergymen and lay notables on the school board established a "work school" to teach religion, reading, writing, and manual arts to girls from poor artisans' families in Saint-Vincent and two adjacent parishes; similar schools were founded also in other parishes in the city.[38]

In the parishes where *petites écoles* already existed, the priests encouraged parents to make their children attend, sometimes resorting to methods that verged on the excessive. Curé Vala of the western village of Saint-Martin-la-Sauveté proudly wrote to the school board in Lyon that he had denied absolution to parents who did not send their children to school; he also refused to admit children to First Communion unless they made an effort to learn to read. "I tried as much as I could," he said, "to get the villagers to send their children to [the schoolmaster]." He offered to pay the tuition for those who could not afford it, and he persuaded the vicar, a native of the parish with great influence among the parishioners, to exhort parents to send their children to school. Convincing them was difficult since they were "not disposed toward schooling," but the struggle was absolutely necessary, for as Vala noted, "there was almost no one who knew how to read when I came into this parish." Thanks to the school, Vala triumphantly claimed, many of his parishioners had learned how to read, although he had to admit that their grasp of the skill was only "partial."[39]

Vestries and Charities

In addition to their new role in schools and devotional confraternities, curés acquired increased responsibilities in old parish organizations. The Tridentine Church demanded, for example, that the curés play a greater role in the parish vestries. Curés in the sixteenth century commonly wielded little power in the vestries, but beginning in the seventeenth century the Church undertook a campaign to reverse this situation and assure the pastors some influence. The campaign was waged throughout France, with the support of the royal government, which wanted to halt the misuse of vestry and community revenues. The pastoral visits of 1654–62, 1700, and 1719 abound with orders that the vestry wardens submit written accounts of the vestry's financial affairs to the curé for his approval, and the diocesan statutes of 1705 reiterated this requirement. By 1719 the ecclesiastics conducting the visits were commanding parishioners to gather up documents and money belonging to the vestry and store them in a doubly locked strongbox. The curé kept one of the keys, and he had to witness any financial transactions or removal of documents. Furthermore, parishioners were warned that the curé's absence from any vestry assembly would mean the "nullification of all decisions the assembly reached."[40] In short, the curés were to enforce the keeping of written records and the separation of public and private funds in the parish vestries. Along with the royal intendants, who approved expenditures voted by village assemblies, the curés thus gave the parish organizations in rural areas their first taste of modern administration, and in the process they vested themselves with no small amount of new legal authority.

Of course, the execution of the Church's commands concerning the curé's role in the vestry was often fraught with difficulty, as the records of the pastoral visits make clear. Vestry wardens refused to turn over the financial accounts, and the vestry's papers frequently remained "in the hands of individuals who refused to give them up." But even if we allow for these complications, it still seems that the curés had gained power in the vestries by the early eighteenth century. Although direct comparison with the sixteenth century is somewhat hazardous (given the scarcity of written documents for the earlier period), there is evidence that curés increased their power in the vestries and that the requirements set down during the parish visits were in force in a number of parishes. When records exist in ample quantities, we can in fact observe the slow ascent of the priests in the vestry records. In Neuville, for instance, a weaver named Antoine Henry gave a perpetual annuity to the vestry in 1534 in order to provide oil for a lamp in the church; his bequest did not even mention the curé. Over a century later, in 1642, a similar foundation by *châtelain* André Mequilly stipulated that the parish curés watch over the vestry wardens to ensure that his pious bequest would actually be used for the upkeep of the lamp.[41]

The curé's increasing influence in the Neuville vestry manifested itself in other ways as well. A 1654 parish assembly agreed that the curé could attend vestry meetings and lease out church pews, and evidence as early as 1665 shows that the priests were indeed giving out pews and also burial places in the church. By 1679 the vestry kept written accounts, signed by the curé. If in 1700 the curé still lacked access to all the vestry's papers, a 1719 parish visit ordered that he preside over the vestry's meetings—a right that, as recently as 1654, the town's seignorial judge had refused to recognize. The curés actually exercised this right. The vestry wardens usually met in the curé's house, his approval was needed for the election of the wardens, and by 1731 he was choosing the visiting preachers for the vestry. Later in the eighteenth century, the curé not only signed the vestry's accounts but did much of the accounting too. In the eyes of Neuville's inhabitants, the curé's hold over the vestry had even come to smack of "despotism." That was the word which several disgruntled parishioners used in 1733 when they protested curé Bricitto's autocratic control over the parish church's treasury.[42]

At times, parish priests even succeeded in vetoing the choice of vestry wardens. In 1676 in the parish of Leguy, the curé rejected a newly elected warden who did not meet with his approval, and pastor Clement of Lentilly did the same in the eighteenth century. To be sure, not all curés wielded such power. In the city of Lyon in particular, curés exercised less influence over parish vestries, and the relationship between the priests and urban notables who served as vestry wardens in Lyon was more evenhanded.[43] But in many parishes in the countryside the curés managed to direct and occasionally even to dominate their vestries.

Seventeenth-century reforms of the hospitals and charities also helped expand the curés' administrative role. Throughout France, secular authorities and local dévots sought to impose their morality and sense of order upon the poor by creating new charities and reforming old ones. The royal government seconded many of these local efforts to reorganize archaic hospitals and almsgiving groups with letters patent and a royal declaration of 1698. Both the royal pronouncements and the local initiatives assured the curés a large role in the direction of a number of the charities. Priests controlled the new parish charities that the dévots established in Lyon in the last decades of the seventeenth century, and they gained considerable authority in the small cities and market towns, when old hospitals or almsgivings were reformed. Curés convoked and presided over meetings, supervised finances, and approved actual disbursements to the poor. The clergymen were in fact among the first to advocate the establishment of new charities or the reorganization of old ones—a role that sometimes pitted them against parishioners who defended time-honored institutions.[44]

By the middle of the eighteenth century, then, the curés had acquired considerable influence in the institutions of their parishes. They wielded power in hospitals and charities and in vestries, schools, and confraternities as well. In many instances, the curés even assumed the role of local functionaries. Besides keeping the registers of baptisms, marriages, and burials, they made inquiries in cases of violent death, secured governmental disaster relief, and provided the intendants with useful social and economic information.[45] Admittedly, the curés' rise to power in their parishes had not come about without occasional resistance, and at times they found themselves locked in conflict with their parishioners. Laymen were not always willing to sacrifice, say, a traditional confraternity banquet for prayers and solemn processions. Yet most parish priests managed to maintain a considerable degree of influence in local institutions, and they used their authority to trumpet both the piety and morality of the Catholic Reformation.

Support for a New Catholic Spirituality

With reformed clergymen in positions of influence throughout the diocese, Catholic spirituality naturally changed in the seventeenth century. The signs of a shift in piety are unmistakable: they range from the growth of the new devotional confraternities to an upsurge of pious bequests in wills. Yet the transformation of Catholic spirituality should not be attributed to the priests alone. In the countryside as well as in the city, Tridentine piety enjoyed the fervent support of lay groups who labored alongside the clergymen to insure the triumph of resurgent Catholicism.

We have noted the proliferation of the new devotional confraternities, which first appeared in the city of Lyon in the 1570s and then spread through the rest of the diocese during the course of the seventeenth century. The link between these Penitents', Blessed Sacrament, and Rosary brotherhoods and new forms of piety is clear. Extolled by the dévots, the confraternities promoted the very practices and devotions that resurgent Catholicism favored. The confraternities of the Blessed Sacrament, for example, granted indulgences for monthly communion, and they cultivated the worship of the Eucharist, one of the focal points of Tridentine piety. Often they supported lamps that burned night and day in churches in honor of the Eucharist, and they made a great effort to put the Holy Sacrament on display—an adoration the Penitents favored as well. Similarly, the confraternities of the Rosary encouraged monthly communion and confession and weekly rosaries. And in general they inspired a growing cult of the Virgin.[46]

The new confraternities may in fact have borne the responsibility for a subtle but important shift in popular devotions—a shift that becomes apparent if we glance at the altars that the confraternities erected. These altars won a substantial following, and they assumed positions of prominence in parish churches, at times shouldering aside the shrines of traditional saintly intercessors whom parishioners had once invoked to cure illness or curry divine favor. In the northeastern part of the diocese, for instance, the Rosary was by far the most popular patron of altars and chapels dedicated in the seventeenth century, especially in mountainous Bugey, where Rosary confraternities abounded. At the same time, altars erected in honor of Saints Antoine, Blaise, Sebastien, and Catherine—all traditional intercessors of the type the Church was discouraging—tended to be abandoned or to disappear from the parish churches.[47] In short, the new confraternities were reshaping Catholic spirituality at the expense, no doubt, of old devotions.

Further evidence of a spiritual transformation comes from our samples of wills and testaments. In rural wills, for example, pious bequests climbed dramatically in the seventeenth century. Whereas no more than 15 percent of the testators in our rural sample left money to the church or to charity in the years 1550–99, by 1625–49 some 54 percent of the wills contained such legacies, and the fraction increased to 90 percent and above after 1700 (table 6). The size of pious bequests jumped as well, from less than 1 percent of the total cash gifts mentioned in the wills in 1575–99 to an astounding 26 percent in 1700–24. They also grew relative to the size of dowries.[48]

It is true that pious bequests dipped somewhat in 1675–99, only to recover thereafter (table 6). This temporary decline did not represent a relaxation of religious fervor, as one might assume, but rather was the result of a traumatic agricultural depression that struck the Lyonnais at the end of the 1670s. For the Lyonnais, this brutal recession marked the onset of the tough times that afflicted the entire French economy from the 1670s to the end of the century, and its devastating effect upon pious donations is borne out by both statistical analysis and a detailed reading of the wills.[49] The consequences of the depression, though, should not mislead us. While economic change explains the brief decline in pious bequests in 1675–99, it does not account for the overall increase in religious and charitable legacies over the course of the seventeenth century. Statistical analysis demonstrates that this rising tide of donations did not result from greater prosperity among the testators, from fewer demands by their heirs, or from any other change in the sample. For a testator of average wealth and with the average number of heirs, the chances of making a pious bequest rose by approximately 4 percent each decade

Table 6 Percentage of rural testators making pious bequests by wealth class

Date	Elite	Coqs du village	Peasants	Total
Before 1550	67% (3)	100% (2)	0% (0)	80% (5)
1550–74	0% (0)	4% (26)	10% (79)	9% (105)
1575–99	71% (7)	14% (28)	10% (79)	15% (114)
1600–24	67% (3)	55% (29)	26% (34)	41% (66)
1625–49	0% (0)	58% (12)	52% (42)	54% (54)
1650–74	60% (5)	36% (14)	50% (10)	45% (29)
1675–99	27% (11)	38% (21)	31% (72)	32% (104)
1700–24	89% (9)	88% (16)	90% (62)	90% (87)
After 1725	100% (6)	100% (6)	100% (24)	100% (36)
Total	66% (44)	41% (154)	38% (402)	41% (600)

Source: Sample of rural wills described in appendix 1.

Note: For this table, information in tax records and marriage contracts was used to arrange occupations in a hierarchy of wealth. Testators were then assigned to one of three broad categories of wealth according to their occupations: elite at the top, *coqs du village* in the middle, and peasants at the bottom. See appendix 1 for details. The figures in parentheses are the absolute number of testators in each category.

during the seventeenth century; the size of his religious and charitable legacies increased by about 2 *livres* every ten years. All of these changes were far too large to be statistical flukes.[50]

Notaries in Lyon also registered an upturn in pious bequests, although the situation in the city was a bit more complicated. As we know, members of the urban elite resumed giving to the Church in the last decades of the sixteenth century. They boosted their donations for a second time in the years 1616–35, when testators such as Claude Poculat, a wealthy bourgeois of Lyon, bestowed enormous sums upon the city's new *hôpital-général*.[51] A third wave of generosity then broke over the city at the end of the seventeenth century. The percentage of wills containing pious bequests rose from 48 percent in 1636–55 to 72 percent in 1676–95 (table 7). The amount of money earmarked for religion or charity grew as well, from 13 percent of the total cash mentioned in wills in 1636–55 to 24 percent in 1696–1715. This time the increase in pious bequests spread beyond the confines of the city's elite, who had borne most of the responsibility for the two earlier waves of donations. For example, among artisans (other than the richest ones) donations climbed from 33 percent in 1636–55 to 64 percent in 1696–1715 (table 7).

Admittedly, the chronological pattern of giving is far more murky in Lyon than in the countryside. Whereas pious bequests rose rather steadily in rural testaments, the urban wills show a series of fitful jumps and starts, first among the urban elite in the late sixteenth century, then again in the years 1616–35, and finally among a broader spectrum of the city's population after 1650. Furthermore, one or two curious anomalies mottle the urban record. Among small-scale merchants, for instance, the rate of charitable and religious giving drops to a mere 33 percent in 1696–1715, and among the elite there is the retreat of 1636–75 (table 7).

As in the case of the rural wills, these inexplicable declines in generosity may have resulted from economic hardship. First of all, a severe depression struck Lyon in the years 1596–1610; the silk industry, which by this time had come to form the backbone of the local economy, was especially hard-hit. Perhaps this depression explains the pause between the first wave of elite giving in the late sixteenth century and the second wave during the years 1616–35. Similarly, war, tariffs, and rising taxes sent Lyon's economy into another tailspin from the late 1630s through the 1650s. This second, mid-century depression could well be what caused even wealthy testators to draw their purse strings again in the years 1636–75. Unfortunately, we will never know for sure because there is no reliable index of the state of the economy in seventeenth-century Lyon.[52]

In any case, both the likelihood and the size of pious bequests did rise among urban testators of all classes over the years 1636–1715. For urbanites

Table 7 Percentage of urban testators making
pious bequests by wealth class, 1596–1715

Period	Officers, large- and medium-scale merchants	Small-scale merchants and officers; richer artisans	Other artisans	Common people	All classes
1596–1615	69%	40%	39%	0%	48%
	(16)	(10)	(18)	(2)	(46)
1616–35	91%	100%	29%	0%	70%
	(22)	(6)	(14)	(1)	(43)
1636–55	69%	40%	33%	0%	48%
	(16)	(10)	(15)	(1)	(42)
1656–75	55%	67%	20%	100%	45%
	(20)	(6)	(15)	(1)	(42)
1676–95	83%	89%	40%	0%	72%
	(23)	(9)	(10)	(1)	(43)
1696–1715	81%	33%	64%	100%	67%
	(21)	(9)	(11)	(1)	(42)

Source: Sample of urban wills described in appendix 1.

Note: For this table, information on tax records was used to arrange occupations in a hierarchy of wealth, just as in chapter 1; testators were then classified by occupation. As in chapter 1, the class of large- and medium-scale merchants includes bourgeois and nobles. Richer artisans include prosperous tradesmen such as goldsmiths and jewelers. The figures in parentheses are the absolute number of testators in each category.

of average wealth, the likelihood of bestowing· money upon religion or charity increased 4.3 percent every ten years during this period, while the size of pious bequests grew by over 26 livres a decade. Statistical analysis confirms that the increase was not a chance result, and it did not stem from greater disposable wealth among the testators or from their having fewer heirs. Nor was it brought on by recovery after the midcentury economic crisis. Indeed, despite a revival in the 1660s and 1670s, Lyon's economy collapsed again in the 1680s. The silk industry and the economy as a whole did not return to life until the second decade of the eighteenth century. This long stretch of economic doldrums, though, occurred at precisely the same time that pious bequests in Lyon reached their peak.[53]

Economic change or shifts in the sample thus do not explain the late-seventeenth-century jump in pious bequests in urban testaments any more than they do in the rural wills. What then does the explosion of giving signify? Perhaps a lust for status or the appeal of fashion; perhaps a return to the past, to the sort of late medieval spirituality that prevailed at the dawn of the sixteenth century in the city of Lyon. But such arguments collapse upon closer inspection.[54] Popular devotions changed as the new confraternities of resurgent Catholicism spread over the diocese, and this shift alone would be enough to distinguish late medieval piety from the spirituality of the Counter Reformation. Further evidence of differences emerges from a consideration of the sort of funerals testators chose. In the wills from early-sixteenth-century Lyon, testators had planned elaborate burial ceremonies, replete with readings from the psalms, legions of attending clergy, and long corteges. Yet by the time of the explosion of giving in the late seventeenth century, testators both rich and poor, urban and rural had abandoned such florid rituals almost completely. The ceremonies of this type simply dropped from the wills.[55]

The disappearance of the traditional funerals points to one of the important distinctions between late medieval piety and the spirituality of Tridentine Catholicism. Clearly, one characteristic of the old ceremonies was that they harnessed group prayer and corporate action to benefit the souls of the dead. After all, the recitation of psalms by a band of priests and the processions by dozens of paupers and clergymen were all instances of collective prayer and mourning for the dead. Counter-Reformation piety, by contrast, placed greater stress upon individual prayer and action. The typical seventeenth-century testator relied not upon group ceremony but upon masses for his own soul. Of course late medieval testators (at least in the city of Lyon) had also commissioned numerous individual masses, and the Catholic Reformation itself hardly banished all collective prayer: the exercises of the new devotional confraternities it spawned immediately come to mind. The change wrought by resurgent Catholicism was therefore one of degree rather than kind. Nonetheless, corporate ritual undeniably assumed a smaller role upon the advent of the Catholic Reformation. Even the new devotional confraternities placed some emphasis on meditation and individualized prayer, and the diocesan hierarchy certainly took care that fraternal undertakings did not dominate the confreres' activities.[56]

More important, seventeenth-century testators themselves seemed to absorb the belief in individualistic salvation. Before the seventeenth century, it had not been uncommon for a testator to ask that votive masses benefit, in addition to his own soul, the souls of his "relatives and friends." Such fraternal gestures disappeared from the wills during the seventeenth century, and testators restricted their attention to their immediate families, or, more likely still, to their own souls.[57] In the new piety, salvation was more the business of individuals than of associations.

What effect this stress on individual sanctification had upon rituals such as the sacraments is difficult to say. Group confessions, we know, were suppressed by the early seventeenth century, and as confessionals appeared in the parishes, penance evidently did become the private dialogue the Tridentine Church desired. But we do not know whether laymen took Communion in a different fashion, whether they meditated on its meaning, or even whether they received it more frequently, as the new devotional confraternities urged.[58]

In any event, Catholic piety had changed by the end of the seventeenth century. Who then supported the spirituality of resurgent Catholicism? Clearly, the new piety received the allegiance of numerous laymen. The statistical analysis suggests that the rise in pious bequests in the seventeenth century was not peculiar to our sample, and it did seem to cut across class lines. Records from the devotional confraternities also testify to the widespread support for Tridentine spirituality. In most parishes, the large number of confreres was a sign that membership extended into many segments of the population. In Lyon, for example, the Confraternity of the Blessed Sacrament in the parish of Notre-Dame-de-Platière distributed candles to 641 confreres for a procession in 1708—a significant number in a parish of fewer than 8,000 souls.[59] Enthusiasm was equally widespread outside of Lyon. When the Rosary confraternity was founded in the village of Sauvain, for example, 144 men and 19 women joined immediately. Saint-Cyr-au-Mont-d'Or, a parish with fewer than 1,700 inhabitants, counted over 300 men and women in its Confraternity of the Blessed Sacrament in 1752, and in the market town of Neuville, which had fewer than 1,200 inhabitants, some 500 adults enrolled in the Confraternity of the Blessed Sacrament during the thirty years after its foundation in 1671. The members in Neuville included both men and women, and they ranged from officers and notables to artisans and persons engaged in the local textile trade: masons, carpenters, furniture makers, butchers, weavers, tailors, cloth washers, and silk workers.[60]

Yet despite signs of widespread allegiance, support for Tridentine spirituality did seem more pronounced among certain groups. The literate in particular showed a strong attachment to the new piety, at least in the countryside. In our sample of rural wills, literate testators gave significantly more to the Church and to charity than did their illiterate brethren. The larger bequests of testators who could read were not chance results, and they did not stem from greater wealth or from greater disposable income either. Indeed, a literate testator in the countryside was 25 percent more likely to make a pious bequest than an illiterate colleague who was equally wealthy and had the same number of children. The literate testator's average bequest exceeded the illiterate's by over 12 livres as well.[61]

Literacy naturally boosted pious bequests in the countryside, for the ability to read exposed a testator to the culture and the literature of the Counter

Reformation. In particular, it increased the chances that he would encounter the voluminous body of works that described how a good Catholic ought to confront death. In Père Crasset's *La douce et la sainte mort* and other books that were reprinted in great numbers and found their way into many private libraries, a reader would learn that making a will was a necessary part of a holy life and a means of advancing his salvation and avoiding damnation. He would read that masses commissioned in his will were "the most effective way" to spare his soul the torments of Purgatory. If he had "his own self-interest at heart," he would follow the urgings of the spiritual literature and reserve a part of his fortune for pious bequests after death. To quote from a text written by a Jesuit who preached and taught in Lyon, this money spent on pious causes would in fact be his own "to enjoy in the other world . . . [wealth] which death could never take away."[62] Clearly, familiarity with such works might influence a testator to make pious bequests. So too would exposure to the whole body of devotional literature produced by resurgent Catholicism in the seventeenth century.

Although the ability to read affected rural testators so dramatically, rising literacy rates do not explain the overall increase in pious bequests in the rural wills. Despite the efforts of the little schools, the real growth in literacy rates did not come until the eighteenth century, long after religious and charitable donations had begun their climb. Our own sample of rural wills confirms this, for despite the effect literacy had on pious donations it does not account for the entire rise in bequests over the course of the seventeenth century.[63]

Inside the city of Lyon, literate testators also showed a predilection for pious bequests, but the effect was not large enough to rule out the possibility of a chance result.[64] The less dramatic findings inside Lyon may seem paradoxical, but they can be explained. First, because literacy was more widespread in Lyon than in the rest of the diocese, an illiterate testator was more likely to have a literate friend or relative who might read to him from the devotional works of resurgent Catholicism, thus masking the effects of his own inability to read. Furthermore, since literacy rates varied less among the population in Lyon, it is harder to isolate the true impact literacy had and more difficult therefore to exclude chance results.

Other groups also rallied to the Counter Reformation, among them various elites. In Lyon, as we saw earlier, wealthy merchants and officers stood at the forefront of the Counter Reformation as early as the late sixteenth century. Slowly but surely, lay notables in the rest of the diocese also began to support resurgent Catholicism. Notaries, merchants, and seignorial officials crop up among the laymen who helped establish early Rosary confraternities outside Lyon, and they were typically among the first members of Blessed Sacrament confraternities as well. By the 1630s, the diary of a doctor from Saint-Bonnet-le-Château reveals that in at least one town the local notables were completely swept up in the devout life. Often such members of the local elite lavished wealth upon the parish churches. Between 1611 and 1669 in the small city of Givors, for example, one of the major benefactors of the parish was the Grimod family—Givors bourgeois who became châtelains and eventually moved to Lyon. In addition to founding numerous masses at the parish church, they paid for a tabernacle, building repairs, candles to burn before the Eucharist, and, finally, a banner depicting the Blessed Sacrament, which parishioners could carry in processions.[65]

In addition to the literate and local elites, urbanites also stood out among the Counter Reformation's supporters. This was obviously the case in Lyon, where the first devotional confraternities had taken root and where groups of dévots had come to cluster. But the laity toiled for resurgent Catholicism in the small cities and market towns too. One mark of their labors was a proliferation of new devotional confraternities: although these groups were found in tiny parishes of less than one hundred inhabitants, they seemed especially popular in small cities and market towns. Among the 108 northeastern parishes, communities with larger populations were far more likely in fact to establish a devotional confraternity, and they generally founded their confraternities earlier than did small villages (table 8). The pattern was much the same in the rest of the diocese, where confraternities sprang up in small cities and market towns like Saint-Germain-Laval before appearing in smaller population centers.[66]

Although historians have tended to overlook this connection between urbanization and the devotional confraternities, the experience of other regions of France was similar.[67] And the connection between cities and Counter-Reformation piety extends beyond the confraternities. Among testators in the countryside, pious bequests were significantly higher, the larger the population of the testator's parish. Moreover, the increase came over and above the effects of the testator's own wealth and ability to read, which suggests that it was not simply a result of larger fortunes and higher literacy rates in the market towns and small cities.[68] One reason the Counter Reformation enjoyed such strong support in the cities was that these communities had more of the lay notables who took an active hand in organizing confraternities and other religious associations. Another factor was that the towns and small cities were subject to more intense proselytizing. They were more likely than villages to summon holiday preachers, and reformed religious orders had begun to appear in the towns and small cities early in the seventeenth century. Furthermore, the male religious orders—the Jesuits in particular—used the small cities as staging grounds for missions.[69] Like literacy, these sermons and missions probably boosted pious bequests.

One final group with extraordinary zeal for the Counter Reformation were women, particularly in the countryside. If we allow for the differences of wealth and literacy, rural women were 10 percent more likely to bestow money upon the Church or charity, and their average gifts exceeded those of

Table 8   The relationship between population and the
probability of having a devotional confraternity
among the 108 northeastern parishes

Parish population range	Number of parishes	Percent with devotional confraternities in 1613–14 or 1654–62	Percent with devotional confraternities in 1700 or 1719	Percent without devotional confraternities for all visits
Below 100	14	14%	21%	79%
100 – 199	17	6%	41%	59%
200 – 299	25	16%	52%	44%
300 – 499	21	19%	62%	29%
500 – 999	23	39%	78%	17%
Over 1,000	7	57%	71%	0%
Population unknown	1	100%	100%	0%
All parishes	108	23%	56%	39%

Sources: Visites; AD Rhône, 1 G 49–53; AD Jura, G 10; Claude Marie Saugrain, *Diction-naire universel de la France ancienne et moderne,* 3 vols. (Paris, 1726).

Note: For the purposes of this table, devotional confraternities were limited to confraternities of the Rosary, Blessed Sacrament, Christian Doctrine, Scapulary, and Penitents. The population figures were derived by comparing Saugrain and the later visit records.

men by nearly 5 livres. Again, the differences defy explanation by mere chance alone.[70]

As for women in Lyon, the wills from 1636 to 1705 give no sign that they were more—or less—generous than men.[71] To be sure, city women did participate enthusiastically in certain charities and new devotions. In 1652, for example, an unnamed priest from the parish of Sainte-Croix in Lyon marveled at the fervor that urban women demonstrated at the opening of a papal jubilee. Although male Penitent confraternities were also engaged in exercises of devotion, what struck this priest as "marvelous" was the "ardor among young women . . . who marched [barefoot] in procession, all dressed in white with candles and veils." In his parish alone, fully 360 young women joined such processions.[72] We should not confuse enthusiasm for particular devotions, though, with extraordinary support for Counter-Reformation piety as a whole. On balance, women in Lyon seemed no more attached to Tridentine piety in the seventeenth century than urban men.

What explains the special appeal of Tridentine piety to women? And why did the new spirituality exert this hold over women only in the countryside? Suffice it to say for now that the Counter Reformation created a host of new opportunities for women, opportunities that seemed unusually attractive outside big cities like Lyon. To understand what these opportunities represented, we must first look at the darker side of resurgent Catholicism, the side which, far from creating a new piety, reshaped and even suppressed older rites and ceremonies. Unlike the new spirituality, this darker facet of the Counter Reformation would not win universal acclaim. Indeed, it would even provoke resistance from defenders of popular culture.

Agents of the Counter-Reformation Ethic

Masters of parish religious organizations and apostles of the new spirituality, the curés were also important cultural intermediaries who helped impose the harsh ethic and the urban sense of order and discipline favored by the post-Tridentine Church. Sermons, parish schools, and catechism classes were the most direct means the curés had to inculcate these values. Certainly, parish clergymen did not devote all their efforts in the pulpit or in catechism class solely to the moral code of resurgent Catholicism. They undoubtedly gave much attention to extolling the new piety, and in any case, the parish schools clearly had to spend some time on teaching children to read. Nevertheless, preaching and instruction were still the obvious way to instill the Counter-Reformation ethic.

About preaching, unfortunately, we know very little, save that curés were encouraged to preach and to use the catechism of Trent in their sermons. Brief marginal notes in parish registers make it clear that they did speak from the pulpit, but with one or two exceptions, we know practically nothing about the content of their sermons.[73]

Much more can be said about the parish schools. From the last chapter we know that Charles Demia and the Company of the Holy Sacrament had in mind a variety of social and ethical goals when they established the little schools. Besides teaching reading and encouraging students to undertake exercises of devotion, little schools were to instill discipline, hostility to popular culture, and sexual restraint, and the curriculum placed considerable stress upon these Tridentine virtues.[74] To the extent that the bureau des écoles managed to impose its will throughout the diocese (it was not always successful), the other primary schools followed a similar curriculum. By encouraging primary education and, in particular, the little schools, curés and vicars thus helped spread the dévots' moral austerity.

Catechism classes may well have had the same effect. Nearly all curés now taught catechism, and the catechism most commonly used was one originally drawn up for the petites écoles by Charles Demia himself. Although this catechism is no longer extant, it no doubt reflected the austere morality that permeated every page of Demia's other works. Had not Demia even instructed the students at his seminary of Saint-Charles to avoid "suggestive" language when they discussed the Incarnation and the sixth commandment in catechism class?[75]

But the priests' role as agents of the Tridentine morality extended far beyond the pulpit and the classroom. The clergymen brought the harsh ethic of the Counter Reformation to bear upon the sacraments and paraliturgical rituals, and they even tried to remake popular culture, particularly in the countryside. Since one of the goals of the Counter Reformation was to separate the sacred from any profane interference, the curés worked to purge the sacraments and parish religious ceremonies of any worldly contamination. Always their aim was to make the ceremonies orderly, disciplined, and subject to clerical control.

Of the sacraments, baptism was perhaps the most notable target of the curés' actions, particularly the social function of baptism. Traditionally, a christening was a mark of membership in the secular community: in rural areas the whole parish celebrated the baptism because it meant that yet another person had joined the community. Believing that these profane celebrations debased the sacrament and spawned horrendous "disorders," some curés sought to stamp them out. Little dramas then ensued before the parish baptismal founts. In the parish of Neuville, for example, curé Gacon had long lamented the rejoicing that accompanied baptisms, and when in 1780 it came time to baptize a child named Claudine, he decided to take drastic action:

> Thoroughly convinced that the baptisms in this parish occasion abuses, expenses, waste of time and disorders, that each day these abuses grow worse, and that this situation must be remedied, . . . I today made the decision, before God and my conscience, to ask the godfather and godmother who brought the child [named Claudine] to the church [for baptism] . . . whether they had not prepared a profane celebration, whether the fiddlers would not be standing at the church door after the baptism, in order to transform the august ceremony of the sacrament into a profane festivity.

When the godparents admitted that this was true, Gacon asked them "with zeal and charity" to send the musicians away. They did so, and the curé thanked them and the entire baptismal party as well, rejoicing that

> everyone went away modestly and decently. The infant's father [even] thanked me for what I had done. . . . [W]ith the help of God, we shall . . . continue to stamp out abuses whose consequences are equally pernicious for religion and society.[76]

Bringing a halt to the baptismal festivities was not enough for the priests, for they also attempted to transform the traditional role of godparents. Although godfathers and godmothers were ostensibly responsible for their godchild's spiritual well-being, the popular conception of their function emphasized their importance for the child's family and the child's material welfare: godparents were chosen to reinforce family friendships and alliances and to help provide for the child's material well-being, should the parents ever be unable to do so. The diocesan hierarchy and the parish clergy, however, took a radically different view of the godfather's and godmother's role. They wanted to reemphasize the godparents' religious responsibilities toward the godchild, at the expense of their traditional role.

With the encouragement of the Church hierarchy, curés began to question godparents, especially godfathers, concerning their knowledge of the catechism, and they refused those who seemed too ignorant of Catholicism to supervise the child's religious upbringing. When Claude Perraud's child was brought to be baptized in the parish of Saint-Cyr-de-Favières, for instance, curé Arnaud spoke in grave terms to the twenty-year-old godfather, Jacques Fleury Mirand, of his religious obligations. He stressed that Mirand's principal obligation would be to teach the child religion, and in order to see whether Mirand was capable of performing this duty, curé Arnaud asked him what were the principal mysteries of the Catholic faith and what was the sacrament of baptism. Mirand said he had never studied the mysteries and remained silent when he was asked about baptism. Dissatisfied with Mirand's responses, curé Arnaud demanded that the infant's father choose another godfather. But Mirand and the godmother then snatched the child and ran from the church, Mirand feeling that the curé had wounded his honor. Furthermore, the child's father supported Mirand and steadfastly refused to replace him. Meanwhile, the godparents (showing a concern for the infant's spiritual health which belied their curé's opinion of them) searched the countryside for a priest who would christen the child. They eventually found a neighboring priest who administered the sacrament, and they filed a criminal complaint against their curé for refusing to baptize the child. Similar events occurred in other parishes in Beaujolais. In each case, the parents and rejected godfathers thought the priest's refusal outrageous, and the godfathers considered it a blot on their reputation.[77]

The other sacraments also became involved in the curés' drive to impose the ethic and spiritual standards of the Counter Reformation. Parish clergymen were supposed to require that brides and grooms know the catechism, and First Communion was sometimes denied children who did not attend school or catechism classes. More important, parish priests took the ominous step of enforcing what they considered "appropriate" behavior for the sacraments and the church: stopping arguments that broke out among the congregation during mass, keeping parishioners from lounging on the altars, halting noisy assemblies of the village young men when the music and laughter from their gatherings disturbed confessions or other church services.[78] Sunday markets, too, often held in front of the church while mass was being said inside, disrupted the services; worse, many people drifted outside during mass in order to talk and joke with their fellow parishioners. In Neuville in 1733, curé Bricitto went so far as to lock the front door of the church to prevent such disruptions of the church services; devout curé Gonjon of Juliénas did the same in 1695. Taverns, which were supposed to close during church services, could cause similar difficulties. In Claveisolles in 1682, curé Jean de Vitry complained to the *bailliage* of Beaujolais that neither attempts at persuasion nor a court injunction had stopped Louis Bellet from keeping his tavern open during mass and vespers. Worse, Bellet hosted games of *boules* and ninepins, and the commotion they caused disrupted the divine services.[79]

To the curés, the talking, joking, and playing outside the church was precisely the sort of scandalous intrusion of the profane into the divine worship which, we know, the entire Counter-Reformation Church found abhorrent. parishioners' slipping outside to laugh, joke, or play when they should have been devoting all of their attention to the Lord ran counter to the whole individualistic thrust of the Counter-Reformation spirituality, which sought to rivet the worshiper's attention on the divine, to the exclusion of secular distractions. Many parishioners, however, did not share this feeling. In Neuville the parishioners complained directly to the bishop when curé Bricitto shut the church doors. In Juliénas one of the parishioners forced the door open right before the curé's eyes, and although not all of the villagers supported this action, a number felt that the curé had no right to close the front door during services. And at Sunday mass in Claveisolles, when curé Vitry stood in the pulpit to read the injunction against games and taverns, Bellet shouted derisively from the back of the church that Vitry should climb "up into the steeple . . . to make himself better understood."[80]

These attempts to discipline behavior caused such furor because the issue was not simply a matter of appropriate conduct, but rather a conflict between two different conceptions of the mass's place in community life. If the priests believed that the mass, like all acts of devotion, was to be rigorously divorced from all contact with secular affairs, the protesting laymen clung to a very different conception of the mass's role. Although they too viewed the mass as an act of worship, they felt that it was entirely proper for the mass to be an occasion for socializing. In their opinion, worship was still compatible with levity and enjoyment, and religion was still woven deeply into the life of the community. While they had absorbed and were no doubt attached to some practices of Counter-Reformation piety (Neuville, for example, had flourishing confraternities of the Rosary and of the Blessed Sacrament), they had not yet fully accepted the prohibition against mixing the sacred and the profane.

Processions also provoked conflict between priests and parishioners. The Church hierarchy took a dim view of the frolicking and amusement that accompanied many of the processions, especially those which led the faithful into the countryside, away from the parish that was supposed to be the focus of religious life. Restrictions were therefore placed upon the amount of time that could be spent on processions away from the parish, and with the Church's encouragement, a number of priests set about to replace treks to distant shrines with shorter processions and to rid the processions of profane diversions. In the 1650s, for instance, pastor Rollet of Odenas banned two customary processions in his village, citing the "scandal, the unseemly and ridiculous conduct they occasioned, and the indecency" they engendered. Sometimes the church hierarchy itself took action against the traditional processions. After a pastoral visit to Neuville in 1719, the archbishop replaced an annual procession to Notre-Dame-de-Fontaine with a much shorter one to Fleurieux-sur-Saône, which was just across the river from Neuville. Similar orders were given the curés in other parishes.[81]

If the parishioners in Neuville and Odenas acquiesced in these changes, others were not willing to give up processions that had been part of local religious life for generations. An incident in the parish of Villié demonstrates this clearly. Like many villages, Villié celebrated Rogations with a procession to a nearby community—in this case, to Chiroubles. But in 1681, when the day for the procession arrived, curé Pierre Michelson of Villié announced in a sermon that he was disturbed by the "disorders" the procession gave rise to. He told his parishioners therefore that the procession henceforth would not venture beyond the parish itself. Instead, the congregation would wind its way around several crosses erected in the village and then return to the parish church.

After the mass was over, Michelson set the newly revised procession in motion. Led by the parish banner and a cross, the congregation filed out of the church, and everything went as Michelson had planned until they reached the cemetery. There the curé directed the banner and crucifix bearers at the front of the procession to go on to the first cross, as he had explained in his sermon; but at that moment, just as the procession was about to deviate from its traditional path, a large group of men from the parish (Michelson later said one hundred) ordered the bearers to go on to Chiroubles. Michelson commanded them to stop, but to no avail: all the parishioners marched off to Chiroubles. Once there, the pilgrims from Villié were stopped by the local curé, who was no doubt aware of Michelson's plans to change the traditional Rogations procession. He asked what they were doing "without their pastor . . . like lost sheep," and they replied that they had come "to pray to God." Shocked, the priest from Chiroubles then told them that a procession without their curé "was not very pious," and he forbad them to make a customary entry into his church. Barred from their usual destination, the faithful of Villié simply knelt down and prayed on the open ground; then they got up and returned home.[82]

Like the struggles over godparents, this incident reveals the potential for conflict between traditional religious practices and the austere, purified spirituality that the curés wanted to impose on their parishes. The laymen of Villié did not cling to the Rogations processions simply out of force of habit. Although meaningless tradition may have weighed heavily on their actions, people do not defend tradition unless it has some importance in their lives, and the Rogations procession to Chiroubles clearly did have such importance. Marching through fields to a nearby parish was believed to help ensure a bountiful harvest and visiting neighbors was a means of ensuring good relations. Moreover, for the congregation of Villié, Chiroubles was clearly a holy place—witness how they knelt and prayed there—and keeping Chiroubles as the procession's destination was thus essential for the ritual's effectiveness. Hence the congregation's steadfast determination to retain the procession's traditional path.

For the curé, however, this hike across the countryside took the faithful away from the parish and caused "disorder." If Michelson, like other curés, did not bother to describe in detail what these disorders were, we can assume that he meant the levity, laughter, and rejoicing that would normally accompany a springtime jaunt to a neighboring village. Although laymen accepted this joviality as part of the ritual, curé Michelson, like a good agent of the Counter Reformation, viewed it as sacrilege.

If the curés and the laity in the countryside were divided over processions and other paraliturgical rituals, the potential for conflict was greatest of all over the issue of the parish festivals and the popular celebrations of the village youth.[83] The Church hierarchy and the dévots of Lyon had instilled in the clergy their hatred for these popular festivities, and they enlisted the curés in their campaign to stamp them out. With the help of the parish priests, the traditional confraternities of the Holy Spirit were suppressed or emasculated, so that they no longer staged banquets or festivals. As for the devotional confraternities that replaced the Holy Spirit associations, the curés' surveillance ensured that they sponsored only pious exercises of devotion, which were actually designed to supplant popular celebrations.[84] With the curés' aid, the royaume ceremonies were also stripped of some of their exuberance. The royaumes sponsored by the new devotional confraternities were devout affairs, and the curés worked to quiet any other royaumes if they grew too raucous. The result seems to have been to transform the royaumes, which had once been communal celebrations, into ceremonies of pure devotion—or at least this is the impression left by several existing descriptions of eighteenth-century royaumes. The cortege escorting the king or queen of the royaume into the church became simply a religious procession, and all elements of secular joviality were kept outside the church building. Since the curé supervised the collection and use of funds from the royaume auction, it became difficult to employ any portion of the revenues to support the parish festivals. In some cases, the money from the royaumes now went exclusively to ornament the church, and the kings and queens no longer had anything to do with hiring musicians and organizing dances.[85]

But the establishment of control over the royaumes and confraternities did not bring a halt to the traditional village festivals, so the Church had to undertake more direct measures. In addition to the bitter campaign against festivals mounted by Lyon's Company of the Holy Sacrament, there were efforts by a number of curés to suppress the festivals in their own parishes. In Saint-Etienne-la-Varenne, irascible curé Deguz refused absolution to young men and women who danced at the parish festival, telling two of the village youths that he would not absolve them unless they promised "to stop dancing, avoid the parish festivals," and acknowledge that these celebrations were immoral. Because the youths helped stage a royaume that was yet another occasion for dancing and frolic, Deguz refused to accept the candle wax that the youths brought him from the proceeds of the royaume, saying that it was "wax from the devil and libertines."[86]

Saint-Etienne-la-Varenne was not the only parish where the curé found himself in conflict with the village youths over the issues of festivals, dancing, and youthful assemblies. Disturbed by the "libertinage of youth," rural priests elsewhere tried to stop the young men from gathering by putting crosses in the public places where the youth assembled. But even this could provoke conflict. When curé Jean Rabot of Saint-Clement-sous-Valsonne erected such a cross in 1681, the village youths retaliated by harassing the workmen who built the cross and by cutting Rabot's vines and ruining his garden. Rabot, a devout leader of the local ecclesiastical conferences, seems to have had somewhat more success in suppressing dancing at festivals in his parish. In 1669 he wrote the seignorial judge, a man with whom he was on close terms, and complained that his parishioners customarily danced on feast days, especially the patron saint's day. Finding this "contrary to the honor due God, and the respect and veneration due the saints," he asked the judge to ban such celebrations. The judge, who would later be active in Lyon's Company of the Holy Sacrament, swiftly obliged and issued an order against the dancing.[87]

Although curés like Rabot who battled against the festivals in the seventeenth century were probably inspired by the Company of the Holy Sacrament (and especially by the retreats the company held for parish priests), the clerical campaign against the festivals and the gatherings of the village youth continued throughout the eighteenth century, well after the company had ceased to be active. In 1753 curé Farjon of the western parish of Champoly called upon the government to suppress the festival of the patron saint's feast day in his parish. The young men of Champoly customarily celebrated this feast day by stringing up a goose by the throat and then vying with one another to strike the animal until its neck was severed and its body fell to the ground; after this gruesome contest, the community staged a huge dance.

Shocked by this display of what he considered debauchery, Farjon wrote the commander of the maréchaussée in Lyon to have him ban the festival in Champoly. The commander, citing royal ordinances against "dangerous public gatherings and festivals with dancing and music," obligingly issued an order against the festival, and he instructed the five cavalrymen in Boen who made up the maréchaussée's nearest brigade to enforce his order. Curé Farjon wrote the head of the Boen brigade to remind him of his commander's order, and on the feast day of the Nativity of the Virgin, the five cavalrymen arrived in Champoly to halt the festival planned for that day. But when they tried to stop the celebrations, the community rioted. A mob forced the cavalrymen to flee to the curé's house, and two hundred angry villagers lay in wait for them through the evening, in case they dared to leave their refuge.[88]

Elsewhere, the priests' campaign extended to the charivaris and other rituals that communal youth groups considered their right. In the small city of Regny, for example, curé Depierre and several parishioners fought against the huge public bonfire that the local youth group customarily built on the first Sunday of Lent. Similarly, the curé of Belmont tried in 1766 to stop a rowdy charivari. The young men of Belmont, armed with muskets and cudgels, had invaded the house of a recently remarried widower, extorted the customary money, food, and drink, and then forced the couple to jump over a bonfire. Arriving in the middle of the charivari, the curé told the youths to bring their indecencies to a halt. They responded to this moralizing by threatening to smash the windows of the vestry if the meddling priest did not shut up and go home![89]

By the end of the Old Regime, curés from throughout France were even asking the *procureur général* of the Paris Parlement to suppress parish festivals and youth celebrations, since local court orders seemed to go unenforced.[90] In the diocese of Lyon, the curés of the four neighboring parishes of Mornant, Taluyers, Saint-Andéol-le-Château, and Chassagny pleaded with the procureur général in 1779 to ban the festivals and youth celebrations in their communities and, if possible, in all of Lyonnais and Forez. The four parishes had all experienced charivaris, raucous parish festivals, and battles between their own young men and the youths of neighboring communities. The four priests complained in particular of the vicious consequences of the charivaris, for afterward the local youths would retire to taverns, where they drank and gambled away their money. Claiming that previous orders against the festivals and gatherings had not been executed, the priests requested a new injunction and asked the Parlement to name two residents of each parish who would inform the Parlement in case anyone violated the ban.[91]

A number of priests in the diocese did not enlist in the campaign against festivals and youth groups. While trained to view the popular festivities as sources of "debauchery" and "disorder," many of the curés no doubt tolerated the festivals and youth rituals in order to preserve peace in their communities and perhaps even for the sake of their own personal safety. The curé of Sorbières, for instance, gave the young men of his village permission to dance at the parish festival in 1781. After a riot broke out when the maréchaussée tried to halt a brawl at the festival, the curé calmed the crowd, but he would not give the cavalrymen the names of the rioters, undoubtedly because he wanted to maintain his own good position in the community.[92]

It also goes without saying that some of the priests who became embroiled in conflict with their communities over the subject of festivals were irascible, difficult men. Even the local archpriest believed this of curé Deguz, the priest from Saint-Etienne-la-Varenne who refused communion to the youthful dancers in his parish, for his measures only drove the young men from the parish church.[93] Yet this charge cannot be levied against the majority of the priests who battled the parish festivals. They were only carrying out the dictates of the Counter-Reformation Church, and some were well known as excellent priests.[94] Indeed, it would be wrong to depict the curés who struggled against the festivals as exceptional. All priests were urged to work to reshape popular culture, and if some tolerated popular celebrations in order to placate their parishioners, those who chose to fight were merely doing what the Tridentine Church wanted.

By the eighteenth century, the reformed clergy was firmly implanted throughout the diocese; austere graduates of seminaries occupied rectories in towns and villages everywhere. But if we ask what these agents of the Counter Reformation accomplished, our judgment must be mixed. Admittedly, the priests put into practice the Tridentine ideals of clerical behavior, and, especially in the countryside, they institutionalized the Counter Reformation, by directing confraternities and parish vestries and by using the pulpit and the classroom as a platform for moral and religious indoctrination. They helped spread the devotional confraternities in rural areas, and they bore partial responsibility for the demise of the traditional village associations of the Holy Spirit and for the transformation of the royaumes into ceremonies of pure devotion. And both in Lyon and elsewhere in the diocese, they helped reform charities and establish schools—accomplishments that aided the poor and somewhat reduced illiteracy.

The reformed parish priests left an intangible legacy as well. Along with pious laymen and the regular clergy, they diffused Counter-Reformation spirituality in the city and countryside. They helped spread the altars and devotions that gained so much favor, and they rallied the faithful to the new piety of the Tridentine Church. Here the clergymen recorded a great triumph, one that left a nearly indelible mark etched upon the wills and confraternity records and upon religion as a whole for decades to come. Their success, though, should not be misunderstood. The priests did not simply impose the victorious elements of Tridentine piety upon the laity, nor were they the only conduits of religious change. The laity as a whole willingly embraced elements of Counter-Reformation spirituality, and certain individuals in particular—urbanites, the literate, and rural women—pledged the Church particularly fervent support. For these ardent believers, the new spirituality (or at least the benign side of it) was a matter of choice, not imposition. In fact, a number of laymen actually worked beside the priests to assure the Counter Reformation's victory. Lay notables in the countryside organized new confraternities, and dévots from Lyon's elite accomplished so much that they seemed at times to steal the initiative away from the clergy.

The consequences of these successes which the priests and their allies obtained cannot be exaggerated, particularly in the countryside. By bringing insular communities outside Lyon into contact with resurgent Catholicism, the clergy helped break down the traditional organizations of parish life. The result was to destroy institutions that isolated the communities and fostered a sense of collective identity. Indeed, one can say more, for the priests were crucial links in a system of social control that extended from the urban lay elite to the lower classes in the cities and the countryside. They were functionaries on behalf of the State, and on behalf of the Church they helped maintain order and impose discipline. Their presence encouraged the keeping of accounts and the separation of public and private funds in the vestries, confraternities, hospitals, and charitable organizations of the diocese. They may have even managed to instill in the urban lower classes and in the rural population some of the Counter Reformation's moral discipline and urban sense of order.[95]

Yet the reformed parish clergymen met with certain failures. Even simple tasks, such as the closing of cemeteries, escaped their grasp, for although the Tridentine Church insisted that the burial grounds be enclosed to keep out markets and secular festivities, most parishes could not afford to maintain cemetery walls, much less build them from scratch. And while the priests managed to popularize the new spirituality and change processions and other religious rituals, they never succeeded in suppressing the parish festivals and other popular celebrations. In the city of Lyon, the festivities of the abbeys of misrule had disappeared, but charivaris continued into the eighteenth century in spite of the opposition of the Church. In the countryside, parish festivals continued into the nineteenth century and beyond, despite the fulminations of the diocesan hierarchy and the curés. The same was true of the gatherings of village youths, for charivaris and brawls between the young men of different parishes lasted into the nineteenth century.[96] The curés tried to suppress all these customs in the market towns and villages, but their efforts to destroy this part of parish culture bore only a bitter fruit, for whenever the priests sought to stamp out the festivals and youth gatherings, they kindled hostility that sometimes exploded into resistance and even violence. In the city of Lyon, such hostility was rare. Many popular festivities in Lyon were already dead when the Church adopted the harsh new ethic in all of its rigor, and in any case the enthusiastic support of the urban elite had helped win acceptance for the Church's campaign. But in the countryside the Counter Reformation's austere morality was imposed in full force, and it battered against beliefs and institutions that were the bulwark of communal solidarity. Not surprisingly, it was rejected by people who saw nothing wrong in combining devotion and gaiety, people whose religion was deeply woven into the fabric of communal affairs. If the rural people accepted the new confraternities and the new devotions of the Counter Reformation, they balked and turned against its austerity and urban sense of order, and they opposed many of its attempts to undermine communal institutions. Their resistance deserves further scrutiny, for it reveals why the curés' appeal for greater powers and moral order rang so hollow at the end of the Old Regime.

5

The Aftermath of the Reforms

Until the end of the Old Regime, parish priests remained faithful to the Tridentine ideals of clerical behavior, and their adherence to these standards continually strained their relationship with the laity. The situation worsened in the second half of the eighteenth century as conflict between priests and parishioners increased, creating a dilemma for the parish clergymen on the eve of the French Revolution.

This antagonism generated by the Counter Reformation raises several questions. What issues kindled strife between priests and parishioners? What social groups led the opposition to the clergy? Which parishes were most likely to witness such instances of hostility and resistance? Curiously, although the tension in the parishes grew more pronounced in the latter half of the eighteenth century, the causes of the conflict did not change. The types of laymen who argued with the priests and the issues they fought over remained the same until the end of the Old Regime. It was not that new problems aggravated the situation after 1750 but that laymen were now more willing to oppose the priests, while the clergymen themselves persevered, almost relentlessly, in their campaign to dominate the parishes and suppress popular culture. Indeed, intellectual and political movements among the lower clergy at the end of the Old Regime may well have led the priests to redouble these efforts despite popular opposition.

Issues and Adversaries

Antagonism between priests and laity, though pronounced locally, did not polarize all parishes: amicable relationships between pastors and their flocks were not uncommon. In Poleymieux, for example, the curé was so beloved that in 1783 his congregation feted the fiftieth anniversary of his arrival in the parish with a banquet, music, and a procession. Elsewhere curés earned the laity's affection through acts of charity and heartfelt concern for the poor. Parish priests founded charitable funds for destitute agricultural laborers, spent their own money to aid jobless spinners and weavers, and worked tirelessly to help people after disaster struck their parishes.[1]

Some curés even stood up for their parishes against outside authorities. In Epercieux the curé led a procession to protest the usurpation of communal property by relatives of the local seignior. At Les-Sauvages, curé Crozier sided with his parishioners against a merchant from Villefranche, Claude Thimonier, who had been taking advantage of poor debtors in the community. The people of Les-Sauvages, who considered Thimonier a despicable usurer, had stoned a house the merchant owned in the parish. When Thimonier tried to have the *maréchaussée* seize the individuals responsible for this action, Crozier demanded that the marshals show a court order justifying the arrests. They could not produce one, and Crozier, acting as the community's defender, gave the outsider Thimonier a vigorous tongue lashing for attempting to arrest the men and for exploiting the poor.[2]

Although the majority of curés probably did not fight with their parishioners, the antagonism between priests and laymen was nonetheless a serious problem. Even clergymen who did not squabble openly with their parishioners must have experienced frequent moments of tension when forced to choose between the harsher of the Tridentine ideals, on the one hand, and the harmony of their parishes on the other. This tension, though far from ubiquitous, bore witness to the sheer difficulty of imposing the more austere Tridentine values on many segments of the population.

Here, certain age-old causes of ill will in the parishes must be distinguished from the relatively new source of conflict that resurgent Catholicism created. The tithe, as we know, had long rankled laymen, but it was far less of a problem for the curés, who collected the tithe in less than 30 percent of the parishes in the diocese, than for the abbeys and collegiate churches, which possessed the vast majority of the tithe rights in the region. Other traditional sore spots were the use of glebe lands and the honorariums which priests received for their services (the *casuel*), and nearly every parish was afflicted by strife over the cost of building or repairing parish rectories.[3]

The Counter Reformation, though, sowed new seeds of discord between priests and parishioners. Many of the new issues are already familiar from the previous chapter. Strife stemming from the Church's campaign against popular customs amounted to conflict between two religions or, indeed, two cultures: the culture of the parish priests, the Church hierarchy, and the urban lay elite, on the one hand, and that of the peasantry on the other. This campaign also involved an assault upon sacred bonds of kinship and peer group solidarity. When curé Deguz of Saint-Etienne-la-Varenne denied communion to two youths in order to force them to renounce dancing at local festivals, the two replied that giving up dancing was unthinkable. They would gladly promise to attend any religious services, but "it was impossible for them not to mingle and rejoice with their parents and friends" at the festivals.[4] The youths' hallowed obligations to kith and kin were far too important to sacrifice for the sake of a meddling curé. Finally, the clergy's drive to dominate parish institutions ran counter to the traditional belief that priests were to be "servants of the parish." It was commonly felt that the curé was obliged to provide the parish with blessings, masses, and magical prayers against blight and bad weather. He had no right to withhold these services or to use them to wield power over the community.[5]

The Catholic Reformation gave rise to other problems as well. The *dévots'* deep concern for children and for their education was one source of trouble. The dévots' solicitude had led to the establishment of schools and catechism classes, but as we have seen it also caused curés to insist that godparents should be capable of supervising their godchildren's spiritual education—a demand that played havoc with traditional family ties. The Church's concern for children could also cause friction when priests interfered in family affairs. In Cogny in 1702, for example, a woman summoned curé Gaspard Girard when her neighbor, a notary named Marchand, began to beat his daughter. When Girard arrived and tried to persuade Marchand to stop, the notary took offense and attacked the curé with a sword. Marchand obviously considered the curé's actions an infringement on his rights as a father. He evidently subscribed to the traditional belief in unlimited paternal authority—an attitude increasingly at odds with the Church's emphasis on parental obligations. Similar conflict over the curé's involvement in parental affairs arose in other parishes as well.[6]

One additional issue evident in much of the conflict generated by the Counter Reformation was communal solidarity. The priests sought to destroy the groups and institutions that reinforced the cultural insularity of the rural community, and parishioners resisted in order to protect their community's sense of identity. The priests' attacks on old confraternities, *royaume* ceremonies, and parish festivals were assaults upon communal solidarity, as were the measures taken against youth groups, for the young men still played a large role in community celebrations. Efforts by clergymen to protect the sacred from the profane and guard the dignity of religion led to strife over the use of the very public places where people socialized and communal solidarity was strengthened. Curés fought with the parish youths to keep them from gathering in the village square, where their noise and music disturbed church services. Attempts to close church doors to prevent the laity from congregating outside during mass also sparked conflict. So did the drive to wall up cemeteries, for burial grounds had once been sites where laymen could barter and talk amidst the graves of their ancestors.[7]

Cabarets, the taverns where villagers met to drink, were among the most important centers of communal solidarity, and we already know that they attracted the priests' attention. Parish youths frequently assembled at the tavern, and there the youths' activities, such as charivaris, began or ended.[8] Often the cabaret was also the site where parish notables met for informal discussions of local affairs. In a tavern owned by the notable Claude Morgue, for example, the parishioners of Vauxrenard talked about their curé, and it was at such a gathering that Morgue voiced his displeasure with the priest for his failure to offer prayers in order to stop a hailstorm. In Claveisolles, when the curé refused to allow Etienne Beranjon to be a godfather at a baptism, Beranjon and the child's parents immediately ran to the cabaret to seek the counsel of the village syndic and other notables who were drinking there.[9]

Besides encouraging communal unity which could easily turn against the curé (as the examples from Vauxrenard and Claveisolles demonstrate), the cabarets were a focus for precisely the sort of activities the clergy detested. Since the sixteenth century, taverns had been viewed as threats to religion, as sources of blasphemy, disorder, ruinous debauchery, and drunkenness. Parish priests eagerly sought to police them, but they could not shut the cabarets down altogether. All they could do was to ensure that the establishments remained closed during divine services, as required by law, so that parishioners would not forsake mass for the camaraderie of a tavern. Even this was never an easy task, despite the body of royal legislation ordering that taverns close on the Sabbath. During the pastoral visits of 1719, curés repeatedly complained that their efforts to shut down the cabarets on Sundays had been unsuccessful, and on numerous occasions priests had to resort to court injunctions against tavern owners—injunctions that were often defied.[10]

A number of groups led the opposition to the priests when disagreement over these various issues erupted into open conflict. The identity of one of these groups is already clear: the parish youths. Their defense of charivaris, rites of passage, and festivals led, as we know, to numerous confrontations with the reformed clergymen. This antagonism between priests and parish youths could lurk behind even innocuous incidents. One Sunday in 1777, for example, a young man named Jean Marie Bonnefond filched a few ripe cherries from a tree belonging to François Gaspard Clerc, the curé of Claveisolles. No more than an innocent prank perhaps, but Clerc did not think so. For months he had watched Bonnefond and other youths cross his plots of wheat and flax to grab fruit from the trees of his orchard. Worse, Bonnefond was one of a number of youths who gathered each Sunday in front of the church to play the flute and pound on wine barrels. On the very day in question Clerc had been forced to tell Bonnefond and his companions to stop their revelry because the noise disturbed confessions he was hearing in the church, but they ignored his admonition. Added to this earlier contumacy, the pilfering of the cherries was too much for Clerc to bear. Grabbing a stick, the curé chased after Bonnefond and finally cornered him in the seignior's courtyard. There he beat the youth and ordered him to beg forgiveness for what he had done.

Bonnefond subsequently filed criminal charges against Clerc, and the priest did the same against Bonnefond when he found himself being harassed by local youths. Bonnefond and his peers danced and sang defamatory songs in front of the curé's house, and one Sunday it was even rumored that they lay in wait for the curé in order to beat him up.[11] The theft of a few cherries thus revealed the terrible hostility smoldering just beneath the surface of Claveisolles, hostility that pitted the parish youths against their curé. The priest's original action was, to be sure, excessive: even he admitted that he had been carried away. But both he and his vicar firmly believed that Bonnefond and his friends deserved to be punished, and both felt that in beating the youth the curé was merely exercising his right to teach the boy a moral lesson.

Local notables in rural communities were also frequently at odds with the curés. In contrast to the urban upper classes, who (as we shall see) lived in relative peace with the clergy, rural notables fought with the priests. Para-doxically, the notables furnished some of the staunchest proponents of Counter-Reformation piety: members of the elite played an active role, we know, in the new devotional confraternities. Support for the new spirituality, though, did not always translate into good relations with the Catholic clergy. In the first place, the notables' role in the confraternities and in parish hospi-tals and vestries was likely to embroil them in conflict with the priests, who were taking control of these local institutions. An influential villager might well protest clerical encroachments upon his traditional prerogatives in local affairs even though he and others of his ilk were sincerely attached to Counter-Reformation devotions. Quite simply, some members of the village elite feared the threat which the curés posed in village politics.

Clearly, too, a rural notable's stature in the community made it easier for him than for others to oppose the curé. It was a notary in Cogny who resisted clerical attempts to meddle in family affairs, and a surgeon-schoolmaster did the same in Saint-Lager. Parishioners with less status or power no doubt resented clerical meddling, but they probably would not have dared to stand up to their curé. Similarly, Claude Morgue, the tavern owner, surgeon, and seignorial agent in Vauxrenard, was probably not alone in resenting his curé's failure to avert a disastrous hailstorm, but after the storm Morgue was by far the most vociferous of the priest's detractors. He even insulted the curé to his face. "Cur! Little bugger of a curé!" he exclaimed, "I would like to have two other men of my opinion. We'd string you up."[12]

Rural merchants formed a third group prominent among the clergy's an-tagonists. A number of economic changes had thrust these merchants into prominence in Lyon's hinterland. Rural industry had expanded tremendously in the diocese, as in the rest of Europe, after 1650: ribbon making around Saint-Etienne, metal working in the same region and in Bugey, the manufac-ture of linens and, later, of cottons in the Monts du Lyonnais and Beaujolais. Industry brought rural parishes into closer contact with merchants who lived in Lyon, the small cities of the diocese, or occasionally even in the villages. The commercialization of the wine trade in northeastern Beaujolais after 1700 had the same effect, as did continued urban investment in land and vineyards in Lyonnais and Beaujolais. The curés' reaction to all of this was complex, but a number of priests grew to suspect the merchants of exploiting the poor. Such an opinion was not entirely unfounded. The merchants and other urbanites often lent money to cash-poor peasants or workers in rural industries, and then, when the borrowers defaulted, they acquired at a cheap price whatever property secured the loans. In this way, merchants and urban lenders had gained possession of great amounts of property since the sixteenth century, and although the merchants' enterprises allowed the peasantry access to larger markets, in the popular mind they were considered usurers.[13]

For the rural curés, suspicion of the merchants gave them the sense that they were protecting the less fortunate among their parishioners. In addition, the curés may have resented the merchants' growing power in the countryside. Thus, curé Crozier of Les Sauvages scolded the merchant Claude Thimonier for exploiting debtors in his parish. In the village of Arbuissonas, a curé rebuked a local merchant in terms that were even more explicit. The priest informed Jean Picard before a Sunday mass in 1754 that he was excommunicated as a usurer and then repeated this denunciation in his sermon. And in Jullié, two local wine merchants alleged that the local pastor had attacked them from the pulpit after they had become engaged in a suit concerning some land bequested to the parish poor.[14]

If youths, notables, and merchants predominated among the parish clergy's antagonists, one group was conspicuously absent: women. Young women, for instance, almost never quarreled with priests. When curé Deguz of Saint-Etienne-la-Varenne threatened to withhold sacraments from both young men and women who danced at festivals, the young women, unlike their male counterparts, gave in to the curé. Older women behaved no differently. A mother might protest when her child's godfather was rejected, and ladies in a Rosary confraternity might refuse at times to accept the curé's tutelage, but in general women could rarely be found among the curé's adversaries.[15]

The predominance of men among the curé's opponents admits of several explanations. First, since males obviously occupied most of the positions of power in the parishes, they would be more likely to argue with the curé over the exercise of his authority, especially in parish organizations. Second, males seemed to be the chief targets of the Church's drive to enforce its new sexual morality. To impose the new sexual ethic, the Church focused on young men, driving away the prostitutes the youths had frequented and condemning their assemblies as debauchery. As for older married men, although the Counter Reformation may have increased their paternal authority, it also expanded their obligations toward their wives and children. Finally, the Catholic Reformation had cost men a fair amount of power. It was by and large their organizations and customs that were the victims of ecclesiastical attacks on popular culture: the youth groups, the festivals, the Holy Spirit confraternities. New confraternities and pious festivals replaced these older institutions, but in the process men, particularly young males, forfeited a bit (though far from all) of their power. They had exercised a monopoly over local young women, a monopoly enforced by ritual violence and—until the sixteenth century—even punishment by gang rape.[16] To the extent that the Church succeeded in suppressing their rituals and diverting them toward pious activities (we have seen that the Church's progress was slow here), the youths lost influence in the communities. Even if the Church failed to suppress their celebrations, the young men, and rural males in general, were certainly threatened by the Counter Reformation. Naturally, they retaliated by arguing with the curés.

Women, on the other hand, made some significant gains during the Counter Reformation. While pre-Reformation Catholicism had afforded lay women only a meager number of outlets, the Counter Reformation Church, with its Rosary confraternities and parish charities, gave them a greatly increased role to play.[17] Even if they remained subordinate to men in both religious and secular affairs, they had nonetheless gained new opportunities for religious activity. This fact helps explain the differences in female and male religious behavior that emerged from our analysis of pious bequests in wills. According to the wills, women outside Lyon gave far more fervid support to Counter-Reformation piety than did rural men. Other studies of pious bequests undertaken elsewhere in France tend to confirm these results: as late as the eighteenth century women usually left more to the Church than men.[18] No doubt the opportunities which the Tridentine Church created helped draw women to Counter-Reformation spirituality.

At the same time, the strife that erupted between priests and males in the parishes in all likelihood drove many men away from the new piety—hence their niggardliness toward the Church in their wills. The divergence between men and women disappeared inside the city of Lyon (a fact with parallels in other large cities such as Paris), but as we shall see, the urban parishes were much less likely to be visited by serious conflict between priests and their male parishioners. One reason is that in Lyon (and in other big cities) the youth groups and festive organizations controlled by men had by and large disappeared or been domesticated by the beginning of the seventeenth century. A major source of contention between laymen and the clergy had thus been eliminated, and with support for the Counter-Reformation morality entrenched among the city's male elite, urban men showed as fervent an attachment to Tridentine piety as their wives and sisters. Outside the big cities, by contrast, domineering male youth groups remained a power in parishes—a power often at odds with reformed curés. Perhaps the strife which the Counter Reformation generated between these rural laymen and their curés was one of the distant causes of the situation that later became so common in the countryside, where men withdrew from the Catholic Church and women remained its staunchest supporters.[19]

Traces of Discord in the Criminal Courts

These examples, culled from criminal records and analyzed here and in the previous chapter, are corroborated by diaries, parish documents, and other qualitative sources. In addition, the criminal records furnish actual quantitative evidence for the growing friction between priests and parishioners. Today, criminal prosecutions are usually initiated by the state, but in the Old Regime, most criminal cases were in fact, if not in theory, adversary proceedings between private parties. Although magistrates and public attorneys prosecuted criminal cases, they rarely acted on their own initiative. Instead, they merely responded to criminal complaints filed by individuals—mostly for insults and cases of physical assault. These complaints represented disputes that could no longer be settled by the private means (ranging from accommodation to fisticuffs) which almost all social classes preferred. The parties involved in these criminal cases covered practically the whole spectrum of society, despite a widespread aversion to court proceedings. Indeed, the profile of the people engaged in criminal cases does not differ greatly from that of the population as a whole. Since the criminal cases thus touched such a broad section of the populace and since they were such a common recourse in arguments that private means could not resolve, they are a superb indicator of social tension, of clashes and disputes that the social system could not contend with.[20]

Because many of our examples of discord have come from criminal cases pitting curés or vicars against parishioners, let us consider these cases as evidence of tension in the parishes. How often then did a curé or a vicar file a criminal complaint against one of his parishioners? How often did parishioners press criminal charges against their parish clergymen? And what proportion of criminal cases were of this type, involving either a priest who filed charges against a member of his congregation or the reverse? Since the parish clergy formed only a tiny fraction of the population, such criminal cases would never be frequent in absolute numbers. But if the reforms of the clergy and the campaigns of the Counter Reformation did aggravate the relationship between priests and parishioners, then such criminal cases would in all likelihood have grown more common relative to the total number of other criminal cases and relative to the priests' small numbers in the populace. Presumably, this increase in relative frequency would first become apparent late in the seventeenth century, when the reformed clergymen began to appear in the countryside in large numbers. Since priests remained faithful to the Tridentine standards throughout the eighteenth century, cases between priests and parishioners would continue to occur with high relative frequency until the end of the Old Regime.

The criminal records of the *bailliage* of Beaujolais, the major criminal tribunal and chief royal court of the region, bear out these presumptions. A survey of all surviving criminal cases heard before 1650 in the bailliage (cases actually existed only from the years 1604 to 1632) plus a large fraction of the surviving cases from the years 1651 through 1788—nearly twenty-two hundred criminal procedures, or two-thirds of those extant[21]—revealed a steady increase in the percentage of criminal cases pitting clergymen against their parishioners (table 9). Indeed, between the early seventeenth century and the last half of the eighteenth century, the frequency of such cases jumped over fourfold, from 0.88 percent before 1650 to 3.86 percent in 1751–88.

Table 9   Criminal complaints before
the *bailliage* of Beaujolais

	Percent of existing *liasses* in sample	Total cases in sample	Priest– parishioner cases	Priest–parishioner cases as percent of total in sample
Before 1650 (1604–32)	100%	114	1	0.88%
1651–1700	52%	760	20	2.63%
1701–1750	41%	695	20	2.88%
1751–1788	82%	621	24	3.86%

Source: Sample of criminal cases from AD Rhône, BBPC. For a description of the sample and a list of the *liasses* chosen, see appendix 2, part a, which also contains statistical evidence concerning the sample's accuracy.

The percentages involved may seem small, but parish priests formed well under 0.5 percent of the population in the diocese. Were priests represented in court cases only in proportion to their small numbers in the population, as seems to have been the case among many other social groups, we would expect to find them matched against their parishioners (either as defendants or as plaintiffs) in less than 1 percent of all criminal cases. The 3.86 percent figure for 1751–88 is so much higher than this that it could hardly be a result of chance—indeed, the odds against the 3.86 percent figure if the priests were drawn from the population at random would be less than one in a thousand.[22] Similarly, although the number of cases involved is small, the fourfold increase in frequency between the first period (before 1650) and the third period (1751–88) is also too large to be explained by chance alone.[23] It thus seems that, beginning in the late seventeenth century, the parish priests stood a greater and greater chance of being embroiled in criminal cases with their parishioners. The chances rose even higher after 1750, a phenomenon we will consider later in greater detail.

The increasing frequency of cases between priests and laymen constitutes one more piece of evidence that the Counter Reformation generated tension between priests and parishioners. Very few of these cases concerned the old, traditional issues that divided clergy and laity. The tithe, for example, was the cause of only a small and declining number of the criminal cases between priests and parishioners heard by the bailliage (table 10). The casuel and disputes over repairs to the rectory were equally insignificant. What was at issue in these cases was the same sort of problems we have been discussing: opposition to the priests' attempts to control local organizations, strife over religious reforms, conflict with local elites and youth groups.

Table 10   Priest–parishioner cases concerned with the tithe

	Priest–parishioner cases	Cases concerned with the tithe	Tithe cases as percent of all cases in sample
Before 1650 (1604–32)	1	1	0.88%
1651–1700	20	4	0.53%
1701–1750	20	3	0.43%
1751–1788	24	0	0.00%

Source: Random cluster sample of criminal cases from AD Rhône, BBPC. For a description of the sample and a list of the liasses chosen, see appendix 2, part a.

It could be objected that these cases concerned only a small number of the Beaujolais's parishes, despite the fact that the survey covered a period of more than a hundred years. Discord between priests and parishioners would thus seem to be only a minor problem. Although only a minority of the communities under the bailliage's jurisdiction reported criminal cases between priests and parishioners, the minority (42 out of 129 parishes) was substantial. Other records would certainly divulge additional instances of strife. In fact, the criminal cases are in many ways like the tip of an iceberg, for they reveal only the most severe cases of strife. Tension of a lower order was far more frequent and hardly a minor problem.

One might also protest that cases omitted from the sample or documents that have been destroyed could easily change or even reverse the results, that the trend we observed merely reflected changes in jurisdiction, such as the decline of ecclesiastical or seignorial courts, or that the Counter Reformation, far from creating strife, merely transformed the curés into litigious elitists who were eager to lodge criminal complaints instead of settling disputes informally. None of these objections, though, can in fact explain the growing frequency of criminal cases between priests and parishioners in the bailliage of Beaujolais.[24]

Criminal cases between priests and their parishioners, far from being unique to the Beaujolais, appeared in court records from spiritually fervid Forez too and in the documents of Lyon's *sénéchaussée*.[25] Indeed, a quantitative survey of criminal cases heard before the sénéchaussée produced results similar to those derived from the bailliage of Beaujolais, at least for the parishes in the sénéchaussée's jurisdiction that lay outside the city of Lyon. The voluminous criminal records from the sénéchaussée permitted a sample of criminal records from only a small number of years. The majority of these involved persons living in Lyon, but if these are set aside, the remaining cases from the rural parishes of the Lyonnais revealed a trend similar to that observed before the bailliage of Beaujolais (table 11). Cases pitting priests against parishioners rose from 2.1 percent to 5.6 percent of all the rural trials. Although the numbers involved here are so small that they could well be the result of chance, it is nonetheless significant that the trend at the sénéchaussée seems to parallel that observed at the bailliage.[26]

Of the cases heard before the sénéchaussée that involved residents of the city of Lyon, not one concerns a parish ecclesiastic (whether a curé, vicar, canon, or stipendiary priest) and one of his parishioners (table 11). Strife between parish clergymen and parishioners in the city of Lyon had commonly found its way into the criminal courts in the sixteenth century, but this no longer seemed to hold true in the 1700s. The city's seignorial courts too seemed free of criminal cases between the parish ecclesiastics and parishioners—or at least a survey of surviving records suggests so. The contrast between Lyon and rural areas of the diocese is striking. During the years 1777–82, for example, when our survey revealed no urban priest–parishioner cases before the sénéchaussée, fully 6.3 percent (8 of 127) of the surviving cases before the bailliage of Beaujolais pitted rural clergymen against their flocks.[27]

The lack of criminal cases between priests and parishioners in the city of Lyon does not mean that discord was completely unknown in urban parishes. Noël Chomel, the priest who played an active role in the Company of the

Table 11   Criminal complaints to the *sénéchaussée* of Lyon:
rural and urban cases

| | Total cases | Priest–parishioner cases | |
		Number	Percent
Before 1650	169		
Rural cases	47	1	2.1%
Urban cases	122	0	0.0%
1777 through 1782	556		
Rural cases	89	5	5.6%
Urban cases	467	0	0.0%

Source: Sample of surviving *plaintes criminelles* from the sénéchaussée of Lyon, at AD Rhône, B. For the period before 1650, all surviving cases were read (5 liasses). For the later period, 15 liasses were selected at random from the 49 surviving liasses. Appendix 2, part a, gives a description of the sampling technique and a list of the liasses chosen.

Note: All but 3 of the 169 cases for the first period were dated after 1609. A criminal case was defined as "rural" if both the defendant and the person filing the criminal complaint lived outside Lyon. In a few cases, the complaint was filed by the prosecutor, and it could not be traced back to any private citizen's accusation. In these instances, the case was "rural" if the defendant lived outside Lyon. All other cases were considered urban.

Holy Sacrament, argued with lay notables in his parish of Saint-Vincent over control of the vestry. The canons of Saint-Nizier fought with the artisans of the Confraternity of Pilgrims of Saint James over the right to name a chaplain for the group, which had its chapel at Saint-Nizier. And in the 1780s curé Demeaux of Saint-Pierre-et-Saint-Saturnin found that his parishioners refused to rebuild the rectory and construct a larger parish hall.[28]

But if conflict did occur from time to time in the parishes of the city, the evidence from the sénéchaussée at least suggests that by the eighteenth century it was less frequent than in the countryside and less likely to erupt into the sort of verbal or physical violence that would attract the attention of the criminal courts. To a large degree, this difference between city and countryside reflected the strong and early support that the Counter Reformation had won in Lyon. Early acceptance of resurgent Catholicism and the values it entailed had done away with the sort of lay–clerical strife that we observed in the sixteenth century. When conflict occasionally did erupt, as in the parish of Saint-Vincent, both sides regretted it and went to great lengths to stop it. This spirit of reconciliation in the city stood in sharp contrast to the mood in rural communities, where grudges and animosity could smolder for years. Moreover, enthusiasm for the Catholic Reformation among the urban elite proved particularly effective in eliminating the discord between priests and parish notables that was so common in rural parishes. Even late in the eighteenth century, after Lyon's elite had lost its cohesiveness and a bit of its religious zeal, after the old alliance between the Church and the city fathers had begun to break down, priests still encountered none of the intransigent hostility from parish notables that was so common in the countryside. Strife between priests and parishioners was therefore minimal in the city. Ecclesiastics in Lyon, as in other cities in France, spent more time feuding with one another than with the laity.[29]

The analysis of criminal records thus confirms that the Counter Reformation generated tension in the parishes but that it was less pronounced in Lyon than in the countryside. This raises the additional question of precisely which rural parishes were most likely to witness conflict between priests and parishioners. Furthermore, the results from both the bailliage and the sénéchaussée suggest that the relationship between priests and rural parishioners continued to worsen in the late eighteenth century. Since the Counter Reformation was firmly in place by this time, perhaps other factors aggravated the situation in the countryside. This conflict in the late eighteenth century does seem to have involved the same issues and the same antagonists as that earlier in the century; no qualitative change in the nature of the parish conflict is evident. But one wonders whether social change further polarized the priests' relationship with the laity. Did laymen grow more willing to resist the clergy? Did the priests' own behavior change and exacerbate their troubles with their parishioners?

At first glance, communities affected by the spread of rural industry or commercialized agriculture would seem most likely to suffer from strife between the clergy and the laity. We know that the manufacturing of textiles and the commercialization of crops such as flax and grapes created a new elite of rural merchants whose relationship with the parish clergy was far from cordial. Rural industry and the cultivation of commercial crops also boosted incomes—an economic change whose social consequences some curés deplored. In the western market town of Feurs, for example, curé Duguet lamented the disruptions brought on by the cultivation of flax. He complained that the traffic in flax "corrupted the peasant, because he wastes the money he gains . . . in the cabaret," and he intimated that the extra income made peasants uppity.[30] In the parish of Azolettes, the curé was even more explicit in his condemnation of the local effects of rural industry. He blamed the influx of money from manufacturing for the "depravity" that was rampant among his parishioners and for the fact that "the common folk" had become "extremely insolent." Rural industry, in his view, undermined the social hierarchy, corrupted the people, and destroyed the old moral order: "the people abandoned themselves to all the excesses of intemperance. . . . Drunk with prosperity, they no longer heeded their pastors. I understood then, better than ever before, why famine or at least scarcity like that of 1770–1771 and 1774 was less of an evil for the people than great abundance."[31] It was thus the destruction of his own authority and of his hold over the laity that most enraged this priest—or so his chilling words suggest. Obviously, if other priests shared the misgivings and fears of the curés of Feurs and Azolettes, we would expect to find more conflict between priests and parishioners in rural communities where industry was growing or agriculture was being commercialized.

The problem, though, is that not all priests viewed rural industry and commercialized agriculture with as much disfavor as the curés of Azolettes and Feurs. Curé Gacon of Neuville, for example, displayed a great interest in winemaking, and he was so favorably disposed to rural industry that, when the manufacture of coarse woolens collapsed in his parish in 1758, he spent his own time and money to reestablish it.[32] More important, the evidence from the bailliage of Beaujolais reveals no significant relationship between priest—parishioner strife, on the one hand, and rural industry or commercialized agriculture on the other. The parishes in the Beaujolais where conflict between clergy and laity broke out were neither more nor less likely than other villages to be engaged in textile manufacturing or the wine trade.[33]

In fact, only negligible social differences existed between those parishes in the Beaujolais where conflict broke out between priests and laymen and those which did not contribute a case to the criminal records we surveyed. The parishes in the Beaujolais which were troubled by such tension were neither more nor less likely to be cities and market towns. They do not appear to have been burdened with larger amounts of ecclesiastical property. And their curés were no more likely to hold tithe rights.[34] All that we can say about the geography of this tension is that the diocese's one large city, Lyon, seemed relatively free of the strife that wracked some rural parishes.

The Period after 1750

Although the issues over which conflicts erupted and the identity of the priests' adversaries did not change, tension between priests and parishioners increased after 1750. The only noticeable difference between parish strife before and after 1750 was that in the latter period a greater proportion of complaints were filed by parishioners than by curés (table 12). Apparently the laity grew more willing to oppose the clergy after 1750, and it was this willingness, not any new, qualitatively different sources of conflict, that accounted for the priest—parishioner cases after 1750.

But what made the laity more inclined to fight? Emmanuel Le Roy Ladurie has noted that peasants in eastern France showed a greater tendency to wrangle with their seigniors in the closing decades of the Old Regime. This contentiousness he considers to be the peasants' answer to the much discussed "seignorial reaction," and he attributes it to a cultural transformation of the peasantry: increased literacy and mobility, loss of respect for traditional authority, and a greater willingness to resort to legal remedies in disputes with local seigniors. Literacy and mobility among peasants in the diocese of Lyon also increased in the eighteenth century, and it seems likely that they underwent a similar cultural transformation.[35] If so, their rebelliousness could just as easily have been directed against the local curé as against (or in addition to) the seignior. And since village notables often led the opposition to the seignior, we would have a ready explanation for their disputes with the curé.

Table 12   Defendants in priest–parishioner criminal cases

	Priest–parishioner cases	Cases with lay defendant	Cases with priest as defendant
Before 1650 (1604–32)	1	1 (100%)	0 (0%)
1651–1700	20	17 (85%)	3 (15%)
1701–1750	20	16 (80%)	4 (20%)
1751–1788	24	10 (42%)	13 (58%)

Source: Random cluster sample of criminal cases from AD Rhône, B, Bailliage de Beaujolais, plaintes criminelles. For a description of the sample and a list of the liasses chosen, see appendix 2, part a.

Changing religious attitudes among the laity in the last half of the eighteenth century also facilitated opposition to the clergy. In studies of late-eighteenth-century testaments from various parts of France, Michelle Vovelle and other historians have detected a decline in the sort of religious stipulations that we associate with Counter-Reformation piety. Especially pronounced after the 1750s, this wholesale abandonment of pious donations, bequests for masses, and invocations of the saints in wills has usually been interpreted as a sign of what French historians call "dechristianization," although Vovelle is quick to point out that forsaking baroque piety did not necessarily mean abandoning Catholicism.[36] Whether it simply meant emphasizing internal religious conviction at the expense of the external gestures that had been so important in Counter-Reformation piety or whether it was indeed a sign of a more serious loss of faith, this dechristianization deeply affected the priests' relationship with the laity. In particular, it probably made conflict between clergymen and their parishioners all the more likely. Once laymen abandoned Tridentine piety, they had less need for their curé, less need for the masses, processions, and rituals that he performed. Opposing a curé whose importance had diminished so would not be so frightening, and resisting him would be even easier if dechristianization meant a serious loosening of religious bonds.

This explanation presupposes, of course, that dechristianization swept over the diocese of Lyon, which may seem an outrageous presumption given the way the phenomenon varied from region to region and from social class to social class in Vovelle's study of Provence.[37] After all, only a massive study of late-eighteenth-century wills for the diocese could determine for certain whether dechristianization touched all the communities where we observed strife between priests and parishioners. Nonetheless, the diocese did exhibit the same symptoms Vovelle and others noticed in Provence, Grenoble, and Paris. Religious vocations in the diocese dropped, both among the regular and the secular clergy. Most notable was the decrease in ordinations after 1760, a pattern with parallels in several other French dioceses. Such a decline no doubt disguised significant regional variations, and it could certainly be the result of economic change, such as expanding opportunities for younger sons, rather than any loss of faith. Yet as Timothy Tackett and other historians have persuasively argued, the decline in ordinations is partly attributable to dechristianization.[38]

Dechristianization in the diocese manifested itself in other ways as well. In the city of Lyon, illegitimate births increased after 1760, and confraternities founded during the Counter Reformation lost their appeal. At Saint-Vincent in Lyon, participation in the Confraternity of the Blessed Sacrament declined after the 1760s. The parish of Sainte-Croix had experienced difficulty in getting parishioners to join in the procession of their Blessed Sacrament confraternity even earlier, in the 1740s. Religious education as envisaged by the dévots also lost support, and by the end of the century, the city's cultural elite seemed to have abandoned some of its commitment to the Church. These lapses so concerned Archbishop Malvin de Montazet that in 1776 he issued a pastoral letter against skepticism.[39]

Symptoms of dechristianization were not confined to the city. In Neuville, the parish celebrated royaumes in honor of six saints at the beginning of the eighteenth century. By the end of the Old Regime, the number had dropped to three. Other rituals and observances characteristic of Counter-Reformation piety also suffered. Curé Jean Roux, the pastor of the village of La Balme, to the southeast of Lyon, complained in 1773 that the chapel of the Virgin in his parish, which had once drawn numerous pilgrims, was no longer popular. Under Roux's predecessor, the devotion had supported four priests, but by 1773 it attracted hardly a soul. Roux lamented the general decline of religion as well. Applauding Montazet's letter on skepticism, he bemoaned the fact that religion no longer "amounts to anything, so to speak. There is none of it among the rich; and among the common people, very little."[40]

Each of these symptoms, from the decrease in the number of vocations and the rise of illegitimacy to the decline of the shrine of La Balme, admits of several explanations, some of which have nothing to do with a decline in Counter-Reformation piety. Increased economic opportunity for younger sons, we mentioned, could account for the decline in vocations. By the same token, a growth in the number of women of childbearing age could inflate the number of illegitimate births, and the popularity of new shrines might have occasioned La Balme's decline. Yet running through all of these various symptoms is a common theme, and men like Roux and the archbishop seem right to have diagnosed them as evidence of dechristianization. Although dechristianization no doubt varied from place to place within the diocese and according to social class, it probably affected many segments of the diocese's population. Since dechristianization entailed diminished need and respect for the parish clergy, it paved the way for greater discord in the parishes.

There are thus several reasons to believe that laymen were more willing to oppose the parish clergy in the late eighteenth century. Conceivably, the clergymen themselves also bore some of the responsibility for the increased conflict after 1750. One possibility is that some change in clerical recruitment or in the priests' social behavior exacerbated their difficulties with the laity. For example, the geographical recruitment of the parish clergy may have changed, leading to greater difficulties with parishioners. We know that priests in the sixteenth century were natives of the regions which they served as pastors and that this fact helped them win acceptance in insular rural communities. By contrast, nonnative clergymen were less likely to sympathize with local customs, and they lacked the kinship ties that might restrain them from making attacks on local institutions. The naming of a pastor from outside the community occasionally unleashed strife between priests intent upon imposing the policies of the Tridentine Church and parishioners resolved to defend local traditions. Jean Genebrier, the first nonnative in living memory to serve as curé of Saint-Just-en-Chevalet, quarreled bitterly with the Penitents of his parish.[41] If nonnative priests tended to behave like this in other parishes, then a sudden influx of such clergymen in the late eighteenth century would help explain the increase in tension we observed.

Some evidence does exist to support this hypothesis. Saint-Just-en-Chevalet was not the only parish which saw outsiders supplant natives in the rectory.[42] Moreover, one of the major sources of native priests in the diocese's towns and small cities—the *sociétés de prêtres*—came under attack from the diocesan hierarchy. Apparently the archbishops wanted to break the sociétés' local roots, and they did so in a way that prevented the sociétés from performing their traditional role of furnishing native clergymen. To begin with, episcopal ordinances of 1678 and 1681 required that the priests in the sociétés serve at least one year as vicars in another parish. A later ordinance of 1749 extended this period to four years and made it extremely difficult to enter a société. The effect was to break the lockstep pattern which saw youths in communities with sociétés enter the priesthood and then join the sociétés in their home parishes.[43] In addition to the new rules affecting the sociétés, a more general shift in the priests' geographic recruitment seems to have taken place between the sixteenth and the eighteenth century. Local recruitment had not disappeared by the eighteenth century, but it had declined in importance (table 13), whereas recruitment from more distant parishes (those more than fifteen kilometers away) had grown more widespread. Unfortunately, the data do not indicate that the decline of local recruitment worsened in the late eighteenth century. The change in the curés' geographical origins helps explain some of the conflict between priests and parishioners, but it sheds little light on the worsening of the situation after 1750.

If changes in geographical recruitment cannot explain the increased tension in the later eighteenth century, could changes in the priests' social origins be the answer? After all, a shift in recruitment toward higher social classes could have aggravated the priests' troubles with the laity. Fortunately, there exist documents, known as patrimonial titles (*titres patrimoniaux* or *titres cléricaux*), that can answer this question. Required of every young man ordained as a subdeacon since the days of the Council of Trent, the patrimonial titles were notarial acts guaranteeing that the cleric had a yearly income sufficient to live on until he received his first benefice. Although the titles were occasionally merely affidavits certifying that the ordinands already had a benefice, the vast majority were annuities that paid a required yearly amount (40 livres in 1577, 100 livres in 1614, and still more in the eighteenth century) and that had usually been funded by the ordinand's father or brother.[44] The titles thus permit us to identify the ordinand's family origins.

Merely setting up a patrimonial title required a substantial amount of capital. The yearly payments alone equaled the incomes of poor families, and this fact served to restrict ecclesiastical recruitment to the well-to-do. Therefore it is understandable that in the late eighteenth century the subdeacons (and apparently those who later became curés were no different) were born into families in what we might call the local economic elite. Only a minority came even from well-to-do peasants' families (*laboureurs,* for example, or in certain regions, like the Monts du Forez, the peasants known as *habitants*). Fewer still belonged to the propertyless army of artisans, sharecroppers, day laborers, and domestics that made up a majority of the population in much of the diocese. They were instead sons of the local elite. Their fathers and brothers were merchants, bourgeois, officeholders, lawyers, and notaries.

Priests from such a background may have encountered difficulties in dealing with peasants and common people, but unfortunately there is no sign

Table 13 Geographic recruitment of curés:
sixteenth and eighteenth centuries

	Sixteenth-century curés	Combined early- and late-eighteenth-century curés	Early-eighteenth-century curés	Late-eighteenth-century curés
Native of parish within 5 kilometers of community served	7 (29%)	4 (12%)	1 (9%)	3 (13%)
Native of parish between 5 and 15 kilometers from community served	8 (33%)	10 (29%)	2 (18%)	8 (35%)
Native of parish more than 15 kilometers from community served	9 (38%)	20 (59%)	8 (73%)	12 (52%)
Column totals	24	34	11	23

Source: All but one of the twenty-four sixteenth-century curés were taken from a study of *prises de possession* in the diocesan *insinuations,* AD Rhône, 4 G 108 (1576–77) and 4 G 111–116 (1579–94). One other was found in an attempt to track down ordinands from the 1586–1601 ordinations, AD Rhône, 1 G 54, by using a file of diocesan curés at A Diana, 2 J 7. For the two later periods the prises de possession are no longer accompanied by documents giving a curé's native parish, and a different method had to be used. What I did was to take young men receiving the tonsure and trace those who later became curés, using A Diana, 2 J 7. Ordination lists provided names and home parishes for those receiving the tonsure. I also used A Diana, 2 J 7, to track down future curés among young clerics who filed *titres patrimoniaux,* an attestation of financial resources required for receipt of the subdeaconate. The early-eighteenth-century curés came from the December 1693 through December 1694 tonsure lists (AD Rhône, 1 G 62) and from titres found in AD Rhône, 4 G 146–149, the ledgers of ecclesiastical insinuations for 1691–1717. Because these curés were all ordained either late in the seventeenth century or early in the eighteenth century, all were serving in the 1720s and 1730s. The late-eighteenth-century curés, men who served in the 1770s and 1780s, were traced from a list of tonsure recipients in 1760 (AD Rhône, 11 G 73) or from titres compiled from the ecclesiastical insinuations for 1759–62 (AD Rhône, 4 G 169–70).

whatsoever that clerical recruitment was any different in the late eighteenth century (table 14). In fact, recruitment of curés from the local elite, which also occurred elsewhere in France, had probably been the practice for nearly two hundred years.[45] The curés' social origins did not shift in the eighteenth century. As in the past, the priests continued to come from the more prosperous classes.

Table 14   Social origins of the secular clergy according to the
Titres Patrimoniaux, 1691–1717 and 1759–62

	Ordinands' families according to 1691–1717 *titres*	Ordinands' families according to 1759–62 *titres*	Families of ordinands known to have become curés (both periods)
Nobles, *officiers,* lawyers, magistrates	17 (25%)	12 (14%)	3 (12%)
Merchants, bourgeois, notaries, surgeons	43 (62%)	52 (63%)	17 (68%)
Master artisans	3 (4%)	5 (6%)	2 (8%)
Laboureurs, fermiers, habitants, vignerons	5 (7%)	11 (13%)	3 (12%)
Artisans	1 (2%)	3 (4%)	0 (0%)
Column totals	69 (100%)	83 (100%)	25 (100%)
Titres bearing no information on ordinand's family	21	6	—

Source: AD Rhône, 4 G 146–149 (1691–1717) and 4 G 169–170 (1759–62). The ordinands known to have become curés were tracked down through the index of diocesan curés, in A Diana, 2 J 7.

Note: The families were classified by father's order or occupation, or, if the father was not mentioned, by the brother's. Some of the rural merchants who appear so frequently in the above tally might in fact have been merely wealthy peasants. In addition, the meaning of some of the other occupational labels varied from place to place in the diocese and over time as well. In the Beaujolais, a *vigneron* was a sharecropper, but the few vignerons in the above list came from areas of the diocese where vignerons were property-owning peasants. *Habitants* were also usually prosperous peasants, but by the late eighteenth century the word had begun to take on its current meaning of "resident."

While the priests' social origins remained the same, their social behavior nonetheless changed in a way that heightened tensions after 1740. As the century wore on, curés acquired a taste for more elegant dwellings that set them apart from the mass of the peasantry. In their view, they were merely claiming the sort of housing that was their right under government regulations. Royal legislation in the late seventeenth century had obliged parishes to find suitable housing for their curés, and in the eighteenth century both royal courts and the intendants, who supervised the construction of rectories, established standards for the curés' lodging. These standards provided for what was, by rural standards, rather sumptuous housing, and we accordingly find eighteenth-century curés inhabiting the sort of dwellings usually reserved for parish notables: large furnished houses with two stories and five or so rooms, hung with tapestries and paintings and well stocked with furniture.[46]

Peasant dwellings in the diocese were far more humble. Even though they had grown more spacious since the sixteenth century—perhaps a second story was added and the stables were separated from the living quarters—it was unusual for an eighteenth-century peasant to inhabit a house with as much furniture or as many separate rooms as the curé's rectory. Peasants actually resented the clergy's expensive lodging, and they considered fancy rectories an extravagance, since they were the ones who had to pay the considerable expenses of construction or remodeling. For these reasons, peasants and other parishioners often resisted when their curé sought to remake a rectory that he considered substandard or when he endeavored to build a spacious new house worthy of his status in the community. They complained to the intendant and often refused to pay the costs of construction. Some of the resulting quarrels lasted for years.[47]

Strife over the parish clergy's quarters goes as far back as the fifteenth century, and many of these disputes merely reflected an impoverished community's inability to pay for even the simplest construction.[48] Nonetheless, the eighteenth-century arguments over housing created a new sort of tension that may well have contributed to the upsurge in priest–parishioner conflict after 1750. The parishioners considered the priests guilty of extravagance, and the priests felt that the laity was denying them their due.

Examples abound to illustrate these divergent views of what was appropriate lodging for a priest in the late eighteenth century. In Brussieu, for instance, curé Beyle encountered stiff resistance when he sought to have the rectory repaired in 1787. Although part of his request concerned simple repairs, Beyle's chief grievance was that his vicar had to sleep in the attic, and many of his other complaints about the rectory seemed largely aesthetic. "No part [of the rectory] is like any other," he said, "neither in width nor in height, which makes it very difficult to use and even dangerous, given the lack of windows to illuminate the interior." The parishioners of Brussieu, evidently not sharing their curé's aesthetic sensibilities, maintained that the vicar's quarters were not an attic but a bedroom (no doubt because they themselves were accustomed to sleeping in lofts), and on the whole they felt that the rectory was completely "suitable." They therefore refused to pay for any repairs, leaving poor Beyle to mutter that "today prisons are larger and have better ventilation. Prisoners who have been condemned to death can breathe pure air in their dungeons, yet a citizen, a priest charged with the service of his parish, finds only putrid air and quarters less salubrious than a jail."[49] Parishioners elsewhere proved equally adamant in resisting the curé's desires for more dignified housing. The inhabitants of Neuville-sur-Ain, including the notables and nonresident property owners, told new curé Bottex in 1777 that the repairs he desired were "exorbitant" and that save for some masonry work, his requests were for "luxuries." In Pizay, when curé Mayfred asked in 1771 that his quarters be enlarged, the town's inhabitants and taxpayers angrily charged that Mayfred was vying with other profligate curés in a reckless contest of conspicuous consumption.[50]

Despite all these troubles with their parishioners, priests after 1750 continued their efforts to dominate the parishes and stamp out popular culture. What motivated them to press on in the last half of the eighteenth century? Was it merely faithful adherence to the ideals of the Tridentine Church, ideals that were still drummed into the priests during their time in the seminary?[51] Or were there additional forces that caused priests to persevere or even to redouble their efforts in the closing decades of the century? If so, we would have yet another partial explanation for the increase in tension after 1750.

Jansenism is one possibility. Stern Jansenist morality would certainly encourage priests to take even stronger stands against festivals and "superstitions" in their parishes, and in some areas of France Jansenist austerity had even driven people from the Church.[52] Jansenist priests and Jansenist influence were certainly not lacking in the diocese of Lyon in the eighteenth century. When in 1736 Jacques Charles Dutillieu, later a wealthy silk maker, came to Lyon as an apprentice, his devout master designated as his confessor an austere priest who made him read Quesnel's *Réflexions morales,* the Jansenist work condemned by the papal bull *Unigenitus* (1713), as well as a number of works by Jansenist authors such as Pierre Nicole and Antoine Arnauld. Perhaps even more Jansenists appeared later in the eighteenth century, for Archbishop Montazet was reputed to have made Lyon a haven for them during his thirty-year tenure as head of the diocese (1758–88). Montazet brought Jansenists to local religious communities and to the faculty of Lyon's seminaries, and he authorized a theology, a catechism, and other works that allegedly showed Jansenist tendencies. In 1782 he even required all candidates for the priesthood to spend a year at the seminary of Saint-Joseph, which was known to be tainted by Jansenism.[53]

Yet the archbishops who preceded Montazet had worked against Jansenism in the diocese, and Montazet could not have done much to reverse their accomplishments and influence large blocks of the parish clergy. More important, Jansenism took so many forms in the late eighteenth century and accusations of Jansenism were tossed about so freely that it is difficult to say what Jansenism encouraged, much less whether it led to greater tension between priests and parishioners.[54]

Finally, we must recognize that some of the curés who were most determined to stamp out festivities were staunch anti-Jansenists. Curé Forestier of Chassagny was such a priest. Disturbed by immorality in the countryside, he was one of four curés from the diocese who sought an injunction from the Parlement of Paris against popular festivities and celebrations of youth groups in the Lyonnais. Yet this dour pastor was deeply opposed to Jansenism. He disliked Archbishop Montazet because of the measures the prelate had taken against the orthodox Sulpicians in Lyon, and upon the death of Christophe de Beaumont, a bishop who had been one of Jansenism's most notorious opponents, Forestier lamented his demise and praised him as the "hammer of Jansenists."[55]

Jansenism may have had some small effect on the priests' determination to carry on the battle in the parishes, but there was a force more powerful than Jansenism that was definitely steeling the curés' resolve as the Old Regime came to a close. This force was a new, more exalted conception of their own importance which was gathering currency in the curés' ranks. The parish priests were gaining the conviction that they had a greater role to play in the secular world. In part, their growing esteem and sense of social mission were results of the Counter Reformation itself. Although the clerical reforms had forced parish priests to withdraw from unseemly contact with the world, they also vested the priests with a great deal of authority, instilled in them a tremendous sense of the clergy's importance, and called on them to exercise their influence in nearly all local organizations, from schools and charities to parish vestries. In part, too, the priest's grander self-conception owed something to the Enlightenment: Voltaire, for one, praised rural curés in his *Dictionnaire philosophique* as potentially useful functionaries in the countryside. Similar assertions occurred in the writings of Turgot and the physiocrats and in the works of a number of minor philosophes. Some parish priests at least were well acquainted with this literature.[56]

But the greatest source of the parish priests' inflated opinion of their own purpose and mission was a noteworthy reform movement gaining adherents among the curés in Lyon and a number of French dioceses. In the last half of the century, curés throughout France leagued together against the Church hierarchy in order to better their material lot and obtain a greater say in Church government. By 1789 this "insurrection of the curés" led the parish priests to ally with the Third Estate, an action that helped to launch the

French Revolution. Clearly, the "insurrection" enjoyed the sympathy of much of the laity, for the members of the Third Estate shared the curés' desire that the lower clergy receive a greater share of the Church's income and that the tithe be spent at the local level instead of being paid to the upper clergy. Throughout France the *cahiers* drawn up by the Third Estate in 1789 supported the curés and their demands.[57]

What is important to us, though, is another, less appreciated aspect of the curés' reform movement. With all due justice for the parish priests and their insurrection, it nevertheless seems that the reform movement encouraged the curés' sense of self-importance and hardened their determination to dominate the parishes and stamp out popular culture. Paradoxically, although the insurrection prepared the way for tactical union with the bourgeoisie in 1789, it also gave the priests additional impetus to defy popular resistance in order to enforce the ideals of the post-Tridentine Church.

To a large extent, this movement among the curés stemmed from their material grievances. In the diocese of Lyon and elsewhere in southeastern France, the main issue was the level of the *portion congrue,* the small salary that tithe owners paid to curés without tithe rights, who formed the majority of the parish clergy in this region. Fixed by royal edict at 300 livres in 1686, the value of the portion congrue had been eroded by inflation in the eighteenth century, and by the 1760s, groups of curés in the Lyonnais and in other southeastern dioceses were petitioning the agents general of the French clergy (the French clergy's legal agents) for an increase in the salary rate. Dissatisfied with their financial situation, the petitioners voiced their resentment of the upper clergy's riches and demanded a more equitable distribution of the Church's wealth. Wryly noting that even the Protestants gave their ministers a living wage, the curés who signed one of the petitions from the diocese of Lyon bemoaned the fact that it was common "for parish priests, who are so useful, to languish in poverty on a 300-livre portion congrue, while for a long time there has not been a single chapter or collegiate church that has failed to do justice to its own lower clergy by increasing wages and honorariums."[58] The curés were angered that they, the most "useful" members of the clergy, wallowed in relative poverty, while canons and priors did nothing and lived in luxury.

In 1768 a royal edict raised the portion congrue by 200 livres, but this amount, a compromise arrived at by the upper clergy, left the curés unsatisfied.[59] Indignation at their own lack of power in the Church only compounded the curés' grievances and led parish clergymen to think of themselves as a body apart from the canons and the rest of the upper clergy. Shared educational experiences, a common social background, and assemblies such as the ecclesiastical conferences encouraged this sense of solidarity. So did the parish priests' habit of socializing with one another: the Counter Reformation had discouraged the clergy from mixing with the laity, so they met with one another to talk, have dinner, or mourn a colleague's death.[60]

As anger and resentment forged the parish clergymen into a movement for reform, the priests began to develop a body of arguments to justify their demands for change. In 1776 in nearby Dauphiné, a province whose clergymen were at the forefront of the insurrection of the curés, one of the leaders of the movement, curé Henri Reymond of Vienne, published a book, *Les droits des curés,* which would become a handbook for disgruntled parish priests throughout France. To defend the curés' demands, Reymond drew, first of all, upon a theological doctrine known as Richerism, which Jansenist priests had invoked in the first half of the eighteenth century in order to resist the upper clergy's attempts to impose the anti-Jansenist bull *Unigenitus.* According to Richerists, the curés were successors of the seventy-two disciples of Christ, just as the bishops were the spiritual heirs of the apostles. The curés were therefore divinely sanctioned ministers in the Church, and, by contrast, the canons and priors, whose wealth the curés resented, merely held posts that had been instituted by man. Reymond also made use of non-theological arguments. In particular, he stressed the utility of the curés, not only to the Church, but to society as a whole. The curés, he claimed, were ideal functionaries, especially in the countryside, where they ensured the people's happiness, guarded against popular sedition, and maintained morality in the face of irreligion.[61]

Among the curés in the diocese of Lyon, the reform movement developed more slowly than it did in Reymond's Dauphiné, in part because Archbishop Montazet was sympathetic to the curés. Nonetheless, parish priests in the diocese were aware of Reymond's work, and they agreed with his arguments concerning the dignity and social utility of the lower clergy. Copies of Reymond's book found their way into curés' libraries, and in 1789, when Montazet had been replaced by the hostile Bishop Marbeuf and open conflict had erupted between the curés and upper clergy, some of the curés of the diocese even wanted to elect Reymond their delegate to the Estates-General in Versailles. Furthermore, at the assemblies where the diocesan ecclesiastics chose delegates for the Estates-General, the curés stridently asserted arguments similar to Reymond's. These curés were influential in drawing up the clergy's cahiers throughout the diocese, and almost without fail the cahiers demanded a redistribution of the Church's wealth to benefit the parish clergy, who were uniformly depicted as functionaries of great utility to society.[62]

The insurrection obviously bolstered the curés' sense of mission and purpose. It also reaffirmed their commitment to the campaign against popular culture, for this campaign, insofar as it was conducive to social stability, constituted ready evidence for the arguments concerning the lower clergy's utility which the curés repeatedly invoked during their insurrection. The battle against popular culture thus served to justify the priests' demands for money and a voice in the ecclesiastical hierarchy, and the curés therefore gave strong support to measures against popular culture in the clergy's cahiers of 1789. Disturbed by the progress of "irreligion," local curés asked in the cahiers that cabarets be policed, that laws against prostitution and gambling be enforced, that festivals with dancing be outlawed, and that "superstitious" practices in rural chapels be stamped out.[63]

This unwavering opposition to popular culture explains why at the end of the Old Regime curés throughout France deluged the *procureur général* of the Paris Parlement and other officials with requests for the suppression of festivals, concubinage, and prostitution. The procureur général, though, was not entirely eager to accede to the priests' demands. Repeatedly, he warned his subordinates and the local magistrates to beware of meddling and "outrageous pretentions" by curés who demanded legal action. He even admonished some of the clergymen that their overzealousness was causing them to interfere in private matters, such as adultery, where governmental intervention was neither prudent nor necessary.[64] Evidently, the procureur and other secular authorities were no longer wholly committed to enforcing traditional morality, no longer dedicated to maintaining the old fusion of civil law and moral obligation which the dévots and the monarchy had created in the seventeenth century. Perhaps the magistrates had been seduced by the Enlightenment or perhaps they had succumbed to the increasingly secularized view of politics that was gnawing away at the monarchy's innards in the last decades of the Old Regime. In any case, their opinions placed them miles apart from the curés, who showed no inclination whatsoever to abandon the harsh old morality created by the Counter-Reformation Church. How ironic that the reform movement among the curés, which originated as a means of enlarging the priests' role in secular society, would create a cultural gap between the clergymen and secular authorities![65]

If the reform movement gave the curés added impetus to press the campaign against popular culture, it may have also contributed to the pernicious elitism prevailing among the parish clergy in the eighteenth century, an elitism that made accommodation with parishioners all the more difficult. The Counter Reformation had of course helped create this paternalistic elitism by forcing the priests to withdraw from contact with the laity and then forming them into a local elite. The curés' insurrection and the other eighteenth-century developments we have examined reinforced this lamentable trend. An eighteenth-century curé who dwelled in a home that suited the local notary and who had no relatives in the region he served obviously found himself at a greater distance from his parishioners than did his predecessors. Were he to imbibe the heady notions of the parish clergy's importance that were circulating during the insurrection of the curés, the social gap and his own sense of superiority would seem greater still. Elitism would be greatest of all in the countryside, given the attachment priests had to urban culture. The curés themselves might have considered their attitude toward the peasants merely a benevolent form of paternalism, but it could easily shade off into hostility, as in the case of curé Duguet of Feurs, who wrote that "the peasant is stupid and lazy." Comparable hostility and elitism permeated a fiery speech that curé Souchon of Sainte-Foy-l'Argentière gave before the Lyonnais clergy at its assembly for the Estates-General of 1789. In what was the most radical address delivered in favor of the Lyonnais curés, Souchon warned that without an increase in the portion congrue, the Church would find it impossible to attract suitable gentlemen who would serve in country parishes and "scour" the souls of recalcitrant peasants.[66]

Despite the extraordinary outpouring of sympathy for the priests in the cahiers of 1789, rural folk considered this priestly elitism an unjustified pretension. Their admiration for a priest's character, education, and high moral standards could thus be tinged with indignation, if they believed that he had risen above his appointed place in the community hierarchy, that of "servant of the parish." Elitist priests, in short, were liable to be considered usurpers who had climbed too fast, and the rural congregations rejected their claims to authority. An incident in the parish of Monsols in Beaujolais was typical. In the midst of a heated dispute before the doors of the parish church, the village curé, one François Ficat, told Benoit Bachot, the peasant's son he was arguing with, that he ought to show some respect for his pastor. This proved too much for youthful Bachot to bear. Cursing, he screamed at the priest that "he did not recognize the curé in any way . . . and that he owed him no respect at all, not even that of extending him his right hand." Warning Ficat that "he had certainly put other curés in their place," he called him a "bum," whereupon the curé plucked off Bachot's hat and flung it to the ground. The gesture carried a message, for French peasants doffed their hats only for authorities they acknowledged. Bachot's refusal to remove his cap only emphasized that he did not recognize the curé's authority.[67] Flinging the hat to the ground was a desperate attempt by the curé to seize the respect that he felt was his due, but Bachot and many other lay people were never willing to accord overweening curés such an honor.

We thus end with one of the tragedies of the Counter Reformation. The Tridentine reforms of the clergy had created a new local elite, an elite for which there was a great need in the fractured society of Old Regime France, and, indeed, of Old Regime Europe. These were priests endowed with confidence and ability, priests devoted to the welfare of their parishes, priests whose commitment to "political" reform was so great that at the end of the Old Regime they were battling with the Church hierarchy. Their alienation from the upper clergy even led them to seek a tactical alliance with the Third Estate at the onset of the Revolution. But these Tridentine reforms were bought at no small expense. Parish clergymen were isolated from society, and at the end of the Old Regime their dogged efforts to enforce the morality of Trent did not even have the support of secular authorities. Worse still, the priests' labors on behalf of the Church risked alienating significant numbers of laymen, despite the goodwill that some reformed priests won in the parishes. By cutting the priests off from the laity, the Counter Reformation crippled their effectiveness as leaders and laid the seeds of future hostility toward the Catholic Church.

6
Conclusion

The Civil Constitution of the Clergy, the radical dechristianization of the Terror, and, in Lyon, the brutal suppression of the federalist rebellion—these and other events of the Revolution marked a dramatic break with the past and drastically affected the relationship between clergy and laity. To be sure, some of the social divisions of Old Regime religion persisted amidst the revolutionary turmoil. In Lyon and in other parts of France, for example, women by and large remained fervently attached to Catholicism, going so far as to defend refractory priests against Jacobin attackers.[1] At the same time, however, the reaction against revolutionary events in many instances completely buried older difficulties between priests and parishioners and even created new bonds of affection between them. In any case, the Revolution raised a host of novel problems for the curés and utterly transformed their lives.

What light then do the experiences of the curés shed upon the Counter Reformation as a whole? We saw that before the Tridentine reforms were put into effect the clergy in parishes outside Lyon enjoyed a close relationship with the laity. Curés and vicars socialized freely with their parishioners, and neither their education nor their behavior set them apart from lay people. They danced at parish festivals, dined at the banquets of the Holy Spirit confraternities, and blessed the *royaumes* and the celebrations of village youth groups. Even their priestly functions drew them closer to the life of the community. The masses they said, the sacraments they administered, and the paraliturgical rituals they performed reinforced communal solidarity. And despite their sacerdotal powers, the rural priests did not elevate themselves above their parishioners.

In the city of Lyon, by contrast, relations between the priests and the laity were far more strained in the pre-Tridentine era. Clerical misbehavior offended broad segments of the city's lay population, while social barriers divided immigrants and the common people from Lyon's secular clergy. Furthermore, Catholicism in Lyon had fallen victim to a spiritual crisis, which cast doubt upon the sacerdotal role played by urban priests. Worst of all, Lyon's laic tradition embittered the clergy's dealings with the city elite.

With the outbreak of the Wars of Religion, though, the clergy's stormy relationship with the elite in Lyon suddenly changed. The need for solidarity against the Protestants and the incipient drive to reform the Catholic Church united the canons and priests who held sway over the city's parishes and the hard-line Catholics who came to dominate the municipal government. The bonds between the city's clerics and the urban elite grew even stronger in the seventeenth century. Lay *dévots* from Lyon's political and social elite shared the urban clergy's commitment to Tridentine spirituality and to the ascetic, rigorous ethic of the Counter Reformation; moreover, they saw in the Catholic Reformation a means of imposing political control and an urban sense of order upon the countryside. Joining Lyon's clerics in organizations such as the Company of the Holy Sacrament, the laymen worked with the diocesan hierarchy to found schools and charitable organizations, and they helped the hierarchy undertake a vast campaign against popular culture.

The lay dévots and the diocesan hierarchy also cooperated in the reform of the parish clergy, striving to establish seminaries and retreats for diocesan priests. The aim of these reforms was not simply to train clergymen who were better educated and better behaved, but to transform the priests into agents who could institutionalize the Counter Reformation in the countryside. These new curés were to promote Counter-Reformation spirituality in the villages and to aid the dévots and the diocesan hierarchy in their battle against popular culture. Trusted intermediaries in the parishes, the reformed curés would assuage the urban elite's fears of the turbulent peasantry and help maintain social control at a time when even the strongest of monarchs lacked armies large enough to patrol every village.

By the eighteenth century, curés who met these standards had finally come to occupy rectories in every corner of the diocese. The reformed priests were far better educated, and their behavior had dramatically improved. They labored to spread Counter-Reformation piety in the parishes, establishing new devotional confraternities and working to prune away older devotions and rituals that had fallen into disfavor. Moreover, they enthusiastically supported the campaign against popular culture. They took steps to suppress royaumes, Holy Spirit confraternities, and parish festivals, and they sought to replace parish celebrations with sober religious ritual. And in the name of resurgent Catholicism, they defended the social and political hierarchy.

Unfortunately, the reform of the clergy and the priests' new sense of mission were all purchased at a high price. Although the new curés and vicars were educated, although they were in many cases men of character, the reforms strained their relationship with the laity, especially in the countryside. Forbidden to socialize with their parishioners, they nevertheless arrogantly tried to dominate village life and sought to reshape it to conform to Tridentine ideals. The result was tension and even overt strife, which left traces in the records of criminal courts. The conflict pitted the priests against village notables and male youth groups, who were determined to protect communal institutions and customs from clerical interference. After 1750, the situation worsened, for dechristianization and, ironically, Richerism only exacerbated the problems the priests faced in adhering to the ideals of Trent.

What then do the priests' experiences say about the Counter Reformation as a whole? In the first place, if the reforms of the clergy are indicative, the Counter Reformation was a long, slow process fraught with setbacks and difficulties. Not until the late seventeenth century were seminaries firmly established and reformed curés common outside the cities. Moreover, the achievement of the Tridentine program produced grave problems for the relationship between priests and parishioners.

Second, it is wrong to say that the Counter Reformation was in its entirety imposed upon the faithful. To be sure, priests and lay dévots attempted to force the Tridentine ethic upon parishioners in the countryside, but popular resistance often condemned this campaign to failure, not just in Lyon but elsewhere in Catholic Europe as well.[2] The more successful undertakings of resurgent Catholicism were those which built upon popular enthusiasm and favor. This was true, for example, of the spread of Counter-Reformation spirituality. It triumphed because the laity as a whole supported elements of the new piety and because certain individuals—urbanites, the literate, rural women—embraced it with particular fervor.

Finally, evidence from Lyon and from the rest of Catholic Europe demonstrates that the Counter Reformation was very much an urban movement.[3] It began in the large cities, where all of its telltale markings, from devotional confraternities to novel devotions, first appeared, and then spread to the small cities and market towns and finally to the villages. It drew enthusiastic support from urban lay elites, and it sowed their religious sensibility and their harsh ethic in the countryside. And it served their interests, both religious and political.

These opinions concerning the Counter Reformation obviously invite comparison with that other great urban movement of religious change, the Reformation. Admittedly, the Counter Reformation and the Reformation were so different that they almost defy comparison. They had radically different theologies, antithetical views of the clergy, and dissimilar bases of social support. Yet despite all of these differences, there were some similarities between the Protestant and Catholic reformations. To begin with, the Reformation itself was not accomplished overnight, and the Protestants encountered their own difficulties, especially when they tried to convince peasants to abandon popish "superstitions." Furthermore, it is evident that both reformations were urban movements. Even if we allow for the guiding hand of the Roman hierarchy, the Counter Reformation, like the Reformation, drew its major support from the cities.[4]

More important, both reformations promoted an urban sense of order and a harsh new ethic that extolled modesty, thrift, diligence, and self-control. In addition, both waged war upon popular culture. To be sure, Calvinist consistories were far more severe in their attack on popular celebrations. Catholics tried to salvage customs that the Protestants denounced as idolatry or vain idleness, and in order to replace what it had suppressed, the Catholic Church promoted religious rituals (processions of the Eucharist, for example) which Protestants considered only new varieties of idolatry. In this sense, the Protestants attempted a far more thorough reform of popular culture. Yet the fact remains that both the Catholic and the Protestant reformations sought to discipline the populace, to rob it of worldly diversions, joy, and levity. The desire to "disenchant" the world, to borrow a phrase from Max Weber, thus cut across confessional lines and was shared by Protestant and Catholic reformers alike, even after we allow for the cult of the saints and the florid Roman ritual. This desire was characteristic of city dwellers in general (save for the common people), not just of those who professed any single creed.[5] Both the Counter Reformation and the Reformation can therefore claim credit for whatever progress the reshaping of popular culture ultimately entailed. But both must also bear responsibility for the gloomy discipline that zealots sought to force upon an unwilling populace.

The Counter Reformation, like the Reformation, thus joins one of the major currents of the social, economic, and political history of early modern Europe: the extension of urban rule over rural communities. Besides saying the mass and administering the sacraments, the parish priests served as agents of urban elites who sought to bring the countryside under control. Along with merchants and tax collectors, curés and vicars helped bind the towns and the villages to the cities.

Appendix 1
Tobit and Probit Analysis of the Wills

At a time of growing disillusionment with quantitative methods, it hardly seems propitious to advocate the use of sophisticated statistical techniques in historical research. Traditional historians argue that historical data (particularly if it antedates the nineteenth century) cannot bear the weight of elaborate statistical analysis, and in any case most quantitative specialists themselves seem to get by with only the crudest of tools.[1] Why waste time then on what some perceive as superfluous and overblown "numerology"?

The fact is, though, that a number of advanced statistical methods could be of great assistance to historians, not the least because they provide an additional source of precious evidence. Chief among these methods are ways of dealing with poorly measured quantities: techniques for so-called limited dependent variables, such as logit, probit, and tobit analysis. Developed chiefly by econometricians, these techniques have proved extremely useful in situations where better-known methods, such as regression analysis, do not really apply. Unfortunately, even many quantitative specialists in the historical profession remain ignorant of these tools, despite the fact that they are ideally suited for historical work. More often than not they are precisely the techniques a historian ought to use when records have been destroyed, the evidence is incomplete, or the matters of interest have been imperfectly recorded. Indeed, these methods belie the argument that rickety preindustrial data cannot bear the weight of advanced statistics. Bad data actually turn out to need the advanced methods more than good data, and crumbling historical records in fact cry out for mathematical sophistication.[2]

In this appendix, I will describe how two of these techniques—tobit and probit analysis—can be applied to the pious bequests and to the other testamentary stipulations discussed earlier in the book. The appendix presumes no knowledge of statistics, and it requires only that the reader be familiar with the treatment of wills given earlier. Readers interested in a more technical approach or desirous of further information about how tobit and probit are used may consult two papers I have written: "Pious Bequests in Wills: A Statistical Analysis" (Social Science Working Paper 393, California Institute of Technology, 1981) and "Wills and Statistics: Tobit Analysis and the Counter

Reformation in Lyon," *The Journal of Interdisciplinary History* 14 (1984): 813–34. We will begin our examination of tobit and probit by looking at the sample of rural wills treated in chapter 4; we will then turn to the urban testaments discussed in chapters 1 and 4. In what follows, I label any demand for masses, any bequest to the Church, or any charitable donation a pious bequest.[3] My reason for doing so is that all such acts were encouraged by the Church, and the testators in both samples were all at least nominal Catholics.

The first factor that influenced a testator's decision to make a pious bequest was wealth. Masses and other pious legacies cost money, and testators noted that their net worth limited their ability to make religious bequests in their wills.[4] Greater wealth therefore rendered pious legacies more likely; it also allowed a testator to reserve more money for any religious and charitable legacies he made. Similarly, unmarried sons and daughters would tend—all other things being equal—to restrain a testator's pious donations, for he would in all likelihood feel compelled to provide more for his children at the expense of his own soul. Pious bequests may also have been related to the testator's age. If religious preferences changed, if men grew to favor religion, for instance, then older testators who were born before the shift might well lag behind and bequeath less to religious causes. Finally, we want to know whether pious bequests changed over time and whether they were more likely to occur (other things being equal) among women or the literate than among men or the illiterate. This means testing whether religious and charitable legacies depended on time, gender, and literacy.

The problem, of course, is to untangle the separate effect of all these factors, from wealth to literacy, which simultaneously influenced each testator. For example, did increased pious donations among the literate merely reflect their greater wealth or were they in fact a sign of a greater propensity to give? Similarly, did pious bequests actually rise over time, apart from any growth in the testators' wealth or any decrease in competing demands by unmarried children? The difficulty is that literacy, wealth, and all the other factors bearing upon a testator's decision were interrelated. As a result, simple techniques, such as tables and graphs, are likely to be deceptive. A table showing that, say, literate testators gave more than the illiterate may suggest something about literacy, but it could also simply reflect the fact that the literate were wealthier. Fortunately, tobit analysis resolves such problems, for it allows us to gauge the independent influence of all the variables which influenced a testator's behavior. And it takes into account the effect of wealth and the other variables both on the likelihood of making a pious bequest and on the size of any bequest made.

Tobit analysis has the further advantage of freeing us from a number of worries about the way wills are sampled: whether the sample is "representative," whether it is random or nearly so, and whether the changes we observe merely result from shifts in the sample's composition. My sample of rural wills, for example, was constructed by first selecting communities in the Lyonnais and Beaujolais where a large number of notarial records had been preserved from the sixteenth, seventeenth, and early eighteenth centuries. From these records, I then drew notarial registers at random and read all or nearly all the testaments in each one. The result was not a random sample of individual wills, and it may well fail to be completely representative. But this does not matter for tobit analysis, which corrects for variations in the composition of the sample. If there are more wealthy testators in one period or one notarial register, for example, tobit takes this into account.[5]

Applying tobit to the rural wills, I recorded for each will the total amount reserved for pious bequests, which was obviously zero if the testator made no religious or charitable legacies. I corrected for the effects of inflation or devaluation by dividing the monetary figures by a ten-year average index of grain prices with the 1590s as a base period.[6] For each testator, I also noted the various explanatory variables of interest: the year, the testator's sex, whether he could sign his name (as a mark of literacy), and the number of his unmarried children (as a measure of the number of dependent heirs whose demands would have to be met out of the estate).[7] The wills do not tell us precisely what a testator's age was, but by noting grandchildren, grandnephews or nieces, or other second generation collateral descendents, I was able to get a crude measure that distinguished the elderly from those middle-aged or younger.

Wealth was more difficult to measure. The wills do not record the total value of a testator's estate, and so we are forced to make do with approximate measures. Fortunately, the wills do provide three excellent approximations. The first uses information on the testators' occupations. Tax records and marriage contracts provide an estimate of the average wealth for any occupation, and the list of occupations in the countryside was full enough to distinguish between, say, landless agricultural laborers (*ouvriers, journaliers*), yeoman farmers (*habitants*), and wealthy landowners (*sieurs villageois*). The tax and marriage records suggest that testators fell into three broad categories of wealth: an elite at the top (including, for example, officials and sieurs villageois); a middle group, the *coqs du village* (among the occupations here were artisans and habitants); and finally the peasants, among whom we find people from *vignerons* to domestics. We simply assign a testator to a wealth category according to his occupation.[8]

The second approximate measure of a testator's wealth—or "wealth proxy"—is the total value of cash bequests to family, friends, and religious or charitable institutions in the will. While this proxy overlooks the value of property not mentioned or given a cash value, evidence from Paris suggests that it was nonetheless roughly proportional to a testator's net worth. Lyonnais tax records and marriage contracts tend to bear this out, and the wealth proxy derived from the total cash in a will is entirely consistent with that derived from the testator's occupation.[9]

The third wealth proxy comes from those wills that mention dowries for unmarried daughters. If we multiply the average dowry by the total number of a testator's heirs, we get an approximate measure of his wealth (or at least something roughly proportional to his net worth), provided the testator did not discriminate inordinately against his daughters. Some testators might indeed have gone out of their way to shortchange girls: they could leave the family farm to one son to keep it undivided, for example. Legal historians might add that such favoritism would be all the more common in the Lyonnais, where the *droit écrit* gave each testator great freedom to favor his "universal heir." In practice, however, the testators were surprisingly egalitarian, so on average this third proxy derived from dowries yields an excellent index of wealth, which agrees with the two other approximate measures. The son who got the undivided family farm, for instance, was usually saddled with the task of paying his sisters' dowries and so ended up with a smaller share of the estate than one might suppose. Even if we assume that each testator departed as far as possible from egalitarianism in the treatment of his daughters by giving each girl only the *legitime* (the minimum fraction of his estate allowed by law), then we still get an index of wealth that is hardly different from our third wealth proxy and that yields nearly identical results.[10]

Approximate measures of wealth affect the tobit results, but not significantly. The proxies are good enough to let us filter out the effects of wealth, and their use does not significantly disturb what tobit reveals about the other variables. There are some complicated statistical reasons for thinking so, but perhaps the best argument is that all three proxies yield nearly identical results with tobit analysis.[11]

Table 15 reveals how closely the tobit results for each of the three proxies agree. For each explanatory variable, tobit generates a coefficient that serves to measure the effect the explanatory variable has on both the size and the likelihood of pious bequests. These are the numbers such as the .701 opposite "year" in the first column of table 15. A positive coefficient means a positive effect: the explanatory variable boosts both the chances of a pious legacy and its magnitude.[12] A negative coefficient implies the reverse, and the larger the size of a coefficient the greater the magnitude of the effect.

The tobit analysis also produces a number called a t-statistic for each coefficient (these are the numbers in parentheses), and the t-statistics reveal whether the effects we observe are likely to be statistical flukes. If a t-statistic is small, then the relationship between the corresponding explanatory variable and pious bequests is likely to have occurred by chance and should be ignored. If, on the other hand, the t-statistic is large, then the effect is probably not a chance result. In particular, if the t-statistic exceeds 1.96, then the odds of the relationship being a statistical illusion are less than 1 in 20, or

Table 15 Tobit estimates for pious bequests in rural wills, 1512–1737

Explanatory variable	Wealth proxy I: occupations	Wealth proxy II: total cash	Wealth proxy III: dowries
Constant	-1198 (-11.26)	-1148 (-10.91)	-1163 (-6.81)
Wealth variables			
X^1 (elite)	46.2 (3.35)	—	—
X^2 (*coqs du village*)	14.0 (1.76)	—	—
T (total cash)	—	3.82 (1.72)	—
D (heirs x dowry)	—	—	12.1 (3.97)
Other explanatory variables			
Y (year)	.701 (10.94)	.674 (10.61)	.678 (6.65)
S (sex−women)	13.5 (1.94)	19.2 (2.77)	20.6 (2.00)
L (literacy)	26.7 (2.33)	47.7 (4.83)	29.3 (2.05)
A (old age)	-28.1 (-1.76)	-29.9 (-1.88)	-40.4 (-1.35)
K (children)	-4.06 (-2.14)	-5.71 (-2.96)	-5.05 (-1.84)
Number of testators	576	544	244
s	61.00	61.37	56.68

Note: The figures in parentheses are t-statistics. The number of testators varies from proxy to proxy because of missing values, and all monetary figures are reduced to constant value *livres*.

X^1 = 1 for members of elite; 0 otherwise
X^2 = 1 for *coqs du village*; 0 otherwise
T = Total bequests which are given a cash value in will (units of value 1,000 livres)
D = Total number of heirs times average dowry (units of 1,000 livres)
Y = Year
S = 0 for males, 1 for females
L = 1 for those who can sign, 0 for those who cannot sign
A = Age dummy; equals 1 if testator has grandchildren, grandnephews or nieces, or second generation cousins
K = Number of unmarried children
s = Estimated standard deviation of equation error term

5 percent. This is what is meant by "statistically significant at the 5 percent level."

In table 15 the coefficient of the year Y is positive for all three wealth proxies. The t-statistics are all large (10.94, 10.61 and 6.65) and significant at better than the 1 percent level. This implies that the relationship between pious bequests and time is not likely to be a fluke. The positive sign of the coefficients means that pious bequests rose over time, and because the wealth of the testators and the demands of their heirs have been taken into account, the increase in bequests cannot result from having more prosperous testators or fewer heirs as time goes on. The fact that the coefficient of Y varies only slightly from wealth proxy to wealth proxy lends credence to the view that our approximate measures are on the average fairly good indexes of a testator's net worth.

The signs and magnitudes of the coefficients of the other variables are also roughly the same for all the proxies, which further confirms our faith in our approximate measures of wealth. In addition, sex and literacy have a positive and statistically significant effect on pious bequests. Women gave more and were more likely to give than men, all other things being equal; similarly, literate testators outdid illiterate ones of equivalent wealth. Finally, the negative coefficient for K is significant at better than 5 percent for the first two wealth proxies, though not for the third. Dependent children evidently did force a testator to choose between them and his soul.

The actual meaning of the coefficients in table 15 is difficult to explain without mathematics, but we can convert the coefficients to numbers that anyone can understand.[13] The coefficients, we noted, measure in some sense the effect a given independent variable has on pious bequests. For each coefficient, we can actually calculate the magnitude of this effect by estimating how much a one-unit difference in the explanatory variable would change both the likelihood and the size of pious bequests. I have done this for selected explanatory variables in table 16. Since the results turn out to be similar for all three proxies, I used the second one (total cash) for the calculations. The calculations assume that all explanatory variables are set equal to their average values and that the one in question is then changed by one unit.[14]

We can see, for example, that on average the likelihood of making a pious bequest rose 0.355 percent each year, or approximately 4 percent each decade. The value of pious bequests increased 0.174 *livres* a year. Women were 10.1 percent more likely to give than men of equivalent wealth, and they gave 4.9 livres more. The literate, *ceteris paribus,* left 12.3 livres more than the illiterate, and a literate testator was 25.1 percent more likely to make pious bequests than an otherwise identical illiterate person. In fact, it is these figures that allow us to make comparisons of testamentary behavior with wealth and the number of heirs held constant.[15]

Table 16 Effect of unit change in selected explanatory variables on pious bequests in rural wills, 1512–1737

Explanatory variable changed by one unit	Resulting change in likelihood of bequest (percent)	Resulting change in size of bequest (constant value *livres*)
Year	0.355	0.174
Sex–women	10.1	4.9
Literacy	25.1	12.3

Note: All independent variables have been set equal to their means. For purposes of comparison, the average pious bequest in rural wills was 36.02 livres, and 50 percent of testators left donations overall.

Several refinements can be made in this analysis of the rural wills. To begin with, we can ask whether variations in the "cost" of religious services influenced the testators. Having a mass said required a certain minimum offering, which served as the "price" of the mass. It may of course seem anachronistic to impose this economic terminology upon a religious decision, but the testators themselves would not have thought so. In fact, they were terribly concerned with the process of paying for masses and the expense of prayers and other religious services.[16] The only reason that the minimum offering needed for a mass was not included earlier in the analysis was that it varied only slightly in real terms. As a first approximation, it was reasonable to treat it as a constant. When the price is added to the tobit analysis, its coefficient is negative, as we would expect—a higher minimum offering would restrict pious bequests. The lack of variation, however, keeps it from being statistically significant (table 17). Treating the cost of a mass as constant and leaving it out of the analysis (as we shall do with our other sample) therefore seems very reasonable indeed.

Two other explanatory variables cannot be dismissed so easily, though. One is the population of the testator's community. Since market towns and small cities had more priests, preachers, and churches per capita, their residents no doubt experienced more frequent proselytizing. As a result, the population of a testator's community had a significant positive effect on pious bequests (table 17).

Similarly, an index of economic expectations also had a noticeable effect on pious bequests (table 17). The reason is easy to understand. Our approximate measures of wealth merely suggest what a testator's fortune was at one time. They do not indicate whether his net worth had been rising or falling or what

**Table 17 Tobit estimates for pious bequests: rural wills
with additional explanatory variables, 1512–1737**

Explanatory variable	Coefficient	T-statistic
Constant	-1259	-11.34
T (total cash)	4.66	2.12
Y (year)	.749	10.93
S (sex–women)	18.8	2.73
L (literacy)	36.8	3.60
A (old age)	-30.2	-1.90
K (children)	-5.13	-2.70
Index	.303	2.64
Population	2.73	2.31
Price	-24.4	-1.03
Number of testators	544	—
s	60.14	—

Note: The estimates have been made with wealth proxy II. "Index," the change in local agricultural lease rates, serves as a rough measure of economic expectations; taken from Joseph Goy and Emmanuel Le Roy Ladurie, *Les fluctuations du produit de la dîme* (Paris, 1972), p. 158, it is the change in the *rente foncière* of the chapter of Saint-Paul. "Population," the number of households in the testator's community at the end of the seventeenth century (units of 1,000 hearths), is an indirect measure of population; it is taken from Maurice Garden et al., *Paroisses et communes de France. Rhône. Dictionnaire d'histoire administrative et démographique* (Paris, 1978). "Price" is the minimum offering needed for a mass in constant value livres. Other variables and units of measurement are as in table 15.

his expectations were for the future. If the economy was collapsing and the future looked grim, a testator might well rein in his pious bequests so that he would have more left to provide for his heirs.

This, in fact, is precisely what testators did when a traumatic agricultural depression struck the Lyonnais at the end of the 1670s. Agricultural output plummeted over 40 percent; it did not recover until the 1690s.[17] Pious bequests dropped too. Only 32 percent of the wills mentioned pious bequests in 1675–99, versus 45 percent in 1650–74, and the drop coincided with the onset of the depression. If we use the fluctuations of local agricultural lease rates as an index of economic expectations (an assumption that makes perfect sense in a rural area), we see that the relationship between economic expectations and pious bequests does seem statistically significant (table 17). Moreover, the index drops enough in the late 1670s to account for most of the temporary decline we observed among pious bequests between 1650–74 and 1675–99. Indeed, given the decline in the index and a shift in some of the other explanatory variables, we would expect a drop in pious bequests of 17 percentage points in the last quarter of the century—a figure very close to the 13 percent drop actually observed. We could expect similar changes in pious bequests whenever the lease index varied: a 100-point drop in the index would translate into an average of 16 percent fewer pious bequests and 7.7 fewer livres for bequests that were made.[18]

Having examined the sample of rural wills at some length, we can quickly present the results of a similar analysis of urban wills. The urban sample was constructed in much the same way as the rural one, except for the fact that I selected notaries from the city of Lyon and read only those wills which had been drawn up by residents of the city. Furthermore, testators who manifested any signs of Protestantism (avowed allegiance to the Reformed Church, requests for burial in the Protestant cemetery, etc.) were excluded; the testators were all nominal Catholics. Once again all monetary figures were deflated using the index of grain prices.[19] The only difference between my treatment of the urban and rural samples was that I divided the urban one into two groups: the wills drafted before 1596 and those drawn up in 1596 or after. I did so because the questions I wanted to ask of the sixteenth-century wills (Did pious bequests decline? Was this decline reversed among the elite?) were quite different from those raised by the post-1595 wills (Was there a broad-based increase in support for the Church?).

Table 18 presents the results of a tobit analysis of pious bequests in wills drawn up before 1596 (i.e., those discussed in chapter 1), using total cash legacies (proxy II) as a measure of wealth.[20] It also contains an analysis of donations to the testator's parish. From the t-statistics and the negative signs of the coefficients for the year, we see that pious bequests as a whole and legacies to parishes in particular declined over the sixteenth century. The depression Lyon suffered in the late sixteenth century does not explain this decline, for when two indexes of the state of Lyon's economy and economic expectations were inserted into the tobit analysis, neither one could account for the drop in pious bequests or legacies to parishes. The two indexes I added were real wages and interest rates. Although neither of these indexes is as good an indicator of economic expectations as the agricultural lease rates used with rural wills, wage and interest rates should suggest what a testator could expect himself or his heirs to earn from labor and capital. When they were included in the tobit analysis of the pre-1596 urban wills, though, their t-statistics were far from significant.[21]

Two other explanatory variables in the tobit analysis deserve explanation. One, "immigrants," measures the difference between newcomers to Lyon and natives. As we can see, immigrants gave significantly less to parishes than did otherwise identical natives (table 18). The second variable, "interaction," tests whether the wealthy behaved differently from the rest of the populace after 1555. The positive sign and significant t-statistic suggest that among the elite

Table 18 Tobit analysis of urban wills, 1521–95

Explanatory variable	Pious bequests	Legacies to parishes
Constant	11300 (2.43)	5450 (9.62)
T (total cash)	38.0 (5.75)	1.79 (2.71)
Y (year)	-7.48 (-2.51)	-3.53 (-9.70)
S (sex–women)	111 (0.86)	32.5 (2.18)
L (literacy)	381 (2.95)	17.3 (1.15)
A (old age)	44.2 (0.19)	36.7 (1.44)
K (children)	-39.1 (-0.73)	2.76 (0.48)
Immigrants	148 (1.03)	-80.8 (-4.30)
Interaction	3.60 (2.88)	0.281 (1.98)
Number of testators	319	319
s	999.55	100.29

Note: The figures in parentheses are t-statistics. Monetary amounts are reduced to constant value livres. All variables and units are as in table 15, save for:

Immigrants = 1 for persons born outside Lyon, 0 otherwise.

Interaction = T times Y for Y greater than or equal to 1555, 0 otherwise (units of 100,000 livre-years). This variable detects a wealth–time interaction after 1555; it is simply a mathematical way of seeing whether pious bequests started to rebound among the rich after 1555, while they were still falling among the poor.

the decline in pious bequests slowed and was even reversed after 1555. Further analysis indicates that this turnaround among the elite probably occurred between 1555 and 1576.[22]

We can, of course, use the tobit coefficients to estimate how much changes in individual explanatory variables would affect pious bequests and legacies to parishes. Table 19 presents the results of such calculations, for variables of interest in chapter 1. We see, for example, that the size of pious bequests dropped approximately 3.6 livres each year, or roughly 72 livres in twenty years. Similarly, an immigrant was some 28 percent less likely to bequeath money to his parish than a native of equal wealth, and he left approximately 24 livres less on average as well. These figures form the basis of the comparisons made in chapter 1.

Table 19 Effect of a unit change in selected explanatory variables: urban wills, 1521–95

Explanatory variable changed by one unit	Resulting change in likelihood of a pious bequest (percent)	Resulting change in size of pious bequest (constant value *livres*)	Resulting change in likelihood of a parish legacy (percent)	Resulting change in size of parish legacy (constant value *livres*)
Year	-0.3	-3.62	-1.2	-1.06
Immigrants	*	*	-28.1	-24.27

*Not significant at 5 percent level.

Note: Variables are defined in tables 15 and 18, and all variables have been set equal to their average values. The mean pious bequest in urban wills before 1595 was 220.62 livres; overall, 70.5 percent of urban testators before 1595 left bequests. For legacies to parishes in the same wills, the averages were 26.34 livres and 42.6 percent.

Finally, we can apply another statistical technique, probit analysis, to the urban testators' requests for processions or other funeral rites. Probit analysis resembles tobit analysis, except that it applies to phenomena like the funeral requests, for which we know whether a testator demanded a certain rite but not how much he spent on it.[23] In short, probit analysis simply tries to explain the likelihood of testators' requesting various funeral rites, given that we lack the sort of monetary information available for pious bequests. In table 20, we find results of a probit analysis for two of the stipulations testators made for their funerals: asking for processions and for the attendance of the secular clergy. The explanatory variables are the same as those in the tobit analysis of pious bequests, and the coefficients and t-statistics have a similar interpretation. In particular, we should note that demands for both processions and secular clergymen dropped in the sixteenth century. Furthermore, immigrants were significantly less likely to request the attendance of secular

Table 20 Probit analysis of requests for selected funeral rituals in urban wills, 1521–95

Explanatory variable	Requests for processions	Requests for secular clergy's attendance
Constant	28.454 (3.83)	41.954 (4.96)
T (total cash)	.231 (1.33)	.00079 (0.096)
Y (year)	-.0190 (-3.96)	-.0278 (-5.10)
S (sex—women)	.222 (1.27)	.225 (1.13)
L (literacy)	.619 (3.53)	.707 (3.68)
A (old age)	.709 (2.35)	.623 (2.00)
K (children)	.121 (1.75)	.128 (1.81)
Immigrants	-.234 (-1.17)	-.573 (-2.26)
Interaction	.00075 (0.42)	.0028 (1.65)
Number of testators	320	322
-2 x log likelihood ratio (chi square, 8 degrees of freedom)	59.56	65.04

Note: The figures in parentheses are t-statistics. Number of cases varies due to missing values. All explanatory variables and units are as in tables 15 and 18.

clergymen; the same holds for a number of other funeral rites as well, such as having psalms said. Differences or changes in wealth do not explain these phenomena, and adding interest rates or real wages to the probit analysis does not account for them either.[24] Nor was there any reversal of the decline in traditional funeral rites among the upper classes, for the interaction terms are insignificant.

Let us finally consider the urban wills drawn up after 1595—wills discussed in chapter 4. Pious bequests in general and legacies to parishes in

Table 21 Tobit analysis of seventeenth-century urban wills

Explanatory variable	All pious bequests 1636–1702	Bequests to parishes 1636–1702	Charitable bequests 1596–1702
Constant	-9150	-9810	20100
	(-2.64)	(-4.93)	(1.62)
T (total cash)	29.3	.868	47.4
	(11.14)	(1.01)	(5.42)
Y (year)	5.39	5.78	-14.0
	(2.59)	(4.86)	(-1.85)
S (sex—women)	3.24	-30.1	195
	(0.04)	(-0.76)	(0.44)
L (literacy)	102	-26.4	1440
	(1.06)	(-0.61)	(2.89)
A (old age)	-162	123	-504
	(-0.97)	(1.88)	(-0.62)
K (children)	-115	-7.55	-309
	(-3.67)	(0.56)	(-1.96)
Immigrant	22.2	-112	-896
	(0.16)	(-1.38)	(-1.30)
1616–35	—	—	1180
			(2.06)
Number of testators	179	179	267
s	503.52	165.08	2655.13

Note: The figures in parentheses are t-statistics. The variable "1616–35" equals 1 for the years 1616–35; 0 otherwise. All other variables and units are as in tables 15 and 18.

particular rose sharply in the last two-thirds of the seventeenth century—
hence the positive and significant coefficients for the year among wills drawn
up after 1635 (table 21). We can calculate that the average testator's pious
bequests grew 26.2 livres per decade; the likelihood of his making religious
or charitable legacies increased nearly 4.3 percent every ten years.[25]

As for the first third of the seventeenth century, it was a time of special-
ized legacies, such as the foundation of new religious houses or charitable
institutions. We see traces of this if we look at the tobit analysis of charitable
bequests, where an additional variable, "1616–35," reveals a special upsurge
of charitable giving during the years 1616–35 (table 21). Finally, unlike the
rural wills, urban wills reveal no sign of any great difference between the
bequests of men and those of women. This holds both for the seventeenth-
century testaments and (with the exception of parish bequests) for the wills
drafted before 1596.

The tobit and probit analyses have thus confirmed a number of important
trends: a decline in bequests in sixteenth-century Lyon, a turnaround among
urban elite, and a more general surge of pious bequests in the seventeenth-
century city and countryside. Tobit and probit have also unearthed a number
of groups who departed from the norm. Besides the well-to-do in the city, we
noted the extraordinary behavior of urban immigrants, the literate, and rural
women, among others. The significance of these results is discussed in chapters 1 and 4.

Appendix 2
The Evidence from Criminal Records

Part a: The Samples of Criminal Records

Since the *plaintes criminelles* of the *bailliage* of Beaujolais and those of the *sénéchaussée* of Lyon were too numerous to read *in toto*, I chose to rely upon samples, which were made large enough to provide me with all the accuracy I needed. An actual random sample of individual complaints was unfeasible, and I therefore decided to resort to cluster samples of the *liasses* in which the complaints were grouped. This involved choosing liasses at random and then reading them in their entirety. For more on the rationale behind this particular sampling process, see Hoffman, "Church and Community," pp. 388–90.

The liasses from the bailliage of Beaujolais were arranged chronologically but not yet permanently classified. In what follows I therefore give both the provisional *cote* for each liasse and the period it covered. I began by reading all the surviving liasses from the period before 1650: there were only two, namely 1 (1604–23) and 2 (1624–32). Second, I selected liasses at random for each of the three subsequent periods (1651–1700, 1701–50, 1751–88) by using a table of random digits and the provisional cotes assigned each liasse. After selecting a liasse, I went through all of the complaints in it. For the 1651–1700 period, I chose the following 12 liasses from the 23 that survived: 3 (1661–70), 4 (1671), 5 (1672), 6 (1673), 8 (1677–81), 9 (1682), 11 (1685), 12 (1686), 13 (1687), 20 (1695), 21 (1696), 24 (1699). For 1701–50, I chose 12 of the surviving 29 liasses: 27 (1702), 28 (1703), 29 (1704), 35 (1711–12), 36 (1713–14), 43 (1728), 44 (1729–30), 47 (1734), 50 (1737–38), 51 (1739–40), 55 (1746–47), 57 (1749–50). Finally, for the 1751–88 period, I read 14 of the surviving 17 liasses: 58 (1751–52), 59 (1753–54), 60 (1755–56), 61 (1757), 63 (1760–61), 64 (1762–63), 65 (1764–66), 67 (1769–70), 68 (1771–76), 69 (1777–78), 70 (1779–80), 71 (1781–82), 73 (1785–86), 74 (1787–88). All of these documents can be found at AD Rhône, B, bailliage de Beaujolais.

Since I read all the surviving liasses for the first period (before 1650), there was no doubt about the percentage of priest–parishioner cases at the bailliage of Beaujolais prior to 1650. For the three subsequent periods, though, the sample was not complete, and one can wonder about the errors which the sampling process introduced into our estimates for the percentage of priest–parishioner cases at the bailliage. A simple way to gauge the magnitude of these errors is to estimate standard deviations for the percentage of priest–parishioner cases in the three periods 1651–1700, 1701–50, and 1751–88. Such standard deviations provide a measure of how much the percentage of priest–parishioner cases would be likely to change were I to include other liasses in the sample, and they can be calculated using an approximation for the standard error from a cluster sample of percentages (see Hoffman, "Church and Community," p. 389, for details). The standard deviations I calculated (0.33 percent for the period 1651–1700, 0.52 percent for 1701–50, and 0.33 percent for 1751–88) all turned out to be very small.

More important, we can use these standard deviations to construct 5 percent lower confidence limits for the percentage of priest–parishioner cases. Intuitively, there is less than a 5 percent chance that the real percentage of priest–parishioner cases lies below these lower confidence limits. For 1651–1700, 1701–50, and 1751–88, the 5 percent lower confidence limits turn out to be, respectively, 1.16 percent, 0.55 percent, and 2.38 percent, if we make a conservative assumption and merely use the Chebyshev inequality. All but one of these very conservative estimates is above the 0.88 percent frequency observed for the cases before 1650; if we assume normality, we get 5 percent lower confidence limits that are higher still: 2.04 percent, 1.96 percent, and 3.28 percent. Thus we can say with great confidence that the observed higher frequencies after 1650 are not quirks of the sampling process.

I also constructed a cluster sample from the voluminous records of the sénéchaussée of Lyon. For the period before 1650, I read all 5 existing liasses of plaintes criminelles (they are listed here with provisional cotes and are to be found in AD Rhône, B, sénéchaussée de Lyon): BP 2838 (1609–24), BP 2839 (1625–29), BP 2840 (1630–38), BP 2841 (1588–1645), BP 2842 (1640–56, which I read through 1650). For the 1777–82 sample (designed to match a preliminary survey of cases from the bailliage of Beaujolais), I read 15 liasses selected at random from the 49 which survived from the years 1777 through 1782: BP 3440 (July 1777), BP 3441 (Aug. 1777), BP 3443 (Nov.–Dec. 1777), BP 3445 (Jan. 1778), BP 3447 (April 1778), BP 3753 (January 1779), BP 3458 (Aug.–Sept. 1779), BP 3459 (Oct.–Nov. 1779), BP 3463 (April 1780), BP 3465 (June 1780), BP 3466 (July–Aug. 1780), BP 3472 (June–July 1781), BP 3476 (1777–82), BP 3479 (March–May 1782), BP 3482 (Aug.–Oct. 1782).

In addition to the samples from the bailliage and the sénéchaussée, I read a number of cases from the *maréchaussée* of Lyon, in AD Rhône, B. I went through liasses B 5 and B 6 (the liasses covering the years 1688–1720), liasse B 10 (the assassination of the curé of Avenas in 1723), and B 76–82 (1777–82). These documents are catalogued chronologically, and the cotes are provisional. Finally I examined the records of several *petites justices*. Some were subject to the bailliage of Beaujolais, and their archives are in AD Rhône, B, unclassified but arranged chronologically: Jarnioux, Juliénas, Montmelas, Oingt, Saint-Lager. For these justices, I examined the records from the periods 1500–1650, 1715–20, and 1777–82. I did the same with the petite justice of Ampuis (also in AD Rhône, B, but subject to the sénéchaussée of Lyon), and with the following seignorial justices whose records are in the ecclesiastical archives at AD Rhône: Anse (10 G 1902–04), Ile-Barbe (10 G 3151), Saint-Just (12 G 362, 386–88, 417), Brignais (12 G 873), and Savigny (1 H 83). Finally, using the excellent printed inventory of the *série* B at the AD Loire, I managed to work through a wide variety of criminal, civil, and police records from royal and seignorial justices in Forez and Roannais, and from the maréchaussées of Forez and Roanne.

Part b: Objections to the Use of the Criminal Records

This section of the appendix answers three objections to the way criminal records from the bailliage of Beaujolais were used in chapter 5. A far more detailed treatment of these matters is available in Hoffman, "Church and Community," pp. 327–34.

The first objection concerns criminal cases omitted from our sample and documents which have been lost or destroyed. Had these missing documents been included in our sample (so the argument goes), they might have changed our results. In particular, they might have reversed the trend we observed toward a greater percentage of cases which pitted clergymen against their parishioners. This objection, though, suffers from some serious flaws. First of all, expanding the sample to include the omitted cases would probably not have yielded significantly different percentages. This follows from the low standard deviations and the high 5 percent lower confidence limits given in part a of this appendix.

It is also unlikely that the loss or destruction of court documents could have affected our findings. Records are undeniably missing, but to assume that the loss and destruction of documents produced the trend we observed would be to suppose that the rats, mold, and unthinking men who ravaged the archives somehow chose to single out cases involving parish priests for preservation in the eighteenth century. If we instead make the more reasonable assumption that documents were preserved through a random process of selection, then we can invoke the same sort of statistical argument used to discuss the possibility of chance results in our sample. And this statistical argument, which remains valid no matter how many thousands of court documents were destroyed, leads to the following conclusion: the likelihood that the random destruction of documents would account for the different frequency of priest–parishioner cases between the first period (before 1650) and the fourth period (1751–88) is only .07.[1] In short, the differences we observed are not likely to be quirks of fate.

A second objection concerns the way in which the increasing percentage of priest–parishioner cases is interpreted. Instead of being a mark of greater tension in the parishes, the higher percentages might simply result from the fact that the Counter Reformation had made the priests more litigious. By improving the curés' education and elevating their status in the parishes (so one could argue), the Counter Reformation would have made it easier for the priests to seek recourse in the courts. In particular, they would have found it easier to bear the monetary and social costs of litigation. As a result, they would have ceased to settle everyday disputes with parishioners by informal means and would have instead simply filed criminal complaints. The problem with this objection, though, is that it does not fit the evidence. If it were valid, we would expect to find a growing fraction of cases in which priests had filed criminal complaints. This was simply not what happened. The percentage of cases with priests as plaintiffs actually declined over the course of the seventeenth and eighteenth centuries. Increasingly, it was laymen who filed the complaints, not priests.[2]

A final objection invokes jurisdictional changes. Perhaps the growing frequency of priest–parishioner cases merely reflects the decline of ecclesiastical courts—a decline that would shift criminal cases in which priests were defendants away from the jurisdiction of the diocesan officiality and toward royal courts like the bailliage. Or perhaps it mirrors a similar decline of seignorial courts as criminal tribunals. The problem here is that the demise of the ecclesiastical courts as criminal tribunals was already an accomplished fact by the beginning of the seventeenth century. They continued to discipline misbehaving priests, but in general they did not hear the sort of priest–parishioner cases of concern to us. Moreover, in a number of the criminal cases between priests and parishioners, the clergyman had filed a complaint against the layman. Such cases with lay defendants would never have been tried by ecclesiastical courts.[3] Similarly, the increasing frequency is not likely to have reflected changes in the influence of other secular courts. The increase was not caused by a movement of criminal cases involving priests from lower courts to the bailliage, and it does not seem to stem from the loss of records in appeals to the Parlement of Paris or other appellate courts.[4]

Abbreviations

AD	Archives Départementales de . . .
A Diana	Archives de la Société de la Diana, Montbrison.
A Diocese	Archives de l'Archevêché de Lyon.
AM	Archives Municipales de . . .
AML	Archives Municipales of the commune in the Loire whose name follows. All citations from these documents have been taken from Claude Chaverondier and J. de Freminville, *Inventaire sommaire des archives départementales antérieures à 1790. Département de la Loire. Serie E supplément: Arrondissement de Montbrison* (Saint-Etienne, 1899).
AMR	Archives Municipales of the commune in the Rhône whose name follows. All citations from these documents have been taken from Georges Guigue, *Inventaire sommaire des archives départementales antérieures à 1790. Rhône. Serie E supplément. Archives anciennes des communes,* 3 vols. (Lyon, 1902–06).
AN	Archives Nationales.
ASEA	*Annales de la société d'émulation de l'Ain.*
A Séminaire	Archives du Séminaire Saint-Irénée, Francheville (Rhône).
BBPC	Serie B, Bailliage de Beaujolais, plaintes criminelles.
BD	*Bulletin de la Diana.*
BHDL	*Bulletin historique du diocèse de Lyon.*
BM	Bibliothèque Municipale de . . .
BN	Bibliothèque Nationale.
DS 1560	*Antiqua statuta ecclesiae lugdunensis a Francisco cardinalis a Turnone anno 1560 promulgata* (Lyon, 1594). This and the other abbreviations beginning with "DS" refer to diocesan statutes or synodal statutes; the number following the "DS" is the year they were adopted.
DS 1566	*Statuta synodalia ecclesiae metropolitanae et primatialis lugdunensis denuo recognita et feliciter adaucta* (Lyon, 1566).
DS 1577	*Statuts et ordonnances synodales de l'église metropolitaine de Lyon. Revues, augmentées et traduites en langue françoyse . . . publiés au sene de Saint Luc MDLXXVII* (Lyon, 1578).
DS 1614a	*Ordonnances et instructions aux curés du diocèse de Lyon faictes par Mgr le révérendissime Archevesque Comte de Lyon, et publiez au synode tenu le 16 avril 1614* (Lyon, 1621).

DS 1614b   *Avertissement de Mgr le Révérendissime Archevêque comte de Lyon, Primat des Gaules, au clergé de son diocèse, touchant la promotion aux ordres et provisions des cures et autres benefices. Publiés au synode de Lyon, le 16 avril 1614* (Lyon, 1621).

DS 1614c   *Ordonnances touchant les prebendes et commissions des messes et aussi touchant ceux qui detiennent des biens ou titres appartenant aux églises et prébendes. Faicte par Mgr le révérendissime Archevesque, Comte de Lyon, au synode tenu le mercredy 16 avril 1614* (Lyon, 1621).

DS 1621   *Ordonnance touchant la publication du décret du S. Concile de Trente, contre les mariages clandestins. Faicte par Mgr . . . l'archevesque . . . au synode tenu le mercredy 28 avril 1621* (Lyon, 1621).

DS 1631   *Statuts et ordonnances de Mgr l'éminentissime Cardinal archevesque de Lion: publiées au Synode, par luy tenu en son palais archiépiscopal, le 7 may, mil six cents trente un* (Lyon, 1631).

DS 1657   *Statuts et règlements généraux faits au synode tenu à Lyon le 27 avril 1657* (Lyon, 1657).

DS 1663   *Règlements et ordonnances faites par Mgr . . . l'archevêque de Lyon* (Lyon, 1663).

DS 1670   *Nouveaux règlements et statuts pour le diocèse de Lyon faits par Mgr l'archevêque . . .* (Lyon, 1670).

DS 1687   *Règlements et ordonnances faites par Mgr . . . l'archevêque de Lyon. Imprimez de nouveaux selon l'ordre des matières . . .* (Lyon, 1687).

DS 1705   *Statuts, ordonnances et règlements synodaux faits par Mgr . . . Claude de Saint George . . . publiés au synode général du diocèse de Lyon . . . le 21 octobre 1705* (Lyon, 1705).

ESFC   E supplément, fonds des communes.

RL   *Revue du Lyonnais.*

Visites   Archives Départementales du Rhône, *Recueil des visites pastorales du diocèse de Lyon aux XVIIe et XVIIIe siècles* (Lyon, 1926).

Notes

Introduction

1. Hubert Jedin, *Geschichte des Konzils von Trient,* 4 vols. (Freiburg-im-Breisgau, 1949–75); Henri Brémond, *Histoire littéraire du sentiment religieux en France depuis la fin des guerres de religion jusqu'à nos jours,* new ed., 11 vols. (Paris, 1967–68). For the existing literature on the Counter Reformation, see the following works: H. Outram Evennett, *The Spirit of the Counter Reformation,* edited and with a postscript by John Bossy (Cambridge, 1968), pp. 1–22, 126–53; Jean Delumeau, *Le catholicisme entre Luther et Voltaire* (Paris, 1971), pp. 9–30; Heinrich Lutz, *Reformation und Gegenreformation* (Munich, 1979), pp. 208–10; Eric Cochrane, "New Light on Post-Tridentine Italy: A Note on Recent Counter-Reformation Scholarship," *Catholic Historical Review* 56 (1970–71): 291–319; A. D. Wright, *The Counter Reformation: Catholic Europe and the Non-Christian World* (New York, 1982), pp. 295–327.

2. Jeanne Ferté, *La vie religieuse dans les campagnes parisiennes, 1622–1695* (Paris, 1962), and Louis Pérouas, *Le diocèse de La Rochelle de 1648 à 1724: Sociologie et pastorale* (Paris, 1964). The earlier study of Thérèse-Jean Schmitt, *L'organization ecclésiastique et la pratique religieuse dans l'archidiaconé d'Autun* (Dijon, 1957), should also be cited, although it spends much less time with religious reform. Subsequent studies of this type include Jean-François Soulet, *Traditions et réformes religieuses dans les Pyrénées centrales au XVII⁰ siècle* (Paris, 1974); Robert Sauzet, *Les visites pastorales dans le diocèse de Chartres pendant la première moitié du XVII⁰ siècle* (Rome, 1975); idem, *Contre-réforme et réforme catholique en Bas Languedoc: Le diocèse de Nîmes au XVII⁰ siècle* (Paris-Louvain, 1979). Other studies cover the pre-Tridentine era: Jacques Toussaert, *Le sentiment religieux en Flandre à la fin du Moyen Age* (Paris, 1963), and François Rapp, *Réformes et réformations à Strasbourg: Eglise et société dans le diocèse de Strasbourg (1450–1525)* (Paris, 1974). One inspiration for these French works were the essays of Gabriel Le Bras, *Etudes de sociologie religieuse,* 2 vols. (Paris, 1955–56). A similar local study for central Europe is Joachim Köhler, *Das Ringen um die tridentinische Erneuerung im Bistum Breslau: Vom Abschluss des Konzils bis zur Schlacht am Weissen Berg, 1564–1620* (Vienna-Cologne, 1973).

3. Delumeau, *Le catholicisme,* pp. 234–37, 256–58; John Bossy, "The Counter Reformation and the People of Catholic Europe," *Past and Present* 47 (1970): 51–70. Cf. Wolfgang Reinhard, "Gegenreformation als Modernisierung? Prolegomena zu einer Theorie des konfessionellen Zeitalters," *Archiv für Reformationsgeschichte* 68 (1977): 226–52.

4. Carlo Ginzburg, *Il formaggio e i vermi: Il cosmo di un mugnaio del '500* (Turin, 1976); idem, *I benandanti* (Turin, 1966); Yves-Marie Bercé, *Fête et révolte: Des mentalités populaires du XVI⁰ au XVIII⁰ siècle* (Paris, 1976); Robert Muchembled, *Culture populaire et culture des élites dans la France moderne (XV⁰–XVIII⁰ siècles)* (Paris, 1978); Peter Burke,

Popular Culture in Early Modern Europe (New York, 1978). One can find further evidence for this point of view in works on popular piety such as L. A. Veit and L. Lenhart, *Kirche und Volksfrömmigkeit im Zeitalter des Barocks* (Freiburg-im-Breisgau, 1956).

5. Natalie Davis, "Some Tasks and Themes in the Study of Popular Religion," in Charles Trinkhaus and Heiko Obermann, eds., *The Pursuit of Holiness* (Leiden, 1973), pp. 307–10. Soulet's work, it should be stressed, is relatively free of this overly hierarchical approach to religion.

6. According to Köhler, *Das Ringen*, pp. 1–2, the same neglect of the sixteenth century is common in work done on the Counter Reformation in central Europe. One recent work that does treat the sixteenth century is Marc Venard, *L'église d'Avignon au XVIᵉ siècle*, 4 vols. (Lille, 1980).

7. Köhler, *Das Ringen*, pp. 89–156.

8. John Bossy, introduction to the English translation of Jean Delumeau, *Catholicism between Luther and Voltaire*, trans. Jeremy Moisier (London, 1977), p. xiii. Hereinafter, citations from Delumeau are to the French original.

9. Evennett, *Spirit of the Counter Reformation*, p. 5.

10. See Bossy's postscript to ibid., pp. 133–42.

Chapter 1. Rapprochement with the Elite

1. The eyewitness was Hippolyte d'Este, the archbishop of Lyon. André Latreille, ed., *Histoire de Lyon et du Lyonnais,* Collection Univers de la France (Toulouse, 1975), pp. 180–81.

2. Ibid.; Georges Guigue, ed., *La magnificence de la superbe entrée de . . . Lyon faicte . . . au roy de France, Henri deuxieme . . . le XXIII de septembre MDXLVIII: Relations et documents* (Lyon, 1927), pp. 3–25, 40–41, 121, 206; AM Lyon, BB 68, fols. 177–208.

3. Pierre Mathieu, *Les deux plus grandes, plus celebres et memorables resjouissances de la ville de Lyon, la premiere pour l'entrée de . . . Henry IIII . . .* (Lyon, 1598).

4. For the population of Lyon, its immigration and commerce, see Richard Gascon, *Grand commerce et vie urbaine au XVIᵉ siècle: Lyon et ses marchands*, 2 vols. (Paris, 1971), 1:55–340, 346–51; Natalie Z. Davis, "The Sacred and the Body Social in Sixteenth-Century Lyon," *Past and Present* 90 (1981): 40–70.

5. Gascon, *Grand commerce*, 1:351–434.

6. These estimates of the number of clergymen and the following descriptions of their churches rely upon a number of sources: the sixteenth-century *pouillé* in August Bernard, *Cartulaire de l'abbaye de Savigny*, 2 vols. (Paris, 1853), 2:980–82; Samuel Chappuzeau, *Lyon dans son lustre* (Lyon, 1656), pp. 52–57; Arthur Kleinclausz, ed., *Histoire de Lyon*, 3 vols. (Lyon, 1939–52), 1:488–89; idem, *Lyon des origines à nos jours: La formation de la cité* (Lyon, 1925); Jean-Marie H. Forest, *L'école cathedrale de Lyon: Le petit séminaire de Saint Jean*, pp. 65, 118–20; René Lacour, *Répertoire numérique détaillé des sous-séries 11 G à 29 G: Archives départementales du Rhône* (Lyon, 1968), pp. vi–xii; idem, *Répertoire numérique de la série H* (Lyon, 1973), pp. v–xxxvi; J. B. Martin, *Histoire des églises et chapelles de Lyon*, 2 vols. (Lyon, 1909); Guillaume Paradin, *Histoire de Lyon* (Lyon, 1573; repr., Roanne, 1973), pp. 253–63.

7. Jean Beyssac, *Les chanoines de l'église de Lyon* (Lyon, 1914); A. Sachet, *Le pardon de la Saint-Jean et de la Saint-Pierre à Saint-Jean de Lyon 1392–1790,* 2 vols. (Lyon, 1914); Paradin, *Histoire de Lyon*, pp. 368–72; Forest, *L'école cathedrale*; Jean Beyssac, "Les custodes de Sainte-Croix," *Bulletin de la société littéraire, historique et archéologique de Lyon* 9 (1922–25): 1–49; L. Bocat, "L'Eglise et les custodes de Sainte-Croix de Lyon

(manuscrit de 1751)," *Revue des questions historiques* 117 (1932): 142–59; Jean Tricou, "Médailles de personnages ecclésiastiques lyonnais du XVᵉ au XVIIIᵉ siècles," *Revue numismatique,* ser. 5, 12 (1950): 177–96; Maurice Pallasse, *La sénéchaussée et siège présidial de Lyon pendant les guerres de religion* (Lyon, 1943), pp. 138–41; and AD Rhône, 10 G 3626.

8. Lacour, *Répertoire numérique des 11 G à 29 G,* pp. ix–xiii; Bernard, *Cartulaire de Savigny,* pp. 980–1007; Nicolas de Nicolai, *Description générale de la ville de Lyon et des anciennes provinces du Lyonnais et du Beaujolais, 1573* (Lyon, 1881), pp. 117–37, 217–61; Réné Fédou, *Les hommes de loi lyonnais à la fin du Moyen Age,* pp. 65–67; Pallasse, *La sénéchaussée de Lyon,* pp. 263–66.

9. AD Rhône, 15 G 33, June 27, 1583; AM Lyon, GG 3–4, GG 434.

10. Jean Beyssac, *Les prévôts de Fourvière* (Lyon, 1908); Kleinclausz, *Lyon des origines,* pp. 76–91; Jean Tricou, "Méraux et jetons armoriés des églises et du clergé lyonnais," *BHDL* (1926): 151–54; idem, *Armorial du chapitre Saint-Nizier de Lyon 1632–1670* (Lyon, 1952). Of seven canons at capitular meetings at Saint-Paul in December 1550 and January 1551 at least three had relatives on the city council and three had family at the *sénéchaussée.* Roughly similar results hold for Saint-Just and Saint-Nizier. See AD Rhône, 12 G 36, fols. 2–3; 13 G 12, fols, 103–20; 15 G 22, fols. 78–79; and fonds Frécon.

11. AD Rhône, 15 G 22, fols. 1–347. Similar evidence appears in 13 G 14–15 (Saint-Paul, 1577–1602) and 15 G 32–34 (Saint-Nizier, 1579–85).

12. AD Rhône, 13 G 14–15, 15 G 32–34.

13. AD Rhône, 12 G 423 (1496, 1498, 1578).

14. AM Lyon, CC 57; Lacour, *Répertoire numérique des 11 G à 29 G,* pp. ix–xiii; Nicolai, *Description de Lyon,* pp. 217–61; Bernard, *Cartulaire de Savigny,* pp. 980–1007; Jean Déniau, *Les nommées des habitants de Lyon en 1446* (Lyon, 1930), pp. 60–62.

15. AM Lyon, CC 309 (1559); Jean Beyssac, *Corévêques, suffragants et auxiliaires de Lyon* (Montbrison, 1910), pp. 67–73; Davis, "The Sacred and the Body Social," pp. 50–51.

16. Davis, "The Sacred and the Body Social," pp. 50–51; AD Rhône, 4 H 25 (1576); Jean Beyssac, *Les prieurs de Notre Dame de Confort, ordre des frères precheurs* (Lyon, 1909).

17. On the education of the Dominicans: Beyssac, *Prieurs de Confort.* On the wealth of mendicant houses: Lacour, *Répertoire de la série H,* pp. v–xvi; Bernard, *Cartulaire de Savigny,* pp. 980–1007; AM Lyon, CC 57 (1555).

18. AM Lyon, GG 384, September 26, 1584; GG 388, January 10, 1593; Beyssac, *Prévôts de Fourvière,* p. 310 (1564); Jean Guéraud, *La chronique lyonnaise de Jean Guéraud, 1536–62,* ed. Jean Tricou (Lyon, 1929), pp. 71, 90, 98 (1553, 1556).

19. The following discussion of politics is based upon AM Lyon, BB 64, 379, 439; CC 309, CC 4257; Gascon, *Grand commerce,* 1:407–35; Paradin, *Histoire de Lyon,* pp. 253–63; Pallasse, *La sénéchaussée de Lyon,* pp. 144–47; Fédou, *Les hommes de loi,* pp. 12–13, 27–28, 62–64, 269–73.

20. AM Lyon, BB 439, November 8, 1558; Gascon, *Grand commerce,* 2:410–11.

21. AM Lyon, CC 309, April 4–5, 1559; Gascon, *Grand commerce,* 2:801–03; Antoine Péricaud, *Notes et documents pour servir à l'histoire de Lyon, 1547–60* (Lyon, 1841), pp. 3–4.

22. AM Lyon, CC 309, April 4–5, 1559; Pallasse, *La sénéchaussée de Lyon,* p. 146; Gascon, *Grand commerce,* 1:430–31. For the city's "laic tradition," see Natalie Z. Davis, *Society and Culture in Early Modern France* (Stanford, 1975), p. 8.

23. Guéraud, *Chronique lyonnaise,* pp. 31, 63, 89, 110; Paradin, *Histoire de Lyon,* pp. 253–63; Pallasse, *La sénéchaussée de Lyon,* pp. 119–20; Beyssac, *Prieurs de Confort,* p. 48; A. Péricaud, *Notes et documents, 1547–60,* pp. 34–35; AM Lyon, AA 138 (letter of March 3, 1556, to Antoine Camus), BB 68 (July 19, 1548), CC 309 (April 4, 1559).

24. My sources here are the death inventories of nine ecclesiastics: AD Rhône, 15 G 336 (1634); 12 G 423 (1483, 1487, 1496, 1498, 1536, 1578, 1588, 1593).

25. Davis, "The Sacred and the Body Social," pp. 45–47, 63–64. For an example, see Gabriel de Saconay, *Discours des premiers troubles advenus à Lyon* (Lyon, 1569), reprinted in F. Danjou, *Archives curieuses de l'histoire de France,* ser. 1, vol. 4 (Paris, 1835), p. 222.

26. AD Rhône, 15 G 29, fols. 215–16 (1573); 15 G 33, fols. 197–99 (1584); 15 G 37, fol. 341 (1593); 4 G 22, fols. 36–38 (1572). See also 15 G 32, fols. 23–24 (1573).

27. AD Rhône, 12 G 362 (1554, 1579, 1603); 12 G 386 (January 2, 1543); 12 G 387 (August 24, 1600). The records from Saint-Just come from its seignorial court, one of the few jurisdictions in the city with substantial criminal records from the sixteenth century.

28. François Garin, *La complainte de François Garin, marchand de Lyon,* Centre d'études et de recherches médiévales de l'Université de Lyon-II (Lyon, 1978), lines 1500–1694; Guéraud, *Chronique lyonnaise,* p. 89.

29. For the 1540 entry, see Guéraud, *Chronique lyonnaise,* pp. 18, 31; Jean Tricou, *Les enfants de la ville* (Lyon, 1938), pp. 6–7, 13–15; AD Rhône, 10 G 116, fol. 273; 10 G 1674; 12 G 693, Comptes, 1539–40, fol. 18, and Comptes, 1540–41, fol. 17; 13 G 562, fol. 27; AM Lyon, BB 58, fols. 67–77. Subsequent entries: Tricou, *Enfants,* pp. 13–15; AM Lyon, BB 74, fols. 60–66 (1552); and BB 78 (June 1, 1556).

30. Marie Thérèse Lorcin, "Les clauses religieuses dans les testaments du plat pays lyonnais aux XIVᵉ et XVᵉ siècles," *Le Moyen Age* 78 (1972): 318–23; idem, *Vivre et mourir en Lyonnais à la fin du Moyen-Age* (Lyon, 1981), pp. 138–40; Nicole Gonthier, *Lyon et ses pauvres au Moyen-Age (1350–1500)* (Lyon, 1978), pp. 229–38; John Bossy, "Essai de sociographie de la messe, 1200–1700," *Annales E.S.C.* 36 (1981): 46, 48. Cf. Steven E. Ozment, *The Reformation in the Cities: The Appeal of Protestantism to Sixteenth-Century Germany and Switzerland* (New Haven, 1975), pp. 15–22.

31. A. Vachet, *Les anciens couvents de Lyon* (Lyon, 1895), pp. 109–10; *La merveilleuse hystoire de l'esprit de Lyon* (Paris, 1528; reedition, Lyon, 1887); Lorcin, *Vivre et mourir,* p. 140; Gonthier, *Lyon et se pauvres,* pp. 52–54, 229–38.

32. AD Rhône, 3 E 4494, fols. 27–31 (1544).

33. Phillippe Ariès, *L'homme devant la mort* (Paris, 1977), pp. 109–10, 164–67; *Merveilleuse hystoire;* Lorcin, "Clauses religieuses," pp. 318–23.

34. Michel Vovelle, *Piété baroque et déchristianisation en Provence au XVIIIᵉ siècle* (Paris, 1973); Pierre Chaunu, *La mort à Paris: XVIᵉ, XVIIᵉ, XVIIIᵉ siècles* (Paris, 1978).

35. For the sample of urban wills, see appendix 1. Elaborate funerals for artisans: AD Rhône, 3 E 3908, fols. 7, 39 (1539); 3 E 350, fol. 114 (1537).

36. On confession and communion: Steven E. Ozment, *The Age of Reform, 1250–1550* (New Haven, 1980), pp. 216–19; Thomas Tentler, *Sin and Confession on the Eve of the Reformation* (Princeton, 1977); and Toussaert, *Sentiment religieux en Flandre,* pp. 104–22, 160–204, for similar figures on communion in urban Flanders. Diocesan statutes recommended communion only at the principal feasts of the year: see DS 1577, p. 10. I calculated the frequency of communion from records for the purchase of hosts at Saint-Paul: AD Rhône, 13 G 592–601 (1490–1678). Until the 1560s, these records usually gave the actual number of hosts purchased. In 1560–61, one of the first years for which we can make a reliable estimate of the parish's population, Saint-Paul bought 36,000 hosts, of which between 500 and 2,000 probably went to the priests who said mass. Baptismal records (AM Lyon, GG 434–35) cover the 1560s only partially, but we do have continuous records for November 1561 through April 1562, when 173 children were christened in the parish. Assuming a birthrate of 36 to 40 per thousand and that 65 to 80 percent of the population were able to take communion, we arrive at between 5,620 and 7,690 communicants and roughly 4 to 6 hosts per year.

Unfortunately, the same calculation was not possible for other parishes of interest in the middle of the sixteenth century, nor could I carry the calculations for Saint-Paul past the 1560s.

37. For the notion that Catholicism was imbedded in holy places, see Davis, "The Sacred and the Body Social." Cf. William Christian, *Local Religion in Sixteenth-Century Spain* (Princeton, 1981). For the examples of this paragraph, see AD Rhône 10 G 47, fols. 435–92; Vachet, *Les anciens couvents,* pp. 647–48; Kleinclausz, *Lyon des origines,* pp. 76–91; Claude Bellièvre, *Souvenirs de voyages en Italie et en Orient: Notes historiques,* ed. Charles Perrat (Geneva, 1956), pp. 27–28; and Martin, *Histoire des églises,* pp. 281–83.

38. AM Lyon, GG 388; AD Rhône, 10 G 47, fols. 453–85 (1559–90).

39. Sainte-Croix: AD Rhône, 10 G 3626. Rogations: Bibliothèque municipale de Lyon, *Entrées royales et fêtes populaires à Lyon du XVe au XVIIIe siècle: Catalogue d'une exposition, du 12 juin au 12 juillet 1970 à la bibliothèque municipale de Lyon,* with an introduction by H. J. Martin (Lyon, 1970), p. 25; Jean Péricaud, "Louis Garon et la fête du cheval fol," *RL,* ser. 1, 5 (1837): 450; AD Rhône, 10 G 47, fol. 485 (1590).

40. Sachet, *Le pardon de la Saint-Jean,* 2:47–62; Bibliothèque municipale de Lyon, *Entrées,* p. 3; Claude de Rubys, *Histoire veritable de la ville de Lyon* (Lyon, 1604), pp. 499–504.

41. AD Rhône, 15 G 29, fols. 194–98 (1573); 10 G 3626, July 25, 1570, and 1571; AM Lyon, GG 388 (July 25, 1593), GG 528 (1595–1604), GG 529 (1588–89); Jean Tricou, *Le Plâtre Saint Esprit de Lyon* (Lyon, 1920), pp. 1–4, 34–52; Natalie Z. Davis, "Protestantism and the Printing Workers in Lyons: A Study in the Problem of Religion and Social Class during the Reformation" (Ph.D. diss., University of Michigan, 1959), p. 112.

42. AM Lyon, BB 24, fols. 7, 440 (1496, 1503); BB 33 (January 17, 1514); CC 57; AD Rhône, 15 G 22, fol. 151; 15 G 27, fols. 131–32, 199–202; 15 G 33, fols. 4–5; 13 H 55, 57; 50 H 84–87; Georges Guigue, ed., *Le livre des confrères de la Trinité de Lyon, 1306–1792* (Lyon, 1898); Jean Tricou, "Enseignes et médailles de dévotion, méreaux et jetons des confréries de Lyon antérieures à 1789," *Revue numismatique,* ser. 5, 14 (1952): 205–28 and 15 (1953): 107–25; idem, *Numismatique des corporations des métiers et du commerce lyonnais de l'ancien régime* (Paris, 1957); Davis, "The Sacred and the Body Social," p. 51; Vachet, *Les anciens couvents,* pp. 78–84. Confraternities were also mentioned in the wills I sampled.

43. Note both Jean Guéraud's hysterical reaction when the confraternities seemed threatened by a royal ordinance in 1561 and the remarks of a visitor to Lyon in 1616: Guéraud, *Chronique lyonnaise,* p. 137, and J. Zinzerling, *Le voyage en France,* trans. by Verdier (Paris, 1665), p. 295.

44. AD Rhône, 3 E 3909, fol. 53 (1552); 4 H 24 (1513, 1579, 1591). Other examples: 3 E 343, fol. 58 (1551), 3 E 7311 (1570), 3 E 2667, fol. 273 (1599).

45. AD Rhône, 4 H 24 (1513, 1579, 1591); 3 E 2667, fols. 273–78 (1599); Guigue, *Trinité,* pp. xxiii–xxix, 20–64. For the vocational brotherhoods, see Rubys, *Histoire de la ville de Lyon,* pp. 499–504, Antoine Fontanon, *Les édits et ordonnances des rois de France,* 2d ed., 3 vols. (Paris, 1611), 1:1086–87 (1561). One exception appears to be the Confraternity of the Trinity, whose well-to-do members invited clergymen to the group's banquets. Perhaps the Confraternity of the Trinity thus helped reduce somewhat the animosity between the clerics and the municipal elite. In any case, the fact that clergymen participated in the banquets of the Trinity confraternity—but not those of most artisans' confraternities—suggests that in terms of status the priests were closer to the elite than to the mass of artisans.

46. Davis, *Society and Culture,* pp. 97–123. See also Bibliothèque municipale de Lyon, *Entrées,* pp. 46–59, 111–17; Jean Tricou, "Les confréries joyeuses de Lyon au XVIe

siècle et leur numismatique," *Revue numismatique* 40 (1937): 293–317; *Recueil des chevauchées de l'asne faites à Lyon en 1566 et 1578* (Lyon, 1862); J. Péricaud, "Louis Garon," pp. 433–56; Rubys, *Histoire de la ville de Lyon,* pp. 370, 409, 499–504; Vachet, *Les anciens couvents,* pp. 71–84.

47. For this and the following paragraph, I am indebted to Davis, "The Sacred and the Body Social." For the mass, see Bossy, "Sociographie de la messe."

48. Davis, "The Sacred and the Body Social," pp. 43 (figures on immigration), 68.

49. AD Rhône, 3 H 3, fol. 26; Vachet, *Les anciens couvents,* pp. 193–209, 385–99; Martin, *Histoire des églises,* p. 377. The burial figures come from the entire sample of urban wills from the period 1520 to 1704. The data on monetary bequests assume a correction for inflation. For details, see appendix 1.

50. These results stem from a tobit analysis of urban wills drawn up before 1596. This statistical technique allows us to disentangle the effects of a number of variables which influenced both a testator's decision to make a pious bequest and the size of the bequest he made, if any. These variables include (among other things) such factors as the testator's wealth, the number of his heirs, and whether he was an immigrant or not. For an elementary explanation of tobit analysis and a complete account of the results, see appendix 1. It turns out that differences in wealth can account for much of the gap between newcomer and native gifts to the mendicants; what remains unexplained could be the result of chance. The same is not true, however, of bequests to parishes. Here the unexplained difference is too large to be a statistical fluke; indeed, a t-test of the difference between immigrants and natives unaccounted for by other variables yields $t = 4.30$, which is significant at better than the 1 percent level. Interested readers will also find an explanation of t-tests in appendix 1.

51. The geographic origins of priests evidently mattered to contemporaries, for even newcomers from villages near Lyon requested priests from their home towns to officiate when they were married in churches in Lyon. See, for example, AD Rhône, 10 G 3626, fol. 2: marriage of Catherine de Belencourt (1570).

52. AD Rhône, 15 G 358–59, 3 H 3; Michel Cormier, *L'ancien couvent des Dominicains de Lyon,* 2 vols. (Lyon, 1898–1900), 2:21–30; Guéraud, *Chronique lyonnaise,* pp. 106–07.

53. Since the poor could not afford all these funeral rituals, I used a statistical technique known as probit analysis to see whether increasing numbers of paupers in the sample could explain the decline in the requests for processions and other ceremonies. I included other explanatory variables as well, such as gender, literacy, and the number of dependent children a testator had. In each case, the decline in requests for the various funeral ceremonies was too large to be explained by chance—indeed, t-tests were significant at better than the 1 percent level. Nor could it be accounted for by the number of paupers or other changes in the sample. See appendix 1 for a summary of the results and an explanation of probit analysis.

54. The comparison of "average" testators is based upon the tobit analysis of pious bequests in urban wills drawn up before 1596. This analysis is described in appendix 1. A t-test of the decline over time yielded $t = 2.51$, significant at the 2 percent level. For a similar decline in demands for masses in Aix-en-Provence, see Claire Dolan, *Entre tours et clochers: Les gens d'église à Aix-en-Provence au XVI* siècle (Sherbrooke, 1981), p. 144.

55. The purchases of hosts at Saint-Paul come from 13 G 592–96 (1490–1569). The population for this period before the first baptismal registers was assumed to follow figures from the city's tax rolls; for these, see Gascon, *Grand commerce,* 1:347–48. For confraternities, see Davis, "The Sacred and the Body Social," p. 51. In my sample of urban wills, the number of testators mentioning confraternities dropped from 9.1 percent in 1520–55 to 5.6 percent in 1556–95, but this decline was too small to be statistically significant.

56. Neither wage rates nor interest rates, which might serve as indexes of expected economic conditions in Lyon, explain the decline in pious giving over time. For the details, see the tobit analysis of pre-1596 urban wills in appendix 1. On the economic crisis at the end of the century, see Gascon, *Grand commerce,* 1:591–674.

57. The number of urban wills that mentioned an attachment to the Roman Catholic Church rose from 8 percent before 1545 to 58 percent during the years 1545–75. It turns out that testators who expressed this attachment were slightly more likely to make pious bequests (all other things being equal), but the difference was small enough so that it could well be a result of chance. In fact, when expressing such an attachment to Catholicism is included in the tobit analysis of pious bequests in urban wills before 1596, we get a t-statistic of only 1.55, which is not significant even at the 10 percent level.

58. See, for example, the profession of orthodoxy that ardent Catholics presented to the city council, BB 82, fols. 46–47.

59. If we compare urban wills drawn up through 1555 with those from 1556–95, we see that the fraction of wills with bequests to parishes fell 49 points, from 70 percent before 1555 to 21 percent in 1556–95; gifts to regular clergy, however, declined only 13 points, from 42 percent to 29 percent. This drop in gifts to parishes was no worse in one parish than another, once we take into account variations in wealth and differences in the number of immigrants between parishes. As for newcomers, they not only showed less inclination to bestow money upon parishes, but they also were less likely to choose elaborate funeral rituals. For this, see the tobit and probit analyses of pre-1596 urban wills in appendix 1.

60. For Protestantism in Lyon, see Davis, *Society and Culture,* pp. 1–16; idem, "The Sacred and the Body Social," pp. 47–50; and Gascon, *Grand commerce,* 2:436–76, 515–19.

61. Gascon, *Grand commerce,* 2:463–92; Pallasse, *La sénéchaussée de Lyon,* pp. 247–61; Ernest Lavisse, *Histoire de France depuis les origines jusqu'à la Revolution,* 9 vols. (Paris, 1903–11), vol. 6, pt. 1: *La Réforme et la Ligue: 1559–98,* by Jean H. Mariéjol, pp. 42–43; Lucien Romier, *La carrière d'un favori, Jacques d'Albon de Saint-André* (Paris, 1909), pp. 311–18.

62. *Histoire ecclésiastique des églises réformées au royaume de France,* ed. G. Baum and E. Cunitz, 3 vols. (Paris, 1883–89), 3:253.

63. The quotation is from the city council deliberations, AM Lyon, BB 82, fols. 46–47. See also Gascon, *Grand commerce,* 2:469–73; Rubys, *Histoire de la ville de Lyon,* p. 389; Pallasse, *La sénéchaussée de Lyon,* pp. 259–60; AM Lyon, CC 1084; Guéraud, *Chronique lyonnaise,* pp. 133–35, 145–46, 149–51.

64. Saconay, *Discours des premiers troubles,* pp. 225–26, 238; AD Rhône, BP 3993, "Mémoire presenté au Cardinal de Tournon"; Pallasse, *La sénéchaussée de Lyon,* pp. 126, 259–61; AM Lyon, BB 82, fols. 55–57, 139; Gascon, *Grand commerce,* 2:464–65, 470.

65. Davis, *Society and Culture,* pp. 152–87; AD Rhône, 10 G 125, fols. 230–33; 10 G 47, fol. 453 (April 3, 1559). The Protestant charges against the canon-counts come from *La juste et saincte défense de la ville de Lyon* (Lyon, 1563), reprinted in F. Danjou, *Archives curieuses,* ser. 1, vol. 4:195–214. This is hardly the most credible source for the Catholics' actions, but Gascon, *Grand commerce,* 2:470, notes that the canons did help circulate a petition demanding a test of faith for city councilors.

66. AD Rhône, BP 3993 (March 17, 1561); 10 G 57, fols. 91–98; 10 G 125, fols. 230–33.

67. For a defense of the Protestant actions and an equally polemical Catholic reply, see *La juste et saincte défense de la ville de Lyon* and Saconay, *Discours des premiers troubles.* See also Gascon, *Grand commerce,* 2:472–79; Guéraud, *Chronique lyonnaise,* pp. 141, 152, 159–61.

68. Gascon, *Grand commerce,* 2:477–92; Kleinclausz, *Histoire de Lyon,* 1:417–22; Antoine

Péricaud, "Notes et documents pour servir à l'histoire de Lyon, 1560–74," *Annuaire du département du Rhône,* pt. 2 (1842): pp. 28–34. Baum and Cunitz, *Histoire ecclésiastique des églises réformées,* pp. 248–97, laments some of the excesses committed by the Protestant soldiers.

69. Catholics such as Saconay, Paradin, Rubys, and Guéraud all agreed on this. See also Davis, *Society and Culture,* pp. 152–87.

70. AM Lyon, BB 83–86 (1563–67), BB 371; Gascon, *Grand commerce,* 2:501–35; and Pallasse, *La sénéchaussée de Lyon,* pp. 289–301.

71. For the journeymen's return to Catholicism and the 1572 massacre, see Davis, *Society and Culture,* pp. 10–16, 152–87. Other sources include AM Lyon, BB 85, fols. 117–37; BB 88, fol. 155; A. Péricaud, "Notes et documents, 1560–74," pp. 53–55, 62–67; Gascon, *Grand commerce,* 2:502–35; Kleinclausz, *Histoire de Lyon,* 1:430–31; and Pallasse, *La sénéchaussée de Lyon,* pp. 295–305.

72. Pallasse, *La sénéchaussée de Lyon,* pp. 263–66, 331–36.

73. AM Lyon, BB 84, fols. 13, 35–40 (1565); BB 87, fols. 110–14 (1568); AD Rhône, 10 G 708 (1598); Gascon, *Grand commerce,* 1:434–35, 2:514–15, 533–34; Pierre Delattre, ed., *Les établissements des Jésuites en France depuis quatres siècles,* 5 vols. (Enghien, 1949–57), s.v. "Lyon"; Henri Fouqueray, *Histoire de la compagnie de Jésus en France des origines à la supression (1528–1752),* 5 vols. (Paris, 1910–25), 1:456–75; Forest, *L'école cathedrale,* pp. 259–60.

74. For the *conseil d'état,* see Pallasse, *La sénéchaussée de Lyon,* pp. 296, 373–86; Henri Hours, "Le 'Conseil d'Etat' à Lyon pendant la Ligue," *Revue historique de droit français et étranger* (1952), pp. 401–20; Jean H. Mariéjol, *Charles Emmanuel de Savoie, duc de Nemours* (Paris, 1938), pp. 91–92, 142, 211; Antoine Péricaud, "Notes et documents pour servir à l'histoire de Lyon pendant la Ligue," *Annuaire du département du Rhône* (1844), pp. 23–24, 37, 144–46; and Robert Harding, *Anatomy of a Power Elite: The Provincial Governors of Early Modern France* (New Haven, 1978), pp. 89–94, who shows that such councils existed in other French cities.

75. P. Richard, *La papauté et la Ligue française: Pierre d'Epinac, archevêque de Lyon (1573–1599)* (Paris, 1901), pp. 167, 186–92, 588; AM Lyon, BB 107, 110; Gascon, *Grand commerce,* 2:534.

76. There is evidence of a sixteenth-century upsurge of Catholicism in other cities as well, although Lyon was a bit precocious: Philip Benedict, "The Catholic Response to Protestantism: Church Activity and Popular Piety in Rouen, 1560–1600," in *Religion and the People, 800–1700,* ed. James Obelkevich (Chapel Hill, 1979), pp. 168–90; idem, *Rouen during the Wars of Religion* (Cambridge, 1981), pp. 190–208; Robert Harding, "The Mobilization of Confraternities against the Reformation in France," *Sixteenth Century Journal* 11 (1980): 92–104; idem, "Revolution and Reform in the Holy League: Angers, Rennes, Nantes," *Journal of Modern History* 53 (1981): 397–410. For the special case of Avignon, see Venard, *L'église d'Avignon au XVIᵉ siècle.*

77. Davis, "Protestantism," pp. 235–39; idem, *Society and Culture,* pp. 30–33; Jean-Pierre Gutton, *La société et les pauvres: L'exemple de la généralité de Lyon, 1534–1789* (Paris, 1970), pp. 270–71; J. D. Mansi, ed., *Sacrorum conciliorum . . . collectio,* 53 vols. (Paris-Leipzig, 1901–27), 32:1095–1140.

78. AD Rhône, 15 G 23–37 (Saint-Nizier, 1550–99); 10 G 47; 12 G 43; 13 G 14–15; Beyssac, *Chanoines,* p. 165; Gabriel de Saconay, *Discours catholiques sur les causes et remedes des malheurs intentés au roy et escheus à son peuple par les Calvinistes* (Lyon, 1568), pp. 30–31, 76–79.

79. AD Rhône, 15 G 29, fol. 215–16 (1573); 15 G 30, fols. 262–63 (1575); 15 G 33, fols. 13–14, 20–21 (1582); 15 G 35, fols. 256–67 (1588); DS 1566, p. 83; DS 1577, pp. 1–2; Leonard Janier, *Probation des saincts sacrements de l'église catholique,* 2d ed. (Paris, 1577).

80. Vachet, *Les anciens couvents,* pp. 181–91, 425–40; J. B. Vanel, *Histoire du couvent des*

Minimes de Lyon (Lyon, 1879), pp. 1–42; Fouqueray, *La compagnie de Jésus,* 1:350–62, 456–75; Delattre, *Les établissements des Jésuites,* s.v. "Lyon"; Rubys, *Histoire de la ville de Lyon,* p. 427, and Theotine de Saint-Just, *Les capucins de l'ancien province de Lyon* (Saint-Etienne, 1951), pp. 28–32.

81. AD Rhône, 10 G 3626, a journal which records events at Sainte-Croix from 1570 to 1581, shows that it was mendicants or Jesuits who preached at Lent and Advent. Even when a hired preacher fell ill, the *custodes* and vicars did not step in for him. See also Antoine Péricaud, "Notes et documents pour servir à l'histoire de Lyon, 1574–1589," *Annuaire du département du Rhône* (1843): 49, 55 (1577); and AD Rhône, 10 G 578 (1551, 1583, 1587); 10 G 1680; 10 G 3626, fol. 9; Jean Beyssac, "Les lecteurs et théologaux de l'église de Lyon," *Bulletin de la société littéraire, historique et archéologique de Lyon* 9 (1922–25): 1–49; Forest, *L'école cathedrale,* pp. 372–73. The information from Saint-Nizier comes from the capitular acts, AD Rhône, 10 G 19–37 (1525–99).

82. Vanel, *Histoire des Minimes,* pp. 155–74; Emond Auger, *Catechismus* (Paris, 1568); Augustin Fliche et al., eds., *Histoire de l'église depuis les origines jusq'à nos jours,* vol. 18, pt. 1: *La restauration catholique, 1563–1648,* by Leopold Willaert (Tournai, 1960), pp. 244–47; Antonio Possevino, *Apparatus sacer* (Venice, 1606); Pierre de Bollo, *Le rosaire de la très saincte Vierge Marie Mère de Dieu* (Lyon, 1604); AD Rhône, 3 H 3; 3 E 283, fol. 135 (1580).

83. AD Rhône, 15 G 23, fols. 8–11 (1550); Vanel, *Histoire des Minimes,* pp. 1–16, 285–88; Fouqueray, *La compagnie de Jésus,* pp. 350–62; Delattre, *Les établissements des Jésuites,* s.v. "Lyon"; Saint-Just, *Les capucins,* pp. 28–32.

84. AD Rhône, 15 G 19–37, the capitular acts for 1525–99. Meetings about preaching first appear in 15 G 21, fol. 170 (1542). For the incident that reveals the laymen were not simply a rubber stamp for the canons, see 15 G 32, fols. 28–37, 83–84 (1579–1580).

85. AD Rhône, 15 G 24, fol. 24 (April 28, 1564). Biographical information on these men was gleaned from Rubys, *Histoire de la ville de Lyon;* AM Lyon, BB 96, fol. 5; BB 370–71; Gascon, *Grand commerce.* For Rouille, see 15 G 29, fols. 194–95.

86. AM Lyon, CC 1184 (1570–71); CC 1272 (1578–79); BB 94, fols. 169–92 (1576).

87. Rubys, *Histoire de la ville de Lyon,* pp. 428–29; A. Péricaud, "Notes et documents, 1574–89," p. 39; AM Lyon, GG 120; AD Rhône, 50 H 11–13, 18, 26.

88. AD Rhône, 50 H 13, fols. 7–9.

89. A. Péricaud, "Notes et documents pendant la Ligue," pp. 46, 53; AM Lyon, GG 120; Richard, *La papauté et la Ligue,* pp. 65–67, 452–54.

90. AM Lyon, BB 127, fol. 96; BB 128, fol. 136; Tricou, *Enfants,* pp. 20–22; A. Péricaud, "Notes et documents pendant la Ligue," pp. 99–100; Philip T. Hoffman, "Church and Community: The Parish Clergy and the Counter Reformation in the Diocese of Lyon, 1500–1789" (Ph.D. diss., Yale University, 1979), p. 67. A copy of this dissertation is available at AD Rhône; it can also be obtained from University Microfilms International, 300 N. Zeeb Road, Ann Arbor, Michigan 48106.

91. See the tobit analysis of pious legacies in urban wills drawn up before 1596 in appendix 1. There was a positive interaction between wealth and time after 1555: $t = 2.88$, significant at the 1 percent level. This means that among the wealthy the decline in pious bequests slowed and was even reversed after 1555. See appendix 1 for a more detailed explanation.

92. AD Rhône, 16 H 1; Vanel, *Histoire des Minimes,* pp. 15–16, 71–96. Among wealthy merchants and officers the percentage who requested funeral processions dropped from 58 before 1555, to 44 in 1556–75, to 24 percent in 1576–95. Figures for other rituals were similar, and the decline cut across class lines. It cannot be explained by varying economic circumstances. For this, see appendix 1 for the probit analysis of funeral procession requests in pre-1596 urban wills.

93. A. Péricaud, "Notes et documents, 1574–89," pp. 887–88 (1582); J. Benedicti, *La*

triomphante victoire de la Vierge Marie, sur sept malins esprits (Lyon, 1611); *Discours véritable des grands miracles de notre Dame de Lucques* (Lyon, 1590); AD Rhône, 3 E 284 (June 13, 1588); Tricou, "Enseignes et médailles de dévotion," p. 114. Although everything we know about the Penitents in Lyon suggests that they were an overwhelmingly elite organization, it is possible that they eventually attracted some members from the lower classes. Unfortunately, the membership lists do not indicate occupations, and by the late sixteenth century there are no longer any reliable urban *taille* rolls which would allow us to determine the socioeconomic position of confrères. The same problems make it difficult to analyze the membership of any confraternity in the city of Lyon during the late sixteenth and seventeenth centuries, and they rule out the sort of study undertaken by Ronald F. E. Weissman in *Ritual Brotherhood in Renaissance Florence* (New York, 1982).

94. Sachet, *Le pardon de la Saint-Jean*, 2:47–62; AD Rhône, 10 G 47, fols. 453–85; 15 G 27, fols. 199–202 (1569).

95. Rubys, *Histoire de la ville de Lyon*, pp. 409, 499–504. For Catholic support of the *chevauchées*, see Davis, "Protestantism," pp. 471–502, 521–53; idem, *Society and Culture*, pp. 121, 309. In 1565 an attempt by a Protestant minister to stop Catholics from dancing at a Pentecost festival sparked a riot: A. Péricaud, "Notes et documents, 1560–74," p. 46, and Rubys, *Histoire de la ville de Lyon*, pp. 405–06.

96. The tobit analysis of pious bequests in pre-1596 urban wills (appendix 1) demonstrates that among the lower classes religious and charitable legacies continued to fall after 1555. The tobit analysis takes into consideration the economic fortunes of individual testators, and when real wage rates are brought into the equation, they do not explain the behavior of the poorer testators either. For the craftsmen's moderation, see Davis, "Protestantism," pp. 521–53. Further evidence comes from the wills. During the years 1556–95, 48 percent of the urban testators mentioned an outspoken attachment to Roman Catholicism, but among artisans (though they were Catholic) this percentage was only 26 percent.

97. Gascon, *Grand commerce*, 2:534.

98. A number of individuals close to the elite gave voice to this fear at various times: Bellièvre, *Souvenirs de voyages*, p. 45; Guéraud, *Chronique lyonnaise*, pp. 61–62; Paradin, *Histoire de Lyon*, p. 285; Rubys, *Histoire de la ville de Lyon*, pp. 370–71, 499–504; Richard, *La papauté et la Ligue*, p. 103.

99. Mariéjol, *La Réforme et la Ligue*, pp. 389, 396–97; Pierre de l'Estoile, *Mémoires journaux de l'Estoile*, ed. Brunet et al., 12 vols. (Paris, 1875–96), 7:3–5, 295–96; Roland Mousnier, *The Assassination of Henry IV*, trans. Joan Spencer (New York, 1973), pp. 158–83, 217–23.

100. Henri Hours, "Les Aventures d'un capucin royaliste après la Ligue," *Bulletin de la société historique, archéologique et littéraire de Lyon* 18 (1952): 55–78; F. Rolle, "Fragments de journal de Ponson Bernard, échevin lyonnais (1592–95)," *RL*, n.s. 31 (1865): 430–44; Pierre Mathieu, *Histoire des derniers troubles de France* (Lyon, 1605), pp. 45–46; Mariéjol, *Nemours*, pp. 165–72; Fouqueray, *La compagnie de Jésus*, 2:256–72, 414–15; Pallasse, *La sénéchaussée de Lyon*, p. 387; Richard, *La papauté et la Ligue*, pp. 531–71; Kleinclausz, *Histoire de Lyon*, 1:458–63; A. Péricaud, "Notes et documents pendant la Ligue," pp. 144–46; Beyssac, *Chanoines*, pp. 171–72.

101. AM Lyon, BB 131, fols. 63–68; A. Péricaud, "Notes et documents pendant la Ligue," pp. 201–13; Mariéjol, *Nemours*, pp. 222–48; Kleinclausz, *Histoire de Lyon*, 1:458–63; Richard, *La papauté et la Ligue*, pp. 568–78.

102. Mathieu, *Les deux plus grandes resjouissances*, p. 11.

103. Mariéjol, *Nemours*, pp. 238–42; A. Péricaud, "Notes et documents pendant la Ligue," p. 166; AM Lyon, AA 146 (1614). For the Penitents, see AD Rhône, 50 H 13 and 50 H 26; and Elie Brackenhoffer, *Voyage en France*, trans. Henry Lehr (Paris, 1925),

pp. 118–20. Even in Paris, where the reaction to the League was so much more bitter, resurgent Catholicism was not snuffed out after the League's collapse. See Denis Richet, "Aspects socio-culturels des conflits religieux à Paris dans la seconde moitié du XVIe siècle," *Annales E.S.C.* 32 (1977): 764–89.

Chapter 2. The Rural Priests from 1500 to 1614

1. Bernard, *Cartulaire de Savigny*, 2:980–1007.
2. Gascon, *Grand commerce*, 1:56–203; Lucien Febvre, *Philippe II et la Franche-Comté* (Paris, 1911; abridged ed., Paris, 1970), pp. 27–28.
3. AD Cote-d'Or, B 11595 (1561); *Visites*, p. 139.
4. Richard Gascon, "La France du mouvement: Les commerces et les villes," in *Histoire économique et sociale de la France*, ed. Fernand Braudel and Ernest Labrousse, 4 vols. (Paris, 1970–), vol. 1, pt. 1: 252, 265; Gascon, *Grand commerce*, 1:56–203, 232–33, 320–23, 881–83; *Visites*, p. 468; Etienne Fournial et al., *Saint-Etienne: Histoire de la ville et de ses habitants* (Roanne, 1976), pp. 76–89; J. B. Galley, *Le pays de Saint-Etienne jusqu'au XVIIe siècle* (Saint-Etienne, 1925), pp. 613–772.
5. Gascon, *Grand commerce*, 1:232–33, 2:814–16; Marie Thérèse Lorcin, *Les campagnes de la région lyonnaise aux XIVe et XVe siècles* (Lyon, 1974), pp. 29, 37–45, 464–65, and maps 4 and 5.
6. AMR, Belleville, GG 2; Samuel Mours, *Le Protestantisme en France au XVIe siècle* (Paris, 1959), pp. 120–21, 168–73; Febvre, *Philippe II*, pp. 297, 324, 340; E. Dubois, "Histoire de Pont-de-Veyle," *ASEA* 33 (1900): 26–32, 121–55; AM Bourg-en-Bresse, BB 45, fols. 5–40 (1567–68); J. Brossard, "Regeste ou mémorial historique de l'église Notre Dame de Bourg, depuis les temps les plus anciens jusqu'à nos jours," *ASEA* 30 (1897): 5–100 (1585, 1594); *Visites*, p. 298; Sylvie Cadier-Sabatier, *Les Protestants de Pont-de-Veyle et lieux circonvoisins au XVIIe siècle* (Trevoux, 1975), pp. 8–10; Jules Baux, *Mémoires historiques de la ville de Bourg*, 2 vols. (Bourg, 1869), 2:282–84.
7. Claude Longeon, "Documents sur la Réforme en Forez," *BD*, 40 (1967): 87–99; Samuel Mours, *Le Protestantisme en France au XVIIe siècle* (Paris, 1967), p. 84; AMR, Belleville, GG 2 (1569–75).
8. Belleville: AMR, Belleville, GG 2. Bresse: [Abbe Dumonet], *Histoire de la révolution de Macon sur le fait de la religion* (Avignon, 1760), p. 144. I thank Robert Harding for this reference. Saint-Etienne: [Simon Goulart], *Mémoires de la Ligue*, new ed., 6 vols. (Amsterdam, 1758), 6:438–53, 460, 467, 475–77. This long complaint concerning mistreatment of Protestants throughout France lists no incidents committed in the part of the diocese outside Lyon, save for the one in Saint-Etienne. The same holds for the *Histoire ecclésiastique des églises reformées*, ed. Baum and Cunitz. For details and for a discussion of two additional incidents of minor religious violence in the countryside, see Hoffman, "Church and Community," p. 87.
9. Pro-Catholic religious associations never sprang up outside Lyon, and the League won only lukewarm allegiance from the small cities and market towns in the diocese. See Claude Longeon, *Une province française à la Renaissance: La vie intellectuelle en Forez au XVIe siècle* (Lille, 1976), pp. 29–42; Jean Beyssac, "La Ligue à Saint-Bonnet-le-Château," *BD* 22 (1924): 87–100; AM Lyon, AA 75–76.
10. A simple calculation illustrates the difference between Lyon and the countryside. In 1743, there were 2.5 *communautés d'hommes* per parish inside Lyon, versus only .027 *communautés* per parish outside the city—a far lower figure. While these ratios would no doubt be closer in the sixteenth century, the gap would still remain. See Hoffman, "Church and Community," p. 89, for a discussion. For friars who preached in the

countryside, see O. Morel, "La vie à Châtillon-en-Dombes, d'après les comptés de syndics (1375–1500)," *ASEA* 53 (1924): 38.

11. *Visites,* passim; Abbé Merle, "La vie religieuse en Forez," Société de la Diana, *Recueil de mémoires et documents sur le Forez,* 16 (Montbrison, 1947), pp. 160–63; AD Loire, G non-classée, paroisses de Saint-Just-en-Chevalet et de Saint-Bonnet-le-Château.

12. AD Loire, G non-classée, paroisse de Saint-Bonnet-le-Château, "Terrier et procès," acte 132, January 17, 1571. For more on the *sociétés,* see Marie Magdeleine Cheyssac, *Saint-Bonnet-le-Château en Forez* (Lyon, 1942), pp. 19–20; [James Condamin and François Langlois], *Histoire de Saint-Bonnet-le-Château par deux prêtres du diocèse de Lyon,* 2 vols. (Paris, 1885); A. de Lateyssoniere, *Recherches historiques sur le département de l'Ain* (Bourg, 1844), p. 271; Pierre-Maxime Relave, *Sury-le-Comptal en Forez: Essai d'histoire et de archéologie* (Montbrison, 1907), p. 99; Jean Canard, *La société des prêtres et les prêtres de Saint-Just-en-Chevalet* (n.p., 1958); and Morel, "La vie à Châtillon-en-Dombes," pp. 45–52.

13. Canard, *Société; idem,* "Liste des curés qui ont administré les paroisses de l'actuel canton de Saint-Just-en-Chevalet," *BD* 43 (1973–74): 281–97; Jean-Pierre Gutton, "Notes sur le recrutement du clergé séculier dans l'archdiocèse de Lyon (1589–1789)," *Bulletin du centre d'histoire économique et sociale de la région lyonnaise* 2 (1974): 1–20.

14. Jean Canard, *Livre d'or de Saint-Romain-d'Urfé* (n.p., 1951); idem, *Promenade à Saint-Priest-la-Prugne* (n.p., 1957); *Visites,* pp. 425–27.

15. AD Rhône, 4 G 108 (1576–77); 4 G 111–16 (1579–94); A Diana 2 J 7. For details, see Hoffman, "Church and Community," pp. 92–93. Cf. Lorcin, *Vivre et mourir,* pp. 76, 85, 113–19.

16. AD Rhône, 4 G 120, fol. 233; 4 G 115, December 21, 1585.

17. Jean Beyssac, *La Paroisse de Montarcher en Forez à la fin du XV* siècle* (Montbrison, 1924), pp. 1–6, 18–24; Charles Signerin, *Histoire de Chevrières* (Saint-Etienne, 1894), p. 245; AML, Chevrières, GG 1–10; Auguste Broutin, *Histoire de la ville de Feurs* (Saint-Etienne, 1867), p. 234; J. Freminville, *Inventaire sommaire des archives départementales antérieures à 1790. Département de la Loire. Série E supplément* (Saint-Etienne, 1899), p. 32.

18. Jean Epinac, "La situation religieuse dans le diocèse de Lyon d'après la visite pastorale de J. de Talaru, 1378–1379," *Cahiers d'histoire* (1961): 217–43. There were only two cases of concubinage in the visits of 1613–14, neither of which involved a curé or a vicar. See *Visites,* pp. 268, 414. For a case of concubinage in Beaujeu, just north of the diocese, see "Journal de Guillaume Paradin, doyen de Beaujeu, pendant les années 1572–1573," *RL,* ser. 1, 6 (1837): 271.

19. *Visites,* p. 66.

20. *Visites,* pp. 21, 84, 155–56, 202, 235, 246, 273–74; DS 1566, pp. 52–54; DS 1577, pp. 1–2, 25–27; J. B. Vanel, "Les curés de Saint-Genest-Malifaux," *BHDL* (1926): 293–327; Jean François Duguet, "Mémoire inédit de l'abbé Jean François Duguet, curé de Feurs," vol. 6, Société de la Diana, *Recueil de mémoires et documents sur le Forez* (Saint-Etienne, 1880); A Diocese, paroisse de Quincié: curé Nague (1540s); AD Rhône, 3 E 666, fols. 20, 27 (1560).

21. *Visites,* pp. 67, 69–70, 110.

22. C. Pepin, "Les chanoines de Notre Dame de Bourg et les syndics," *ASEA* 61 (1939): 3–32; AD Rhône, B, Bailliage de Beaujolais, Scellés et inventaires 1606–07, May 28, 1605; DS 1577. Cf. Lorcin, *Vivre et mourir,* pp. 156–59.

23. AD Rhône, B, Bailliage de Beaujolais, Scellés et inventaires 1517–96, June 11, 1587.

24. AD Rhône, B, Bailliage de Beaujolais, Scellés et inventaires, 1517–96, June 11, 1587; 1606–07, May 28, 1605; AD Ain 2B, Inventaires 1628–30, April 28, 1629.

25. For the sample of rural wills, see appendix 1 and chapter 4. In the communities I selected for my sample of rural wills (communities well endowed with notaries), I leafed

through a number of notarial registers which antedated 1550 but unearthed only five wills. To be sure, rural testators did make pious bequests in the fourteenth and fifteenth centuries, as evidence from ecclesiastical and civil courts shows: Lorcin, "Clauses religieuses," pp. 287–323; idem, *Vivre et mourir,* pp. 133–47; Marguerite Gonon, "La vie religieuse en Forez au XIVe siècle et son vocabulaire, d'après les testaments," *Bulletin du Cangé* 30 (1960): 233–86; idem, *La vie quotidienne en Lyonnais d'après les testaments, XIVe–XVIe siècles* (Macon, 1969), p. 9; idem, *Les institutions et la société en Forez au XIVe siècle d'après les testaments* (Macon, 1960), pp. 60, 117–27. However, nearly all of Lorcin's wills were registered with the *officialité* precisely because they contained pious bequests, and the same holds for a large number of the testaments from Forez which Gonon used—a fact that makes statistical analysis very different and rules out comparisons with my wills from notarial registers. We therefore cannot be certain that rural pious bequests declined from a late medieval peak, as Lorcin's work suggests. One conclusion, however, does seem more sure: late medieval votive masses were predominantly an urban phenomenon. On this point, see Lorcin, "Clauses religieuses," p. 322; idem, *Vivre et mourir,* p. 145; and Bossy, "Sociographie de la messe," p. 46. Finally, if pious bequests did subside in the countryside from a late medieval peak, the decline may have been a purely economic phenomenon. In the first place, the late medieval peak (which Lorcin situates in the years 1340–80) may have been an economic result of the plague: survivors had fewer heirs and so were free to leave more of their wealth to the Church. Furthermore, while economic crisis does not explain the drop in pious bequests in mid-sixteenth-century Lyon, it could well account for the near disappearance of pious bequests outside the city. An index of agricultural lease rates dropped by 47 points between 1550 and 1573, and according to the calculations in appendix 1, this would be enough to cut pious bequests by roughly 8 percent.

26. DS 1577; Jean Canard, *Folklore Chrétien: Coutumes d'origine religieuse disparues ou en voie de disparition en Forez et en Lyonnais* (Roanne, 1952), pp. 35–38; AML, Saint-Just-en-Chevalet, GG 1 (1580, 1581); Duguet, "Mémoire inédit," p. 99; AD Rhône, ESFC, Belleville, liasse 19, October 25–27, 1621: a youth accused of ringing the tocsin that touched off a "sédition populaire" claims that he thought the bells were to be rung for a baptism.

27. Richard, *La papauté et la Ligue,* p. 79; L. Perrat, "Mon vieux Châtillon," *ASEA* 40 (1907): 352; *Saint Vincent de Paul: Correspondance, entretiens, documents,* ed. Pierre Coste, 14 vols. (Paris, 1920–25), 13:50.

28. Gonon, "Vie religieuse," p. 263; Merle, "Vie religieuse en Forez," p. 167; Morel, 55 (1927–28): 224–29; *Visites,* pp. 246, 289; Cf. Toussaert, *Sentiment religieux en Flandre,* pp. 161–80.

29. For examples from other parts of France, see *Journal manuscrit d'un sire de Gouberville: Gentilhomme campagnard au Cotentin de 1553 à 1562,* ed. Abbé Tollemar (Rennes, 1879), pp. 556–65, and Roger Vaultier, *Le folklore pendant la guerre de cent ans d'après les lettres de remission du trésor des chartes* (Paris, 1965), pp. 13–16.

30. See, for example, AD Rhône, 3 E 1004, fols. 28, 315 (1536, 1538); 3 E 8721, February 5, 1560; Lorcin, "Clauses religieuses," pp. 292–96; Gonon, "Vie religieuse," pp. 241–43; AD Loire, G non-classée, paroisse de Saint-Just-en-Chevalet, no. 6, terrier de l'eglise avant 1568; Duguet, "Mémoire inédit," pp. 100–01; AMR, Quincié, GG 1 (1602); A Diocese, paroisse de Quincié, liste de pensions, fols. 82–93 (1548); AD Ain, G 90, paroisse de Dommartin (1550), and "Inventaire analytique des archives de la confrérie du Saint-Esprit de Virieu-le-Petit," legs testamentaires.

31. Signerin, *Histoire de Chevrières,* pp. 25, 48–51.

32. AD Loire, G non-classée, paroisse de Saint-Bonnet-le-Château, liasse M16, fol. 65: fondations de 1506, 1537, 1538, 1549; *Visites,* p. 457; Duguet, "Mémoire inédit," pp. 103–04.

33. Duguet, "Mémoire inédit," pp. 102, 107–10, 251–52; AML, Epercieu, GG 1–6 (1696); Gonon, "Vie religieuse," pp. 264–66. As in the rest of Catholic Europe, the holy places that laymen marched to were frequently sites where special paraliturgical rituals were performed or where statues of the Virgin had miraculously been found. In Montmerle, for instance, legend had it that local boatmen had once discovered a bronze statue of the Virgin in the waters of the Saône and had hidden the statue on a river island. Miraculously, though, the statue then moved to the parish church of Montmerle, where the Virgin made it known that she wanted her own separate chapel built on a nearby hill. Once constructed, the chapel became an important place of pilgrimage. For this and other examples, see de Nicolai, *Description générale de Lyon*, p. 240; Jean Claude Schmitt, *Le saint lévrier: Guinefort, guérisseur d'enfants depuis le XIIIe siècle* (Paris, 1979); Abbé Renon, "Notre Dame des Minimes à Montmerle," *Bulletin d'histoire et d'archéologie du diocèse de Bellay* 7, no. 16 (1952): 15–31; Pierre Louvet, *Mémoires contenant ce qu'il a de plus remarquable dans la ville de Villefranche* (Lyon, 1671), pp. 17–18. Cf. Christian, *Local Religion*, pp. 70–125.

34. AML, Saint-Bonnet-le-Château, GG 1 (1609); Condamin and Langlois, *Histoire de Saint-Bonnet-le-Château*, 2:143; *Visites*, p. 471; Merle, "Vie religieuse en Forez." Cf. Brossard, "Mémorial historique de Notre Dame de Bourg," p. 37 (1565); AMR, Grigny, GG 2 (1717); Vernaison, GG 1 (1665); Paradin, *Histoire de Lyon*, p. 357; Broutin, *Histoire de Feurs*, p. 172.

35. AMR, Belleville, GG 1. Many priests recorded such events in their parish registers; in the countryside, the registers are at times as good as diaries.

36. Canard, *Folklore Chrétien*, pp. 71–76; Duguet, "Mémoire inédit," pp. 98–100; AD Loire, G non-classée, paroisse de Saint-Bonnet-le-Château, liasse M16, fol. 65; AD Rhône, ESFC, Belleville, liasse 19, October 25–27, 1621; AMR, Orliénas, GG 1 (1610); Sainte-Foy-les-Lyon, GG 1 (1607); Vaugneray, GG 1.

37. *Visites*, p. 451; AMR, Longes, GG 1 (1598); Chambost-Longessaigne, GG 1 (1603); Canard, *Folklore Chrétien*, pp. 40–42; Duguet, "Mémoire inédit," p. 102; AD Rhône, ESFC, Saint-Cyr-au-Mont-d'Or, registres 9, 18a; BM Roanne, 3 G 56.

38. AML, Feurs, GG 1–GG 25 (May 2, 1599); Longeon, *Une province française*, pp. 187–90.

39. DS 1577, pp. 2–3; 18–23; *Visites*, pp. 255, 261, 297, 302. Cf. Tollemar, p. 541.

40. *Visites*, p. 157; DS 1577, pp. 1–3, 22–23, 25–28.

41. Noel du Fail, *Propos rustiques*, new ed. (Paris, 1921), pp. 52–53; Tollemar, *Journal manuscrit d'un sire*, pp. 170–79.

42. Jean-Pierre Gutton, *Villages du Lyonnais sous la monarchie (XVIe–XVIIIe siècles)* (Lyon, 1978); idem, *La sociabilité villageoise dans l'ancienne France* (Paris, 1979). This paragraph and the subsequent two are based upon Gutton's works and upon my own reading of village records in AD Rhône, 2 E and ESFC; AD Ain, E; A Diana, 4 E; BM Roanne, 4 E; and notarial registers. For details, see Hoffman, "Church and Community," pp. 113–14.

43. See, for example, *Visites*, pp. 206, 212, and AD Ain, E 493.

44. Vincent Durand, "Lettres patentes de Charles IX pour la fondation du collège de Boen," *BD* 7 (1893–94): 200–05; Lorcin, *Les campagnes*, pp. 160–66; AD Rhône, ESFC, Saint-Cyr-au-Mont-d'Or, registre 9, fols. 13–15, 27, 128; AD Ain, "Inventaire analytique . . . Virieu-le-Petit," pt. 4 (1399).

45. AD Rhône, 10 G 2743 (1733); for a similar case, see AD Ain, C 133. For the Holy Spirit confraternities, see Felix Bernard, "Les confréries communales du Saint Esprit," *Mémoires de l'académie des sciences, belles-lettres et arts de Savoie*, ser. 6, 7 (1963): 16–79; Pierre Duparc, "Confréries du Saint Esprit et communautés d'habitants au Moyen-Age," *Revue historique de droit français et étranger* (1958): 348–67, 555–85; Merle, "Vie religieuse en Forez," pp. 164–65; Lorcin, *Les campagnes*, pp. 160–66;

J. J. A. Pilot de Thorey, *Usages, fêtes et coutumes en Dauphiné* (Grenoble, 1882; repr. Marseille, 1977), pp. 48–50, 67–68; M. Gonon, *La vie quotidienne*, pp. 41–42; idem, "La vie religieuse," pp. 259–61; and Gutton, *Villages du Lyonnais*, pp. 17–18, 82–83.

46. V. Durand, "Lettres patentes de Charles IX," p. 200–05; J. Manissier, *Histoire de Ceyzeriat* (Bourg, 1967), p. 58; J. B. Chambeyron, *Recherches historiques sur la ville de Rive-de-Gier* (Lyon, 1844), pp. 25–27.

47. *Visites*, p. 106; AD Ain, C 133; A Diana, 5 G 6 (1535–80); M. Cochard, "Notice historique et statistique du canton de Saint-Symphorien-le-Château," *Archives historiques et statistiques du département du Rhône* 4 (1826): 279–90, 388–406; AD Rhône, 50 H 127; ESFC, Saint-Cyr-au-Mont-d'Or: GG 13, fols. 139–41, 156–60 (1534, 1597); registre 9, fols. 118–20, 185–86 (1607); registre 18b (1610).

48. AD Rhône, 3 E 8724 (May 16, 1581); BM Roanne, 5 G 30.

49. AD Ain, E 436.

50. Lorcin, *Les campagnes*, pp. 160–66; Duparc, "Confréries du Saint Esprit," pp. 348–67, 555–85; AD Rhône, ESFC, Saint-Genis-Laval, liasse 2; Saint-Cyr-au-Mont-d'Or, liasse 18a.

51. AD Rhône, D 354; Guigue, *Trinité*, pp. lvii–lx; A. Vachez, *Etude historique sur le canton de Mornant* (Lyon, 1871), p. 77; Duparc, "Confréries du Saint Esprit"; AD Rhône, 10 G 2743 (1733); Jean Canard, "Les confréries de Saint-Just-en-Chevalet," *BD* 43 (1973–74): 93–120.

52. Jean Prajoux, *Notes et documents sur Renaison* (Lyon, 1905), pp. 13–14; AD Rhône, 2 E 157–60, 166; 10 G 2743 (1733); ESFC, Saint-Genis-Laval, liasse 2 (1658).

53. Beyssac, *La paroisse de Montarcher*, pp. 14–16; AML Montarcher, GG 1–10; A Diana, 5 G 6; AD Loire, B 1529 (1538); B 1179 (September 21, 1550); Gonon, "Vie religieuse," pp. 259–62.

54. Lorcin, *Les campagnes*, pp. 164–65; Bercé, *Fête et révolte*, pp. 13–16; Vaultier, *Le folklore*, pp. 45–47; Gutton, *Villages du Lyonnais*, p. 85; idem, "Reinages, abbayes de jeunesse et confréries dans les villages de l'ancienne France," *Cahiers d'histoire* 21 (1976): 446; Alice Taverne, *Coutumes et superstitions foréziennes*, 9 vols. (Lyon, 1973–74), 8:44–46; AD Loire B 1317 (August 21, 1680); BM Roanne, 3 G 42.

55. Du Fail, *Propos rustiques*, pp. 52–58; Bercé, *Fête et révolte*, pp. 11, 127–30; Beyssac, *La paroisse de Montarcher*, pp. 14–16; AD Loire, B 1529 (1538).

56. Beyssac, *La paroisse de Montarcher*, pp. 14–16; Gutton, *Villages du Lyonnais*, pp. 84–86; idem, "Reinages"; Lorcin, *Les campagnes*, pp. 164–65; Vaultier, *Le folklore*, p. 125. Professional confraternities also held *royaumes*: Canard, "Confréries de Saint-Just-en-Chevalet," pp. 99–103, 116–17, and Gonon, "Vie religieuse," pp. 260–65.

57. AD Loire, B 1529 (1538).

58. AMR, Saint-Rambert-l'Ile-Barbe, GG 6; Lorcin, *Les campagnes*, pp. 164–65; Gutton, "Reinages"; AD Loire, B 1317, August 21, 1680; Canard, *Folklore Chrétien*, pp. 53–57; Vaultier, *Le folklore*, p. 125; Arnold van Gennep, *Manuel de folklore français contemporain*, 8 vols. (Paris, 1937–58), vol. 1, pt. 1:202–13, pt. 4:1716; Cochard, "Notice historique," pp. 282–90; Bercé, *Fête et révolte*, pp. 28–31, 128–29; Davis, *Society and Culture*, pp. 97–125; Mikhail Bakhtin, *Rabelais and his World*, trans. Helen Iswolsky (Cambridge, Mass.: 1968), pp. 4–12.

59. AMR, Couzon-au-Mont-d'Or, GG 1 (1604); Lentilly, GG 1 (1616); Orliénas, GG 1 (1603–06); Oullins, GG 1 (late sixteenth century); Saint-Rambert-l'Ile-Barbe, GG 6 (1571, 1579); Quincieux GG 1 (1630s); AD Rhône, ESFC, Fleurieu, liasse 2 (1625–26).

60. Gutton, "Reinages"; idem, *Villages du Lyonnais*, pp. 85–86; Davis, *Society and Culture*, pp. 97–123; Canard, *Folklore Chrétien*, pp. 27–29; Bercé, *Fête et révolte*, pp. 13–53;

Vaultier, *Le folklore,* pp. 29–36, 40, 45–57, 88; and Paul Fortier-Beaulieu, *Mariages et noces campagnardes dans les pays ayant formé le département de la Loire* (Paris, 1945), pp. 233–37, discuss the youth in the diocese and the rest of France. For local examples of their activities, see D. P. Benoit, *Histoire de l'abbaye et de la terre de Saint-Claude,* 2 vols. (Montreuil-sur-Mer, 1892), 2:427–28; AD Loire, B 1521 (1664), B 1586 and B 1589; Abbé Reure, "Anciennes moeurs foréziennes," *BD* 12 (1901): 24–42; and Pilot de Thorey, *Usages, fêtes et coutumes,* pp. 97–124.

61. Gutton, "Reinages," pp. 448–50; idem, *Villages du Lyonnais,* p. 85; Taverne, *Coutumes et superstitions,* pp. 44–46; van Gennep, *Manuel de folklore,* vol. 1, pt. 1:202–13; V. Durand, "Lettres patentes de Charles IX," pp. 200–05; Beyssac, *La paroisse de Montarcher,* pp. 14–16; AMR, Oullins, GG 1 (1588, 1590, 1599); AD Rhône, 4 G 24, fols. 23–27 (1683); 10 G 2804 (1605); A Diocese, paroisse de Saint-Martin-en-Haut, livre de compte; AD Loire, B 1317 (August 21, 1680).

62. J. B. Galley, *L'Election de Saint-Etienne à la fin d'ancien régime* (Saint-Etienne, 1903), pp. 47, 53; Gutton, "Reinages," pp. 448–50; van Gennep, *Manuel de folklore,* vol. 1, pt. 1:202–13, pt. 4:1716.

63. *Montaillou, village occitan de 1294 à 1324* (Paris, 1975).

64. Roger Doucet, *Les institutions de la France au XVIᵉ siècle,* 2 vols. (Paris, 1948), 2:787–88; Michel Mollat, *La vie et la pratique religieuse au XIVᵉ siècle et dans la première partie du XVᵉ principalement en France* (Paris, 1965), pp. 75–77.

65. Dubois, "Histoire de Pont-de-Veyle," pp. 403–05; AD Rhône, ESFC, Belleville, liasse 19 (February 28, 1599); AM Bourg-en-Bresse, GG 182; AD Rhône, ESFC, Belleville, liasses 14 and 25 (late sixteenth century), Fleurieu (1606); BM Roanne, 4 E 7 (1627); and AD Ain, E 485 (1577–1699). In some cities, of course, the priests did select preachers; for such exceptions, see Hoffman, "Church and Community," pp. 135–36.

66. AD Rhône, ESFC, Saint-Cyr-au-Mont-d'Or, registres 2, 9, 18a, and 18b; 2 E 154, 157–58, 164–66; BM Roanne, 5 G; A Diana, 5 G; and AD Ain E 436. One of the few examples of priests as witnesses comes from AD Ain, "Inventaire . . . Virieu-le-Petit," Comptabilité (1458, 1459, 1472).

67. AM Bourg-en-Bresse, GG 222–GG 226; Canard, "Confréries de Saint-Just-en-Chevalet"; AD Rhône, 3 E 8722 (August 19, 1571); A Diocese, paroisse de Quincié, pensions, fols. 82–93, 117–19; *Visites,* pp. 179–84. The parish visits of 1613–14 abound with incidents of usurped revenues, as do those of the region around Roanne in 1596 (AD Rhône, 10 G 538). For one of the rare vestries in which the clergy did exercise some authority, see Brossard, "Mémorial historique de Notre Dame de Bourg," pp. 5–100 (1549).

68. Cf. Gutton, *Villages du Lyonnais,* pp. 86, 99. As for the Holy Spirit confraternities, we have already seen the difficulties experienced by the one in Neuville. Testamentary bequests to the confraternities, which had been fairly common in the fourteenth and fifteenth centuries, nearly disappeared from our sixteenth-century rural wills. See Lorcin, *Les campagnes,* pp. 185–90, 510; Gonon, *Vie quotidienne,* pp. 41–42; AD Ain, "Inventaire analytique . . . Virieu-le-Petit," legs testamentaires.

69. AD Rhône, 2 E 166, fol. 3 (1585). Cf. 3 E 8722 (August 19, 1571).

70. Samuel Popkin, *The Rational Peasant: The Political Economy of Rural Society in Vietnam* (Berkeley, 1979).

71. Examples of troubles over the *casuel* and the tithe: AD Rhône, 13 G 809 (1566); 13 G 894 (1552–54); 15 G 528 (1566); A Diocese, Quincié, pensions, fols. 82–93 (1548); August Cornet, "Varennes-Saint-Sauner à travers les siècles," *ASEA* 42 (1909): 178–80. Examples not involving the curé are even more numerous; for these and for a general discussion, see Hoffman, "Church and Community," pp. 141, 306; Gutton, *Villages du Lyonnais,* pp. 67–73; Victor Carrière et al., *Introduction aux études d'histoire ecclésiastique locale,* 3 vols. (Paris, 1936), 3:287–352.

72. Brossard, "Mémorial historique de Notre Dame de Bourg," pp. 5–100 (1549, 1562); Pepin, "Les chanoines de Notre Dame de Bourg," pp. 3–32; Gutton, *Villages du Lyonnais*, p. 145; AD Rhône, 4 G 22 (1580).

73. The evidence here comes from criminal court records discussed below in chapter 5. While officiality and royal court records are admittedly meager before 1600, documents have survived from seignorial courts, in the series B of AD Rhône and AD Loire. Parish and communal archives and the curés' own comments in parish registers provide additional evidence. In none of these sources, though, do we find any signs before the seventeenth century of conflict between laymen and priests who were opposed to communal institutions. See Hoffman, "Church and Community," pp. 142–43.

74. For evidence from French, German, Austrian, and Italian sources, see Hoffman, "Church and Community," pp. 143–44.

Chapter 3. Christian Discipline: The Reforms of the Clergy

1. Perrat, "Mon vieux Châtillon," p. 352.

2. Ibid.; *Visites*, pp. 335–37; Coste, ed., *Vincent de Paul: Correspondance*, 13:45–54; Pierre Coste, *Le grand saint du grand siècle, Monsieur Vincent*, 2d ed., 3 vols. (Paris, 1934), 1:93–110.

3. Brackenhoffer, *Voyage en France*, pp. 116–20; Chappuzeau, *Lyon dans son lustre*, pp. 60–75; Martin, *Histoire des églises*; Gutton, *La société et les pauvres*, pp. 298–303. Charitable bequests (largely to the new hospital, which was established in the years 1614–22) jumped significantly in the period 1615–35; see appendix 1.

4. Delumeau, *Le catholicisme*, pp. 62–65; Doucet, *Les institutions de la France*, 2:675–76; and Victor Martin, *Le Gallicanisme et la Réforme catholique: Essai historique sur l'introduction en France des décrets du Concile de Trente (1563–1615)* (Paris, 1919; repr., Geneva, 1975), pp. 167–71, 398, which shows that even staunch Gallicans accepted most of the moral and dogmatic decrees of Trent. For parallels between royal legislation and the decrees of Trent, see Hoffman, "Church and Community," p. 151.

5. AD Rhône, 50 H 7, 21, 44, 53; Vachet, *Etude historique sur Mornant*, pp. 202–05, 621–26; Maurice Garden, *Lyon et les Lyonnais au XVIIIᵉ siècle* (Paris, 1970), pp. 531–32; Yves Poutet and Jacqueline Roubert, "Les 'Assemblées' secrètes des XVIIᵉ–XVIIIᵉ siècles en relation avec l'*AA* de Lyon," *Divus Thomas* 70 (1967): 153–54, 321–22; 71 (1968): 73–76. It is not clear what "AA" stood for. Besides "assemblée anonyme," Poutet suggests "anima" and "associatio amicorum."

6. René de Voyer d'Argenson, *Les annales de la Compagnie du Saint Sacrement*, ed. Beauchet-Filleau (Marseille, 1900); Raoul Allier, *La cabale des dévots* (Paris, 1902); Emmanuel Chill, "Religion and Mendicity in Seventeenth-Century France," *International Review of Social History* 7 (1962): 400–25; Kathryn Norberg, "Rich and Poor in the Old Regime: Grenoble 1600–1804" (Ph.D. diss., Yale University, 1978), pp. 33–66; Charles Berthelot du Chesnay, "La spiritualité des Laics," *XVIIᵉ siècle* 62 (1964): 31–46. For Lyon, the basic documents include Georges Guigue, ed., *Les papiers des dévots de Lyon: Recueil de textes sur la Compagnie secrète du Saint-Sacrement 1630–1731* (Lyon, 1922), and AD Rhône, 50 H 115–16.

7. Guigue, *Les papiers des dévots*, pp. 76–100. Many members were active in other religious organizations; see ibid., pp. 120, 161–66, and AD Rhône, 50 H 7, 44–68.

8. Guigue, *Les papiers des dévots*; AD Rhône, 50 H 115–16; Gutton, *La société et les pauvres*, pp. 377–93; Allier, *La cabale des dévots*, pp. 48–49, 322–46, 356–431.

9. A. Dégert, *Histoire des séminaires français jusqu'à la Révolution*, 2d ed., 2 vols. (Paris, 1912), 1:117–54, 2:354–55; P. Broutin, *La réforme pastorale en France au XVIIᵉ siècle*, 2 vols. (Tournai, 1956), 1:16–19.

10. Delumeau, *Le catholicisme,* pp. 59–60; Dégert, *Histoires des séminaires,* 1:41–57, 117–57; Roland Mousnier, *Les institutions de la France sous la monarchie absolue,* vol. 1: *Société et état* (Paris, 1974), p. 268.

11. P. Broutin, *La réforme pastorale,* 2:181–267; Dégert, *Histoires des séminaires,* 1:117–254. Cf. Michael Arneth, *Das Ringen um Geist und Form des Priesterbildung im Säkularklerus des siebzehnten Jahrhunderts* (Wurzburg, 1970).

12. Dégert, *Histoires des séminaires,* 1:1–29, 41–117; Delumeau, *Le catholicisme,* pp. 68–75. Cf. Soulet, *Traditions et réformes,* pp. 131–49, and Ferté, *La vie religieuse,* pp. 147–69.

13. Forest, *L'école cathedrale,* pp. 260–77.

14. For examples from Lyon and other dioceses, see Jean Marie H. Forest, "Messire Jean Rabot, curé de Saint-Clement-sous-Valsonne," *BHDL* (1912): 485; Pérouas, *Le diocèse de La Rochelle,* pp. 194–205; Soulet, *Traditions et réformes,* pp. 131–49.

15. DS 1577, pp. 17–18; DS 1614a, pp. 10–11; DS 1614b, pp. 4–13; Gutton, "Le recrutement du clergé," p. 4.

16. Kleinclausz, *Histoire de Lyon,* 2:100; Jean Soulcié, "La formation des clercs au séminaire Saint-Irénée de Lyon de 1659 à 1905" (Thèse de doctorat, Faculté de droit canonique de Lyon, 1955), pp. 28–34, 52–62, 95–102; Guigue, *Les papiers des dévots,* pp. 79–80; Jean Marie de La Mure, *Histoire ecclésiastique du diocèse de Lyon* (Lyon, 1671), pp. 222–23.

17. *Dictionnaire de spiritualité ascétique et mystique, doctrine et histoire* (Paris, 1954–), s.v. "Jacques Cretenet"; Soulcié, "La formation des clercs," pp. 95–102; Poutet, "Les 'Assemblées' secrètes," pp. 149–51, 187–88.

18. Roger Chartier, Marie Madelein Compère, Dominique Julia, *L'éducation en France du XVIᵉ au XVIIIᵉ siècle* (Paris, 1976), pp. 60–77; Gutton, *La société et les pauvres,* p. 384; *Dictionnaire de spiritualité,* s.v. "Charles Demia"; Guigue, *Les papiers des dévots,* pp. 70, 87, 104, 120, 188–94; AD Rhône, 50 H 115 (August 20, 1682).

19. DS 1657, pp. 13–14; DS 1687, pp. 37–41; DS 1705, pp. 61–69; Soulcié, "La formation des clercs," pp. 34–51, 75–86, 152–66.

20. Chartier, *L'éducation en France,* pp. 71–77.

21. A Séminaire, "Mémoire de tous ceux qui ont fait retraitte . . . depuis le 1 novembre 1670" and "Retraittés"; Soulcié, "La formation des clercs," pp. 34–51, 102–04.

22. Soulcié, "La formation des clercs," pp. 95–102; Poutet, "Les 'Assemblées' secrètes," pp. 187–88; *Dictionnaire de spiritualité,* s.v. "Jacques Cretenet"; Gutton, "Le recrutement du clergé," p. 3.

23. Soulcié, "La formation des clercs," pp. 63–94, 117–51; Chartier, *L'éducation en France,* pp. 67–69; Brémond, *Histoire littéraire,* vol. 3, pt. 1:142–52.

24. A Séminaire, "Mémoire de tous ceux qui ont fait retraitte . . ." and "Retraittés" (1671, 1672, 1674, and 1678); Guigue, *Les papiers des dévots,* pp. 110, 122; AD Rhône, 50 H 115 (February 2, 1682, and April 29, 1683), 50 H 116 (May 15, 1698); Soulcié, "La formation des clercs," pp. 34–51, 102–04.

25. A Séminaire, Retraite générale de MM les curés, 1664–1698 et 1704–1758; Soulcié, "La formation des clercs," pp. 102–04; DS 1670, p. 14; DS 1687, pp. 41–46; AD Rhône, 50 H 115 (April 9, 1682, and April 29, 1683).

26. La Mure, *Histoire ecclésiastique,* p. 216, 222–23; DS 1663, p. 6; Forest, "Messire Jean Rabot," p. 482; AMR, Sourcieux-sur-l'Arbrêle GG 1 (1652) and Haute-Rivoire GG 6 (1721). Cf. P. Broutin, *La réforme pastorale,* vol. 1, and Delumeau, *Le catholicisme,* p. 271.

27. On synods and visits in general, see Delumeau, *Le catholicisme,* pp. 52–57, 66, 71–75, 199–205, 208–10; and the works by P. Broutin, Ferté, Pérouas, and Sauzet, which provide examples from other dioceses. For Lyon, see Richard, *La papauté et la Ligue,*

pp. 87–88, 594; AD Rhône, 1 G 48–52; 10 G 538; AMR, Lentilly GG 3–4, Létra GG 2–3, Chassagny GG 4, Chausson GG 1–2.

28. Pérouas, *Le diocèse de La Rochelle,* pp. 228–34; Norberg, "Rich and Poor," pp. 149–50; P. Broutin, *La réforme pastorale,* 1:233–53; La Mure, *Histoire ecclésiastique,* pp. 216–24; Kleinclausz, *Histoire de Lyon,* 2:97–99.

29. This was probably true of Camille de Neuville's ban on parish festivals; see the discussion below.

30. DS 1560, p. 219; DS 1566, pp. 55–57; DS 1577, pp. 25–27; DS 1614a, p. 15; Pierre d'Epinac, *Advertissement de la part de Monseigneur le Révérendissime Archevesque de Lyon au clergé de son diocèse* (Lyon, 1585), p. 7.

31. Mollat, *La vie et la pratique religieuse,* pp. 42–47; Odette Pontal, *Les statuts synodaux* (Biepols, 1975), pp. 87–88; Rapp, *Réformes et réformations,* pp. 131–33, 150–60.

32. DS 1560, pp. 75, 150, 165, 170; DS 1566, pp. 52–56; DS 1577, pp. 25–27; DS 1614b, p. 4; DS 1657, p. 9–11; Janier, *Probation des saincts sacrements.* Cf. Delumeau, *Le catholicisme,* pp. 59, 266; Soulet, *Traditions et réformes,* pp. 190–201; Pérouas, *Le diocèse de La Rochelle,* pp. 194–205, 272–94; Ferté, *La vie religieuse,* pp. 147–69, 170–95.

33. Charles Demia, *Trésor clérical ou conduites pour acquérir et conserver la sainteté ecclésiastique* (Lyon, 1682), pp. 340–43.

34. DS 1577, p. 25; Demia, *Trésor,* pp. 340–43; AMR, Sourcieux-sur-l'Arbrêle GG 1 (1652); DS 1705, p. 28. Cf. Soulet, *Traditions et réformes,* pp. 231–61.

35. Jean Benedicti, *La somme des pechez et les remedes d'iceux,* 2d ed. (Lyon, 1594), p. 58; DS 1577, pp. 29–30; DS 1614a, pp. 7–10; DS 1663, pp. 4–5; DS 1687, pp. 47–49; d'Epinac, *Avertissement au clergé,* p. 7.

36. DS 1577, pp. 29–30; *Instructions des curés et vicaires pour faire le prône* (Lyon, 1578).

37. Noël Chomel, *Recueil de plusieurs lettres familières d'un curé adressées à d'autres curés contenant diverses pratiques pour sanctifier les paroisses* (Lyon, 1693), preface and pp. 113–15.

38. For Chomel and Colembet, see Chomel, *Recueil de plusieurs lettres;* idem, *Dictionnaire oeconomique contenant divers moyens d'augmenter et conserver son bien et meme sa santé,* 2 vols. (Lyon, 1709); Guigue, *Les papiers des dévots,* pp. 84, 90, 102–03; AD Rhône, D 253, E 177–79, 44 H 10–17; Gutton, *La société et les pauvres,* pp. 103, 381–400; C. P. Testnoire Lafayette, *Histoire de Saint-Etienne* (Saint-Etienne, 1902), pp. 132–37. See also Hoffman, "Church and Community," p. 179.

39. Pérouas, *Le diocèse de La Rochelle,* pp. 353–409.

40. Davis, *Society and Culture,* pp. 74–76; Brémond, *Histoire littéraire,* 9:45–128; Delumeau, *Le catholicisme,* pp. 282–84; Ferté, *La vie religieuse,* pp. 294–335; DS 1614a, pp. 14–15; Evennett, *Spirit of the Counter Reformation,* pp. 36–42; Janier, *Probation des saincts sacrements,* pp. 209–13.

41. Richard, *La papauté et la Ligue,* p. 79; Perrat, "Mon vieux Châtillon," p. 352; Coste, ed., *Vincent de Paul: Correspondance,* 9:50; Benedicti, *La somme des pechez,* p. 972; DS 1663, p. 11; DS 1687, pp. 45–58; Chomel, *Recueil de plusieurs lettres,* preface and pp. 7–13.

42. DS 1577, pp. 18–21; DS 1566, p. 81; Chomel, *Recueil de plusieurs lettres,* pp. 62–71; DS 1687, pp. 69–75; Janier, *Probation des saincts sacrements,* p. 109.

43. DS 1577, pp. 2–3; DS 1687, p. 23. Cf. Delumeau, *Le catholicisme,* p. 84; Brémond, *Histoire littéraire,* 9:156.

44. Emile Mâle, *L'art religieux de la fin du XVIᵉ siècle, du XVIIᵉ siècle et du XVIIIᵉ siècle: Etude sur l'iconographie après le concile de Trente* (Paris, 1951), pp. 72–86; *Lexikon für Theologie und Kirche,* 2d ed. (Freiburg-im-Breisgau, 1964), s.v. "Sakramenthäuschen"; *Visites,* passim; DS 1631, pp. 7–8; DS 1687, p. 23; DS 1705, pp. 110–13; Demia,

Trésor, pp. 501–05; Guigue, *Les papiers des dévots,* pp. 64, 67, 72, 116, 174; Chomel, *Recueil de plusieurs lettres,* pp. 230–74; *Catéchiste des peuples de la campagne et des villes par un prêtre missionaire,* 6 vols. (Lyon, 1706), 4:29; *Dictionnaire de spiritualité,* s.v. "Confréries."

45. Burke, *Popular Culture,* pp. 177, 232; Mâle, *L'art religieux,* pp. 145–201, 313–25, 365–82; *Dictionnaire de théologie catholique* (Paris, 1923–), s.v. "Saints (Culte des)" and "Jacques de Voragine."

46. Brémond, *Histoire littéraire,* 9:249–89; Demia, *Trésor,* pp. 501–05; DS 1705, pp. 110–13; *Catéchiste des peuples,* 4:69; *Lexikon für Theologie und Kirche,* s.v. "Rosenkranz"; Kleinclausz, *Lyon des origines,* pp. 80–92; AM Lyon, GG 113.

47. Delumeau, *Le catholicisme,* pp. 280–81; Chomel, *Recueil de plusieurs lettres,* pp. 93–102, 129–173; DS 1670, pp. 7–8.

48. AD Rhône, 50 H 21.

49. DS 1566, pp. 65, 72–73; DS 1577, passim; DS 1614a, p. 14. In 1609 the canon-counts mounted their own drive to reform the festival of the Innocents at the cathedral; see Forest, *L'école cathedrale,* pp. 169–75.

50. DS 1670, p. 11; DS 1687, pp. 28, 82; DS 1705, pp. 110–13.

51. *Catéchiste des peuples,* 1:140–69; Chomel, *Recueil de plusieurs lettres,* pp. 26–34, 40–41.

52. Demia, *Trésor,* pp. 464–71. For the other rituals of mourning he condemned, see Hoffman, "Church and Community," pp. 190–91.

53. AD Rhône, 50 H 115–16, and Guigue, *Les papiers des dévots,* passim.

54. Guigue, *Les papiers des dévots,* pp. 64, 108–20; Gutton, *La société et les pauvres,* p. 386; AD Rhône, 50 H 115 (November 19, 1682); D 346, fol. 23.

55. AD Rhône, 50 H 115 (May 13 to July 8, 1683; August 17, 1686; February 8, 1687).

56. AD Rhône, 50 H 115 (January 30, 1682; April 29, 1683; June 3, 1686).

57. DS 1614a, p. 8; Guigue, *Les papiers des dévots,* pp. 10–11; Chartier, *L'éducation en France,* pp. 113–14.

58. Burke, *Popular Culture,* p. 226.

59. AD Rhône, ESFC, Neuville, GC 18, fols. 162–90 (1671–73); BM Roanne, 5 G 24, 26. Cf. Thérèse Schmitt, *L'organization ecclésiastique,* pp. 196–209.

60. Burke, *Popular Culture,* pp. 217–18; Muchembled, *Culture populaire,* pp. 194–96; John T. McNeill and Helena M. Gamer, eds., *Medieval Handbooks of Penance* (New York, 1938), pp. 321–45; Jean-Claude Schmitt, *Le saint lévrier;* Davis, *Society and Culture,* pp. 119–20; Bellièvre, *Souvenirs de voyages,* pp. 20, 108.

61. Burke, *Popular Culture,* pp. 220–21; Davis, *Society and Culture,* pp. 119–21; Bercé, *Fête et révolte,* p. 150.

62. Davis, *Society and Culture,* pp. 119–21; idem, "Protestantism," pp. 534–53; Rubys, *Histoire de la ville de Lyon,* pp. 370–71, 409, 499–504. For similar views elsewhere, see Bercé, *Fête et révolte,* p. 70.

63. Rubys, *Histoire de la ville de Lyon,* p. 501; J. Péricaud, "Louis Garon," pp. 433–56; Tricou, "Les confréries joyeuses," pp. 293–317; Bibliothèque municipale de Lyon, *Entrées.*

64. DS 1577, pp. 2–3; DS 1663, p. 11; *Visites,* p. 99; Chomel, *Recueil de plusieurs lettres,* p. 31.

65. Benedicti, *La somme des pechez,* pp. 58–71.

66. The Council of Trent banned the depiction of nudes in religious art, and Paul IV and Clement VIII sought to efface nudes in Michelangelo's ceiling in the Sistine Chapel—a work that the papacy itself had commissioned not long before! For further evidence of the new sexual morality, see Muchembled, *Culture populaire,* pp. 230–40; Jean-Louis Flandrin, *Familles: Parenté, maison, sexualité dans l'ancienne société* (Paris, 1976), pp. 176–88, 202–03. One of the practices that the urban elites had once tolerated was

prostitution: see Jacques Rossiaud, "Prostitution, jeunesse et société dans les villes du Sud-Est au XVᵉ siècle," *Annales E.S.C.* 31 (1976): 289–323.

67. AD Rhône, 50 H 115–16, passim; Guigue, *Les papiers des dévots*, pp. 44, 64–71, 106–20. Another sign of the harsher sexual morality occurs in DS 1705, pp. 45–58, which makes concubinage a sin that only the bishop can absolve; earlier diocesan statutes had not done so.

68. AD Rhône, D 346; Demia, *Trésor*, p. 353.

69. Guigue, *Les papiers des dévots*, p. 68, 112; Chomel, *Recueil de plusieurs lettres*, pp. 28, 44–62, 74; *Catéchiste des peuples*, 1:140–69; Burke, *Popular Culture*, pp. 186–87, 212. For similar sentiments elsewhere, see Esprit Flechier, *Mémoires de Flechier sur les grands-jours d'Auvergne en 1665*, ed. M. Cheruel (Paris, 1856), pp. 242–43.

70. Bibliothèque municipale de Lyon, *Entrées*, pp. 15–16, 56–58; Burke, *Popular Culture*, pp. 243, 270–81; Muchembled, *Culture populaire*, pp. 197, 225–28, 342–45.

71. Muchembled, *Culture populaire*, pp. 159, 176–228; Bercé, *Fête et révolte*, pp. 13–18, 74–82. For legislation against festivals and confraternities that cites their seditiousness and lumps together charivaris and revolts, see René Pillorget, *Les mouvements insurrectionnels de Provence entre 1596 et 1715* (Paris, 1975), pp. 146–51; Yves-Marie Bercé, *Histoire des Croquants: Etude des soulevements populaires au XVIIᵉ siècle dans le sud-ouest de la France*, 2 vols. (Geneva, 1974), 1:206–23; Delamare, *Traité de la police*, 3d ed., 3 vols. (Amsterdam, 1729), 1:347–52; Fontanon, *Edits et ordonnances*, 1:819, 836, 1086–89; Joseph N. Guyot, *Répertoire universel et raisonné de jurisprudence civile, criminelle, canonique et bénéficiale*, 18 vols. (Paris, 1784), s.v. "fêtes"; Flechier, *Mémoires*, pp. 279, 283–87. For further details, see Hoffman, "Church and Community," pp. 204–05.

72. Bercé, *Fête et révolte*, pp. 13–18, 75–82; idem, *Histoire des Croquants*, pp. 206–23, 674–98; Emmanuel Le Roy Ladurie, "Les masses profondes: La paysannerie," in *Histoire économique et sociale de la France*, ed. F. Braudel and E. Labrousse, 4 vols. (Paris, 1970–), vol. 1, pt. 2:822–59; idem, *Le carnaval de Romans* (Paris, 1979), pp. 102–18, 202, 315–31. For the diocese's brief outburst of peasant unrest, see Gutton, *Villages du Lyonnais*, pp. 40–41, 121–22; Richard Bonney, *Political Change in France under Richelieu and Mazarin: 1624–1661* (Oxford, 1978), pp. 227, 232. There were also urban revolts in the city of Lyon: Boris Porchnev, *Les soulèvements populaires en France de 1623 à 1648* (Paris, 1963), pp. 151–56, 661–64. As for disturbances after festivals, numerous examples will be cited in the following two chapters.

73. Evennett, *Spirit of the Counter Reformation*, pp. 24–42; D. François Le Tellier de Bellefons, *Sermons pour les prières de quarante heures contre les debauches du Carnaval* (Lyon, 1694); Gutton, *La société et les pauvres*, p. 385; Chartier, *L'éducation en France*, p. 61.

74. AD Rhône, D 346.

75. For this and the following paragraph, see Delumeau, *Le catholicisme*, pp. 46–49, 88–92; Evennett, *Spirit of the Counter Reformation*, pp. 31–42; *Dictionnaire de spiritualité*, s.v. "Charité." References to the evils of the world of the flesh and to the need for self-control abound in the spiritual literature and in sermons by regular clergymen: Le Tellier de Bellefons, *Sermons contre Carnaval*, pp. 72–84; idem, *Octave des morts* (Lyon, 1695), sermon 6; Estienne Bertel, *Discours choisis sur plusieurs matières importantes de la foy et des moeurs* (Lyon, 1687), pp. 625–29.

76. For the free rider problem, see Mancur Olson, *The Logic of Collective Action* (Cambridge, 1965), and Popkin, *The Rational Peasant*, pp. 253–57. One might doubt that "free riding" occurred in traditional societies such as early modern Europe, but one can think of numerous examples—for instance, canons who favored seminaries yet refused to contribute to their establishment. Moreover, organizations that were involved in the campaign for social control, such as the Company of the Holy Sacrament, typically resorted

to tactics that minimized free riding: focusing on local goals, for example, or breaking undertakings down into small tasks so that each member could feel that his contribution made a difference. A modern reader might also ask why elites did not simply resort to force to achieve social control and political order. The answer is that unlike soldiers and police forces clergymen were numerous and also cheap, for their salaries were already paid. Moreover, sin and impiety were widely considered to be the causes of rebellion; religious reform was therefore the obvious remedy.

77. Coste, ed., *Saint Vincent de Paul: Correspondance,* 9:43; Guigue, *Les papiers des dévots,* pp. 145–46. Cf. Martin, *Histoires des églises,* p. 278.
78. The metaphor of Lent's victory over Carnival appears in Burke, *Popular Culture.*
79. DS 1577, pp. 50–52; DS 1614a, p. 5; DS 1663, p. 4; Janier, *Probation des saincts sacrements;* Chomel, *Recueil de plusieurs lettres,* pp. 4–5, 33–34, 113–14.

Chapter 4. Agents of Counter Reformation

1. AD Rhône, 4 G 24, fols. 47–60 (1684).
2. For Saint-Just, see AD Rhône, 12 G 362, "Information faites contre les clercs de Saint-Just, 1511–1725." For the other parishes, I relied upon the criminal registers from the urban jurisdiction of Ainay (11 G 302–05, 11 G 395) for the years 1777–82; the records of the *officialité* (4 G 22–30); and samples taken from the voluminous records of the *sénéchaussée* of Lyon—a subject discussed in the next chapter. Concerning the intellectual level of the parish clergy in Lyon, we know that canons were well educated, and in Lyon, as in all cities and walled towns, curés were required to have university diplomas or at least three years of law or theology to maintain possession of their benefices. See Guyot, *Répertoire universel,* s.v. "curé"; and for the canons, the biographies in Tricou, *Armorial de Saint-Nizier,* and Beyssac, *Chanoines.*
3. AD Rhône, 1 G 48–53; AD Jura, G 10, and *Visites.* These are the major surviving *procès-verbaux* of pastoral visits made after the late sixteenth century. For details on these and other visits, see Hoffman, "Church and Community," pp. 214–15.
4. Pierre Durand de Maillane, *Dictionnaire de droit canonique et de pratique bénéficiale,* 6 vols. (Lyon, 1787), s.v. "pluralisme" and "curé"; Beyssac, *Chanoines.*
5. AD Rhône, 1 G 53, fols. 1, 15, 19, 45, 59, and passim.
6. AD Rhône, ESFC, Saint-Cyr-au-Mont-d'Or, registre 16, fol. 937; 4 G 30 (1756–77); 12 G 362.
7. Gutton, "Le recrutement du clergé," pp. 1–20. The number of *bénéfices à âmes* vacant for extraordinary reasons dropped from 24 per decade (in 1645–55) to 1 or 2 per decade after 1705.
8. For problems with death inventories, see Hoffman, "Church and Community," p. 222.
9. Books recommended by the *dévots:* Demia, *Trésor,* pp. 64, 403–08.
10. The rural priests in the diocese were still not likely to be university graduates. For this, see Hoffman, "Church and Community," pp. 224–25, and the sources cited there.
11. Sources for the events in Saint-Germain-Laval include BM Roanne, 3 G 55, 4 E 34, 5 G 18, 5 G 22, 5 G 24–26; AD Rhône, 1 G 52, fol. 485; *Visites,* pp. 382–84; A Séminaire, Retraite générale de MM les curés (1667).
12. *Visites,* pp. 10, 32; AD Jura, G 10, fols. 149, 198. Cf. Robert Chanaud, "Folklore et religion dans le diocèse de Grenoble à la fin du XVIIe siècle: Les visites pastorales de Mgr Le Camus," *Le monde alpin et rhodanien* 5 (1977): 33–103.
13. A Diana, 3 G 1, 5 G 1–3.
14. AD Ain, C 133; Adrien Faure, *Histoire de Pérouges* (n.p., 1970), pp. 43–45; A Séminaire, Retraite générale de MM les curés, 1664–1698 et 1704–1758.
15. For examples from four villages, see AD Rhône, 2 E 151, 155, 156, 158, 160; 28 G

89, 93; ESFC, Saint-Cyr-au-Mont-d'Or, registres 2, 3, 9, 12, 18b; Canard, "Confréries de Saint-Just-en-Chevalet," pp. 98, 111–12; BM Roanne, 5 G 27; AD Rhône, 10 G 538 and 1 G 52, fol. 348.

16. AD Rhône, 10 G 2743 (February 26, 1733); 1 G 51, fol. 70 (1749). Another example: Benoit, *L'abbaye de Sainte-Claude,* 2:658–61.

17. AD Rhône, 1 G 151, fol. 70 (1749).

18. Paul Brune, *Histoire de l'ordre hospitalier du Saint-Esprit* (Lons-le-Saunier, 1882), pp. 427–35.

19. AD Rhône, 10 G 2743, letter of Archbishop Malvin de Montazet (1761).

20. Jean Tricou, "Enseignes et médailles de dévotions," 14 (1952): 205–28 and 15 (1953): 107–25; AD Rhône, 10 G 1688, 13 G 287, 13 G 649, 2 H 16, 27 H 405, 50 H 119. A detailed study of the membership of these confraternities would be very difficult, given the lack of occupational information in the confraternity records and the absence of suitable tax records in which members could be traced during the seventeenth century.

21. AMR, Chassagny, GG 1; Dracé, GG 1; Duerne, GG 1; AD Rhône, 3 H 3, fols. 134–39; AD Ain G 90 (1644); A Diocese, Vendranges (1615); J. G. Trolieur de la Vaupière, *Histoire de Beaujolais,* ed. Leon Galle and Georges Guigue (Lyon, 1920), p. 281. For these confraternities elsewhere in Europe see *Lexikon für Theologie und Kirche,* 2d ed., s.v. "Rosenkranz" and "Corporis-Christi Bruderschaft"; *Dictionnaire de spiritualité,* s.v. "Confréries" and "Doctrinaires"; T. Schmitt, *L'organization ecclésiastique,* pp. 199–201; Delumeau, *Le catholicisme,* p. 146; Pérouas, *Le diocèse de La Rochelle,* pp. 165–68, 382–84, 424, 454–64; Ferté, *La vie religieuse,* pp. 336–69.

22. AMR, Tassin, GG 2, June 6, 1721; Saint-Genis-les-Ollières, GG 1, September 21, 1668; AML, Sauvain, GG 1, October 1, 1623; Saint-Barthelemy-Letra, GG 1, August 15, 1700. Cf. Ferté, *La vie religieuse,* pp. 336–69.

23. *Visites;* AD Rhône, 1 G 49–53. The Rosary confraternities tended to cluster in the hilly regions on the eastern and western fringes of the diocese—a tendency with parallels elsewhere in France. One possible reason the Rosary confraternities predominated in these regions was that the mountains abounded in small cities and market towns. With more small cities, the mountainous fringes of the diocese would (as I explain below) have experienced Counter-Reformation spirituality well before the center of the diocese, and it would be only natural that they witnessed a flourishing of Rosary confraternities, for the Rosary confraternities were promoted at an earlier date than the Blessed Sacrament confraternities. For a discussion, see Hoffman, "Church and Community," p. 244.

24. Examples from urban parishes: AD Rhône, 13 G 287 (Saint-Paul, 1654–96), 13 G 649 (Saint-Vincent, 1708–09), 10 G 1688 (Sainte-Croix, 1636–1789), and BP 3629 (Sainte-Croix, 1740s). Brotherhoods of Christian Doctrine: AMR, Duerne, GG 1 (October 21, 1640); Givors, GG 1 (January 24, 1642).

25. A Diocese, paroisse des Ardillats, Règles générales de la confrérie du Très Sainct Sacrement.

26. Demia, *Trésor,* pp. 501–05; DS 1705, pp. 110–13; AD Rhône, 1 G 53, fols. 5, 17, 19, 21, 27, 35; AD Jura, G 10, fols. 72, 98, 129, 131, 204.

27. AD Rhône, 10 G 1425 (1710–17); 1 G 50, fol. 152; AD Ain E 496. Cf. Maurice Agulhon, *Pénitents et Francs-Maçons de l'ancienne Provence* (Paris, 1968), pp. 92–93, 106–07, 116.

28. DS 1705, pp. 110–13; Demia, *Trésor,* pp. 501–05; Philippe Pouzet, "Les anciennes confréries de Villefranche," *Revue d'histoire de Lyon,* 3 (1904): 428; AD Rhône, 2 E 198; ESFC, Neuville, liasse 3, fols. 165–90 (1671, 1673); AMR, Neuville, GG 16 (August 15, 1753).

29. AD Rhône, 50 H 21 (1658). For parishes where curés did have power over the Penitents, see AD Ain E 470 (1673), E 498 (1641), and Condamin and Langlois, *Histoire de Saint-Bonnet-le-Château,* 2:231–34.

30. AD Loire, B 781 (February 23, 1682).
31. One of the five belonged to a family that furnished two of the Penitents' rectors, and the other four were probably enrolled in the confraternity or associated with its members. See Hoffman, "Church and Community," pp. 255–56.
32. Sources for the incidents in Saint-Just include AD Loire, B 781, which contains the curé's complaint (February 23, 1682), an agreement between Dubessey and the curé (February 17, 1683), and letters from Dubessey and his accomplice, Jean Chastre (September 1683 and August 25, 1683); Jean Canard's article "La confrérie des pénitents blancs de Saint-Just-en-Chevalet," *BD* 43 (1973–74): 205–21, and his *Société*, pp. 37–40.
33. AMR, l'Arbrêle, GG 3 (1748).
34. AD Rhône, BBPC, 44 (1729–30): July 20 and December 17, 1730.
35. Gutton, *La société et les pauvres,* pp. 385–86; idem, *Villages du Lyonnais,* pp. 57–62; Garden, *Lyon et les Lyonnais,* p. 446; Latreille, *Histoire de Lyon,* p. 268; August Cornet, "Les petites écoles de Charles Demia dans l'Ain," *ASEA* 44 (1911): 50–78.
36. A. Balland and F. Balland, "Saint-Julien-de-Reyssouze: Résumé des principaux événements survenus dans cette commune de 1300 à 1852," *ASEA* 43 (1910): 5–44; AMR, Pollioney, GG 3 (1781); AD Rhône, ESFC, Saint-Cyr-au-Mont-d'Or, registre 7; Gutton, *Villages du Lyonnais,* pp. 58, 61.
37. Garden, *Lyon et les Lyonnais,* pp. 447–48; AD Rhône, ESFC, Saint-Cyr-au-Mont-d'Or, registre 7 (1780s).
38. AD Rhône, D 353; Garden, *Lyon et les Lyonnais,* p. 448; AM Lyon, GG 114; Gutton, *La société et les pauvres,* pp. 432–33, 471–75.
39. Thomas Malley, "Sentiments d'un curé sur l'école primaire," *BHDL* (1911): 310–14.
40. AD Rhône, 1 G 53, fol. 11. Similar orders can be found throughout 1 G 49–53; and in AD Jura, G 10; DS 1705, p. 101; and DS 1687, pp. 115–17.
41. AD Rhône, 1 G 53, fol. 159; ESFC, Neuville, GG 14. Cf. Gutton, *Villages du Lyonnais,* p. 75.
42. AD Rhône, 28 G 86; 28 G 89; ESFC, Neuville, GG 14, GG 17, GG 21, GG 24–25, GG 27–28; AD Jura, G 10, fol. 255. For a similar accusation in Pont-de-Veyle, see Dubois, 34 (1901): 34–47.
43. AMR, Leguy, GG 1, and Lentilly, GG 5. Additional rural examples are cited in Hoffman, "Church and Community," p. 265. For urban examples, see AD Rhône, 13 G 645 and 11 G 544–48. Even in rural parishes the curé could not always veto the choice of a vestry warden: see Gutton, *Villages du Lyonnais,* p. 75.
44. Gutton, *La société et les pauvres,* pp. 375–77, 410, 482–84; A Diocese, fonds de Saint-Nizier, Dames de Charité, liasses I, II, and III, pts. 3, 4, and 5; AD Rhône, ESFC, Saint-Cyr-au-Mont-d'Or, registres 2, 3, 9, 12; Dubois, 34 (1901): 17–22; AD Ain, fonds de la commune de Pont-de-Veyle, non-classé, cote provisoire 290, "Inventaire raisonné . . . des titres de l'hôtel de ville," and "Notes sur les registres de l'hôtel de ville de Pont-de-Veyle," entries for 1700. For more on hospitals and charities, see Hoffman, "Church and Community," pp. 265–67.
45. Guyot, *Répertoire universel,* s.v. "curé"; AMR, Denicé, GG 5 (1741); AD Rhône, ESFC, La Guillotière (March 22, 1767); C 1–2; AD Ain, C 221; Kleinclausz, *Histoire de Lyon,* 2:82–91. See also Hoffman, "Church and Community," pp. 268–70.
46. AD Rhône, ESFC, Neuville, liasse 3, fols. 178–98 (July 26, 1671); *Visites,* p. 11; BM Roanne, 5 G 24, 5 G 26; Guigue, *Les papiers des dévots,* pp. 211–13; Gutton, *Villages du Lyonnais,* p. 82; AD Rhône, 3 H 3, fols. 134–39; de Bollo, *Le rosaire de la Vierge Marie,* pp. 37–53.
47. The information on the Rosary and the saints is taken from a study of the altars and chapels of the twenty-five most popular saints and devotions among the 108 northeastern parishes which had three successive parish visits. For each parish, I noted which altars

and chapels disappeared and which were newly founded over the course of the successive visits. See Hoffman, "Church and Community," pp. 240, 385–87, for details. Further evidence for the popularity of the devotion to the rosary comes from *découvertes de cadavres*—judicial investigations of drownings and other accidental deaths. In both Lyon and the countryside, victims of the accidents often carried rosaries in their pockets: AD Rhône, 11 G 313 (January 8, 1745); AD Ain, B unclassified, justice of Echallon, assises (August 9, 1707). Unfortunately, death inventories—a better source—usually omitted rosaries.

48. These results come from my sample of rural wills, which is described in appendix 1.

49. See the statistical analysis in appendix 1; Philip T. Hoffman, "Pious Bequests in Wills: A Statistical Analysis" (California Institute of Technology, Social Science Working Paper No. 393, June, 1981), pp. 34–41, contains a more detailed analysis. In particular, the momentary decline in bequests was not the result of Protestants who sneaked into the sample or of the Church's slackening its efforts of reform.

50. All of these calculations rely on the tobit analysis in appendix 1. They correct for inflation and assume that wealth and other economic factors are held constant.

51. Poculat left 9,000 *livres* to the *hôpital-général* in 1620: AD Rhône, 3 E 4001, fol. 326. Bequests to charity (chiefly to the *hôpital-général,* which was founded in the years 1614–22) jumped significantly during the period 1616–35: see appendix 1 for a statistical test.

52. For the economic troubles, see Kleinclausz, *Histoire de Lyon,* 2:4–5, 28–39, 50–52, 63–67; E. Pariset, *Histoire de la fabrique lyonnaise* (Lyon, 1901), pp. 54–59, 71–76; Marcel Vigne, *La banque à Lyon du XVe au XVIIIe siècle* (Lyon, 1903), pp. 217–26. Whereas we can use series of land leases to gauge rural economic expectations, we have no comparable quantitative index for the urban economy, especially in the seventeenth century. Even the wage and interest rate series we used for the sixteenth century are lacking or of dubious value for seventeenth-century Lyon. Interest rates at the fairs, for example, were fixed in the seventeenth century, and so they reveal nothing about economic expectations. Tax records are equally useless.

53. A tobit analysis yields $t=2.59$, significant at the .01 level, for an increase in pious bequests over time among the urban wills drawn up after 1635. Again, this test controls for other factors that could affect the making of a will, such as the testator's wealth, the number of his dependent children, etc. See appendix 1 for details. For the economic troubles after 1680, see Kleinclausz, *Histoire de Lyon,* 2:63–76; Pariset, *La fabrique lyonnaise,* pp. 114–21.

54. See Hoffman, "Pious Bequests," pp. 45–50, where I consider and reject a number of other possible explanations, including easier access to churches, "cheaper" masses, changes in inheritance taxes, etc.

55. In chapter 1 we noted that urban testators began to abandon the elaborate burials in the 1540s. Rural testators had rarely shown (or perhaps could rarely afford) such lavish funerals; even so, the fraction of rural wills mentioning elaborate funerals dropped from over 8 percent in the sixteenth century to under 1 percent after 1700.

56. For meditation in the Rosary confraternity, see de Bollo, *Le rosaire de la Vierge Marie,* passim.

57. If we restrict ourselves to those wills that contained bequests for masses or prayers and that actually said for whom the masses or prayers were intended, we can calculate the percent of these wills which mentioned "relatives and friends" in addition to the testator himself. Among the urban wills with a specific intention, 8 percent (15 of 193 testaments) mentioned "relatives and friends" in the sixteenth century, but none (0 of 31) did so in the eighteenth century. Among rural testaments, the corresponding figures for the sixteenth and eighteenth centuries are 38 percent (5 of 13) and 0 percent (0 of 62), respectively. For the urban wills, this difference is significant at only the 10 percent level

(by Fisher's exact test), but for the rural ones it is significant at well below the .001 level.

58. For group confession, see chapter 3. Confessionals were common in the visits of 1700 and 1719: AD Jura, G 10; AD Rhône, 1 G 53. Unfortunately, evidence about actual communion practices is unavailable for the seventeenth and early eighteenth centuries.

59. AD Rhône, 2 H 16; Garden, *Lyon et les Lyonnais,* p. 41.

60. AML, Sauvain, GG 1, October 1, 1623; AD Rhône, ESFC, Saint-Cyr-au-Mont-d'Or, registre 11, fol. 5; Neuville, liasse 3, fol. 165 (1671) and GG 25. The population estimates come from birth figures; see Hoffman, "Church and Community," p. 242, for details.

61. Tests for the effects of literacy in the rural wills yield t-statistics of 2.05 or better, depending on the wealth measure used in the tobit analysis. These are significant at the 5 percent level or better. Since the tobit analysis takes into account the wealth, sex, age, and family size of the testators, we can be confident that we are measuring the actual impact of literacy on pious donations and not the effects of other differences between the literate and the illiterate.

62. Chaunu, *La mort à Paris,* pp. 331–37, 371; Daniel Roche, "La mémoire de la mort," *Annales E.S.C.* 31 (1976): 76–119; Le Tellier de Bellefons, *Octave des Morts,* p. 176; Bertel, *Discours choisis,* pp. 601–03. Bertel, a Jesuit, preached in Lyon and taught at the city's College of the Trinity.

63. The tobit analysis in appendix 1 shows that pious bequests rose over and above any increase caused by changing literacy.

64. A t-test yields only t=1.06 for the effect of literacy on pious bequests in urban wills, 1636–1705. This is not significant at the 10 percent level. See appendix 1 for details. On literacy rates, see Latreille, *Histoire de Lyon,* pp. 267–68; Gutton, *Villages du Lyonnais,* pp. 62–64.

65. AD Rhône, 3 H 3, fol. 135–39; AMR, Lissieu, GG 1 (April 1, 1663); AM Bourg-en-Bresse, GG 211; A. Vachez, ed., "Documents inédits: Le livre de raison de messire Pierre Boyer, docteur en medecine à Saint-Bonnet-le-Château (1620–34)," *RL,* 5th ser., 8 (1889): 207–19, 291–99, 378–86, 450–60; AD Rhône, 3 E 2235 (September 8, 1669).

66. *Visites;* AD Rhône, 1 G 49–52.

67. Vovelle, *Piété baroque en Provence,* p. 165, provides examples from Provence. For others, see Hoffman, "Church and Community," p. 247.

68. The tobit analysis yields t=2.31 for the effects of population among the rural testators. This is significant at the .05 level. See appendix 1.

69. Delattre, *Les établissements des Jésuites,* s.v. "Macon, Bourg-en-Bresse, Trévoux, Saint-Etienne, Saint-Chamond, Roanne, Pont-de-Veyle, Lyon"; Perrat, "Mon vieux Châtillon," pp. 317–66; Trolieur de la Vaupière, *Histoire de Beaujolais,* p. 281.

70. A t-test for the differences between men and women in the rural wills yielded t-statistics of 1.94, 2.77, and 2.00, depending on the wealth measure used. The last two are significant at the .05 level, and the first is very nearly so. See appendix 1 for details.

71. The tobit analysis (appendix 1) of urban wills, 1636–1705, yields t=0.04 for the effect of sex on pious bequests.

72. AM Lyon, GG 394, fols. 80–81.

73. For an analysis of one surviving sermon, see Hoffman, "Church and Community," pp. 274–76. The marginal notations in parish registers suggest that many curés confined themselves to the sort of simple preaching that the Church hierarchy recommended. The same appears to have been the case in other dioceses. See AMR, Haute-Rivoire, GG 5; Ferté, *La vie religieuse,* pp. 196–230; and Pérouas, *Le diocèse de La Rochelle,* pp. 272–94. On the other hand, some curés were capable of more elaborate sermons:

AMR, Charly, GG 7 (1722); La-Tour-de-Salvigny, GG 3; Saint-Symphorien-sur-Coise, GG 2 (1645–46).

74. AD Rhône, D 346; Charles Demia, *Reglemens pour les écoles de la ville et du diocèse de Lyon* (Lyon, n.d.). See chapter 3.

75. Demia, *Trésor*, p. 352. A search at the BM Lyon, the BN, and other libraries failed to uncover a copy of Demia's *Catéchisme pour les petites écoles du diocése de Lyon*. For references to it and evidence that it was the most commonly used catechism in the diocese, see Hoffman, "Church and Community," p. 278.

76. AMR, Neuville, GG 11 (1780).

77. DS 1663, pp. 7–8; AD Rhône, BBPC, 69 (1777–78), October 31, 1777. Other examples can be found in BBPC, 73 (1785–86), June 16 through August 17, 1786, and February 3, 1786, respectively. See Hoffman, "Church and Community," p. 281, for details.

78. DS 1705, pp. 69–75; AD Rhône, BBPC, 71 (1781–82), June 1, 1781; 50 (1737–38), November 18, 1737; 69 (1777–78), December 30, 1776, through January 4, 1777, and August 1 through August 21, 1777; and 70 (1779–80), March 18, 1778.

79. AD Rhône, 28 G 86 (1732–33); BBPC, 21 (1696), December 9, 1695; 9 (1682), June 2, 1682.

80. AD Rhône, 28 G 86 (1732–33); BBPC, 21 (1696), December 9, 1695; 9 (1682), June 2, 1682.

81. AMR, Odenas, GG 1; AD Rhône, 28 G 89 (1719); 15 G 491 (1720); BBPC, 21 (1696), December 9, 1695.

82. AD Rhône, BBPC, 8 (1677–81), May 22, 1681.

83. Among other sorts of strife, I might mention conflicts over religious rituals that peasants believed would protect their crops or their livestock. A number of curés grew skeptical of these ceremonies and incurred the wrath of peasants for refusing to perform them. See AMR, Grigny, GG 2 (1718); Létra, GG 6 (1753); Bessenay, GG 6 (1753); AD Rhône, BBPC, 6 (1673), Vaux-en-Beaujolais; 12 (1686), February 27, 1686; 21 (1695), December 9, 1695; and Hoffman, "Church and Community," pp. 288–90.

84. In Neuville, for example, the Blessed Sacrament confraternity sponsored a round of devotions and prayers during Carnival, in order to divert the faithful from the pre-Lenten celebrations: AD Rhône, ESFC, Neuville, liasse 5, fol 23 (1672).

85. AMR, Pommiers, GG 2 (1731), Saint-Symphorien-sur-Coise, GG 2 (1667–71); AD Rhône, ESFC, Neuville, GG 18, fols. 167–74, 188–90 (1671–73), GG 20, GG 21, GG 25, GG 27; Fleurieu-sur-l'Arbrêle, liasse 1; AD Rhône, 1 G 50, fol. 36; 4 G 24, fols. 23–27 (1683); 13 G 649. Cf. Gutton, "Reinages," pp. 443–53.

86. AD Rhône, 4 G 24, fols. 23–27 (1683).

87. AMR, Pouilly-le-Monial, GG 2 (1725); Forest, "Jean Rabot," pp. 482–90. The judge, Jean Terrasson, joined the Company of the Holy Sacrament in 1678 (Guigue, *Les papiers des dévots,* p. 70), and the company once arranged to have him personally try the case of a blasphemer in the parish of Saint-Clement-sous-Valsonne (AD Rhône, 50 H 115, January 30, 1682) so as to make an example of the sinner. Other curés also cooperated with seignorial judges to suppress festivals: AD Rhône, 2 B 66, Bois d'Oingt (August 16, 1724).

88. AD Loire, B 358, August 20, 1753.

89. AD Loire, B 1586, justice seigneuriale de Regny, February 1, 1769, and B 1589, February 28, 1778; B 842, maréchaussée de Roanne, August 28, 1766. Cf. Ferté, *La vie religieuse,* p. 327.

90. Bercé, *Fête et révolte,* pp. 171–74; BN, manuscrits Joly de Fleury, Correspondance administrative et affaires locales.

91. The priests' request is in BN, manuscrits Joly de Fleury, no. 1395, Affaires locales, fols. 322–24 (1779). In 1786 the court did prohibit festivals, charivaris, and other gatherings of parish youths in the Lyonnais, but there is no evidence connecting the curé's request and the 1786 court order; see Hoffman, "Church and Community," p. 297.

92. AD Loire, B 390, maréchaussée de Forez, August 19, 1781.

93. AD Rhône, 4 G 24, fols. 23–37, (1683).

94. For example, Jean Rabot, the curé of Saint-Clement-sous-Valsonne who worked against festivals and youth assemblies despite the resistance of the local *garçons,* was the leader of the regional ecclesiastical conference, and he was judged by contemporaries to be one of the best curés in the diocese. See Forest, "Jean Rabot," pp. 481–82, 487–88.

95. Perhaps some of the faithful outside Lyon adopted the austere Counter-Reformation sexual morality: in the market town of Pont-de-Vaux, one of the few communities for which figures are available, illegitimacy rates dropped during the period 1570–1670. The same pattern has been observed in other French communities, but it existed in Protestant England as well. See Flandrin, *Familles,* p. 179.

96. AM Lyon, FF, Proces-verbaux et contraventions: charivaris continue up to 1777; Henri Hours, "Emeutes et émotions populaires dans les campagnes du Lyonnais au XVIIIᵉ siècle," *Cahiers d'histoire* 9 (1964): 137–53; Fortier-Beaulieu, *Mariages et noces campagnardes,* pp. 233–37, 314–18; Taverne, *Coutumes et superstitions,* 4:63; 8:22, 44–46.

Chapter 5. The Aftermath of the Reforms

1. *Fête villageoise donnée au curé de Poleymieux* (Lyon, 1783); AD Ain, C 502 (1780); AMR, Tarare, GG 10 (1766); AD Rhône, ESFC, Neuville, *liasse* 11, fols. 81–82; Louis Charrier de la Roche, *Lettre pour exhorter ses paroissiens à l'aumône* (Lyon, 1780).

2. AML, Epercieux, GG 1–6 (1711–12); Gutton, *Villages du Lyonnais,* pp. 90, 162; AD Rhône, BBPC, 59 (1753–54), April 25, 1753.

3. Gutton, *Villages du Lyonnais,* pp. 67–73, is excellent for all aspects of strife over material issues. Cf. Timothy Tackett, *Priest and Parish in Eighteenth-Century France: A Social and Political Study of Curés in a Diocese of Dauphiné, 1750–1791* (Princeton, 1977), pp. 170–221. Gutton estimates that in 1728–29 only 18 percent of the diocesan curés held tithe rights, but his sources omit the eastern half of the diocese. I came up with a figure of slightly under 30 percent by using a different source: the "Pouillé général des paroisses du diocèse de Lyon au XVIIIᵉ siècle," Société de la Diana, *Mémoires et documents sur le Forez,* vol. 5 (Saint-Etienne, 1879), pp. 114–98. See Hoffman, "Church and Community," p. 306, for details. There are, of course, occasional examples of conflict between priests and parishioners over the tithe. For these, and for examples of strife over housing, the *casuel,* and glebe lands, see Hoffman, "Church and Community," p. 306.

4. AD Rhône, 4 G 24, fols. 23–27, April 17, 1683.

5. For the belief that curés were supposed to be "valets" of the parish, see AD Rhône, 1 H 83 (March 21, 1745) and BBPC, 6 (1673), parish of Vaux, date of complaint unreadable.

6. AD Rhône, BBPC, 28 (1703), January 11, 1703. Another example: Hoffman, "Church and Community," p. 308. For the Church's concern with children and parental obligations toward children, see Flandrin, *Familles,* pp. 128–308.

7. Cf. AD Rhône, BBPC, 20 (1695), August 15 through 30, 1695, parish of Blacé.

8. Fights on parish feast days between youths from neighboring villages often began in taverns, and the youths typically met in taverns before or after charivaris and bonfires on the first Sunday of Lent. Furthermore, the cabaret owners were frequently ringleaders in these affairs. My generalizations here are drawn from the following incidents: AD Loire,

B 832 (December 26, 1760), B 851 (August 5, 1770), B 1589 (February 28, 1778); AD Rhône, Sénéchaussée de Lyon, BP 3445 (January 18, 1778); AD Rhône, BBPC, 70 (1779–80), October 26, 1779, and 74 (1787), May 13, 1788; BN, manuscrits Joly de Fleury, 1395, Affaires locales, fols. 322–24.

9. AD Rhône, BBPC, 12 (1686), February 27, 1686, and 73 (1785–86), June 26 through August 17, 1786.

10. Roger Dion, *Histoire de la vigne et du vin en France depuis les origines au XIXe siècle* (Paris, 1959), pp. 472–91; Guyot, *Répertoire universel,* s.v. "cabaretier"; AD Rhône, 1 G 53, fols. 1, 59; 28 G 86, July 18, 1733; BBPC, 6 (1673), August 30, 1673; 9 (1682), June 3, 1682.

11. BBPC, 69 (1777–78), August 21, 1777, and 70 (1779–80), March 18, 1778. It is clear that parish youths still had a major hand in parish festivals and in defending the parish against outsiders: AD Loire, B 832, December 26, 1760; B 1521, July 14, 1664; AD Rhône, B, Maréchaussée, July–December 1779, November 18 and December 26, 1779; BBPC, 67 (1769–70), August 8, 1770, and 70 (1779–80), September 17, 1779.

12. BBPC, 12 (1686), February 27, 1686. Saint-Lager: BBPC, 73 (1785–86), March 24, 1786.

13. For local sources on these economic changes and more general works in French, German, and English, see Hoffman, "Church and Community," pp. 314–15. Land transactions and lending: Gascon, *Grand commerce,* 2:811–72; Gutton, *La société et les pauvres,* pp. 165–67; Garden, *Lyon et les Lyonnais,* pp. 361–63.

14. AD Rhône, BBPC, 59 (1753–54), October 11 through 19, 1754; 69 (1777–78), January 22, 1778.

15. AD Rhône, 4 G 24, fols. 23–27, April 17, 1683; AMR, L'Arbrêle, GG 3 (1748); AD Rhône, BBPC, 69 (1777–78), October 31, 1777. In my sample of criminal court cases from the *bailliage de Beaujolais* (described below), over 90 percent of the parishioners embroiled in difficulties with their curés were male.

16. Flandrin, *Familles,* pp. 124, 184–87, 203, 212; Vovelle, *Piété baroque en Provence,* p. 609; Rossiaud, "Prostitution, jeunesse et société," pp. 289–323; Jacques Rossiaud, "Fraternités de jeunesse et niveaux de culture dans les villes du Sud-Est à la fin du Moyen-Age," *Cahiers d'histoire* 21 (1976): 67–102.

17. Davis, *Society and Culture,* pp. 75, 292–93; Kathryn Norberg, "Women, the Family, and the Counter Reformation: Women's Confraternities in the Seventeenth Century," *Proceedings of the Western Society for French History* 6 (1979): 55–63; Jean Claude Schmitt, "Apostolat mendiant et société: Une confrérie dominicaine à la veille de la Reforme," *Annales E.S.C.* 26 (1971): 101–03.

18. Vovelle, *Piété baroque en Provence,* pp. 608–09; Norberg, "Rich and Poor," pp. 294–97; Chaunu, *La mort à Paris,* pp. 434–35. See chapter 4 for the wills from the diocese of Lyon.

19. Cf. Agulhon, *Pénitents et Francs-Macons,* pp. 53–54, 124–32. The differences between male and female testators were least pronounced in Paris: Chaunu, *La mort à Paris,* pp. 434–35. For the decline and domestication of male youth groups and festive bodies, both in Lyon and in other cities, see chapter 3 and Rossiaud, "Fraternités de jeunesse," pp. 85–102. Traditional forms of popular culture did not disappear entirely in big cities like Lyon: charivaris, for example, continued in Lyon well into the eighteenth century. The point is simply that male youth groups remained a serious power not in the cities but in market towns and villages. Cf. Nicole Castan, *Justice et répression en Languedoc à l'époque des lumières* (Paris, 1980), pp. 60–64, 205–08.

20. For this view of criminal justice, see Yves Castan, *Honnêteté et relations sociales en Languedoc (1715–1780)* (Paris, 1974), pp. 63–114, 541; A. Abbiatecci et al., *Crimes et criminalité en France aux XVIIe et XVIIIe siècles* (Paris, 1971); Alfred Soman, "The

Parlement of Paris and the Great Witch Hunt (1565–1640)," *Sixteenth Century Journal*
9 (1978): 30–44; Nicole Castan, *Justice et répression;* idem, *Les criminels de Languedoc:*
Les exigences d'ordre et les voies du ressentiment dans une société pré-révolutionnaire
(1750–1790) (Toulouse, 1980). In some ways, of course, the plaintiffs and defendants
in criminal cases did differ from the population as a whole. For this, see the two works
by Nicole Castan.

21. The records used consist of liasses of loose documents, arranged in chronological order.
For a given trial, one usually finds a criminal complaint and other pieces of criminal pro-
cedure. The final disposition of the cases is often unknown: in the Old Regime, criminal
proceedings were often dropped to avoid court costs, and the differences between the
plaintiff and the defendant were then settled out of court. I have used the complaints to
count the criminal cases. For my survey, I read all surviving liasses before 1650 and then
selected liasses at random and read them in their entirety for the periods after 1650. See
appendix 2, part a, for a description of this sample and a list of the liasses chosen.

22. Messance, *Recherches sur la population des généralités d'Auvergne, de Lyon, de Rouen, et de*
quelques provinces et villes du royaume (Paris, 1766; repr., Paris, 1973), pp. 28–29,
39–55, gives population figures and the number of clergymen for various parts of the
diocese. See Hoffman, "Church and Community," pp. 322–24, 391, for details and the
calculation of the probabilities. One might object that the priests' greater daily contact
with parishioners would cause them to be overrepresented in criminal cases, but this
objection ignores the fact that the Tridentine Church urged priests to avoid dealings
with laymen.

23. The probability that chance alone (i.e., random sampling) would generate differences in
observed frequencies as great as those observed between the first period (before 1650: 1
case in 114) and the fourth period (1751–88: 24 cases in 621) is only .07, by a one-
sided Fisher's exact test. The fact that my sampling scheme is not random might raise
somewhat this probability of a spurious result, but only by a very small amount. See
Hoffman, "Church and Community," pp. 391–92, for details, a discussion, and calculations.

24. See appendix 2, part b.

25. Both this and the previous chapter have cited examples from the Forez, examples
discovered through the use of the excellent inventory for the AD Loire, série B. There are
also examples in AD Ain.

26. Cf. N. Castan, *Criminels de Languedoc,* p. 128.

27. Cases between parish ecclesiastics and parishioners were fairly common in the sixteenth
and early seventeenth century before the justice of Saint-Just; after the early seventeenth
century, though, criminal cases involving clerics at Saint-Just were almost all concerned
with moral offenses. Practically none concerned strife with parishioners. At the justice of
Ainay a survey of all the surviving criminal cases for the years 1777–82 also failed to
turn up incidents pitting ecclesiastics against their parishioners. Ainay and Saint-Just were
not the only remaining jurisdictions in the city, but the results are nonetheless indicative.
See AD Rhône, 11 G 302–305, 395 and 12 G 362, 386–388, 417. The figures for
1777–82 for the *bailliage* of Beaujolais are from AD Rhône, BBPC, 69 (1777–78), 70
(1779–80), 71 (1781–82).

28. Camille de Neuville, *Règlements faits par Monseigneur l'archevêque de Lyon au sujet des*
differens . . . entre le curé de la paroisse de Saint Vincent de Lyon et les marguilliers et
fabriciens de ladite paroisse (Lyon, 1690); AD Rhône, 13 G 649 (September 2, 1709);
15 G 158–159; 27 H 416.

29. Cf. John McManners, *French Ecclesiastical Society under the Ancien Regime: A Study of*
Angers in the Eighteenth Century (Manchester, 1960). For late-eighteenth-century
developments in Lyon, see Louis Trénard, *Histoire sociale des idées: Lyon de l'Encyclopédie*
au préromantisme, 2 vols. (Paris, 1958), 1:211–13, and Garden, *Lyon et les Lyonnais,*
pp. 487–592.

30. Duguet, "Mémoire inédit," pp. 29–31.
31. François Vermale, *Département du Rhône: Essai sur la répartition sociale des biens ecclésiastiques nationalisés* (Paris, 1906), p. 118.
32. AD Rhône, ESFC, Neuville, *liasse* 11, fols. 44–54, 81–82.
33. Hoffman, "Church and Community," pp. 342–46, contains details and statistical tests.
34. "Pouillé général des paroisses du diocèse de Lyon au XVIIIe siècle"; Vermale, *Biens ecclésiastiques nationalisés;* Sebastien Charléty, *Documents relatifs à la vente des biens nationaux dans le département du Rhône* (Lyon, 1906), pp. 147–71.
35. Emmanuel Le Roy Ladurie, "Révoltes et contestations rurales en France de 1675 à 1788," *Annales E.S.C.* 27 (1974): 12–15; Gutton, *Villages du Lyonnais,* pp. 63–64, 88.
36. Vovelle, *Piété baroque en Provence,* pp. 610–14; Norberg, "Rich and Poor," pp. 286–340; Chaunu, *La mort à Paris,* pp. 432–62; Delumeau, *Le catholicisme,* pp. 293–330; Jean Quéniart, *Les hommes, l'église et dieu dans la France du XVIIIe siècle* (Paris, 1978), pp. 203–306.
37. Vovelle, *Piété baroque en Provence,* pp. 481, 601.
38. Garden, *Lyon et les Lyonnais,* pp. 473–76; Gutton, "Le recrutement du clergé," pp. 5–6; Tackett, *Priest and Parish,* pp. 65–71; idem, "L'histoire sociale du clergé diocésain dans la France du XVIIIe siècle," *Revue d'histoire moderne et contemporaine* 27 (1979): 204–08; Quéniart, *Les hommes, l'église et dieu,* pp. 297–306.
39. Garden, *Lyon et les Lyonnais,* pp. 36–37, 446–48, 641; AD Rhône, 13 G 649; BP 3629; Trénard, *Histoire sociale des idées,* pp. 90–91, 211–13; Chartier, *L'éducation en France,* p. 67; *Dictionnaire de théologie catholique,* s.v. "Antoine Malvin de Montazet"; and Montazet's letter, *Instruction pastorale sur les sources de l'incrédulité et les fondaments de la religion* (Lyon, 1776).
40. AD Rhône, ESFC, Neuville, GG 21–22; Marius Riollet, ed., "Le journal d'un curé de campagne, 1768–1790," *Revue d'histoire de Lyon* 10 (1911): 289–93.
41. See chapter 4.
42. In Saint-Romain-d'Urfé, the vicars were apparently all natives until the eighteenth century; see Canard, *Livre d'or de Saint-Romain-d'Urfé.*
43. Relave, *Sury-le-Comptal,* pp. 374–77, 497–98, 507–14.
44. Durand de Maillane, *Dictionnaire de droit canonique,* s.v. "titre"; DS 1577, pp. 17–18; Janier, *Probation de saincts sacrements,* p. 146; DS 1614b, pp. 5–6.
45. A qualitative examination of the *titres* in AD Rhône, 4 G 124 (1630–31) and 4 G 129 (1639–41) reveals similar backgrounds. Before the 1630s the *titres* are not recorded in the *insinuations ecclésiastiques*—a fact that makes research on social origins before the early seventeenth century very difficult, at least in the diocese of Lyon. For similar results from other regions and different centuries, see Tackett, *Priest and Parish,* pp. 54–65; idem, "Histoire sociale," pp. 209–16; Charles Berthelot du Chesnay, "Le clergé diocesain français au XVIIIe siècle et les registres des insinuations ecclésiastiques," *Revue d'histoire moderne et contemporaine* 10 (1963): 241–70; Marc Venard, "Pour une sociologie du clergé au XVIe siècle: Recherche sur le recrutement sacerdotal dans la province d'Avignon," *Annales E.S.C.* 23 (1968): 987–1016.
46. Gutton, *Villages du Lyonnais,* pp. 70–73. This is also the impression left by death inventories. See, for example, AD Rhône, B, Scelles, tutelles, inventaires, June 11, 1587, and May 28, 1605, where priests live in simple housing. Compare these with AD Rhône, ESFC, Bron, February 2, 1675, and AD Ain, B 852, December 20, 1712, where the furnishings are far more prosperous and the quarters more roomy.
47. Taverne, *Coutumes et superstitions,* 2:46; Gutton, *Villages du Lyonnais,* pp. 70–73. Cf. Gerard Bouchard, *Le village immobile: Sennely-en-Sologne au XVIIIe siècle* (Paris, 1972).
48. Gutton, *Villages du Lyonnais,* pp. 70–73; Antoine Lugnier, *Cinq siècles de vie paysanne à Roche-en-Forez (1440–1940)* (Saint-Etienne, 1962), pp. 277–84.
49. AMR, Brussieu, GG 4 (1787–89).

50. AD Ain, C 127 (1777); C 137 (1771–72).

51. Quéniart, *Les hommes, l'église et dieu,* pp. 55–77, 85–87, 148–54, 173, 200, 270–73.

52. William H. Williams, "The Significance of Jansenism in the History of the French Catholic Clergy in the Pre-Revolutionary Era," in *Studies in Eighteenth-Century Culture,* ed. Roseann Runte, American Society for Eighteenth-Century Studies, vol. 7 (New York, 1978), pp. 290–91.

53. Jacques-Charles Dutillieu, "Le livre de raison de Jacques-Charles Dutillieu," ed. F. Breghot du Lut (Lyon, 1886), pp. 25–26; Kleinclausz, *Histoire de Lyon,* 2:197; E. Préclin, *Les jansénistes du XVIIIᵉ siècle et la constitution civile du clergé* (Paris, 1928), pp. 296–304; *Dictionnaire de théologie catholique,* s.v. "Antoine Malvin de Montazet"; Charles Monternot, *L'église de Lyon pendant la Révolution: Yves-Alexandre de Marbeuf* (Lyon, 1911), pp. 40–44; and Soulcié, "La formation des clercs," pp. 163–87, who points out that not all of the accusations of Jansenism lodged against Montazet should be taken at face value.

54. Kleinclausz, *Histoire de Lyon,* 2:195–96; Williams, "Significance of Jansenism," pp. 289–303.

55. AMR, Chassagny, GG 7 (1777–81); BN, manuscrits Joly de Fleury, 1399, affaires locales (Lechelle-Lyon), fols. 322–24.

56. Pierre Sage, *Le bon prêtre dans la literature française* (Geneva-Lille, 1951), pp. 209–33, 273–95; Préclin, *Les jansénistes,* pp. 385–86; Tackett, *Priest and Parish,* pp. 95, 154–55, 169, 227.

57. For the insurrection of the curés, see John McManners, *The French Revolution and the Church* (New York, 1970), pp. 12–13, 16–22: idem, *French Ecclesiastical Society,* pp. 129–239; Tackett, *Priest and Parish,* pp. 225–68; and idem, "The Citizen Priest: Politics and Ideology among the Parish Clergy of Eighteenth-Century Dauphiné," in Runte, ed., *Studies in Eighteenth-Century Culture,* 7:307–28. For additional works on this subject, see Hoffman, "Church and Community," pp. 367–68. The local *cahiers* for the Estates-General: Claude Faure, ed., *Cahiers de doléances du Beaujolais pour les Etats Generaux de 1789* (Lyon, 1939); Raoul de Clavière, *Les assemblées des trois ordres de la sénéchaussée de Beaujolais en 1789* (Lyon, 1935); Charles Dementhon, "L'Abbé J. B. Bottex et l'assemblée du bailliage de Bourg-en-Bresse en 1789," *ASEA* 36 (1903): 25–54; E. Dubois, "Cahiers de doléances des bailliages de Bourg, Bellay et Gex et de la sénéchaussée de Trévoux," *ASEA* 44 (1911): 93–136, 173–212, 269–331; 45 (1912): 4–47, 77–121, 169–211, 277–309; Etienne Fournial and Jean-Pierre Gutton, eds., *Etats généraux de 1789: Cahiers de doléances de la province de Forez* (Montbrison and Saint-Etienne, 1975); *Journal historique des assemblées de l'ordre ecclésiastique pour la députation aux états généraux* (Lyon, 1789).

58. Tackett, *Priest and Parish,* p. 230; idem, "The Citizen Priest," p. 313; AN G8 637, dossier 38.

59. Durand de Maillane, *Dictionnaire de droit canonique,* s.v. "portion congrue"; Tackett, *Priest and Parish,* pp. 231–32.

60. See, for example, Riollet, "Le journal d'un curé," p. 298; AMR, Haute Rivoire, GG 6 (1727); Riviere, GG 2 (1770).

61. Tackett, *Priest and Parish,* p. 244; idem, "The Citizen Priest," p. 315.

62. Préclin, *Les jansénistes,* p. 296; AD Rhône, B, petite justice de Jarnioux, inventaire du curé Jean Souchon, January 22 through 24, 1778; *Journal historique,* pp. 93–97; Monternot, *L'église de Lyon,* pp. 58–70; Clavière, *Les assemblées des trois ordres,* pp. 196–203, 241–42; Fournial and Gutton, *Etats généraux de 1789,* pp. 461–90, 537; Dubois, "Cahiers de doléances"; Dementhon, "J. B. Bottex"; Charles Jarrin, *La Bresse et le Bugey, leur place dans l'histoire* (Bourg, 1886), pp. 336–39; Philibert Le Duc, *Curiosités historiques de l'Ain,* vol. 2 (Bourg, 1877), pp. 648–73. Strife between

the lower and upper clergy was particularly pronounced at the meeting of the estates of the Lyonnais and the Beaujolais. See Hoffman, "Church and Community," pp. 371–72.

63. Le Duc, *Curiosités historiques*, pp. 648–73; Dubois, "Cahiers de doléances," 45 (1912): 170–74; and Fournial and Gutton, *Etats généraux de 1789*, p. 488.

64. Bercé, *Fête et révolte*, pp. 172–76. Examples abound in BN, manuscrits Joly de Fleury. See, for example, 1399, affaires locales, Lechelle-Lyon, fols. 322–24; 2415, droit et administration, fols. 3–26; and 2418, fols. 1–37. Cf. N. Castan, *Justice et répression*, p. 205.

65. Quéniart, *Les hommes, l'église et dieu*, pp. 270–79.

66. Duguet, "Mémoire inédit," p. 240; *Deux cahiers oubliés par les commissaires . . . du tiers état de Lyon: avec le discours prononcé dans l'assemblée des trois ordres . . . le 14 mars 1789 par M. Souchon, curé de Sainte-Foy-l'Argentière* (Lyon, 1789). Some curés found Souchon a bit too radical.

67. AD Rhône, BBPC, 37 (1715–20), September 27 through October 6, 1717. Cf. Y. Castan, *Honnêteté et relations sociales*, pp. 89, 109.

Chapter 6. Conclusion

1. Latreille, *Histoire de Lyon*, p. 293; Gabriel Le Bras, *Introduction à l'histoire de la pratique religieuse en France* (Paris, 1942), pp. 99–101. A brief account of the Revolution in and about Lyon can be found in Latreille, *Histoire de Lyon*, pp. 285–313. For a useful discussion of the dramatic break between the opposition to Catholicism under the Old Regime and the radical dechristianization of the Revolution, see John McManners, *Death and the Enlightenment: Changing Attitudes to Death among Christians and Unbelievers in Eighteenth-Century France* (Oxford, 1981), pp. 440–43.

2. For the Tridentine campaign against popular culture in Italy, see Ginzburg, *Il formaggio*, pp. 145–48. For incidents of resistance in southwestern France, see N. Castan, *Justice et répression*, pp. 43–44, 205–08.

3. AD Haute Garonne, B 92i, fol. 320, October 31, 1548 (attempts by Catholic magistrates in Toulouse to reform the clergy and crack down on abuses of popular religion); Harding, "Revolution and Reform," pp. 397–410 (early support for the Counter Reformation in the cities of Angers, Rennes, and Nantes); Benedict, *Rouen*, pp. 190–208 (the case of Rouen); Ginzburg, *Il formaggio*, pp. 145–46 (urban roots of the Italian Counter Reformation).

4. Urban support for the German Reformation: Ozment, *The Reformation in the Cities*; Bernd Moeller, *Reichstadt und Reformation* (Gutersloh, 1962). With a few exceptions (such as the Cévennes), French Protestantism also drew its support from the cities. The differences between the social appeal of Protestantism and that of Catholicism were, however, far from simple. Calvinism in France drew more adherents from literate crafts and from urban immigrants, but apart from a few social groups (sovereign court judges, for example), it attracted men and women from nearly all social classes. See Davis, *Society and Culture*, pp. 1–16; Benedict, *Rouen*, pp. 71–94; A. N. Galpern, *The Religions of the People in Sixteenth-Century Champagne* (Cambridge, Mass., 1976); and Emmanuel Le Roy Ladurie, *Les Paysans de Languedoc*, 2 vols. (Paris, 1966), 1:333–56, for case studies. As for the setbacks that Protestants encountered when they attempted to reform popular religion and culture, see Veit and Lenhard, *Kirche und Volksfrömmigkeit*, pp. 6–9, and Gerald Strauss, "Success and Failure in the German Reformation," *Past and Present* 67 (1975): 30–63.

5. This is not to say that Max Weber's *The Protestant Ethic and the Spirit of Capitalism*, tr. Talcott Parsons (London, 1930), was completely wrong. It may well have been the anxieties born of the theology of predestination that spurred individual Calvinists to

collective action. If so, then the doctrine of predestination was what overcame the "free rider" problem among Calvinists, just as the antithetical belief in good works did among Catholics. Once mobilized by their own distinctive theology, though, the Calvinists pursued a goal—social control—that was nearly identical to that sought by the Catholic *dévots*. Both among Protestants and Catholics, therefore, religious zeal spurred individuals to work in unison for common goals.

Appendix 1. Tobit and Probit Analysis of the Wills

1. Oscar Handlin, *Truth in History* (Cambridge, 1979), pp. 11–14. Cf. Morgan H. Kousser, "Criticisms of Quantitative Social Scientific History," paper delivered at the First International Conference on Quantitative History, Washington, 1982.

2. Cf. Kousser, "Criticisms," p. 12, and Robert W. Fogel, "The New Economic History: Its Findings and Methods," in *The Reinterpretation of American Economic History,* ed. Robert W. Fogel and Stanley Engerman (New York, 1971), p. 8. A computer program for probit is available with the statistical package *SAS,* and programs for logit and tobit exist in some econometric packages, such as *QUAIL* and *TROLL.* In addition, the author will furnish *FORTRAN* probit and tobit programs to interested readers.

3. The only exceptions were small, involuntary fees required by parish vestries in a small number of rural wills. Since these were not a matter of choice, they were excluded.

4. AD Rhône, 3 E 3690 (April 17, 1600). Cf. Vovelle, *Piété baroque en Provence,* p. 112.

5. For the rural sample (but not the urban one), I relied upon microfilms made by the Mormon Church. The Mormons are in the process of filming all the notarial registers in the AD Rhône, and the registers filmed so far are not unusual in any respect. In total I read 600 wills from the eastern Lyonnais and Beaujolais in the following notarial registers: 3 E 1–5, 38, 56–57, 1004, 1027–30, 1415, 2190–92, 2235–39, 8721–22, 8858, 8892, 8895–97, 8901, 8907, 8913. Readers may wonder why this sample is smaller than, say, Vovelle's. The answer is that statistics allowed me to answer questions (and to provide firmer answers than Vovelle could give) with much less data. For an extended examination of the sample and an explanation of why tobit and similar techniques do not require a random or perfectly representative sample of testators, see Hoffman, "Pious Bequests," p. 56.

6. Alternative deflators (such as converting prices to silver) produced nearly identical results. See Hoffman, "Pious Bequests," p. 56.

7. Testators too ill to sign or not asked to sign were considered illiterate unless they belonged to a literate profession such as the judiciary.

8. See Hoffman, "Pious Bequests," pp. 12–14, for a complete description.

9. See ibid., pp. 14–20, for statistical evidence concerning the consistency of the wealth proxies. Again, grain prices were used to correct the total cash in the wills for inflation; converting prices to silver yielded similar results.

10. See ibid., pp. 17–20, 58–62, for a more detailed treatment of legal practices, inheritance customs, and use of the dowries to estimate wealth.

11. Ibid., pp. 12, 31–32, 64–66.

12. What if a growing number of testators began making very small religious legacies, so that the likelihood of pious bequests went up over time but the size diminished? I would argue that such an increase in token donations signified no upsurge in religious behavior, and a tobit analysis would lead us to the same conclusion. Fortunately, such a turn of events never occurred in the wills. The likelihood and the size of pious bequests moved together, and I payed attention to both in order to glean the most possible information from the wills.

13. For a mathematical explanation, see Hoffman, "Pious Bequests," pp. 10–12, or G. S.

Maddala, *Econometrics* (New York, 1977), pp. 162–82. Readers familiar with statistics should know that I always assume the explanatory variables enter the tobit equation linearly; obvious nonlinearities (a fall and then a rise in pious bequests over time, for example) I dealt with by adding dummy variables and interaction terms or by dividing the sample into separate groups. The assumption of linearity is as good an approximation as any, and in any case other functional forms yield similar results.

14. Complete calculations for all variables are in Hoffman, "Pious Bequests," pp. 25–26. Needless to say, it may not make much sense to set dummy variables for sex and literacy equal to their average values and then change them by one unit. This is what I did, though, both for consistency and for comparisons with actual results. Doing the calculations any other way would not have made much difference.

15. Strictly speaking, the figures in table 16 are valid only for small changes of the explanatory variables, but they provide good approximations for larger changes as well.

16. AD Rhône, 3 E 38 (June 21, 1679). Cf. Vovelle, *Piété baroque en Provence,* p. 112.

17. Georges Durand, *Vin, vigne, vignerons en Lyonnais et Beaujolais* (Lyon, 1979), pp. 495–97.

18. These calculations assume that all explanatory variables are set equal to their mean values; see Hoffman, "Pious Bequests," pp. 34–42, for a more detailed examination of the dip in pious bequests at the end of the seventeenth century. Vovelle observes similar fluctuations in his data, but without statistical tools to separate what is religious from what is economic, he inevitably attributes the fluctuations to religious causes.

19. Converting prices to silver yielded similar results. In selecting urban notaries, I tried to get roughly the same number of wills from each decade in the sixteenth century and from every second decade in the seventeenth century. To gather as wide a spectrum as possible of the urban populace, I sampled from a large number of notaries, reading at most thirty wills per register. I ended up with 593 wills from the following notaries: AD Rhône, 3 E 283, 286, 336, 342–43, 349–50, 540, 547, 555, 557, 666, 759, 909, 911–13, 2667, 2932, 3181, 3482, 3690, 3755, 3908–11, 4001–02, 4161, 4475, 4494, 4553, 4670, 4786, 4789, 4793, 4991, 5001, 5378, 5388, 5418, 5453, 6228, 6717, 6729, 6762, 6942, 6983, 7184, 7311, 7541, 7690, 7759, 7764, 7969, 7982, 8125, 8288, 8293.

20. Fewer urban wills mentioned dowries and so it was not feasible to rely upon them as a measure of wealth in the tobit analysis. Similarly, occupations provided much less precise information in the urban wills. On the other hand, the index of wealth based on total cash bequests was entirely consistent with what little we do know from occupations, and it was also highly correlated with measures of wealth based on dowries (in those wills mentioning dowries) and with other information in the wills, such as the amount of money entering the testator's own marriage contract.

21. For example, when a real wage index is added to the tobit analysis of pious bequests and parish legacies, the t-statistics are 0.29 and 0.58, respectively. Similar results hold for interest rates, and they are no different if we substitute changes in wage rates. My source for real wages and interest rates is Gascon, *Grand commerce,* 1:261 and 2:933–34.

22. Multicollinearity makes measuring the exact magnitude of the interaction effects difficult. With the second wealth proxy (total cash bequests), the coefficient of the interaction term suggests that pious bequests began to rise after 1555 only among the truly wealthy. The wealth measure based on occupations suggests, however, that the turnaround took place in slightly less refined social strata, among the merchants and officers who made religious foundations in the late sixteenth century. As for pinpointing the timing of the turnaround, a test for different behavior among the wealthy after 1565 (instead of 1555) was positive and significant ($t=2.17$); a similar test for different behavior after 1575, though, was not significant. This indicates that the reversal among the elite took place between the late 1550s and 1575.

23. For a formal explanation, see Maddala, *Econometrics*, pp. 162–82.

24. When added to the probit analysis of processions, real wages has a t-statistic of only 0.61. Similar results hold for interest rates.

25. A sharp-eyed reader may ask why we excluded from the tobit analysis of pious bequests and parish legacies those wills dating from the years 1596–1635. If these legacies jumped late in the century, why not use "dummy" variables to create a different coefficient for the variable "year" after 1635, much as we created an interaction term for the sixteenth-century wills? The answer is that multicollinearity (born of the fact that by the seventeenth century our sample skips every other decade) made this impossible. We therefore had to split the sample.

Appendix 2. The Evidence from Criminal Records

1. Hoffman, "Church and Community," pp. 328–29, 391–92.

2. See table 13 in chapter 5.

3. By the end of the sixteenth century the criminal jurisdiction of ecclesiastical tribunals extended only to the cases in which ecclesiastics were defendants. Even with an ecclasiastical defendant, though, the ecclesiastical courts were to proceed in concert with royal judges in nearly all criminal cases. This was the rule established by the Ordonnance of Melun (1580), and although this *ordonnance* was not followed everywhere in France, it was the rule in the bailliage of Beaujolais and the sénéchaussée of Lyon. Secular courts had the right to try ecclesiastics, and all the Church courts could do was to go along with the lay judges. One finds examples of such dual proceedings involving both the bailliage and the *officialité*, but in general it seems that the criminal cases heard by the officialité were of a very different nature from those heard before the bailliage. With a few exceptions, the officiality cases did not involve a priest's control of local organizations or strife over religious reform. Instead they concerned ecclesiastical misbehavior or immorality. Such cases were relatively rare before the bailliage. See Doucet, *Les institutions de la France*, 2:691, 783–86; Gaston Zeller, *Les institutions de la France au XVI*e* siècle* (Paris, 1948), p. 358; Mousnier, *Les institutions*, 1:235; Claude Le Brun de la Rochette, *Le Procès criminel, divisé en deux livres, le premier contenant les crimes, le second la forme de procèdes aux matières criminelles*, 2 vols. (Lyon, 1610), 2:66–69 (Le Brun de la Rochette was an "avocat en la sénéchaussée et siège présidiel de Lyon, et au bailliage de Beaujolais" and so could speak with some authority concerning local judicial practices); Pallasse, *La sénéchaussée de Lyon*, pp. 116–17; DS 1687, pp. 154–65; Guyot, *Répertoire universel*, s.v. "Officialité," "Juridiction"; Durand de Maillane, *Dictionnaire de droit canonique*, s.v. "Officialité," "Juridiction." The officialité proceedings, which I have also consulted, are in AD Rhône, 4 G 22–30.

4. If criminal cases involving priests had shifted from lower courts to the bailliage, then criminal cases between priests and parishioners would appear in the sixteenth- or early-seventeenth-century records of these courts, but an investigation failed to turn up any such cases. The investigation involved the records of the *petites justices* listed at the end of part a of this appendix. As for the loss of documents from appeal to the Parlement of Paris, see Hoffman, "Church and Community," p. 331, where I argue that this would not be likely to produce the trend of more and more priest–parishioner cases. Appeals were also possible to the *sénéchaussée et présidial* of Lyon, but a search failed to reveal any.

Bibliography

The large body of archival records which forms the basis of this book is identified in the notes, and I have therefore given only an abbreviated list of my major primary and secondary sources below. Readers who are interested in a more detailed description of my manuscript and printed sources can consult the bibliographic essay and bibliography of my dissertation: Hoffman, "Church and Community," pp. 395–422. Copies of the dissertation are available at AD Rhône or from University Microfilms International, 300 N. Zeeb Road, Ann Arbor, Michigan 48106. Although I have done considerable research since the dissertation was completed, most of this additional research was conducted in the same archives and drew upon the same archival series described in the bibliographic essay. The only major exception was the sample of rural and urban wills, which came from AD Rhône, 3 E, a series of notarial registers.

1. Manuscript Sources

Archives Nationales: G⁸*, G⁸ 637.

Bibliothèque Nationale: Collection Joly de Fleury.

AD Loire: B (royal and seignorial justices); G (parishes of Saint-Just-en-Chevalet and Saint-Bonnet-le-Château).

AD Jura: G 10 (parish visits).

AD Ain: B (*bailliage et siège présidial* of Bourg-en-Bresse); C (intendancy records); G (parishes); E (communes and confraternities—this series is now the *sous-série* 1 E); documents from the commune of Pont-de-Veyle (now listed as part of the series E *dépot*); manuscript inventory of documents from Virieu-le-Petit.

AD Rhône: B (*sénéchaussée et présidial* of Lyon, *bailliage* of Beaujolais, *petites justices,* and the *maréchaussée*); C 1–2, C 157–60 (intendancy records); D (schools); E (family documents); E supplément, fonds des communes; 2 E (communes of Franc-Lyonnais); 3 E (notaries); 1 G–29 G (secular clergy, including records of diocesan administration, the officiality, parish and collegiate churches, confraternities and seignorial justices); 1 H–50 H (regular clergy, including documents from parishes, seignorial justices, confraternities, and the Company of the Holy Sacrament); fonds Léon Galle. Since I did my research, series B and C have been broken up into *sous-séries,* but finding the documents from my references should pose no problem.

AM Bourg-en-Bresse: BB (municipal deliberations); GG (religious matters); HH (professional confraternities).

AM Lyon: AA (correspondence); BB (deliberations); CC (fiscal records); FF (police); GG (religious matters); HH (professional confraternities).

AM Trévoux: GG.

BM Roanne: 4 E (communes); 3 G (parishes); 5 G (confraternities).

A Diana: 4 E (communes); 3 G (parishes); 5 G (confraternities); 2 J 7 (card file of curés from the diocese of Lyon).

A Diocese: Documents concerning Saint-Nizier and rural parishes.

A Séminaire: Documents concerning the Saint-Irénée Seminary and retreats.

2. Printed Primary and Secondary Sources

The following bibliography comprises only those printed works which are mentioned in more than one chapter; diocesan and synodal statutes and other frequently cited works which are included in the list of abbreviations are all omitted.

Agulhon, Maurice. *Pénitents et Francs-Maçons de l'ancienne Provence.* Paris, 1968.

Baum, G., and E. Cunitz, eds. *Histoire ecclésiastique des églises réformées au royaume de France.* 3 vols. Paris, 1883–89.

Bellièvre, Claude. *Souvenirs de voyages en Italie et en Orient: Notes historiques.* Edited by Charles Perrat. Geneva, 1956.

Benedict, Philip. *Rouen during the Wars of Religion.* Cambridge, 1981.

Benoit, D. P. *Histoire de l'abbaye et de la terre de Saint-Claude.* Montreuil-sur-Mer, 1892.

Bercé, Yves-Marie. *Fête et révolte: Des mentalités populaires du XVI*^{e} *au XVIII*^{e} *siècle.* Paris, 1976.

Bernard, August. *Cartulaire de l'abbaye de Savigny.* Paris, 1853.

Bertel, Estienne. *Discours choisis sur plusieurs matières importantes de la foy et des moeurs.* Lyon, 1687.

Beyssac, Jean. *Les chanoines de l'église de Lyon.* Lyon, 1914.

Bibliothèque municipale de Lyon. *Entrées royales et fêtes populaires à Lyon du XV*^{e} *au XVIII*^{e} *siècle: Catalogue d'une exposition du 12 juin au 12 juillet 1970 à la bibliothèque municipale de Lyon.* Lyon, 1970.

Bollo, Pierre de. *Le rosaire de la très saincte vierge Marie mère de Dieu.* Lyon, 1604.

Bossy, John. "The Counter-Reformation and the People of Catholic Europe." *Past and Present* 47 (1970): 51–70.

———. "Essai de sociographie de la messe, 1200–1700." *Annales E.S.C.* 36 (1981): 44–70.

Brackenhoffer, Elie. *Voyage en France, 1643–44.* Translated by Henry Lehr. Paris, 1925.

Brémond, Henri. *Histoire littéraire du sentiment religieux en France depuis la fin des guerres de religion jusqu'à nos jours.* 11 vols. New edition, Paris, 1967–68.

Burke, Peter. *Popular Culture in Early Modern Europe.* New York, 1978.

Canard, Jean. *Livre d'or de Saint-Romain-d'Urfé.* N.p., 1951.

———. *La société des prêtres et les prêtres de Saint-Just-en-Chevalet.* N.p., 1958.

———. "Les confréries de Saint-Just-en-Chevalet." *BD* 43 (1973–74): 92–120.

Castan, Nicole. *Justice et répression en Languedoc à l'époque des lumières.* Paris, 1980.

Chappuzeau, Samuel. *Lyon dans son lustre.* Lyon, 1656.

Chartier, Roger, Marie Madeleine Compère, and Dominique Julia. *L'éducation en France du XVIᵉ au XVIIIᵉ siècle.* Paris, 1976.

Chaunu, Pierre. *La mort à Paris.* Paris, 1978.

Christian, William A. *Local Religion in Sixteenth-Century Spain.* Princeton, 1981.

[Condamin, James, and François Langlois.] *Histoire de Saint-Bonnet-le-Château par deux prêtres du diocèse de Lyon.* 2 vols. Paris, 1885.

Davis, Natalie Zemon. "Protestantism and the Printing Workers of Lyons: A Study in the Problem of Religion and Social Class during the Reformation." Ph.D. diss., University of Michigan, 1959.

———. *Society and Culture in Early Modern France.* Stanford, 1975.

Delattre, Pierre, ed. *Les établissements des Jésuites en France depuis quatre siècles.* 5 vols. Enghien, 1949–57.

Delumeau, Jean. *Le catholicisme entre Luther et Voltaire.* Paris, 1971.

Demia, Charles. *Trésor clerical ou conduites pour acquérir et conserver la sainteté ecclésiastique.* Lyon, 1682.

Dictionnaire de spiritualité ascétique et mystique, doctrine et histoire. Paris, 1954–.

Dictionnaire de théologie catholique. Paris, 1923–.

Doucet, Roger. *Les institutions de la France au XVIᵉ siècle.* 2 vols. Paris, 1948.

Dubois, E. "Histoire de Pont-de-Veyle." *ASEA* 33 (1900): 5–44, 121–93, 253–325, 365–449; 34 (1901): 5–48.

Duguet, Jean François. "Mémoire inédit de l'abbé Jean François Duguet, curé de Feurs." Edited by Vincent Durand. *Recueil de mémoires et documents sur le Forez,* volume 6. Published by Société de la Diana. St. Etienne, 1880.

Durand de Maillane, Pierre. *Dictionnaire de droit canonique et de pratique bénéficiale.* 6 vols. Lyon, 1787.

Evennett, H. Outram. *The Spirit of the Counter Reformation.* Edited and with a postscript by John Bossy. Notre Dame, 1975.

Ferté, Jeanne. *La vie religieuse dans les campagnes parisiennes, 1622–1695.* Paris, 1962.

Flandrin, Jean-Louis. *Familles: Parents, maison, sexualité dans l'ancienne société.* Paris, 1976.

Fontanon, Antoine. *Les édits et ordonnances des rois de France.* 3 vols. 2d ed. Paris, 1611.

Forest, Jean-Marie H. *L'école cathédrale de Lyon: Le petit séminaire de Saint-Jean.* Lyon, 1885.

———. "Messire Jean Rabot, curé de Saint-Clement-sous-Valsonne." *BHDL* (1912): 481–97.

Garden, Maurice. *Lyon et les Lyonnais au XVIIIᵉ siècle.* Paris, 1970.

Gascon, Richard. *Grand commerce et vie urbaine au XVIᵉ siècle: Lyon et ses marchands.* 2 vols. Paris, 1971.

Ginzburg, Carlo. *Il formaggio e i vermi: Il cosmo di un mugnaio del '500.* Turin, 1976.

Guigue, Georges, ed. *Le livre des confrères de la Trinité de Lyon, 1306–1792.* Lyon, 1898.

————. *Les papiers des dévots de Lyon: Recueil de textes sur la compagnie secrète du Saint-Sacrement, 1630–1731.* Lyon, 1922.

Gutton, Jean-Pierre. *La société et les pauvres: L'exemple de la généralité de Lyon, 1534–1789.* Paris, 1970.

————. "Notes sur le recrutement du clergé séculier dans l'archdiocèse de Lyon (1589–1789)." *Bulletin du centre d'histoire économique et sociale de la région lyonnaise* 2 (1974): 1–20.

————. "Reinages, abbayes de jeunesse et confréries dans les villages de l'ancienne France." *Cahiers d'histoire* 21 (1976): 443–53.

————. *Villages du Lyonnais sous la monarchie (XVIᵉ–XVIIIᵉ siècles).* Lyon, 1978.

Guyot, Joseph N. *Répertoire universel et raisonné de jurisprudence civile, criminelle, canonique et bénéficiale.* 18 vols. Paris, 1784.

Harding, Robert. "Revolution and Reform in the Holy League: Angers, Rennes, Nantes." *Journal of Modern History* 53 (1981): 379–416.

Hoffman, Philip T. "Church and Community: The Parish Clergy and the Counter Reformation in the Diocese of Lyon, 1500–1789." Ph.D. diss., Yale University, 1979. A copy of this dissertation is available at AD Rhône or from University Microfilms International, 300 N. Zeeb Road, Ann Arbor, Michigan, 48106.

————. "Pious Bequests in Wills: A Statistical Analysis." Social Science Working Paper No. 393, Division of the Humanities and Social Sciences, California Institute of Technology, 1981.

Janier, Leonard. *Probation des saincts sacrements de l'église catholique.* 2d ed. Paris, 1577.

Kleinclausz, Arthur, ed. *Lyon des origines à nos jours: La formation de la cité.* Lyon, 1925.

————. *Histoire de Lyon.* 3 vols. Lyon, 1939–52.

Latreille, André, ed. *Histoire de Lyon et du Lyonnais.* Collection Univers de la France, Toulouse, 1975.

Le Tellier de Bellefons, D. F. *Octave des morts.* Lyon, 1695.

Lexicon für Theologie und Kirche. Fribourg in Brisgau, 1957–.

Lorcin, Marie Thérèse. "Les clauses religieuses dans les testaments du plat pays lyonnais aux XIVᵉ et XVᵉ siècles." *Le Moyen Age* 78 (1972): 287–323.

————. *Vivre et mourir en Lyonnais à la fin du Moyen-Age.* Lyon, 1981.

Martin, J. B. *Histoire des églises et chapelles de Lyon.* 2 vols. Lyon, 1909.

Mollat, Michel. *La vie et la pratique religieuse au XIVᵉ siècle et dans la première partie du XVᵉ principalement en France.* Paris, 1965.

Mousnier, Roland. *Les institutions de la France sous la monarchie absolue.* Volume 1: *Société et état.* Paris, 1974.

Muchembled, Robert. *Culture populaire et culture des élites dans la France moderne (XVᵉ–XVIIIᵉ siècles).* Paris, 1978.

Nicolai, Nicolas de. *Description générale de la ville de Lyon et des anciennes provinces du Lyonnais et du Beaujolais, 1573.* Lyon, 1881.

Norberg, Kathryn. "Rich and Poor in the Old Regime: Grenoble, 1600–1804." Ph.D. diss., Yale University, 1978.

Ozment, Steven E. *The Reformation in the Cities: The Appeal of Protestantism to Sixteenth-Century Germany and Switzerland.* New Haven, 1975.

Pallasse, M. *La sénéchaussée et siège présidial de Lyon pendant les guerres de religion.* Lyon, 1943.

Péricaud, Jean. "Louis Garon et la fête du cheval fol." *RL,* ser. 1, 5 (1837): 433–56.

Pérouas, Louis. *Le diocèse de La Rochelle de 1648 à 1724: Sociologie et pastorale.* Paris, 1964.

Perrat, L. "Mon vieux Châtillon." *ASEA* 39 (1906): 205–60; 40 (1907): 317–66; 41 (1908): 82–104, 251–311.

Popkin, Samuel L. *The Rational Peasant: The Political Economy of Rural Society in Vietnam.* Berkeley, 1979.

Rapp, François. *Réformes et réformations à Strasbourg: Eglise et société dans le diocèse de Strasbourg (1450–1525).* Paris, 1974.

Relave, Pierre-Maxime. *Sury-le-Comptal en Forez: Essai d'histoire et d'archéologie.* Montbrison, 1907.

Richard, P. *La papauté et la Ligue française: Pierre d'Epinac, archevêque de Lyon (1573–1599).* Paris, 1901.

Rossiaud, Jacques. "Prostitution, jeunesse et société dans les villes du Sud-Est au XVe siècle." *Annales E.S.C.* 31 (1976): 289–323.

Rubys, Claude de. *Histoire véritable de la ville de Lyon.* Lyon, 1604.

Schmitt, Jean-Claude. *Le saint lévrier: Guinefort, guérisseur d'enfants depuis le XIIIe siècle.* Paris, 1979.

Schmitt, Thérèse-Jean. *L'organisation ecclésiastique et la pratique religieuse dans l'archidiaconé d'Autun.* Dijon, 1957.

Tackett, Timothy. *Priest and Parish in Eighteenth-Century France: A Social and Political Study of Curés in a Diocese in Dauphiné, 1750–1791.* Princeton, 1977.

Taverne, Alice. *Coutumes et superstitions foréziennes.* 9 vols. Lyon, 1973–74.

Toussaert, Jacques. *Le sentiment religieux en Flandre à la fin du Moyen Age.* Paris, 1963.

Tricou, Jean. "Les confréries joyeuses de Lyon au XVIe siècle et leur numismatique." *Revue numismatique* 40 (1937): 293–317.

———. *Armorial du chapitre Saint-Nizier de Lyon 1632–1670.* Lyon, 1952.

———. "Enseignes et médailles de dévotion, méreaux et jetons des confréries de Lyon antérieures à 1789." *Revue numismatique,* ser. 5, 14 (1952): 205–28 and 15 (1953): 107–25.

Vachet, A. *Les anciens couvents de Lyon.* Lyon, 1895.

Vanel, J. B. "Les curés de Saint-Genest-Malifaux." *BHDL* (1926): 221–39, 293–327; (1927): 28–45, 99–111, 154–63, 196–208.

Veit, L. A., and L. Lenhart. *Kirche und Volksfrömmigkeit im Zeitalter des Barocks.* Freiburg-im-Breisgau, 1956.

Venard, Marc. *L'église d'Avignon au XVIe siècle.* 4 vols. Lille, 1980.

Vovelle, Michel. *Piété baroque et déchristianisation en Provence au XVIIIe siècle.* Paris, 1973.

Index

Abbeys of misrule, 26, 41, 72, 91, 93, 137
Art, religious: and Tridentine reform, 85, 92, 210
Artisans, 18, 21, 23, 25-26, 41, 121, 124, 200
Assemblies, village, 58-59, 60, 66, 67, 68
Associations, lay religious, 73-74. *See also* Confraternities
Auger, Edmond, 36, 38, 41

Bailliage of Beaujolais. *See* Courts
Banquets, confraternity, 26, 61, 111-12, 118, 195
Baptism. *See* Rituals: specific
Bells, church: in rural parishes, 53, 54, 55-56, 203
Benedicti, Jean, 40, 84, 92
Bequests, pious, 136, 207; tobit analysis of, 171-84 *passim*, 196, 197, 199, 200, 215, 216, 224-26; probit analysis of, 171-72, 181-83, 184, 196, 224, 225; defined, 172
—rural, 52-53, 118-21, 124-27, 145, 153, 172-79, 184, 202-03, 215, 216, 224
—urban, 22-24, 27-28, 29, 40, 41, 52, 121-23, 125, 145, 153, 179-84, 196, 197, 199, 200, 203, 215, 216, 219, 224, 225
Bérulle, Pierre de, 71, 78, 85
Bollo, Pierre de, 37, 41
Borromeo, Bp. Carlo, 5, 75, 90
Bricitto, curé, 117, 131
Burial and mourning rites. *See* Rituals: specific

Calvinism, 41, 47, 94, 223-24; in Lyon, 30-32, 33; and attack on popular culture, 170-71

Canon-counts, 11, 25, 41, 74; role of, 13; and city government, 16, 34, 197; wealth of, 17; and Protestantism, 31-32; and Tridentine reform, 71, 75; and pluralism, 99
Canons: social background of, 13, 18; education of, 14, 212; duties of, 16; and reform, 35-38. *See also* Clergy, parish
Capuchins, 36, 37, 42, 104, 109
Casuel, 69, 140, 148, 206, 218
Catechism, 3, 50, 82, 83, 90, 93, 100, 105, 110, 128-29, 130, 141, 160
Catholic League, 39-40, 42-43, 48, 201
Cemeteries, 91, 137, 141
Charities: bequests to, 72, 139, 172, 173, 184, 207, 215; reform of, 117-18, 136, 168; clerical control of, 117, 137, 161; and women, 145
Charivaris, 26, 64, 69, 113, 141, 142, 211, 218, 219; and Tridentine reform, 87, 88, 94, 135, 137
Chomel, Noël, 79, 86-89, 91, 93, 97, 149-50
Clergy, parish: sixteenth-century reform of, 1, 4, 5, 71-97 *passim;* as agents of Tridentine reform, 3, 4, 5, 6, 83-84, 128-38, 139, 141, 168, 169; behavior of, 71-72, 81, 82, 91, 98, 136, 167, 168; societies of, 72; education and training of, 72, 74-79, 81, 167, 168, 188, 212; role of, 82, 83, 163, 165, 170; and confraternities, 89, 105-14; and education, 115-16, 128; as administrators, 116-18; preaching of, 82-83, 128, 216; ratio of to population, 147; and French Revolution, 161-62; reform movement among (post-1750), 161-65; and conflicts with upper clergy, 162, 163, 165; libraries of, 163; *see also* Priests,

Clergy, parish (*continued*)
stipendiary
—conflict with laity: causes of, 131-38,
139, 217, 218; and family groups, 140,
141, 218; and parish institutions,
140-41, 207; and communal solidarity,
140, 141-42, 168-69; and tithe, 140,
148, 218; and taverns, 141-42, 218;
and youth groups, 142-43, 145, 168-
69; and village notables, 143; and merchants, 143-44, 151-52; and men vs.
women, 144-45, 146, 219; and urban
vs. rural, 145, 149-51, 152; and criminal cases, 146-52, 153, 154, 168,
185-88, 219, 220, 226; and rural industry, 151-52; and agriculture, 151, 152;
and 'dechristianization,' 153-55, 167,
169; and social origins of priests, 155,
156-59; and rectories, 159-60, 218; and
Jansenism, 160-61; and clerical reform
movement, 161-65; and clerical elitism,
164-66; and French Revolution, 167;
and Richerism, 169
—in rural areas: and laity, 44, 48, 103,
105, 140, 151, 167; community and
family ties of, 48-50, 51-52, 53, 82,
99, 155, 158; as godfathers, 49-50;
behavior of, 50, 52, 71-72, 98-101,
151; and Tridentine reform, 50, 71-72,
82, 83-97 *passim*, 103, 137; and absenteeism, 50, 98, 99; education of, 50-51,
82-83, 98, 99, 101-03; libraries of, 51,
101-03; wealth of, 52, 188; role of (sixteenth century), 56-70 *passim*; and confraternities, 66-67, 104, 107, 108-14;
and communal solidarity, 68-70; preaching of, 82-83; and pluralism, 99; dress
of, 99-100; and changes of benefice, 100-01; role of (seventeenth vs.
eighteenth century), 103-08, 116, 118,
167; dwellings of, 159-60
—in urban areas: role of (sixteenth century),
8, 10, 16, 30, 57, 167-68; and urban
elite, 8, 34-35, 42-44, 167-68, 195;
recruitment of, 11, 13; education of, 11,
14, 103, 212; and pluralism, 13, 14,
15; background of, 13-14; libraries of,
14; family and community ties of,
15-16, 34, 52, 155, 158, 193, 196;
conflict with laity (sixteenth century),
16-21; and city council, 16-18, 20-21,
33, 34; and immigrants, 18-19, 27;

behavior of, 19-20, 35-36, 98-99, 167;
and confraternities, 26, 74; wealth of,
27, 28, 34, 52; and lower classes, 27,
30, 42; and Protestantism, 31, 32-34,
168; reform of, 35-36; as godfathers,
52; as missionaries, 87
Clergy, upper, 3, 34; and conflict with parish clergy, 162, 163, 165, 222-23. *See
also* Canon-counts; Canons; Ecclesiastical
hierarchy
College of the Trinity, Lyon, 34, 38, 75
Collegiate churches: rural, 48
—in Lyon, 11; clergy of, 13-14, 25, 35-
36, 81, 162; wealth of, 14, 15, 17, 18
Colombet, Guy, 79, 83
Common people. *See* Lower classes
Communal solidarity, village, 68-70, 94,
108, 137-38, 140, 141-42, 155-56,
167. *See also* Institutions, communal
Communauté d'habitants: assembly of, 58-
59; and confraternities, 59-60, 61
Communion. *See* Rituals: specific
Communities (only those mentioned on
more than one page are included): Azolettes, 151, 152; Beligny, 51, 102; Belleville, 47, 55, 56, 66, 114; Boen, 64,
102, 135; Bourg-en-Bresse, 45, 51, 64,
66, 67, 111; Ceyzeriat, 59, 60-61;
Chassagny, 135, 161; Chevrières, 49-50,
54; Chiroubles, 132, 133; Claveisolles,
131, 142-43; Cogny, 141, 143; Condrieu, 60, 65; Feurs, 50, 54-55, 55-56,
151, 152, 162; La Balme, 154, 155;
Les-Sauvages, 140, 144; l'Hôpital-le-
Grand, 60, 62, 63; Montarcher, 49, 62,
63, 65; Montbrison, 56, 62; Neuville,
61, 66-67, 68, 112, 117, 124, 129,
131, 132, 152, 154, 206, 217; Pérouges, 60, 106; Pont-de-Veyle, 47, 66;
Saint-Amour, 47, 57; Saint-Bonnet-le-
Château, 46, 47, 48, 54, 55, 64, 125;
Saint-Claude, 64, 111; Saint-Clement-
sous-Valsonne, 134, 217, 218; Saint-
Cyr-au-Mont-d'Or, 60, 66, 100, 115,
124; Sainte-Foy-les-Lyon, 61-62, 107,
108; Saint-Etienne, 46, 47-48; Saint-
Etienne-la-Varenne, 134, 136, 140,
143, 144; Saint-Genest-de-Malifaux,
50, 102; Saint-Genis-Laval, 60, 61;
Saint-Germain-Laval, 55, 103-05, 109,
112, 113, 126; Saint-Just-en-Chevalet,
48-49, 54, 67, 112-14, 155; Saint-

Symphorien-le-Château, 60, 61; Sauvain, 109, 124; Taluyers, 69, 135; Treffort, 101, 102; Vauxrenard, 142, 143; Villié, 132, 133

Company of the Holy Sacrament, 73-74, 76, 77, 79, 81, 83, 88-89, 90, 92-93, 97, 128, 134, 149-50, 168, 210-11, 217

Concubinage, priestly, 50, 69, 81, 92, 202, 211

Confession. *See* Rituals: specific

Confraternities: professional, 25-26, 27, 29, 39, 41, 61, 67, 141, 195; female, 72 (*see also* Confraternities: of the Rosary)
—devotional, 3, 42, 52, 73, 85-87, 90, 94, 108-14, 118-19, 123, 124, 126, 127, 133, 136-38, 143, 154, 168, 169, 200, 206, 213
—specific: 26, 39-40, 73, 74, 108, 110, 127, 150, 195; of the Blessed Sacrament, 90, 104, 108, 109, 110, 111, 112, 114, 118, 124, 125, 127, 131, 154, 213, 217; of the Holy Spirit, 59, 60, 66, 68, 88, 103, 104-08, 111, 133, 136, 145, 167, 168, 206; of Penitents, 38-39, 41, 42, 44, 86, 103, 104, 108, 109, 110, 111-14, 118, 119, 127, 200, 213-14; of the Rosary, 85-86, 103, 108, 109, 110, 111, 112, 114, 118, 119, 124, 125, 127, 131, 144, 145, 213
—village, 54-55, 59-63, 64, 66-67, 68-69, 105-14

Conseil d'état, 34, 42-43

Cordeliers, 26, 41. *See also* Orders, religious

Council of Trent. *See* Trent, Council of

Courts: *Maréchaussée*, 113, 135, 136, 140, 186-87; *Bailliage* of Beaujolais, 147-49, 151, 152, 185-86, 187, 188, 219, 226; seignorial, 149, 188, 194, 207, 217; ecclesiastical, 188, 226
—*Sénéchaussée:* 10, 11, 74, 89, 193, 212, 226; and Protestantism, 31, 33; and priest-parishioner cases, 149, 150, 151, 152, 185, 186

Criminal cases: and priest-parishioner conflicts, 113-14, 130-36, 146-52, 185-88, 207, 219, 220, 226

Crosses, village, 56, 61, 132, 134

Dancing: clerical restriction of, 87, 88, 93, 98, 111, 134, 136, 140, 144, 164, 200

"Dechristianization," 153-55, 167, 169

Deguz, curé, 134, 136, 140, 144

De la Barge, Etienne, 39, 42

Demia, Charles, 79, 82, 83; and education, 77, 81, 88-89, 93, 95, 114, 115, 128; and rituals, 88, 90, 92; catechism of, 128-29, 217

De Paul, Vincent: and campaign against popular culture, 71, 84, 87, 96, 97; as exemplar, 81, 82

De Sales, François, 79, 80, 85, 86, 90, 103

D'Este, Abp. Hippolyte, 8, 20, 34, 192

Devotions, 37, 127, 128, 136, 138, 168, 169; and confraternities, 26, 119, 123, 217; to the Rosary, 37, 119, 215; to the Eucharist, 85, 86, 89-90, 118-19, 170; to the Virgin Mary, 85-86, 114, 154, 155; to saints, 85, 86, 119, 214-15

Dévots, 1, 74; and education, 77, 83, 102-03, 114, 115, 141, 154, 212; and confraternities, 85-86, 89, 118; and campaign against popular culture, 86-97 *passim*, 128, 133, 137, 168, 169, 224; urban role of, 97, 126; associations of, 73. *See also* Company of the Holy Sacrament; Confraternities: devotional

Dominicans, 109. *See also* Orders, religious

Dowries, 174, 224, 225

Dubessey, Etienne Joseph, 113-14, 214

Duguet, curé, 151, 165

Ecclesiastical hierarchy: and campaign against popular culture, 2-3, 6, 84, 86-97 *passim*, 106, 109, 130, 132, 133-34, 140; and clerical reform, 6, 76, 80-81, 82, 98, 102-03, 155-56, 161-62; in sixteenth-century Lyon, 10-16

Education: secondary, 17, 34, 38; clerical, 74-79. *See also* Schools, "little"; Schools, primary; Seminaries

Elite, urban, 7-8, 10; and city council, 7, 16; and alliance with clergy, 8, 37-38, 42-44, 74, 170; and clerical recruitment, 11, 13, 34, 37-38, 156-58; and conflict with clergy, 18, 34-35, 44, 150-51, 167-68, 195; and Protestantism, 30-31, 169; and Tridentine reform, 35-36, 37-38, 40, 43-44, 72, 73-74, 125, 126, 137-38, 145, 154, 169; and confraternities, 38-39, 52, 73-74, 195; pious bequests of, 40, 41, 52, 53,

Elite, urban (*continued*)
179-80; vs. lower classes, 41-42, 93-94, 140; and education, 77, 78; and campaign against popular culture, 84, 91, 93-95, 96-97, 170. *See also* Lower classes, urban
Epinac, Abp. Pierre d', 38, 42, 80, 84
Eucharist, 23; and confraternities, 113, 124. *See also* Devotions: to the Eucharist
Exorcisms, 21-22, 35, 40

Family groups: and conflict with clergy, 2, 3-4, 140, 141, 155; clerical ties with, 15-16, 34, 49-50, 51-52, 82
Feast days: suppression of, 134-35
Festivals, popular: clerical suppression and reform of, 2, 41, 87, 88, 96, 133-36, 137, 141, 142, 145, 160, 161, 164, 168, 217, 218, 219; and confraternities, 26, 62, 89, 111; role of, 62, 63; clerical toleration of, 62-63, 64, 65, 135-36; and military activities, 62, 64; government suppression of, 88, 89, 135; of inversion, 91, 93; and *dévots,* 91-92; and sexual morality, 92, 93; and political disorder, 94
Franciscans of Saint-Bonaventure. *See* Cordeliers
"Free rider" problem, 96, 211-12, 224
French Revolution: and clergy, 139, 161-62, 167, 223
Funerals. *See* Rites: specific, of burial and mourning

Gacon, curé, 112, 129, 152
Genebrier, Jean, 112-14, 155
Godparents, 23; clergy as, 49-50, 52, 82; role of and Tridentine reform, 129-30, 141, 142, 144
Good works: and Tridentine reform, 95-96, 224
Grolée, Antoinette de, 21-22, 35
Guéraud, Jean, 18, 20, 28, 195, 198

Hospitals: in Lyon, 14, 72, 215; in Belleville, 55; village, 66, 143; reform of, 117-18, 137

Illegitimacy: rates of, 154, 155, 218
Immigrants: and parish clergy, 18-19, 52; acceptance of, 27, 167; and religious orders, 27-28, 196; pious bequests of,
27-28, 179, 196; and traditional piety, 30
Institutions, communal: and parish clergy, 57-70 *passim,* 104-08, 140-41, 168-69, 207; overlapping of, 59-60; and communal solidarity, 68-69; and Tridentine reform, 90, 103-05, 136-38. *See also* Communal solidarity, village; Towns; Vestries, parish

Jacobins. *See* Dominicans
Jansenism, 6, 78, 160-61, 163, 222
Jesuits, 36, 42, 73, 199; as local missionaries, 4, 6, 126; and education, 34, 38, 75; and confraternities, 108, 109

Laity: and "insurrection of the curés," 161-62; pre-Tridentine relationship with clergy, 167-68; *see also* Bequests, pious
—conflict with clergy, 1, 2, 3, 4, 69-70, 71, 103, 105; urban vs. rural, 16-21, 65-66, 129-38, 145, 149; and clerical reform, 98, 161-65; and parish institutions, 118, 140-44, 168-69; and family groups, 140, 141; and communal solidarity, 140, 141-42; and taverns, 141-42, 218; and youth groups, 142-43, 145, 168-69; and village notables, 143; and merchants, 143-44, 151-52; men vs. women, 144-45, 146; court records as evidence of, 146-52, 153, 154, 168, 186-88, 207; and rural industry, 151-52; and commercialization of agriculture, 151, 152; post-1750, 152-66 *passim;* and "dechristianization," 153-55, 169; and nonnative priests, 155-56; and social origins of priests, 156-59; and rectories, 159-60; and Jansenism, 160-61; and clerical elitism, 164-66; and French Revolution, 167; and Richerism, 169
—piety of, 6, 35, 124, 136-37, 169; and preaching, 36-37; and seminary retreats, 79; and devotional confraternities, 108, 109, 118, 126, 127; in towns, 125-26; and role of women, 126-28; and "dechristianization," 153-55
Latin: clerical knowledge of, 51, 76, 77, 83
Libraries, personal: of clergy, 14, 51, 101-03, 163; of laity, 125
Literacy: of parish clergy, 51, 76, 82-83, 101-03; and pious bequests, 124-25,

126, 216, 224; and Tridentine reform, 137, 153, 169

Lower classes: and campaign against popular culture, 2; and Tridentine reform, 2, 27, 30, 40-42; clerical recruitment, 18, 156-58; rural, 44, 84-85, 94, 97, 152-53, 159-60; and clerical elitism, 164-65

—urban: vs. urban elite, 10, 41-42, 93, 140, 200; and parish clergy, 18, 42, 167; and Tridentine reform, 97, 137, 170

Lyon, visits of Henry II and Henry IV, 7, 8; in sixteenth century, 9-10; and Protestantism, 31-32

—abbeys and convents of: Augustinians' Convent, 12, 15, 25-26, 27; Carmelites' Convent, 12, 15, 27, 36; Dominicans Convent, 12, 15, 27, 28, 36, 43; Franciscans of Saint-Bonaventure Convent, 12, 15, 26, 27, 36

—churches and parishes of: Notre-Dame-de-Platière, 12, 14, 22, 124; Sainte-Croix, 11, 12, 24, 25, 36, 74, 127, 154, 199; Saint-Etienne, 11, 12, 47-48, 83, 201; Saint-Georges, 12, 14, 19, 20, 25, 74, 77; Saint-Irénée, 12, 14, 24; Saint-Jean, Cathedral of, 11, 12, 13, 15, 17, 18, 25, 32, 35, 36, 74; Saint-Just, 12, 13-14, 18, 19-20, 24, 32, 74, 98, 193, 194; Saint-Michel, 12, 14, 76; Saint-Nizier, 12, 13, 14, 15, 19, 25, 26, 27, 31, 32, 35, 36, 37, 38, 40, 41, 74, 89, 150, 193; Saint-Paul, 12 13, 14, 15, 18, 23, 32, 74, 193, 194-95, 196; Saint-Pierre-et-Saint-Saturnin, 12, 14, 25, 57, 74, 150; Saint-Pierre-le-Vieux, 12, 14, 74; Saint-Thomas-de-Fourvière, 12, 13, 74; Saint-Vincent, 12, 14, 31, 74, 83, 89, 115, 150, 154

—city council of, 7, 8, 75, 193; conflict with clergy, 8, 16-18, 20-21, 33, 34; and religious toleration, 31-32; and confraternities, 38, 40; and urban lower classes, 41-42

Lyon, diocese of: churches and religious orders in, 11-16, 72; described (sixteenth century), 45-48; Protestants in, 47-48

Magic, 92, 93
Maistret, Bp. Jacques, 37, 38, 39, 42
Maréchaussée. See Courts

Marquemont, Abp. Denis-Simon de, 50, 75, 79, 80, 81, 85, 99
Marriage. *See* Rituals: specific
Mass. *See* Rituals
Massacres: of Protestants, 33, 48
Men: monopoly of over women, 64, 145; pious bequests of vs. women, 126-27, 145, 176; as prime opponents of clergy, 144-45; and Tridentine reform, 144-45, 146. *See also* Youth groups: village
Mendicants: in Lyon, 15-16; as immigrants, 15, 19; as preachers and missionaries, 36-37, 42, 48, 199, 201. *See also* Orders, religious
Merchants: in Lyon, 7, 10; and religious orders, 27-28, 37; rural and clergy-parishioner conflict, 143-44, 151-52
Minimes, 36, 37, 40. *See also* Mendicants; Orders, religious
Miracles, 40-41, 55
Missions: by religious orders to rural laity, 4, 6, 37, 77, 104, 126; and Tridentine reform, 87, 97, 109
Montazet, Abp. Malvin de, 154, 155, 160-61, 163, 222
Morgue, Claude, 141-42, 143

Neuville, Abp. Camille de: and seminaries, 76, 77; and parish visitations, 80, 99; and Tridentine reform, 79, 80, 81, 87, 89; and primary schools, 114-15
Notables, town: and parish clergy, 67, 68, 141-42, 143, 153, 159; and Tridentine reform, 125-26, 137

Oratorians, 75, 103; seminary of (Lyon), 76, 78. *See also* Orders, religious
Orders, religious: and Tridentine reform, 2-3, 6, 85, 114, 160; in Lyon, 11, 14, 15, 72; wealth of, 15, 38; and pious bequests, 22, 184, 196; and immigrants, 27-28; in rural areas, 104, 109, 126, 201-02. *See also* Mendicants
Ordination: requirements for, 74, 75, 76, 77; and seminary retreats, 77-78, 79; decrease in, 154
Organizations, parish. *See* Institutions, communal; Vestries, parish

Pain bénit, 56, 61
Parades, entry, 20, 26, 93
Parishes. *See* Communities

Parish priests. *See* Clergy, parish

Peasants. *See* Lower classes: rural

Penance. *See* Rituals: specific, of confession

Piety, traditional: medieval basis of, 21-28; urban decline of, 28-30; and immigrants, 30; in rural areas (sixteenth century), 52-57, 202-03; Tridentine reform of, *see* Piety, Tridentine

Piety, Tridentine: and reform of traditional piety, 3, 4, 95-96, 118-19, 123-24, 129-38, 140, 145, 150-51, 168, 169; laic rejection of, 153-55

Pluralism, 13, 14, 15, 99

Poorhouses, 83, 95, 104, 121, 144. *See also* Charities

Popular culture: support for, 3-4, 70, 90-91, 128, 219; and rural clergy, 26, 56-70 *passim;* and the sacraments, 84-85; "counterfeiting" of, 90; and political disorder, 94, 135, 136, 137; and "insurrection of curés," 162, 163-64
—clerical campaign against, 2, 3, 4, 71-72, 86-97 *passim,* 128, 129, 131, 139, 140, 144-45, 160-61, 168; and confraternities, 88-89, 108, 111-12; and Protestants, 90, 91, 169-70; roots of, 91-97; and sexual morality, 92-93; and work ethic, 94-95

Portion congrue, 162, 165

Possevino, Antonio, 36, 37, 41

Preachers, 42, 43, 199; and Tridentine reform, 3, 36-37; selection of, 66, 110, 117, 126; rural parish clergy as, 82-83, 128, 216

Priests. *See* Clergy, parish

Priests, stipendiary, 13-14; behavior of, 19, 81, 98, 100

Probit analysis. *See* Bequests, pious: probit analysis of

Processions: for King Henry II (1548), 7-8; for King Henry IV (1595), 8; pre-Tridentine, 24-25, 27, 38, 41, 42, 54-55, 57; and anti-Protestantism, 31, 47; and Tridentine reform, 41, 85, 86, 88, 90, 127, 131-33, 137; "White," 47; of the Eucharist, 170

Property, communal: and village confraternities, 59-61

Protestantism: in Lyon, 5, 30-31, 32; and Catholic solidarity, 6, 8, 30-34, 168; and attack on popular culture, 71, 90, 91, 200, 224; in rural areas, 47-48; and Tridentine reform, 73, 75, 84; as urban

movement, 169, 223; and pious bequests, 179. *See also* Calvinism; Protestants; Reformation, Protestant

Protestants: 21, 31-32, 162, 215; repression of and attacks on, 16, 30-34, 41, 47-48, 201; reconversion of, 33, 41, 47, 71.

Purgatory, 21, 22, 54

Rabot, Jean, 134, 218

Rajat, Jean, 103-04, 108

Reformation, Protestant: social and economic effects of, 1, 2; compared with Counter Reformation, 169-70. *See also* Calvinism; Protestantism; Protestants

Retreats, seminary: for ordinands, 77-78, 79; for laity, 78, 79; for parish clergy, 78, 79, 83, 101, 104, 134, 168; and campaign against popular culture, 89, 97

Richerism, 163, 169

Riots, 10, 42, 200, 203; anti-Protestant, 31, 33, 200; and Tridentine reform, 94, 135, 136, 137, 211, 212

Rituals, 21-25; *see also* Sacraments
—paraliturgical: clerical participation in, 51, 53-57, 58, 61, 62, 63, 65, 167; in villages, 53-54, 56-57, 204; and communal solidarity, 68-69, 167
—specific: of baptism, 23, 27, 53, 57, 129-30, 194; of burial and mourning, 21-22, 23, 27, 28-29, 30, 40, 52, 53-54, 88, 92, 123, 172, 177, 178, 181-83, 196, 197, 199, 203, 215; of communion, 23, 53, 84, 130, 194, 196, 216 (*see also* Eucharist); of confession, 21, 23, 38, 53, 65, 66, 71, 84, 124; of marriage, 23, 27, 53, 57, 84-85, 130, 196
—traditional: and Tridentine reform, 2, 71, 94, 123, 129, 131-36, 137, 145, 154-55, 164, 168, 217; attitudes toward, 8, 21-22, 27, 28, 87, 170; decline in, 29-30, 199; replacement of, 88, 89-90

Rouille, Guillaume, 33, 38

Royaumes: pre-Tridentine, 25, 26, 62-65, 71-72, 87-88, 90, 91, 94, 107, 111, 133-34, 136, 141, 154, 168

Rubys, Claude de, 38, 41, 42, 90-91, 198

Sacraments: traditional role of, 23; and Penitents' confraternities, 38-39; and paraliturgical rituals, 53-54; as social vs.

religious acts, 84-85; and individual salvation, 87, 124; and Tridentine piety, 129-31; and communal solidarity, 167. *See also* Rituals

Saint Bartholomew's Day massacre, 33, 48

Saint Georges, Abp. Claude de, 77, 87, 99

Schools, "little": 74, 77, 83, 88-89, 93, 95, 114, 115, 125, 128, 141, 154, 168

Schools, primary: types of, 114-15; and parish clergy, 114-16, 136, 161; curriculum of, 128

Seignior: role of in village affairs, 58, 60

Seignorial courts. *See* Courts

Seminaries, 3-5, 35, 51-52, 72, 75-79, 80-82, 97, 101, 104, 136, 160, 168-169, 211; Saint-Charles, Seminary of (Lyon), 77-79, 81, 82, 88, 129; Saint-Irénée, Seminary of (Lyon), 76, 77, 78-79, 81, 82, 83, 89, 104, 106; Saint-Joseph, Seminary of (Lyon), 76-77, 78, 160; Saint-Sulpice, Seminary of (Paris), 76, 78, 81

Sénéchaussée. See Courts

Sexual morality: of parish clergy, 50, 69, 81, 82, 98, 202, 211; in villages, 62, 64, 128, 144, 218; and campaign against popular culture, 92-93, 95, 164, 165, 210-11

Shrines: pre-Tridentine role of, 23-24, 55, 204. *See also* Processions

Sociétés de prêtres, 48, 54, 155-56

Sulpicians, 76, 78, 81, 161

Syndics, 60, 61, 66

Synods: and Tridentine reform, 4, 80

Taverns: and parish clergy, 50, 131, 141-42, 218

Theater, religious, 26, 56

Thimonier, Claude, 140, 144

Tithe rights, 13, 69, 140, 148, 152, 162, 206, 218

Titles, patrimonial (*titres patrimoniaux*), 156, 158, 221

Tobit analysis. *See* Bequests, pious: tobit analysis of

Towns: government of, 58, 60; "little" schools in, 88-89. *See also* Communities

Trent, Council of, 1; and episcopal reform, 3, 4, 6, 50, 70, 75, 80, 81-82, 95, 99, 210; catechisms of, 14, 82, 83, 103, 128; publication of decrees of, 38, 42; enforcement of decrees of, 72-73, 207

Valentin, Charles, 104-05, 113

Valliezy, Jehan, 51, 102, 103

Vestries, parish: role of, 54, 58-59, 87; and confraternities, 60, 104, 106; control of, 67, 103, 105, 116-17, 136, 137, 143, 144, 148, 161, 206

Villages. *See* Communal solidarity, village; Institutions, communal

Virgin Mary: devotions to, 37, 85-86, 114, 119, 154, 155; statues of, 55, 204

Visitations, ecclesiastical: purposes of, 4, 99, 116, 142; to rural parishes, 50-51, 52, 56, 67, 80, 85, 202, 206; seventeenth and eighteenth centuries compared, 99-100, 101; and confraternities, 106, 109, 110

Vocations, religious, 81-82; decline in (eighteenth century), 154, 155

Weber, Max, 94, 223-24

Wills. *See* Bequests, pious

Witchcraft. *See* Magic

Women: pious bequests of, 23-24, 126-27, 145, 172, 175, 176, 177, 178, 180, 181, 183, 184, 216, 219; and confraternities, 72, 114, 124; and Tridentine reform, 126-28, 136, 144, 145, 146, 167, 169

Youth groups: urban, 7, 20, 145-46

—village: and festivals, 62, 64-65, 69, 87, 219; and communal solidarity, 68, 69, 94; and parish clergy, 69, 70, 135, 141, 142-43, 145, 161, 167, 168-69, 218, 219; and Tridentine reform, 88, 130, 133-36, 137, 219; vs. urban, 145-46